CHILD ABDUCTION WITHIN THE EUROPEAN UNION

The first part of the book critically evaluates the evolution of the separate intra-EU child abduction regime and examines to what extent the European Union complied with its standards of good legislative drafting during the negotiations on the Brussels II bis Regulation. It seeks to demonstrate that there was no real legal need for the involvement of the European Union in the area of child abduction and for the tightening of the 1980 Hague Abduction Convention return mechanism. The second part of the book presents findings of a statistical survey into the operation of child abduction provisions of the Brussels II bis Regulation in the first year of the functioning of the instrument and reveals how effectively the intra-EU return mechanism operated in that year. Based on the findings of the statistical survey, the book identifies and discusses a number of points of concern in respect to the functioning of the new child abduction scheme. Finally, the book investigates whether the Brussels II bis Regulation has added any value in the area of child abduction.

Volume 11 in the series Studies in Private International Law

Studies in Private International Law

Volume 1: Electronic Consumer Contracts in the Conflict of Laws
Sophia Tang

Volume 2: Foreign Currency Claims in the Conflict of Laws
Vaughan Black

Volume 3: Jurisdiction and Judgments in Relation to EU Competition Law Claims
Mihail Danov

Volume 4: Cases and Materials on EU Private International Law
Stefania Bariatti

Volume 5: International Commercial Disputes: Commercial Conflict of Laws in English Courts
Jonathan Hill and Adeline Chong

Volume 6: International Child Abduction: The Inadequacies of the Law
Thalia Kruger

Volume 7: Mediating International Child Abduction Cases
Sarah Vigers

Volume 8: International Antitrust Litigation: Conflict of Laws and Coordination
Edited by Jürgen Basedow, Stéphanie Francq and Laurence Idot

Volume 9: The Governing Law of Companies in EU Law
Justin Borg-Barthet

Volume 10: Intellectual Property and Private International Law: Comparative Perspectives
Edited by Toshiyuki Kono

Child Abduction within the European Union

Katarina Trimmings

· HART ·
PUBLISHING
OXFORD AND PORTLAND, OREGON
2013

Published in the United Kingdom by Hart Publishing Ltd
16C Worcester Place, Oxford, OX1 2JW
Telephone: +44 (0)1865 517530
Fax: +44 (0)1865 510710
E-mail: mail@hartpub.co.uk
Website: http://www.hartpub.co.uk

Published in North America (US and Canada) by
Hart Publishing
c/o International Specialized Book Services
920 NE 58th Avenue, Suite 300
Portland, OR 97213-3786
USA
Tel: +1 503 287 3093 or toll-free: (1) 800 944 6190
Fax: +1 503 280 8832
E-mail: orders@isbs.com
Website: http://www.isbs.com

British Library Cataloguing in Publication Data
Data Available

ISBN: 978-1-84946-397-3

Typeset by Compuscript Ltd, Shannon
Printed and bound in Great Britain by
MPG Printgroup Ltd

SERIES EDITORS' PREFACE

This book grew out of Katarina Trimmings' PhD thesis. Paul Beaumont was her main supervisor. She had the excellent idea of building on the empirical research she had done while working for Professor Nigel Lowe at Cardiff University. Nigel and she had collected comprehensive data on the global operation of the Hague Child Abduction Convention in 2003. Katarina decided to do a follow up study for 2005–6 focusing only on child abductions within the European Union to see what impact the newly-in-force Brussels IIa Regulation had made. For a private study by a PhD student she did remarkably well in getting the cooperation of the Central Authorities in the EU in filling in her questionnaire. Her almost completely comprehensive results provided a good basis for an initial assessment of the practical significance of the additions to the Hague Child Abduction Convention created by Brussels IIa for intra-EU child abductions. For the book she has been able, with the consent of Professor Lowe, to make use of the findings of a global study on the Hague Child Abduction Convention for the year 2008 by extracting the data relevant to intra-EU cases and comparing it to the data from 2003 and 2005–6. Thus her empirical findings are based on good data with one year taken from before the operation of Brussels IIa and two years taken from the period of the operation of that Regulation. One interesting finding that was expertly drawn out by Katarina, who is from Slovakia, is that the new EU Member States in Central and Eastern Europe experienced much longer delays before decisions were reached on child abduction cases and made far fewer return orders than the EU average. Her explanation for this deserves to be taken seriously as it comes from an insider's perspective.

Dr Trimmings has added to her empirical study several strands of library-based analytical work. First, she carefully considered whether the EU complied with its own standards for better lawmaking, including respect for subsidiarity and proportionality, and convincingly concludes that the EU fell far short of those standards. Good evidence was not there to support some of the specific changes that were made by Brussels IIa and insufficient efforts were made to respect reverse subsidiarity by seeking evidence-based reforms to the treatment of international child abduction cases at the global level in The Hague. Second, she used comparative law case analysis to investigate whether it confirmed or denied some of the more significant indications from the empirical research. Therefore the book contains excellent case-law analysis, which takes account of the academic literature on the Article 13(2) Hague Convention exception based on a child's views and the impact on it of Brussels IIa, on the fundamental rights exception in Article 20 of the Hague Convention, on the grave risk of harm exception in Article 13(1)(b) and the impact on it of Article 11(4) of Brussels IIa, and on the meaning of 'habitual residence' in this context.

For anyone doing serious academic study on the Hague Child Abduction Convention and/or the Brussels IIa Regulation provisions on child abduction this book is a must read. In addition it will make an interesting read for anyone interested in EU lawmaking, the voice of a child in litigation affecting that child, the link between domestic violence and mother's fleeing with their children, the relationship between human rights and private international law, the risk that judges manipulate statutory provisions to achieve the results they believe do justice in individual cases, and the usefulness and meaning of 'habitual residence' as a connecting factor.

Paul Beaumont, University of Aberdeen
Jonathan Harris, King's College, University of London

PREFACE

This book is based on the author's doctoral thesis, which was presented for the degree of PhD at the University of Aberdeen in April 2010. The thesis was researched between November 2006 and February 2010. For the purposes of this book, the thesis was later updated to include relevant materials, including case law for the period until the beginning of November 2011. The thesis was generously funded by the University of Aberdeen Law School Studentship for which the author is very thankful. The author was also the grateful recipient of a travel grant from the CB Davidson Bequest Fund which enabled her to undertake several research trips.

The author is particularly indebted to her supervisor, Professor Paul Beaumont. Not only did he provide countless words of wisdom and the benefit of his experience but untold patience and encouragement, without which this thesis would not have been completed.

Gratitude is also extended to Professor Nigel Lowe of the Cardiff University. By his kind permission the author was granted access to a set of extremely valuable information that enabled her to conduct her statistical survey in the form of a comparative study.

The author would also like to thank the many academics and practitioners who provided her with help and assistance during the course of her research; including the staff at the Central Authorities of Austria, Belgium, Cyprus, Czech Republic, England & Wales, Estonia, Finland, France, Germany, Hungary, Ireland, Italy, Latvia, Lithuania, Luxembourg, Malta, Northern Ireland, Poland, Portugal, Scotland, Slovakia, Slovenia and Sweden.

Last but not least, the writer would like to express her sincere gratitude to her husband Mark for his support and encouragement throughout her doctoral studies.

CONTENTS

TABLE OF CASES

Australia

Canada

Ireland

United Kingdom

England and Wales

Northern Ireland

Scotland

United States

European Court of Human Rights

Court of Justice of the European Union

TABLE OF LEGISLATION

International Conventions

EC Legislation

National legislation

Other Documents

EC

European Commission

European Council

European Parliament

Economic and Social Committee

Committee of the Regions

Other

Hague Conference on Private International Law

Special Commissions Reports

Preliminary Documents

Other

UN

1

Introduction

The key instrument providing for a worldwide regulation of international parental child abduction has long been the Hague Convention of 25 October 1980 on the Civil Aspects of International Child Abduction. The Convention has been in force since 1983 and has proved a phenomenal success.[1] Thanks to this treaty many thousands of children have been successfully returned to their habitual residence. The main object of the 1980 Convention is to secure the prompt return of children wrongfully removed from or retained in any Contracting State.[2] The countries that are parties to the 1980 Convention have agreed that a child who is habitually resident in one Contracting State, and who has been removed to or retained in another Contracting State in violation of the left-behind parent's rights of custody, shall be promptly returned to the country of his/her habitual residence. The Contracting States' undertaking to re-establish the *status quo* changed by a one-sided decision of the abductor rests upon a conviction that, because of its close proximity to the child, the best suited court to take a decision on the merits of the case, that is, custody and access rights, is the competent court in the State of the child's habitual residence prior to his/her removal or retention.[3] There is a treaty obligation to return any abducted child below the age of 16[4] if an application is made within one year from the date of the wrongful removal or retention,[5] unless one of the exceptions to return provided for in Articles 12, 13 or 20 of the 1980 Convention applies.[6]

[1] There are 86 Contracting States to the Convention as of September 2011.

[2] Hague Convention on the Civil Aspects of International Child Abduction (1980) (Hague Abduction Convention) Art 1.

[3] E Pérez-Vera, 'Explanatory Report on the 1980 Hague Child Abduction Convention' (1982) para 19, available at www.hcch.net/upload/expl28.pdf.

[4] Hague Abduction Convention (1980) Art 4.

[5] Hague Abduction Convention (1980) Art 12.

[6] According to Art 12 the court of the requested State need not return the child to the country of his/her habitual residence if a period of more than one year has elapsed from the date of the wrongful removal or retention and it is demonstrated that the child is settled in his/her new environment; Art 13 provides that the court need not return the child to the country of his/her habitual residence if at least one of the following preconditions is met: the left-behind parent was not actually exercising his/her custody rights at the time of the abduction; he/she had consented or subsequently acquiesced to the abduction; the return would expose the child to physical or psychological harm or otherwise place the child in an intolerable situation and the child who has attained a sufficient age and degree of maturity objects to being returned; and finally, under Art 20 the seized court may refuse to return the child if the return would violate fundamental principles of the requested State relating to the protection of human rights and fundamental freedoms.

Within the European Union, the operation of the 1980 Convention has been modified by certain provisions of the Council Regulation (EC) No 2201/2003 of 27 November 2003 Concerning Jurisdiction and the Recognition and Enforcement of Judgments in Matrimonial Matters and the Matters of Parental Responsibility, repealing Regulation (EC) No 1347/2000 (Brussels II bis Regulation). The Regulation entered into force on 1 March 2005 and applies to child abduction cases between the EU Member States except for Denmark.[7] This regional instrument aims at creating even more ambitious rules on child abduction by imposing stricter obligations to assure the prompt return of a child. It reinforces the first principle of the 1980 Convention that the question of the custody of the child should be decided by the Member State of the habitual residence of the child.

Despite the ambitious goal of strengthening the deterrence of child abduction within the borders of the Union, the new child abduction regime did not receive a warm welcome by commentators. Quite the contrary, it provoked a storm of criticism as the value of parallel international instruments was questioned.[8] Serious concerns were voiced at the 'risk of disharmony between regulations emanating from Brussels and a convention negotiated at The Hague'.[9] It was rightly argued that the 1980 Convention had been working well and that there was no legal need for a regional legislative intervention into the sphere of child abduction.[10] As a result, the motivation behind the Union's decision to move into the domain of child abduction was questioned and it was suggested that this choice was more of a political than a practical nature.[11]

[7] Denmark has opted out from most Justice and Home Affairs matters and therefore does not participate in measures adopted by the Union in the area of visas, asylum, immigration and judicial co-operation in civil matters.

[8] Legitimate objections were raised against the phenomenon of 'parallelism', ie the existence of parallel sets of rules of private international law, the one to be applied to intra-EU cases only and thus to accord uneven treatment to cases that are in principle identical, *mutatis mutandis*. See N Lowe *et al* (eds), *The New Brussels II Regulation: A Supplement to International Movement of Children* (Bristol, Jordan Publishing Limited, 2005) 45; and P McEleavy, 'The New Child Abduction Regime in the European Union: Symbiotic Relationship or Forced Partnership?' (2005) 1 *Journal of Private International Law* 5, 6. The Hague Conference itself voiced legitimate concerns about parallelism, warning of the danger of 'proliferation of instruments dealing with cross-frontier family matters'. P Lortie, 'The Communitarisation of Family Law—The Hague Conventions and the New Brussels II Regulation' (2005) 10 *Judges' Newsletter* 47, 48. Generally on parallelism see I Fletcher, *Conflict of Laws and European Community Law: with Special Reference to the Community Conventions on Private International Law* (Amsterdam, North-Holland Publishing Company, 1982) 82.

[9] The Right Honourable Lord Justice Thorpe, 'The Second UK Family Law Conference: London, England' (2002) 4 *Judges' Newsletter* 32, 33.

[10] It is, however, not to suggest that there were no difficulties associated with the operation of the Convention. The most serious problem was an increasingly apparent tension between the Convention objective to secure the return of the child and the lack of safety of the returned child and/or the returning parent, especially in abductions committed against the background of domestic violence.

[11] A particularly harsh criticism came from P McEleavy in McEleavy, 'The New Child Abduction Regime' (n 8) 6 : 'Experience of law making in the field of family law within the EU has shown that project initiation and development has often very little to do with pressing legal needs or indeed finding the most appropriate solution.... The reason, in large part, is that the EU is a forum where political considerations can prevail over legal reality.'

The question of desirability of separate intra-EU child abduction rules, and the underlying issue of motivation behind the Union's involvement in the area, however, did not arise only retrospectively—after the adoption of the Brussels II bis Regulation. In fact, the issue marked the entire negotiation process, being at the heart of a schism that arose between the EU Members at the very early stage of the drafting procedure, and accompanied the entire negotiations. Much of the blame for the division was attributed to the reputed efforts of the pro-European Member States led by France to bring discredit on the Hague child abduction regime by pressing for a separate Brussels solution. Also, it was rightly argued that the proposed scheme was overly complicated and, as a result, very likely to lead to confusion for the parties, practitioners and judges.[12] The pro-reformists, in contrast, sought to justify the indispensability of the new child abduction rules by claiming indications of an alleged misuse of the exceptions to return provided for by the 1980 Convention, particularly Article 13(1)(b).[13] The conflict between the two camps inevitably affected the drafting procedure and ultimately had a negative impact on the quality of the relevant provisions of the Regulation.

This book starts with the premise that there was no real need for tightening the operation of the Convention return mechanism. It is based on a belief that the real problem with the operation of the Convention was not an overuse of the grave risk of harm defence as claimed by the drafters of the Regulation. Rather, the actual issue has been the lack of effective safeguards to secure the protection of the child and the abducting parent upon their return to the requesting State, especially in Article 13(1)(b) cases involving domestic violence.[14] Consequently, the book questions the viability of the argument of the misuse of Article 13(1)(b), seeking to demonstrate that this rationale was erroneous and without any foundation in empirical reality. The book critically assesses the development of the Brussels II bis initiative and looks at how, despite the opposition of a substantial

[12] Lortie, 'The Communitarisation of Family Law' (n 8) 48.

[13] Commission (EC), 'Mutual recognition of decisions on parental responsibility' (Working Document) COM (2001) 166 final, 8, 27 March 2001. The argument of a misuse of Art 13(1)(b) was, however, presented only at a later stage of the negotiations. The early rationale, underlying among others the issue of child abduction, was an ambitious goal of the Union to better respond to the European citizen's special needs by a deeper involvement into the international family law matters. See M Jänterä-Jareborg, 'Unification of International Family Law in Europe—A Critical Perspective' in K Boele-Woelki (ed), *Perspectives for the Unification and Harmonisation of Family Law in Europe* (Antwerp, Intersentia, 2003) 194–216, 194.

[14] See, eg, MH Weiner, 'International Child Abduction and the Escape from Domestic Violence' (2000–2001) 69 *Fordham Law Review* 593; M Freeman, 'Primary Carers and the Hague Child Abduction Convention' [2001] *International Family Law* 140; R Lamont, 'International Child Abduction and Domestic Violence in the European Union' in H Stalford *et al* (eds), *Gender and Migration in 21st Century Europe* (Farnham, Ashgate Publishing 2009) 27–43; R Hoegger, 'What If She Leaves? Domestic Violence Cases Under the Hague Convention and the Insufficiency of the Undertakings Remedy' (2003) 18 *Berkeley Women's Law Journal* 181; M Kaye, 'The Hague Convention and the Flight from Domestic Violence: How Women and Children are Being Returned by Coach and Four' (1999) 13 *International Journal of Law, Policy and the Family* 191; and C Bruch, 'The Unmet Needs of Domestic Violence Victims and Their Children in Hague Child Abduction Convention Cases' (2004–2005) 38 *Family Law Quarterly* 529.

number of Member States, the Union managed to move into the domain of child abduction. The book further reproaches the Union for the lack of compliance with its law-making policy, aspiring to show that the child abduction provisions of the Brussels II bis Regulation were drafted in a rather unprofessional manner that fell short of the Union's standards of good legislative drafting. The second part of the book is based on acceptance of the reality of the new intra-EU child abduction regime. Applying methods of empirical research, it examines how the Regulation operates in the area of child abduction and to what extent the instrument has fulfilled the expectations of its drafters. It also identifies areas that cause particular concern with respect to the practical operation of the child abduction provisions of the Regulation. The final part of the book to some extent departs from the overall critical attitude as it seeks to acknowledge those aspects of the Regulation that represent an added value in the area of child abduction.

Accordingly, the book addresses four interrelated objectives. First, it aims at critically evaluating the evolution of the new intra-EU child abduction regime, and examining to what extent the Union complied with its standards of good legislative drafting during the negotiations on the Brussels II bis Regulation. Second, it seeks to demonstrate that there was no real legal need for the involvement of the European Union in the area of child abduction, and tightening the Convention return mechanism. Third, it aspires to reveal how effectively the new return mechanism operates, and what are the points of concern in respect to the functioning of the new child abduction scheme. Finally, it investigates whether the Regulation has any added value in the area of child abduction.

I. Structure and Methodology

The book begins with the historical development of the Brussels II bis legislative initiative, focusing in particular on the evolution of the child abduction provisions of the new instrument. A detailed review of the key milestones on the road to the separate intra-EU child abduction regime (from the Tampere European Council Meeting in October 1999 to the adoption of the Brussels II bis Regulation in November 2003), is intermingled with critical observations on legislative practices employed by the European Commission throughout the negotiations on the Brussels II bis Regulation. The law-making policy of the European Union is then examined and the level of compliance with the Union's principles of good legislative drafting throughout the negotiations on the new child abduction regime is assessed. The scrutinised principles are the principle of subsidiarity, the principle of proportionality, and the rule of mandatory consultation. Finally, a comprehensive study of resources relevant to the interpretation and the application of Article 13(1)(b) from the early 1990s until the adoption of the Brussels II bis Regulation is included.

The main body of the book is represented by an empirical survey of the practical operation of the child abduction provisions of the Brussels II bis Regulation. The survey takes the form of a statistical and analytical study, evaluating the effectiveness of the intra-EU child abduction regime. The analysis commences with information on the numbers of applications for return made within the researched period (1 July 2005 to 30 June 2006) under the Regulation; and information on the profile and the nationality of the abductor. It then turns to the outcome of the applications, the reason for judicial refusal and the timing of the cases. The rationale behind the choice of the researched period was that 2005/06 (being the first year of the operation of the Brussels II bis Regulation) had been the only year of the functioning of the separate intra-EU child abduction regime prior to the commencement of this research in November 2006. The findings of the survey are assessed by means of comparison with corresponding data obtained through the 2003 Statistical Analysis of Applications Made in 2003 under the Hague Abduction Convention.[15] The 2003 statistical analysis was a research project conducted by the Centre of International Family Law Studies at Cardiff University Law School under the directorship of Professor Nigel Lowe. The author was involved in this project as a research assistant.

The statistical analysis is followed by an examination of areas that, as indicated by the results of the survey, appear to be of concern with respect to the practical operation of the child abduction provisions of the Brussels II bis Regulation.

With a view to acknowledging the Regulation's contribution towards an increased understanding of the importance of the voice of the child, the final part of the book is devoted to the analysis of the obligation to hear a child in return proceedings, contained in Article 11(2). An examination of relevant recent legal developments in EU jurisdictions (England and Wales in particular) is followed by analysis of current approaches toward the defence of child's objections in major non-EU jurisdictions: Australia, Canada and the United States. The focus on England and Wales, Australia, Canada and the United States is due to the fact that among the published case law, the jurisprudence of these countries predominates and is without doubt the most elaborate.

This book is based on the author's doctoral thesis, which was presented for the degree of PhD at the University of Aberdeen in April 2010. The thesis was researched between November 2006 and February 2010. For the purposes of this book, the thesis was later updated to include relevant materials, including case law for the period until the beginning of November 2011. The thesis was funded by the University of Aberdeen Law School Studentship which covered fees as well as maintenance. Additionally, the author was awarded a contribution towards travel expenses from the CB Davidson Bequest Fund. In March 2007, the author carried

[15] N Lowe, E Atkinson, K Horosova and S Patterson, 'A Statistical Analysis of Applications Made in 2003 under the Hague Convention of 25 October 1980 on the Civil Aspects of International Child Abduction' Preliminary Document No 3 (2006) 41, available at www.hcch.net/upload/wop/abd_pd03e2006.pdf.

out empirical research at the Child Abduction Unit in London (the Central Authority for England and Wales), whilst in April and May 2007 she visited and interviewed personnel at the Office for International Legal Protection of Children in Brno, Czech Republic (the Central Authority for the Czech Republic) and the Centre for International Legal Protection of Children and Youth in Bratislava, Slovakia (the Central Authority for the Slovak Republic).

The book has sought to include all relevant primary and secondary resources.

2

Milestones on the Road to the Separate Child Abduction Regime within the European Union

This Chapter analyses the development of the Brussels II bis initiative to explore how, despite the opposition of a substantial number of Member States, the European Union has been able to move into the area of child abduction. It examines in detail significant milestones on the road to the separate intra-EU child abduction rules, whilst with a critical eye assesses legislative practices employed by the European Commission throughout the negotiations on the Brussels II bis Regulation. The Chapter also observes the effects of the drafting procedure on the substantive quality of the new child abduction provisions, arguing that the Regulation has failed to address real problems among which the most pressing has been the protection of domestic violence victims and their children upon the return to the requesting State. It is in this context that the Chapter represents a historical practice-oriented study concerned with a comprehensive comparison of the final text of the relevant provisions of the Brussels II bis Regulation with the original proposals including a detailed analysis of the legislative history.

I. October 1999: The Tampere European Council Meeting

It was the European Council meeting held in Tampere on 15 and 16 October 1999 which set in motion a chain of initiatives that have led to the European Union's active participation in enacting legislation to regulate family law matters. The initial issue raised was the recognition and enforcement of judicial decisions throughout the Union, in particular a need for reduction of intermediate measures.[1] The aim was to ensure automatic recognition and direct enforcement of judgments throughout the Union, without any intermediate proceedings or grounds for refusal of enforcement. As a first step these intermediate procedures

[1] See 'Tampere European Council: Presidency Conclusions' (15–16 October 1999) para 34, available at www.europarl.europa.eu/summits/tam_en.htm.

were to be abolished for selected types of judgments, including certain judicial decisions in the area of family law. No exhaustive list of the family law judgments to be targeted was drawn up on this occasion; nevertheless, two examples were stated: decisions in respect of maintenance claims and decisions granting visiting rights. Though originally the Union did not have the remotest intention to get involved in the issue of child abduction, rather unforeseeably the visiting rights later became a bridge to the new Union-wide child abduction regime.

The principle of mutual recognition of judicial decisions was recognised by the Tampere meeting as 'the cornerstone of judicial co-operation in both civil and commercial matters within the Union'.[2] The meeting highlighted the need to establish a genuine European area of justice where all EU citizens would have the same access to justice throughout the Union.[3] The ultimate goal of the Tampere programme was the creation of the genuine area of freedom, security and justice in the European Union—an objective already set out in the Treaty of Amsterdam, which entered into force on 1 May 1999, a few months before the Tampere European Council meeting took place. The Treaty of Amsterdam provided a legal framework for the use of the Union's legislative powers for certain key policies in the area of justice and home affairs, including judicial co-operation in civil matters. The provisions on judicial co-operation in civil matters were included into a new Title IV which the Treaty of Amsterdam inserted into the Treaty establishing the European Community.[4] The issue was thus transferred from the third to the first pillar, which opened the door for the Union's deeper involvement in the area.

II. May 2000: Council Regulation (EC) No 1347/2000 of 29 May 2000 on Jurisdiction and the Recognition and Enforcement of Judgments in Matrimonial Matters and in Matters of Parental Responsibility for Children of Both Spouses (the Brussels II Regulation)

Following the Tampere meeting, in the area of family matters Council Regulation No. 1347/2000[5] was adopted in May 2000 and entered into force on 1 March 2001. The Brussels II Regulation represented an important first step towards a mutual

[2] *Ibid*, para 33.

[3] *Ibid*, para 5.

[4] EC Treaty (Treaty of Amsterdam, as amended) Title IV (Visas, Asylum, Immigration and Other Policies Related to Free Movement of Persons) Arts 61(c) and 65 state that in order to establish an area of freedom, security and justice, the Council shall adopt measures in the field of judicial co-operation in civil matters having cross-border implications and insofar as necessary for the proper functioning of the internal market. These measures include improving and simplifying the recognition and enforcement of decisions in civil and commercial matters.

[5] Council Regulation (EC) 1347/2000 of 29 May 2000 on jurisdiction and the recognition and enforcement of judgments in matrimonial matters and in matters of parental responsibility for children of both spouses [2003] OJ L160/19 ('Brussels II Regulation').

recognition of judgments in the field of family law litigation. It set out uniform rules on jurisdiction and on recognition and enforcement for divorce cases and on certain aspects of parental responsibility. With respect to the latter, the scope of the Regulation was, however, too narrow. It was limited to the judgments issued in the context of divorce proceedings and concerned only children common to both spouses. This entailed that the Regulation was applicable neither to relationships other than marriage nor to judgments other than those rendered on the occasion of divorce, separation and marriage annulment.[6] In addition, the Regulation was of no use in cases concerning children not common to both spouses, such as step-children or adopted children of the family. This could lead to unfortunate situations where different sets of rules had to be applied to different children within the family. Moreover, the Regulation did not abolish the *exequatur* procedure; this intermediate measure was still required before a judgment issued in one Member State could be enforced in another.

The Brussels II Regulation was a direct predecessor of the Brussels II bis Regulation. Interestingly, however, the former did not make even a glancing reference to the issue of child abduction, which soon after was claimed to be pressing.

III. July 2000: Initiative of the French Republic with a View to Adopting a Council Regulation on the Mutual Enforcement of Judgments on Rights of Access to Children

On 1 July 2000 France took over the six-month rotating Presidency of the Council of the European Union from Portugal. France, as a founder member of the European Union, took a determined and ambitious approach to the period of its Presidency. The agenda included the reform of the EU institutions, which was at that time desirable so as to give effectiveness to the process of enlargement of the Union, the development of a closer relationship between Europe and its citizens, and the reinforcement of the EU social model by prioritising growth and employment in Europe.[7] Last but not least was the task to go on with the process of establishing an area of security, freedom and justice,[8] which was to be achieved among other means by the free circulation of judgments within Europe. As recognised by the Tampere meeting, it was the concept of mutual recognition of judgments through which this aim was to be attained. Seeking to apply this principle in the scope of

[6] Commission (EC), 'Mutual recognition of decisions on parental responsibility' (Working Document) COM (2001) 166 final, 4, 27 March 2001.

[7] 'The French Presidency of the European Union July–December 2000' (Ministry of Foreign Affairs, Label France, Magazine No 40, 07/2000, Editorial), available at www.diplomatie.gouv.fr/label_france/English/DOSSIER/presidence/edito.html.

[8] *Ibid.*

family law France put forward on 3 July 2000 a proposal aiming at the abolition of *exequatur* for certain judgments on parental responsibility concerning rights of access.[9] The scope of this initiative was defined by reference to the Brussels II Regulation. The proposal therefore applied only to judgments falling under the Brussels II Regulation granting cross-border rights of access to one of the parents of one of the children under 16 years of age.[10] The point where the proposed scheme departed from the Brussels II Regulation was the introduction of the principle of mutual recognition of the enforceability of the judgments in question.[11] It was suggested that these judgments, if even provisionally enforceable in the Member State where they had been rendered, could be enforced in all other Member States without any special procedure being requested.[12] The automatic recognition of the judicial decision was, however, to be distinguished from enforcement itself which was to be carried out under the law of the requested Member State; nevertheless, under the same conditions as if the judgment was given in the Member State of enforcement.[13]

The proposal reinforced a number of well-established principles of private international law of family law, such as the co-operation principle,[14] the encouragement of the voluntary exercise of rights of access[15] and the protection of both the best interests of the child and the interests of the custodial parent.[16] The protection of the latter interests was to be safeguarded by the guarantee for the automatic return of the child at the end of the period of access.[17] To this effect the authorities of the Member State where the child was staying might not assume jurisdiction during the child's visit to modify the foreign judgment which was being enforced and they should have been in a position to order the prompt return of the child.[18] The proposal did not contain any detailed provisions on how this mechanism would operate; nevertheless, from the wording of Article 11 it is evident that no flexibility was permitted in the proceedings, that is, no defences, including Article 13 of the 1980 Hague Abduction Convention, could have been invoked to oppose the return of the child.

[9] Initiative of the French Republic of 3 July 2000 with a view to adopting a council regulation on the mutual enforcement of judgments on rights of access to children [2000] OJ C 234/08.

[10] *Ibid*, Art 1.

[11] *Ibid*, ch II.

[12] *Ibid*, Art 2.

[13] *Ibid*, Art 3.

[14] *Ibid*, ch VI. See, eg, Art 7 of the 1980 Hague Abduction Convention and Art 30 of the 1996 Hague Convention on Jurisdiction, Applicable Law, Recognition, Enforcement and Co-operation in Respect of Parental Responsibility and Measures for the Protection of Children.

[15] *Ibid*, para 15. See, eg, Art 7(c) of the 1980 Hague Abduction Convention.

[16] *Ibid*, para 11. See Art 1(a) of the 1993 Hague Convention on Protection of Children and Co-operation in Respect of Intercountry Adoption for an example of the reference to the principle of the best interests of the child, and Art 1(b) of the 1980 Hague Abduction Convention for an example of the reference to the principle of the protection of the interests of the custodial parent.

[17] French Initiative on Rights of Access (n 9) ch V.

[18] *Ibid*, para 13.

The proposal for the automatic return of the child at the end of the period of access became a cornerstone of the new intra-EU child abduction regime. Though representing an early embryonic stage of development of the new rules on child abduction, the proposed provision was highly significant for the future quality of the new Regulation. Regrettably, the vague character of the proposed return mechanism applicable to wrongful retentions gave an unpromising start to the negotiations, which later abruptly covered all situations of parental child abduction, regardless of their connection with visiting rights.[19]

There was a general consensus among the EU Member States that international regulation of cross-border access was rather unsatisfactory,[20] with at least four different instruments potentially applicable, of which none provided an adequate remedy.[21] Nevertheless, despite the high desirability of a creative solution to the trans-frontier access problems, the French proposal attracted a dual criticism. First, there was strong disapproval of the inclusion of the provisions on the prompt return of the child in the proposed Regulation expressed by a group of the EU Member States under the leadership of the United Kingdom and Germany. These Members rightly argued that the problem of wrongful removals and retentions had long been satisfactorily regulated by and dealt with under the 1980 Hague Abduction Convention and that there was no need for the European Union to meddle in the domain of child abduction. The second contingent was paradoxically represented by the supporters of the proposal as a whole.[22] The objections raised by these Member States were directed only towards the limited scope of the proposed Regulation. This group aimed at the extension of the proposed instrument's scope while approving the incorporation of the presented answer to wrongful retentions. This aspiration soon received active encouragement from the European Parliament and the Economic and Social Committee.

[19] Art 3 of the 1980 Hague Abduction Convention recognises two forms of child abduction: a wrongful removal and a wrongful retention. Wrongful retentions normally occur as a consequence of non-return of the child by the non-custodial parent at the end of the period of access.

[20] W Duncan, 'Transfrontier Access/Contact and the Hague Convention of 25 October 1980 on the Civil Aspects of International Child Abduction—Final Report', Preliminary Document No 5 (2002) para 14, available at www.diplomatie.gouv.fr/label_france/English/DOSSIER/presidence/edito.html. For a full analysis see N Lowe and K Horosova, 'Good Practice Report on Access Under the Hague Convention of 25 October 1980 on the Civil Aspects of International Child Abduction', National Center for Missing & Exploited Children (2007), available at www.diplomatie.gouv.fr/label_france/English/DOSSIER/presidence/edito.html.

[21] Brussels II Regulation; 1980 Hague Abduction Convention; 1980 Council of Europe Convention on Recognition and Enforcement of Decisions Concerning Custody of Children and on Restoration of Custody of Children; and 1961 Hague Convention Concerning the Powers and Authorities and the Law Applicable in Respect of the Protection of Minors. For an analysis of the international instruments governing cross-border access see N Lowe, 'Regulating Cross Border Access to Children' in S Hofer, D Klippel and U Walter (eds), *Perspektiven des Familienrechts: Festschrift fur Dieter Schwab* (Bielefeld, Gieseking Verlag, 2005).

[22] Belgium, Greece, Italy, Luxembourg, Portugal, Spain and obviously France. See P McEleavy, 'The New Child Abduction Regime in the European Union: Symbiotic Relationship or Forced Partnership?' (2005) 1 *Journal of Private International Law* 5 fn 15.

In their opinions from October 2000,[23] while acknowledging that the French initiative contributed to the slow reinforcement of the principle of judicial co-operation in civil matters, both institutions expressed concerns about the limited scope of this pilot project. At the same time they emphasised the need to broaden the scope of the Brussels II Regulation. The positive approach adopted by the European Parliament and the Economic and Social Committee produced a climate that was favourable to a further movement of the Community into the family law domain. As a result, the Justice and Home Affairs Council meeting on 30 November 2000 concluded that the work on the French initiative should continue and that the project should be done in parallel with the work on extending the scope of the Brussels II Regulation.[24]

France was heavily criticised for benefiting from agenda-shaping powers during the period of its Presidency from July to December 2000.[25] The coalition led by the United Kingdom and Germany justly accused the country of arrogance for promoting without precaution its national interests.[26] France, however, saw the six months in the office of President in a different light and, convinced of a number of considerable achievements, concluded that its Presidency contributed to the genuine establishment of the European judicial area through mutual recognition of court decisions.[27]

IV. December 2000: The Draft Programme of Measures for Implementation of the Principle of Mutual Recognition of Decisions in Civil and Commercial Matters

In December 2000 the Council and the Commission adopted a Draft programme of measures for implementation of the principle of mutual recognition of decisions in civil and commercial matters.[28] This document was developed

[23] Economic and Social Committee (EC), 'Initiative of the French Republic with a view to adopting a Council Regulation on the mutual enforcement of judgments on rights of access to children' (Opinion) 2001 C14/17, 19 October 2000; and European Parliament (EC), 'Initiative of the French Republic with a view to adopting a council regulation on the mutual enforcement of judgments on rights of access to children' (Report) A5-0311/2000, 24 October 2000.

[24] European Community, 'Justice, Home Affairs and Civil Protection: 2314th Council Meeting, Brussels, 30 November and 1 December 2000' 13865/00 (Presse 457), available at www.diplomatie.gouv.fr/label_france/English/DOSSIER/presidence/edito.html.

[25] For more details see McEleavy, 'The New Child Abduction Regime' (n 22) fn 22.

[26] Ch Lequesne, 'French Presidency of the European Union: a Dull Response to the Challenge of Growth' (2001) II *Annuaire français de relations internationales*, available at www.diplomatie.gouv.fr/label_france/English/DOSSIER/presidence/edito.html.

[27] French Embassy in the United Kingdom, 'Achievements of the French Presidency of the European Union' (1 January 2001), available at www.ambafrance-uk.org/Achievements-of-the-French.html.

[28] Commission notice (EC) on draft programme of measures for implementation of the principle of mutual recognition of decisions in civil and commercial matters [2001] OJ C12/01.

in response to the call of the Tampere Council meeting on the Council and the Commission to draw up a programme of measures to implement the principle of mutual recognition.[29]

The Draft programme identified four areas of work, while family law was recognised as the field where progress was most needed.[30] The ultimate aim was an abolition of *exequatur* in the areas of family law covered by the Brussels II Regulation as well as in family situations arising through relationships other than marriage. This objective was to be achieved progressively in three stages. At the first stage, the French initiative on rights of access should have been implemented and *exequatur* abolished for judgments on rights of access.[31] It is to be noted, however, that despite addressing the French initiative as a whole, the Draft programme did not touch on the particularly problematic issue of wrongful retentions. No indication was provided of the possible further development with regard to child abductions.

V. March 2001: Commission Working Document: Mutual Recognition of Decisions on Parental Responsibility

The direction was, however, soon indicated by the Commission working document on the mutual recognition of decisions on parental responsibility adopted on 27 March 2001.[32] The working document dealt in depth with the striking provisions of the French initiative. It not only approved the need to strengthen the protection of the custodial parent against wrongful retentions but recommended going beyond the French proposal and revising the issue of wrongful retentions to a greater extent than initially suggested. It concluded that France offered only a partial solution to the 'problems encountered in practice with Article 13(1)(b),[33] whose application is allegedly prone to abuse'.[34] Though no details of the alleged abuse of the grave risk of harm exception of Article 13(1)(b) were specified, nor was any evidence presented in the document, two alternative suggestions were made as to how to solve the 'problem' in question. First, the custodial parent was to be better protected through further limitations on the ability of the

[29] Tampere European Council Presidency Conclusions (n 1) para 37.
[30] Draft Programme of Measures (n 28) I and III.
[31] *Ibid*, III.
[32] Commission Working Document on Mutual Recognition (n 6).
[33] Art 13(1)(b) of the 1980 Hague Abduction Convention. This Article provides an exception to the obligation to return the child where there is a grave risk that return would expose the child to physical or psychological harm or otherwise place him/her in an intolerable situation.
[34] Tampere European Council Presidency Conclusions (n 1) 8.

non-custodial parent exercising his/her rights of access to invoke the grave risk of harm exception when refusing the return of the child.[35] The working document, however, did not make clear how to facilitate this increased protection and it thus remained open whether a new formulation of Article 13(1)(b) in relation to wrongful retentions should be provided or whether it would suffice to rely on a narrower interpretation of the 1980 Hague Abduction Convention. The alternative proposition to safeguard the protection of the custodial parent, described as 'more proactive', suggested that before the actual exercise of the rights of access the custodial parent was to obtain a recognition of the custody decision or an undertaking to this effect from the relevant authority of the Member State of access or from the non-custodial parent.[36]

The Commission's declared aim was the preparation and submission of a proposal for a Council Regulation on parental responsibility and the working document was to be one of the instruments through which this intention was to be accomplished.[37]

As a follow-up to the working document, a public hearing was held on 27 June 2001. The hearing was open to Member States and other interested parties who were given an opportunity to express their views and pass comments on the preliminary considerations for the extension of the scope of the Brussels II Regulation, the corresponding rules on jurisdiction and related issues including the proposed guarantees of the return of the child after his/her stay abroad at the end of the exercise of the cross-border rights of access.

VI. September 2001: The Commission Proposal for a Council Regulation on Jurisdiction and the Recognition and Enforcement of Judgments in Matters of Parental Responsibility

Building on the working document and having taken account of the comments expressed at the public hearing, the Commission prepared a proposal for a Council Regulation on jurisdiction and the recognition and enforcement of judgments in matters of parental responsibility.[38] The proposal was presented on 6 September 2001. The scope of the proposal, however, came as a surprise. Whilst lacking any explanation whatsoever, it completely departed from the scope of

[35] *Ibid*, 17.
[36] *Ibid*.
[37] *Ibid*, final remarks.
[38] Commission proposal (EC) for council regulation on jurisdiction and the recognition and enforcement of judgments in matters of parental responsibility [2001] OJ C332/269.

the preceding texts. Alongside wrongful retentions, the proposal also addressed wrongful removals as the second category of child abduction, quite unrelated to the exercise of access rights. This rather unexpected marked shift in approach suggested that the Union's aspiration was no longer just to facilitate the safe exercise of access rights through deterring unilateral acts of wrongful retentions, but also to strengthen the protection of the custodial parent against both unlawful acts—retentions as well as removals.

According to the proposal the alleged abductor was no longer able to invoke any of the exceptions to return of the child provided for by the 1980 Hague Abduction Convention.[39] The court of the Member State where the child had been removed to or retained in was obliged to order the immediate return of the child to the State of the habitual residence of the child, that is, the requesting State.[40] To provide a certain balance to the exclusion of the possible exceptions to return, the proposal allowed for provisional measures to protect the child to be taken by the court of the State of refuge which would suspend the return of the child until the court of the child's habitual residence decided on the substance of the matter.[41] The time limit for this court to be seized was one month; otherwise the provisional measures ceased to apply.[42] The possibility of the application of the provisional measures was restricted only to cases where there was an urgent need to protect the child. No definition of 'urgent cases' was, however, provided by the proposal. Neither were the provisional measures further specified, apart from a rather vague phrase 'as may be available under the law of that Member State' included in the first paragraph of Article 9.

As can be seen, the basic rule on jurisdiction was the habitual residence of the child. As in the case of the 1980 Hague Abduction Convention, the future of the child was to be determined by the relevant court of his/her habitual residence immediately before the removal or retention.[43] This court would, however, lose jurisdiction to decide on custody and related matters once the child acquired a habitual residence in another Member State and each holder of parental responsibility acquiesced in the abduction, or failed to request the return of the child after having obtained the information on the child's whereabouts for at least a year and the child was settled in his/her new environment.[44]

[39] These exceptions are: custody rights actually not exercised at the time of wrongful removal or retention or wrongful removal or retention consented to or subsequently acquiesced in (Art 13(1)(a)); grave risk that return would expose the child to physical or psychological harm or otherwise place the child in an intolerable situation (Art 13(1)(b)); and fundamental principles of the requested State relating to the protection of human rights and fundamental freedoms (Art 20).

[40] Proposal for Regulation on Jurisdiction, Recognition and Enforcement (n 38) Art 5(3).

[41] *Ibid*, Art 9(1).

[42] *Ibid*, Art 9(2).

[43] *Ibid*, Art 3.

[44] *Ibid*, Art 5.

Overall, the proposal extended the rules on recognition and enforcement of the Brussels II Regulation to all decisions on parental responsibility[45] based on common jurisdictional rules.[46] The principal aim of the Commission was to facilitate the fundamental right of the child whose parents live in different European countries to maintain regular contact with both parents, regardless of whether they lived in a marital or non-marital union.[47] In the explanatory memorandum accompanying the proposal the Commission expressed a general satisfaction with the document, concluding that, construed in conjunction with the French initiative, these two documents implemented the first stage of the second area of the programme of mutual recognition.[48]

VII. October 2001–May 2002: Consultations on the Commission Proposal

The proposal was followed by debates in the Council which emphasised the undesirability of two separate documents and strongly recommended merging the Commission's proposal and the French initiative into a single instrument.[49] The same view was expressed by the Economic and Social Committee, which had been approached by the Council, which was seeking advice through the optional consultation procedure.[50] In its opinion from 16 January 2002, the Economic and Social Committee defended the need to merge the existing Draft documents by the exigency of increased clarity, coherency and consistency of jurisdictional rules and procedures.[51] In the light of these recommendations, the Commission decided to revise the existing proposal and formally withdrew the original text on 6 June 2002. Under these circumstances, the European Parliament expressed its preference not to give its opinion before the new revised proposal was presented.

[45] *Ibid*, Art 1 in conjunction with Art 15.

[46] *Ibid*, ch II Arts 3–14.

[47] European Community, 'Area of freedom, security and justice (14/22), 1.4.14' (Bulletin EU 9-2001), available at www.europa.eu/bulletin/en/200109/p104014.htm.

[48] Commission (EC), 'Explanatory memorandum to the proposal for a council regulation on jurisdiction and the recognition and enforcement of judgments in matters of parental responsibility' COM (2001) 505 final, 4, 6 September 2001.

[49] Commission (EC), 'Explanatory memorandum to the proposal for a council regulation concerning jurisdiction and the recognition and enforcement of judgments in matrimonial matters and matters of parental responsibility repealing Regulation (EC) No 44/2001 in matters relating to maintenance, COM (2002) 222 final/2, 3, 17 May 2002.

[50] Economic and Social Committee (EC), 'Proposal for a council regulation on jurisdiction and the recognition and enforcement of judgements in matters of parental responsibility' (Opinion) 2002 C80/09, 16 January 2002.

[51] *Ibid*, para 2.9.

VIII. May 2002: The Commission Proposal for a Council Regulation Concerning Jurisdiction and the Recognition and Enforcement of Judgments in Matrimonial Matters and in Matters of Parental Responsibility Repealing Regulation (EC) No 1347/2000 and Amending Regulation (EC) No 44/2001 in Matters Relating to Maintenance

The new revised proposal was adopted by the Commission and put before the Council on 3 May 2002. On the same day the document was transmitted to the European Parliament for a mandatory consultation. The revised proposal brought together not only the original Commission proposal and the French initiative, as recommended by the Council and the Economic and Social Committee in January 2002, but went even further. It also incorporated the Brussels II Regulation, thus facilitating divorce and parental responsibility.

On the subject of child abductions the revised proposal greatly expanded the scope of its predecessor, both formally and substantively. A separate chapter was incorporated into the text containing provisions on jurisdiction, the return of the child, provisional protective measures not to return the child, judgments on custody and financial aspects of the proceedings.[52] These provisions were preceded by a short introduction which, while recognising that the 1980 Hague Abduction Convention provided for a successful answer to the issue of child abduction, at the same time criticised the provisions of the Convention which allowed for a transfer of jurisdiction by abduction as an unlawful act if an exception to return was successfully invoked by the abductor. In order to overcome the perceived weakness of the 1980 Convention and thus to prevent the abductors from successfully creating artificial jurisdictional links for the purpose of instigating custody proceedings, the revised proposal excluded all possible exceptions to return granted by the 1980 Convention. The child must have been returned within a strict time limit of one month from having been located.[53] The obligation to return the child was imposed not on a relevant court of the requested Member State but on the Central Authority of this State. The only way to prevent the immediate return of the child was to institute proceedings for a protective measure. A protective measure not to return the child could, however, have been adopted only on the basis of the grave risk of harm exception or the objections of the child.[54] Moreover, the

[52] Commission proposal (EC) for council regulation concerning jurisdiction and the recognition and enforcement of judgments in matrimonial matters and matters of parental responsibility repealing regulation (EC) No 44/2001 in matters relating to maintenance [2002] OJ C203/155–78.

[53] *Ibid*, Art 22.

[54] *Ibid*, Art 23.

protective measure was just temporary; it was valid only until the court of law of the requesting Member State (that is, the Member State of the habitual residence of the child immediately before the removal or retention) issued a custody decision. If this decision entailed the return of the child, there was no excuse for any further delay in returning the child to the requesting State since the judgment was automatically recognised and enforced in the requested Member State.[55] It was only required that the judgment was certified by the court of origin to the effect that it fulfilled all procedural requirements.[56]

Additionally, the document introduced a principle of the mandatory hearing of the child by laying down that the child of a sufficient age and maturity must be heard in the proceedings.[57] No less importantly, it emphasised the importance of active co-operation between Central Authorities.[58]

In contrast to the original Commission proposal the revised proposal made it clear that the Regulation under negotiations once adopted would take precedence over the 1980 Convention[59] and thus supersede the existing summary return mechanism. More and more resembling the final version of the Regulation, the revised proposal, in its own words, aimed at reinforcement of the principle that the most competent court to deliver a judgment on custody is the relevant court of the Member State of the child's habitual residence immediately before the removal or retention.[60]

IX. November 2002: Report of the European Parliament on the Revised Commission Proposal

Notwithstanding the shortcomings of the Commission's action the European Parliament expressed satisfaction with the revised proposal.[61] Express approval was given to the proposed Union-specific solution for child abduction ('applicable to all children in all cases'), particularly to the abolition of the *exequatur* procedure in cases of wrongful removal and retention. Overall, the new child abduction regime was described as a set of comprehensible rules greatly facilitating the protection of the best interests of the child. Certain amendments were, however, suggested in order for the proposal to be approved by the Parliament. First, it called for a direct

[55] *Ibid*, Art 24.
[56] *Ibid*, Art 47.
[57] *Ibid*, Art 24.
[58] *Ibid*, Art 22.
[59] *Ibid*, Art 61.
[60] *Ibid*, Art 24.
[61] European Parliament (EC), 'Proposal for a council regulation concerning jurisdiction and the recognition and enforcement of judgments in matrimonial matters and matters of parental responsibility repealing Regulation (EC) No 44/2001 in matters relating to maintenance' (Report) A5-0385/2002, 7 November 2002.

reference to the primacy of the child's interests in all court proceedings relating to children.[62] Second, the principle of the mandatory hearing of the child in the return proceedings was to be improved by providing for alternatives for recording the views of the child. This was to protect especially younger children from inevitably stressful participation in court hearings by easier options of expressing their views to a child psychologist or a social worker. Certain modifications were also suggested to the return procedure itself. First, it was suggested to make it clear that the Central Authorities should not have a quasi-judicial role but would only be responsible for mediating a voluntary return of the child.[63] If no agreement was achieved, the Central Authority would institute legal proceedings by submitting a return application to the relevant court.[64] This solution replicated obligations imposed on the Central Authorities by Articles 7(c) and 7(f) of the 1980 Convention.

Second, in order to guarantee a speedy resolution of the case, the requested Member State was required to decide on the application for a protective measure within a period of two months, wherever possible.[65] A third substantive change to the return proceedings related to the judgment entailing the return of the child issued by the requesting Member State. It was required so that this judicial decision was more specific and hence spelt out details of the actual return of the child—namely, the period within which the child must be returned and potential consequences of a failure to actually return the child.[66] Finally, acknowledging that the child abduction issues are very complex, and that, unfortunately, not all courts possess the skills and experience necessary for dealing with this type of cross-border family matter, it was suggested to introduce a consultative procedure whereby a judge could discuss the case with the Central Authorities before taking a final decision.[67]

Last but not least, recognising that, inevitably, in different Member States different procedural standards apply and aiming at an increased consistency in these standards, it was suggested to establish guidelines in special cases such as in cases of domestic violence.[68]

The amendments suggested by the European Parliament were, however, not looked upon favourably by the Commission and were rejected.[69]

62 *Ibid*, amendment 7.
63 *Ibid*, explanatory statement.
64 *Ibid*, amendment 9.
65 *Ibid*, amendment 11.
66 *Ibid*, amendment 13.
67 *Ibid*, amendment 19.
68 *Ibid*, amendment 17.
69 Commission (EC), 'Monitoring of the decision-making process between institutions: proposal for a council regulation concerning jurisdiction and the recognition and enforcement of judgments in matrimonial matters and in matters of parental responsibility repealing Regulation (EC) No 1347/2000 and amending Regulation (EC) No 44/2001 in matters relating to maintenance.' (PreLex 2002/0110/CNS) COM (2002) 222, available at www.ec.europa.eu/prelex/detail_dossier_print.cfm?CL=en&DosID=173360.

X. November 2002–November 2003: Heated Negotiations

This stage of negotiations was marked by extremely heated debates on the desirability of the new Union-wide child abduction rules. A strong opposition against the suggested regime and an urgent call for a compromise solution between the Hague and the Union *modus operandi* was expressed by the group of Member States led by the United Kingdom and Germany. Their concerns can best be described in the following statement:

> The proposal set out to replace the 1980 Convention for intra-community cases with a scheme that consultees thought was complex, likely to increase litigation and overburden the authorities and, crucially, took insufficient account of the interests of the child. Moreover, replacing the Hague Convention was seen as likely to send an extremely damaging message of lack of support from Europe that would undermine the Convention's effectiveness worldwide.[70]

Like the opponents of the reform, its proponents were also convinced of their solution. Consequently, it seemed that a compromise was unachievable.[71] In order to prevent the failure of the proposed instrument, efforts were intensified to identify the most problematic provisions and the file was passed to the Council with an expectation that it would find a solution that could eventually be accepted by both camps.[72] The discussions held at the Council resulted in an agreement which was reached at the meeting on 28 and 29 November 2002.[73] According to the agreed text, the 1980 Hague Abduction Convention remained in force but was supplemented by extra provisions for intra-Union cases to reinforce the summary return mechanism. To this effect, if the return proceedings result in a judicial refusal to return, the courts of the requesting State will be allowed to make a custody order. Such an order will be enforceable without any special procedure, providing that the concerns of the court that refused the return of the child were taken into account and procedural safeguards, such as the mandatory hearing of the child and the applicant, were observed. The requested court has a strict obligation to issue its decision within six weeks from being seized with the matter, save in exceptional circumstances.

This agreement was considered an important step forward in the debate on the new intra-Union child abduction regime[74] and opened the door to a final stage of

[70] UK Parliament: European Standing Committee B of the House of Commons, 'Debate on matrimonial matters and parental responsibility' (22 January 2003), available at www.publications.parliament.uk/pa/cm200203/cmstand/eurob/st030122/30122s01.htm.

[71] See McEleavy (n 22) 13.

[72] *Ibid.*

[73] European Community, 'Justice, Home Affairs and Civil Protection, 2469th Council Meeting, Brussels, 28 and 29 November 2002' 14817/02 (Presse 375), available at www.consilium.europa.eu/ueDocs/cms_Data/docs/pressData/en/jha/73439.pdf.

[74] *Ibid.*

negotiations on the Draft Regulation as a whole. The final talks were held at the Council meeting in Luxembourg on 5 and 6 June 2003 and resulted in a conclusion that it would be possible to formally agree upon the Regulation in November 2003, subject to finalisation of certain technical aspects[75] and revision of the text by the Legal Linguistic Experts of the Council.[76] The Regulation was finally adopted on 27 November 2003, entered into force on 1 August 2004 and applied from 1 March 2005.[77]

XI. The Brussels II bis Regulation

The Brussels II bis Regulation emphasises protective measures to nullify a defence under Article 13(1)(b) of the Convention; sets up a special procedure in the event of a refusal under Article 13 of the Convention by the requested State; and promotes automatic enforcement of return orders throughout the region. The key provision is Article 11(4), according to which a court is no longer allowed to refuse a return of the child on the basis of Article 13(1)(b) of the Convention, if it is established that adequate arrangements have been made in the requesting State to secure the protection of the child upon his/her return. Further, according to Article 11(6)–11(8), if a return was refused under Article 13 of the Convention, the court must immediately transmit a copy of the non-return decision to the relevant court in the requesting State.[78] This court must then notify the parties and invite them to make submissions within three months of the day of notification so that the issue of the custody of the child could be examined.[79] A judgment entailing the return of the child is then directly enforceable in the requested Member State.[80]

The relationship between the Regulation and the 1980 Convention is based on a seemingly simple formula that in matters covered by the Regulation this new law prevails over the provisions of the 1980 Convention.[81] Hence, where there has been a wrongful removal or retention, the 1980 Hague Convention continues to apply, however, not in its original form, but as supplemented by the new

[75] European Community, 'Justice, Home Affairs and Civil Protection, 2514th Council Meeting, Luxembourg, 5 and 6 June 2003' 9845/03 (Presse 150), available at www.consilium.europa.eu/ueDocs/cms_Data/docs/pressData/en/jha/73439.pdf.

[76] European Community, 'Justice, Home Affairs and Civil Protection, 2529th Council Meeting, Brussels, 2 and 3 October 2003' 12762/03 (Presse 278), available at www.consilium.europa.eu/ueDocs/cms_Data/docs/pressData/en/jha/77479.pdf.

[77] Council Regulation (EC) 2201/2003 of November 2003 concerning jurisdiction and the recognition and enforcement of judgments in matrimonial matters and the matters of parental responsibility, repealing regulation (EC) No 1347/2000 [2003] OJ L338/1 ('Brussels II bis Regulation').

[78] Brussels II bis Regulation Art 11(6).

[79] Brussels II bis Regulation Art 11(7).

[80] Brussels II bis Regulation Art 42.

[81] Brussels II bis Regulation Art 60(e).

Brussels II Regulation.[82] In relation to the national law of the Member States this EU instrument takes precedence over the domestic legislation.[83] It is directly applicable in the Member States, without a need for implementing statutes.

No doubt, the Regulation deserves credit for reinforcing the first principle of the 1980 Convention that the question of the custody of the child should be decided by the Member State of the habitual residence of the child. It has, however, rightly been argued that, whilst doing so, the scheme upsets the balance between the general obligation of requested courts to return abducted children and the protection of the best interests of an individual child. That balance was successfully achieved by the 1980 Convention through providing for a limited number of exceptions to the obligation to return.[84] Legitimate objections have also been raised against the mechanism established by Articles 11(6)–11(8) which allows the court of the child's habitual residence to review a non-return order made by the requested court pursuant to Article 13 of the Convention. In particular, it was correctly suggested that by allowing non-return orders to be 'trumped' by subsequent return orders, the scheme undermines the principle of mutual trust between the Member States as one of the key principles of the operation of private international law instruments.[85] Last but not least, given the extent of changes made to the Convention summary return mechanism by the Regulation, the instrument has justly been criticised for essentially altering the Convention scheme rather than only complementing it.[86]

XII. Conclusions

The quality of any legislative initiative depends largely upon the conduct of the drafting procedure. Qualities such as general respect for negotiators' views, research and specialist consultation are of the utmost importance in negotiations and an essential prerequisite for a carefully thought through international instrument. Unfortunately, however, it appears that none of these qualities were present during the negotiations on the child abduction provisions of the Brussels II bis Regulation. Quite the contrary, the negotiations were disturbingly marked by a

82 Brussels II bis Regulation recital [17].

83 Commission (EC), 'Practice guide for the application of the new Brussels II Regulation', available at www.ec.europa.eu/civiljustice/publications/docs/guide_new_brussels_ii_en.pdf.

84 McEleavy (n 22) 5.

85 *Ibid*, 31. Given the content of Arts 11(6)–11(8) it is somehow paradoxical that par 21 of the recital to the Brussels II bis Regulation refers to the principle of mutual trust as being a basis for the Regulation's recognition and enforcement procedure.

86 Officially, it was submitted that the Regulation only complements the 1980 Convention mechanism. See recital 17 of the Brussels II bis Regulation. McEleavy (n 22) 6. See also P McEleavy, 'Brussels II bis: Matrimonial Matters, Parental Responsibility, Child Abduction and Mutual Recognition' [Notes] (2004) 53 *International & Comparative Law Quarterly* 503.

self-assured attitude of the Commission and the pro-reformist Member States led by France, and were characterised by a lack of expert involvement.

In particular, the drafting procedure suffered from several defects. The first fault was the sudden appearance of the subject in the Commission proposal from September 2001 and the subsequent disregard for the opposition against the initiative on the side of some of the Member States. Undoubtedly, the way the matter was brought on the scene was highly unusual, considering particularly the fact that wrongful retentions had been at the centre of the dispute since the early stage of the negotiations. Moreover, having pushed for the further extension of the reform of child abduction provisions regardless of strong disagreement of some of the Member States, the Union, sadly, did not present itself as an organisation placing a high value on its Members' opinions.

Second, the proposed Regulation was brought forward without the Commission's experts having conducted any empirical research to justify the need for the Union-specific solution for child abduction. During the consultations on the Commission proposal this deficiency in the approach was later raised by the Economic and Social Committee questioning the necessity to lay down new rules in the Regulation.[87] The reproach, however, was not heeded. Not surprisingly, therefore, the quality of the proposed scheme became a serious concern. It is submitted here that had a properly grounded empirical investigation been carried out, an opportunity would have arisen to identify real problems, and by addressing them, to improve the operation of the Convention at the regional level. Presumably, it would have transpired that there had been no need for tightening the Convention summary return mechanism. Rather, the pressing issue that needed to be addressed was the problem of the safety of the child and the abductor parent upon their return to the requesting State, in particular in abductions motivated by spousal abuse.

Finally, several valuable provisions that appeared in the proposals were for some unexplained reason omitted from the final version of the scheme. This slip only substantiated the claim that the intra-EU child abduction regime was drafted in a highly unprofessional and confused manner, with the quality of the proposed scheme being at the bottom of the drafters' list of priorities. In particular, the revised proposal from May 2002 guaranteed better protection to the child than its successor, the final version of the Regulation. This safeguard was provided through the provision of Article 23, termed 'Provisional protective measure not to return the child'. According to this Article, if an application for the protective measure was granted, the child could stay in the requested State, as the return was delayed pending the adjudication of custody in the requesting State. The preventive measures were, however, unwisely omitted from the final Regulation. It is submitted here that had the provision of Article 23 been incorporated into the Brussels II bis Regulation, the instrument would have significantly alleviated the

[87] Opinion of the Economic and Social Committee (n 50) para 2.4.

major drawback of the Convention return mechanism—the problem of the safety of the child and the returning parent, applicable especially in Article 13(1)(b) cases involving domestic violence.

In a similar manner, the report of the European Parliament on the revised Commission proposal from November 2002 made a useful recommendation that a consultative procedure be introduced whereby a judge could discuss the case with the Central Authorities before taking a final decision.[88] The report also suggested the establishment of guidelines in special cases such as cases involving domestic violence.[89] It is submitted here that both provisions, if they had been included in the final version of the regulation, would have improved the quality of the new scheme, the former in terms of outcomes whereas the latter in terms of the safety of the child and the abducting parent. The consultation procedure would be of great assistance in the Member States where the jurisdiction for hearing child abduction cases has not been concentrated.[90] The guidelines for cases of domestic violence would be of immense value, given the vague wording of Article 11(4) of the Regulation.[91]

[88] Report of the European Parliament (n 61) amendment 19.

[89] *Ibid*, amendment 17.

[90] Contracting States to the 1980 Hague Abduction Convention have been recommended to take measures to concentrate jurisdiction for Convention cases in a limited number of courts. Permanent Bureau of the Hague Conference, 'Conclusions and Recommendations of the Fourth Meeting of the Special Commission to Review the Operation of the Hague Convention of 25 October 1980 on the Civil Aspects of International Child Abduction, 22–28 March 2001' Part III, para 3.1, available at www.hcch.net/upload/concl28sc4_e.pdf. The key advantages to be gained by such a concentration of jurisdiction are: '[A]n accumulation of experience among the judges concerned; and as a result, the development of mutual confidence between judges and authorities in different legal systems; the creation of a high level of interdisciplinary understanding of Convention objectives, in particular the distinction from custody proceedings; mitigation against delay; and greater consistency of practice by judges and lawyers.' Permanent Bureau of the Hague Conference, 'Guide to Good Practice under the Hague Convention of 25 October 1980 on the Civil Aspects of International Child Abduction: Part II—Implementing Measures' at 29, available at www.hcch.net/upload/abdguide2_e.pdf. It has, nevertheless, been recognised that despite the considerable benefits of the concentration of jurisdiction, in some Contracting States this arrangement was not possible. See Fourth Special Commission Meeting (n 90).

[91] For a detailed analysis see section entitled 'Flaws of Article 11(4)' below.

3

Principles of Good Legislative Drafting vs Child Abduction Provisions of the Brussels II bis Regulation

The quality of law-making is of great concern to the European Union. Since the Edinburgh European Council in December 1992, it has been a declared intention of the EU institutions involved in the legislative process to work towards the improvement of legislative processes and outputs.[1] In December 1998 the Interinstitutional agreement on common guidelines for the quality of the drafting of Community legislation[2] was adopted. A further action was stimulated by the 2000 Lisbon European Council, which called on the Community institutions and Member States to develop a strategic plan for improving the regulatory environment.[3] As a result, in 2002 the Commission's Action plan for better regulation[4] was prepared. The action plan became a foundation for the Interinstitutional agreement on better lawmaking published on 31 December 2003.[5]

The ultimate aim of the initiative to improve the quality of the EU legislation is a greater effectiveness and acceptability of Community law-making activities in the eyes of Member States and European citizens. Snappy slogans such as 'better lawmaking' or 'legislate less to act better' have become catchwords of this policy.[6]

[1] R Baldwin, 'Is Better Regulation Smarter Regulation?' [2005] *Public Law* 485, 488.

[2] Parliament, Council and Commission (EC), Interinstitutional agreement of 22 December 1998 on common guidelines for the quality of drafting of community legislation [1999] OJ C73/1.

[3] 'Prodi Presents Initiatives Aimed at Improving EU's Working Methods' (Editorial) (2002) 112 EU Focus 19, 19.

[4] Commission (EC), 'Action plan on simplifying and improving the regulatory environment' (Communication) COM (2002) 278 final, 5 June 2002.

[5] Parliament, Council and Commission (EC), Interinstitutional agreement of 16 December 2003 on better lawmaking [2003] OJ C321/01. It is to be noted that the above list of the Community measures aimed at improving the quality of the regulatory environment is not exhaustive. Between the mid-1990s and the adoption of the Interinstitutional agreement on better lawmaking in 2003 the Community institutions produced a number of other documents relevant to the "better lawmaking" strategy. For some examples see L Senden, 'Soft Law, Self-Regulation and Co-Regulation in European Law: Where Do They Meet?' (2005) 9 *Electronic Journal of Comparative Law* 1, fn 19. For a more detailed review see H Xanthaki, 'The Problem of Quality in EU Legislation' (2001) 38 *Common Market Law Review* 615.

[6] Senden, 'Soft Law, Self-Regulation and Co-Regulation' (n 5) 5.

Chapter 2 indicated that the legislative procedure for the new intra-EU child abduction mechanism was marked by certain non-standard techniques. In particular, these included a flagrant disregard for the reservations of a number of Member States against the proposed scheme, and a lack of expert involvement in the drafting procedure. This Chapter therefore characterises the European Community's law-making policy valid between July 1999 and November 2003[7] and investigates to what extent the process of adoption of the new child abduction regime complied with the Community's principles of good legislative drafting, in particular, the principles of subsidiarity and proportionality, and the rule of mandatory consultation. The Chapter provides background information on each of the principles and then critically assesses to what extent these principles were applied throughout the negotiations on the new child abduction regulation.

I. The Principles of Subsidiarity and Proportionality

Guiding principles of the European Union's long-term plan to improve the quality of regulatory environment, so called 'better law making', are the principle of subsidiarity and its 'brother principle', proportionality.[8] Precise criteria for applying these principles are set out in the Protocol on the Application of the Principles of Subsidiarity and Proportionality, annexed to the Treaty of Amsterdam.[9]

Subsidiarity and proportionality were, however, not born with the Treaty of Amsterdam.[10] Both principles had already been enshrined in Article 3b of the EEC Treaty as amended by the Maastricht Treaty[11] (later Article 5 of the EC

[7] The Chapter looks at the European law-making policy as it stood at the time of the drafting of the Brussels II bis Regulation. It is therefore to be understood that all references to the EC Treaty mean the Treaty on European Union as amended by the Treaty of Amsterdam (in force between 1 May 1999 and 30 November 2009). Occasionally, however, reference has been made to the Treaty of Lisbon (Treaty of Lisbon amending the Treaty on European Union and the Treaty Establishing the European Community, signed at Lisbon, 13 December 2007, in force since 1 December 2009), so as to provide the reader with an overview of the most significant changes introduced to the issues under the discussion by the Treaty of Lisbon. (With the entry into force of the Treaty of Lisbon, the EC Treaty (ie the Treaty Establishing the European Community) has been replaced by the Treaty on the Functioning of the European Union (TFEU).

[8] European Community, 'Edinburgh European Council: Presidency Conclusions' (11–12 December 1992), available at www.europarl.europa.eu/summits/edinburgh/default_en.htm; and Commission (EC), 'The principle of subsidiarity' (Communication) SEC (92)90 final, 27 October 1992.

[9] Protocol (No 30) on the application of the principles of subsidiarity and proportionality, annexed to the Treaty of Amsterdam (Protocol No 30) [1997] OJ C340/105. Now Protocol (No 2) on the application of the principles of subsidiarity and proportionality, annexed to the Treaty of Lisbon (Protocol No 2, annexed to the Treaty of Lisbon).

[10] In this context, it has been suggested in general terms that 'the concept of subsidiarity has always permeated the European Community'. JW Bridge, 'Constitutions, Powers and the Doctrine of Subsidiarity' (1999) 31 *Bracton Law Journal* 49, 51.

[11] Treaty on European Union (the Maastricht Treaty) [1992] OJ C191.

Treaty).[12] Article 5 of the EC Treaty is a three-part provision covering in the first clause the principle of attribution (also called 'the principle of conferral'), in the second clause the principle of subsidiarity and in the third clause the principle of proportionality. Each principle integrates with the others and together they furnish all aspects of the distribution of competences. A particularly strong link is between the principle of subsidiarity and the principle of proportionality.[13] The notion of attribution lays down the rule of limited Community competence, that is, that the Community may only act within the limits of jurisdiction granted to it by the Treaty.[14] The concept of subsidiarity aims to guarantee that decisions in Europe are taken at the most relevant level.[15] The principle of proportionality then further limits the scope of the Community's powers to only those actions that are indispensable for the achievement of the objectives of the Treaty.[16]

Protocol No 30 to the EC Treaty imposes on the Commission an obligation to justify its legislative proposals having regard to the principles of subsidiarity and

[12] AG Toth, 'Legal Analysis of Subsidiarity' in D O'Keeffe and P Twomey (eds), *Legal Issues of the Maastricht Treaty* (London, Wiley Chancery Law, 1994) 37–8. For a summary of the historical legacy of subsidiarity see N Emiliou, 'Subsidiarity: An Effective Barrier against the Enterprises of Ambition' (1992) 17 *European Law Review* 383. Other earlier literature on subsidiarity includes V Constantinesco, 'Who's Afraid of Subsidiarity?' (1991) 11 *Yearbook of European Law* 33; J Delors, *Subsidiarity: the Challenge of Change (Proceedings of the Jacques Delors Colloquium 1991)* (Maastricht, Institute of Public Administration, 1991); DZ Cass, 'The Word That Saves Maastricht? The Principle of Subsidiarity and the Division of Powers Within the European Community' (1992) 29 *Common Market Law Review* 1107; AG Toth, 'The Principle of Subsidiarity in the Maastricht Treaty' (1992) 29 *Common Market Law Review* 1079; J Steiner, 'Subsidiarity Under the Maastricht Treaty' in D O'Keeffe and P Twomey (eds), *Legal Issues of the Maastricht Treaty* (London, Wiley Chancery Law, 1994) 49 (the implementation of the principle by the Community under the Maastricht Treaty); N Emiliou, 'Subsidiarity: Panacea or Fig Leaf?' in D O'Keeffe and P Twomey (eds), *Legal Issues of the Maastricht Treaty* (London, Wiley Chancery Law, 1994) 65; K Lenaerts, 'The Principle of Subsidiarity and the Environment in the European Union: Keeping Balance of Federalism' (1994) 17 *Fordham International Law Journal* 846; PD Marquardt, 'Subsidiarity and Sovereignty in the European Union' (1994) 18 *Fordham International Law Journal* 616; I Pernice, 'The Framework Revisited: Constitutional, Federal and Subsidiarity Issues' (1995–1996) 2 *Columbia Journal of European Law* 403.

[13] Committee of the Regions, *The Committee of Regions and the Implementation and Monitoring of the Principles of Subsidiarity and Proportionality in the Light of the Constitution for Europe* (Brussels, Office for Official Publications of the European Communities, 2006) 53. In this respect, it has been pointed out that subsidiarity and proportionality have a cumulative effect. Steiner, 'Subsidiarity Under the Maastricht Treaty' (n 13) 49 and 60.

[14] For a detailed analysis of the principle of conferral see, eg, A Dashwood, 'The Relationship Between the Member States and the European Union/European Community' (2004) 41 *Common Market Law Review* 355, 357–66.

[15] Committee of the Regions (EC), 'Application and monitoring of the subsidiarity and proportionality principles: the Committee of the Regions' political and operational role' (Report) 2006 R/CdR 191, 02 August 2006. Also G Davies, 'Subsidiarity: The Wrong Idea, In the Wrong Place, at the Wrong Time' (2006) 43 *Common Market Law Review* 63, 67; and GA Bermann, 'Taking Subsidiarity Seriously: Federalism in the European Community and the United States' (1994) 32 *Columbia Law Review* 331, 338.

[16] Edinburgh European Council: Presidency Conclusions (n 8) 8–9. N Emiliou, *The EU Principle of Proportionality in European Law: Comparative Study* (London, Kluwer Law International, 1996) 140; and ET Swaine, 'Subsidiarity and Self-Interest: Federalism at the European Court of Justice' (2000) 41 *Harvard International Law Journal* 17, 56 ('subsidiarity generally concerns the propriety of Community actions, and proportionality the degree or scope of that action').

proportionality.[17] The Commission is also required to submit a yearly report on the implementation of the principle of subsidiarity to the European Council, the European Parliament and the Council.[18] In these reports, the Commission annually advises of progress made in the area and reaffirms its commitment to the 'better law making' process.[19] Among other achievements the Commission declares a steady decrease in the number of its proposals for new legislation.[20] This trend is to demonstrate that there is a 'new legislative culture'[21] in the Union as an expression of a general policy 'do less, but do it better'.[22]

A. Subsidiarity[23]

The principle of subsidiarity is a guide to the exercise of Community powers.[24] It was at the relevant time formulated in the second clause of Article 5 of the EC Treaty:[25]

> In areas which do not fall within its exclusive competence, the Community shall take action, in accordance with the principle of subsidiarity, only if and in so far as the objectives of the proposed action cannot be sufficiently achieved by the Member States and can therefore, by reason of the scale or effects of the proposed action, be better achieved by the Community.

[17] Protocol No 30, provision 9.

[18] *Ibid.* This obligation was first imposed on the Commission by the Edinburgh European Council in December 1992 with a view to monitoring the application of the principle. It was reiterated in 1993 in the Interinstitutional agreement between the European Parliament, the Council and the Commission on procedures for implementing the subsidiarity principle (concluded on 29 October 1993; Bull 10-1993, [2.2.2]); and later incorporated into provision 9 of Protocol No 30.

[19] The annual reports cover not only subsidiarity and proportionality but also other measures aimed at better lawmaking. These include codification, simplification of legal acts, efforts towards more advanced dialogue with Member States, and a better access by citizens to information on European law. R von Borries and M Hauschield, 'Implementing the Subsidiarity Principle' (1998–1999) 5 *Columbia Journal of European Law* 369, 382.

[20] See the 1997 and 1998 reports: Commission (EC), 'Better Lawmaking 1997' (Report) COM (97) 626 final; and Commission (EC), 'Better Lawmaking 1998' (Report) COM (98) 715 final.

[21] Better Lawmaking 1997 (n 20) 9.

[22] I Cooper, 'The Watchdogs of Subsidiarity: National Parliaments and the Logic of Arguing in the EU' (2006) 44 *Journal of Common Market Studies* 281, 286.

[23] The principle of subsidiarity is particularly important for the purpose of examining compliance with the standards of good legislative drafting in the case of the Brussels II bis Regulation. For an in-depth analysis of the principle of subsidiarity see Bermann, 'Taking Subsidiarity Seriously' and A Estella, *The EU Principle of Subsidiarity and Its Critique* (Oxford, Oxford University Press, 2002). The above materials represent leading secondary resources on the subject. It is, however, to be noted that, for the purposes of this thesis, the utility of Bermann's article is to some extent diminished. The reason for this is that the article, having been published in 1994, represents an older writing on subsidiarity and is therefore partly outdated.

[24] Estella, *The EU Principle of Subsidiarity* (n 23) 103. Estella points out that subsidiarity is a principle regulating the exercise—as opposed to the attribution—of Community competences.

[25] The definition of the principle of subsidiarity is reiterated in provisions 3 and 5 of Protocol No 30. Under the currently valid Treaty of Lisbon, the definition of subsidiarity is enshrined in Art 5 of the Treaty on European Union (consolidated version).

The above Article implies that where the Community does not have exclusive powers,[26] the Commission examines the feasibility of its action on the two related criteria. It has to assess: first, whether the intended objectives can be attained sufficiently well by the Member States (the criterion of necessity); and second, whether these objectives can be better achieved at the Community level (the criterion of efficiency).[27] This analysis is called the 'subsidiarity test'.

i. 'Upward' Application of the Principle of Subsidiarity

In certain instances the objectives of the proposed action can, however, be better achieved at an international level rather than at Community or national level.[28] The Commission itself has repeatedly acknowledged this fact and instructed that in such cases subsidiarity be applied analogously (so called 'reverse' or 'upwards' application of the principle of subsidiarity).[29] Therefore, when it is appropriate that decision making take place in an international framework rather than in the context of the European Union, subsidiarity must be applied in the 'upward' fashion and the Community must restrain from legislative action in the area. Doubtless, considering an increasingly significant external dimension of the European Union, the 'upward' subsidiarity is an important element of the ongoing debate about appropriate levels of legislative action in the framework of the

[26] Quite surprisingly, however, neither the Treaty nor the Protocol defines the notions of non-exclusive competence or states the spheres covered. It has therefore, never been straightforward to determine which policy fields are covered (Estella (n 23) 104). Nevertheless, the currently valid Treaty of Lisbon specifies principal areas that are subject to non-exclusive (ie shared) competence. According to Art 4(2) these areas are: the internal market; social policy, for the aspects defined in the Treaty; economic, social and territorial cohesion; agriculture and fisheries, excluding the conservation of marine biological resources; the environment; consumer protection; transport; trans-European networks energy; the area of freedom, security and justice; and common safety concerns in public health matters, for the aspects defined in the Treaty. For a detailed analysis of the problem of competences between the EU and its Member States under the Lisbon Treaty see P Craig, 'The Treaty of Lisbon, Process, Architecture and Substance' (2008) 33 *European Law Review* 137, 144–49; 'Legislative Comment: Oh Brave New World! Lisbon Enters Into Force' [2010] *EU Focus* 1, 13; and R Schutze, 'Lisbon and the Federal Order of Competences: A Prospective Analysis' (2008) 33 *European Law Review* 709.

[27] Commission (EC), 'Better Lawmaking 1996' (Report) CSE (96) 7 final, 2. The criteria of necessity and efficiency are reiterated by provision 5 of Protocol No 30.

[28] In the context of family law, this fact was first acknowledged some 16 years ago by Beaumont and Moir in their article 'Brussels Convention II: A New Private International Law Instrument in Family Matters for the European Community?'. In particular, the authors suggested: '[T]here is scope for arguing that subsidiarity should compel the Union to consider whether action could be better taken at an international level rather than a European level.' P Beaumont and G Moir, 'Brussels Convention II: A New Private International Law Instrument in Family Matters for the European Community?' (1995) 20 European Law Review 268, 284.

[29] Better Lawmaking 1997 (n 20) 4; and Commission (EC), 'Better Lawmaking 2000' (Report) COM (2000) 772 final 4. The term 'reverse subsidiarity' was suggested by P Beaumont and G Moir in Beaumont and Moir, 'Brussels Convention II'. See also P Beaumont, 'International Family Law in Europe—the Maintenance Project, the Hague Conference and the EC: A Triumph of Reverse Subsidiarity' (2009) 73 *Rabels Zeitschrift* 509, fn 1.

European Union.[30] At this point, it is considered essential to point out that the 'upward' application of subsidiarity is relevant in the context of child abduction.[31]

ii. Subsidiarity Test and Child Abduction

Article 5 of the EC Treaty[32] established two criteria for implementing subsidiarity: the necessity criterion and the efficiency criterion (also called the 'sufficiency' and the 'value-added' criteria[33]). In the context of child abduction, these criteria must be applied in the 'upward' fashion. In this case, according to the necessity criterion, the Community shall act 'only if and so far as the objectives of the proposed action cannot be sufficiently achieved by a relevant international treaty'.[34]

According to the efficiency criterion, the Community shall act 'if by reason of the scale or effects of the proposed action, the objective can be better achieved by the Community'.[35]

For a Community legislative action to be legitimate, both aspects of the principle of subsidiarity must be met cumulatively.[36] The burden of proof lies on the Union institutions to demonstrate the justification for Union legislative action in preference to action taken at the international level.[37] This implies that, to give a good reason for the new child abduction regime, the Union had to demonstrate that the existing international legislation, that is, the 1980 Hague Abduction Convention, was not achieving the aims of the proposed child abduction scheme

[30] Ch Timmermans, 'Subsidiarity and Transparency' (1998–1999) 22 *Fordham International Law Journal* S106, S112. Timmermans acknowledges in general terms that the concept of the 'upwards' application of the principle of subsidiarity is 'not new' and of 'rapidly growing importance'. See also P McEleavy, 'The Brussels II Regulation: How the European Community Has Moved into Family Law' (2002) 51 *International and Comparative Law Quarterly* 883, fn 78, arguing for 'reverse subsidiarity' in the context of parental responsibility. Also G De Búrca, 'Reappraising Subsidiarity's Significance after Amsterdam', NYU School of Law & Jean Monnet Center—Harvard Jean Monnet Working Paper 7/99, at 10–11 and 19, available at www.centers.law.nyu.edu/jeanmonnet/papers/99/990703.html. De Búrca accepts that subsidiarity covers also the 'upwards' application of this principle, but is not of the view that Art 5 of the EC Treaty implies reverse subsidiarity.

[31] Importantly, reverse subsidiarity worked successfully in the context of maintenance. See P Beaumont, 'International Family Law in Europe—the Maintenance Project, the Hague Conference and the EC: A Triumph of Reverse Subsidiarity' (2009) 73 *The Rabel Journal of Comparative and International Private Law* 510. Persuasive arguments in favour of a global rather than a regional solution included the fact that 'globalisation has led to more families with an international dimension not just within the EU but throughout the world and the large movements of people have often followed different patterns than those prompted by European integration, eg Asians from the British Commonwealth moving to the United Kingdom, Turkish people seeking employment in Germany, North Africans migrating to France, etc.' Also, it was rightly pointed out that 'with the increased diversity in approaches to family law … it would not be possible to reach deeper agreements at the EU level than it would globally in the Hague', *ibid*, 511.

[32] See now Art 5 of the Treaty on European Union post the entry into force of the Treaty of Lisbon.

[33] Estella (n 23) 93.

[34] Protocol No 30, provision 5, 'upwards' application.

[35] *Ibid*.

[36] *Ibid*, provision 5. See also Ch Henkel, 'The Allocation of Powers in the European Union: A Closer Look at the Principle of Subsidiarity' (2002) 20 *Berkeley Journal of International Law* 359, 370.

[37] The Principle of Subsidiarity (n 8) 4.

and that these aims could have been better achieved by action on the part of the European Union.

a. The Term 'Objectives of the Proposed Action'

Prior to the analysis of the application of the subsidiarity principle to the new intra-EU child abduction regime, it is considered important to take a closer look at the term 'objectives of the proposed action' in the context of the Brussels II bis Regulation.

The term 'objectives of the proposed action' contained in the second clause of Article 5 is not an easy expression to interpret. Generally, it is rightly considered to be fairly ambiguous.[38] The obscurity of the expression was also apparent in the case of the Brussels II bis Regulation. None of the proposals made during the negotiations, nor the final text of the Regulation, specifically addresses the issue of the objectives of the Community action in question. The Preamble to the French initiative on rights of access from July 2000 only implicitly stated that the objective of the proposed Regulation was to contribute to the establishment of a genuine European judicial area, in which, amongst other things, judgments relating to visitation rights would be directly enforceable in the Member States.[39]

The Commission proposal from September 2001 did not contain any mention of the objectives of the proposed Regulation. Neither did the revised Commission proposal from May 2002. Only the explanatory memorandum to the revised proposal clarified that the general aim of the proposal was recognition and enforcement of judgments in matrimonial matters and in matters of parental responsibility within the Union.[40] The explanatory memorandum also stated that a specific objective of the Community action in this context was the protection of the child's best interests, through safeguarding the child's fundamental right to maintain contact with both parents.[41]

The final version of the Brussels II bis Regulation is also far from being clear about its objectives. Indeed, there is no provision dealing with this issue contained in the Regulation. It is only the Practice guide for the application of the new Brussels II Regulation where some aims of the Regulation are worded. This list is,

[38] It has been suggested that the way the objective of the proposed Community measure is defined in a particular case largely affects the result of the efficiency test. J Snell, 'European Constitutional Settlement, An Ever Closer Union, and the Treaty of Lisbon: Democracy or Relevance?' (2008) 33 *European Law Review* 619, 629. It is, however, submitted here that it is not only the result of the efficiency test but also the result of the necessity test that depends on how the 'objectives of the proposed action' are defined.

[39] Initiative of the French Republic of 3 July 2000 with a view to adopting a council regulation on the mutual enforcement of judgments on rights of access to children [2000] OJ C 234/08, preamble, recital 2.

[40] Commission (EC), 'Explanatory memorandum to the proposal for a council regulation concerning jurisdiction and the recognition and enforcement of judgments in matrimonial matters and matters of parental responsibility repealing Regulation (EC) No 44/2001 in matters relating to maintenance, COM (2002) 222 final/2, 3, 17 May 2002.

[41] *Ibid*, 5.

however, utterly non-exhaustive as the issue has not been dealt with in a systematic way. According to the guide, one of the primary objectives of the Regulation is 'to ensure that a child can maintain contact with all holders of parental responsibility after a separation, even when they live in different Member States (Articles 40, 41)'.[42] The guide also gives specific aims of the Regulation concerning child abduction. In this context, the Regulation aims at deterring parental child abduction within the Union and, if a child abduction takes place, ensuring the prompt return of the child to the Member State of his/her habitual residence.[43]

As can be seen from the above examination, there was no comprehensive definition of the 'objectives of the proposed action' given during the negotiations on the Brussels II bis Regulation. The fact is that it cast doubts on the overall reliability of the results of the necessity test, as it could hardly have been possible to carry out this examination without first having clearly defined the proposed objectives.

It is believed that, apart from the lack of a clear definition of the 'objectives of the proposed action', the uncertain quality of the necessity test in the case of the Brussels II bis Regulation can be assigned to the 'multi-layer' character of the proposed objectives. The 'multi-layer' describes the fact that there are main objectives, sub-objectives, and possible further sub-sub-objectives contained in the proposals as well as in the Regulation itself.[44] For example, as noted before, the main objective of the Regulation is to guarantee a child's fundamental right to maintain contact with both parents, even when they live in different EU Member States. In addition, the Regulation has several sub-objectives, including the aim to tackle parental child abduction within the Union and, if a child abduction takes place, to ensure the prompt return of the child to the Member State of his/her habitual residence. At first sight, the relationship between these two 'layers' of objectives appears to be that of the objective of an action and the means to achieve that action.[45] In other words, the aim to deter child abduction and to ensure the prompt return of the child, if the child is abducted within the Union, seems to be one of the means to guarantee the child's fundamental right to maintain contact with both parents. This approach has, however, negative practical implications, which adversely affect the performance of the necessity test. This adversity consists in the fact that the test is carried out only in relation to the primary objectives of the proposed action. The sub-objectives, being only the means to attain the main goals, are not subject to the necessity test. In the light of these thoughts this approach appears to be clearly misguided. Rather, it is suggested that every 'layer' of objectives be viewed as individual aims, which themselves must be checked against necessity. At this point, one feels a compelling urge to ask which approach

[42] Commission (EC), 'Practice guide for the application of the new Brussels II Regulation', available at www.ec.europa.eu/civiljustice/publications/docs/guide_new_brussels_ii_en.pdf.

[43] *Ibid*, 28.

[44] De Búrca refers in this context to the problem of 'the degree of specificity' with which a particular objective of the proposed action is defined. De Búrca, 'Reappraising Subsidiarity's Significance' (n 30) 25.

[45] It implies that the more specifically we define an objective, the more it can also be described as the action taken to accomplish a broader objective. *Ibid*.

was taken in the case of the Brussels II bis Regulation. Neither the preparatory documents nor the Regulation provide an answer to this question. Nevertheless, the hasty character of the negotiations indicates that the Commission might not have had enough time to carry out the necessity test in relation to all objectives of the Regulation. Hence, it can be assumed that only the main aims were checked against the necessity, and that the sub-objectives of the Regulation, including the objectives in the area of child abduction, were regrettably overlooked.

b. Necessity Test

In order for the new child abduction regime to pass the necessity test, the Commission had to prove that the 1980 Hague Abduction Convention was not 'sufficiently' efficient in attaining the objectives of the proposed Regulation.
The result of the necessity test can be found in recital 32 of the Preamble to the Regulation. The recital states:

> Since the objectives of this Regulation cannot be sufficiently achieved by the Member States ... the Community may adopt measures, in accordance with the principle of subsidiarity as set out in Article 5 of the Treaty.

The self-assured character of the above statement gives the impression that the Commission had no doubts as to whether the necessity criterion was applied correctly. Let us therefore presume that the Commission took the right approach and conducted the necessity test in relation to each objective of the proposed Regulation separately. Subsequently, in the area of child abduction, recital 32 states:

> The objective of deterring parental child abduction within the Union and, if a child abduction takes place, ensuring the prompt return of the child to the Member State of his/her habitual residence, cannot be sufficiently achieved by the 1980 Hague Abduction Convention.

In more familiar language, the above paragraph claims that the 1980 Hague Abduction Convention was not operating sufficiently well and thus not attaining the objective of the prompt return of abducted children to the country of their habitual residence. This statement, however, has hardly any persuasive power, unless it is backed up by supporting evidence. Indeed, Protocol No 30 of the Amsterdam Treaty imposes on the Commission the obligation to justify proposed legislation with regard to the principle of subsidiarity:

> For any proposed Community legislation, the reasons on which it is based shall be stated with a view to justifying its compliance with the principles of subsidiarity and proportionality.[46]

[46] Protocol No 30, provision 4. Notably, the procedural obligation of provision 4 applies not only to the Commission but to all Community institutions which have the power to propose legislation as well as to Member States (in the context of the Member States' right to propose legislation); see Estella (n 23) 124. A compliance with the principle of subsidiarity is required also from the Council and the European Parliament when making amendments to the Commission proposals (Protocol No 30, provision 11). Another responsibility imposed on the Council and the European Parliament in the context of subsidiarity is an obligation to examine the proposals submitted to them by the Commission for their consistency with subsidiarity (Protocol No 30, provision 11).

> Without prejudice to its right of initiative, the Commission should justify the relevance of its proposals with regard to the principle of subsidiarity; whenever necessary, the explanatory memorandum accompanying a proposal will give details in this respect.[47]

In other words, every proposal and, if necessary, also the explanatory memorandum, must contain a description of how the proposed legislation has been measured against subsidiarity.[48] Nevertheless, in contravention of this legal duty, the Commission did not provide any explanation of how the suggested intra-EU child abduction regime was justified in the light of the necessity criterion. Indeed, neither the first Commission proposal from September 2001 nor the revised Commission proposal from May 2002 includes any details on the necessity test.[49] An explanatory memorandum to the Regulation, as a potential source of information, is also out of the question as, unfortunately, none has been drafted in this case.

The only argument as to why there was a need for the new child abduction regime is found in the Commission working document on the mutual recognition of decisions on parental responsibility from March 2001.[50] This document asserts that there have been practical problems with the application of the 1980 Hague Abduction Convention. Particularly, there is a claim of a frequent abuse of the Article 13(1)(b) exception to return. Evidence to support this contention was drawn from the 1999 statistical survey on the operation of the Convention conducted by the Cardiff Law School in co-operation with the Permanent Bureau of the Hague Conference.[51] However, it is submitted here that this evidence was obtained through only a superficial examination that led to incorrect analysis and interpretation of the 1999 statistical survey.[52]

Moreover, the credibility of the Commission's reasoning was paradoxically undermined by another Community institution, the Economic and Social Committee. In its opinion from January 2002, the Committee concluded that: '[I]t is not at first sight clear why there should be a need to lay down new rules [on

[47] Protocol No 30, provision 9.

[48] European Parliament (EC), 'Resolution on the Commission report to the European Council on better lawmaking 2000 and on the Commission report to the European Council on better lawmaking 2001' P5_TA(2003)0143, [21].

[49] Given the fact that the obligation to justify proposed legislation in the light of the principle of subsidiarity applies not only to the Commission but also to Member States (n 46 above), the French initiative on the rights of access from July 2000 was also deficient in this respect. Indeed, no justification for compliance with subsidiarity was given by France in the document.

[50] Commission (EC), 'Mutual recognition of decisions on parental responsibility' (Working Document) COM (2001) 166 final, 8, 27 March 2001.

[51] N Lowe, S Armstrong and A Mathias, 'A Statistical Analysis of Applications made in 1999 under the Hague Convention on the Civil Aspects of International Child Abduction' Preliminary Document No 3 (2001), available at www.hcch.net/upload/abd2001pd3e.pdf ('1999 statistical survey').

[52] For a detailed analysis of the 1999 statistical survey see Chapter 4, section entitled 'The Statistical Analysis of Applications made in 1999 under the Hague Convention on the Civil Aspects of International Child Abduction'.

child abduction] in the Regulation'.[53] Undoubtedly, this statement indicates that the Committee did not find the Commission's evidence to justify the need for the new child abduction regime compelling. The above analysis inevitably leads to the conclusion that, in the case of the new child abduction regime, the Commission neglected its duty to sufficiently justify the need for the proposed legislation.

c. Efficiency Test

In order for the new child abduction regime to pass the efficiency test, the Commission had to prove that the objectives of the proposed Regulation could, by reason of the scale or effects of the proposed action, be better achieved by the Community.

Like the result of the necessity test, the outcome of the efficiency test is set out in recital 32 of the Preamble to the Regulation:

> [The objectives of this Regulation] can be better achieved at the Community level. [Therefore,] [t]he Community may adopt measures, in accordance with the principle of subsidiarity as set out in Article 5 of the Treaty.

Assuming again that the Commission conducted the necessity test in relation to each objective of the proposed Regulation separately, in the area of child abduction recital 32 asserts:

> The objective of deterring parental child abduction within the Union and, if a child abduction takes place, ensuring the prompt return of the child to the Member State of his/her habitual residence, can be better achieved at the Community level [than it is achieved by the 1980 Hague Abduction Convention].

Unfortunately, as with the necessity test, the preparatory documents are silent on the reasons behind the results of the efficiency test. It is therefore to be questioned what made the Commission believe that the new regime envisaged at the Community level would tackle child abduction more efficiently and effectively than the 1980 Hague Abduction Convention.

It has been suggested that careful attention must be paid to the 'scale and effects of the proposed action'.[54] In other words, it must be demonstrated that there will be benefits in scale or effect as a consequence of Community action. Hence, let us retrospectively examine what could have been viewed as potential benefits of the new intra-EU child abduction regime.

The Abduction Convention signed in The Hague on 25 October 1980 has long been a key international instrument for protecting children from harmful effects of wrongful removals and retentions. The Convention has been in force since 1983 and as of September 2011 boasts 86 Contracting Parties, including all EU

[53] Economic and Social Committee (EC), 'Proposal for a Council regulation on jurisdiction and the recognition and enforcement of judgments in matters of parental responsibility' (Opinion) 2002 C80/09, par 2.4, 16 January 2002.

[54] R Dehousse (ed), *Europe After Maastricht: An Ever Closer Union?* (Munich, Law Books in Europe, 1994) 113.

Member States.[55] The Convention has proved a phenomenal success and at the relevant time (that is, 2001–2003) was rightly considered to be the most successful family law instrument completed under the auspices of the Hague Conference on Private International Law.[56] In the Contracting States, the Convention achieved a fundamental change in the attitude of the judiciary towards cases of wrongful removal and retention. Prior to the adoption of the Convention, the general perception was that the child should not be returned to the country of his/her habitual residence, especially if the abduction was committed by the mother of the child.[57] Though this opinion is still widely shared by the general public in the Contracting States, the courts have altered their way of thinking and accepted that the most appropriate jurisdiction to decide on the child's best interests is the country of the child's habitual residence.[58]

Logical reasoning suggests that a worldwide solution to a problem is better than regional rules, especially if the worldwide regulation already exists and operates reasonably effectively. Indeed, there are a number of projects, for example the 1958 Convention on the Recognition and Enforcement of Foreign Arbitral Awards (also known as the New York Convention), proving that worldwide solutions can be more effective than merely regional harmonisations.[59]

In contradiction with this common sense and despite the Convention's accomplishments, however, the pro-reformist camp, supported by the Commission, insisted that the Treaty was not working efficiently. The alarming fact is that no empirical research whatsoever was conducted by either the Commission or the Member States to support this assertion. Against this background, one feels tempted to question why no effort was made to prove the credibility of the given statement.

Last but not least, it ought to be noted that it is not solely the Commission that should be blamed for the failure to meet its obligations related to the principle of subsidiarity. The Council and the European Parliament should also be held

[55] See Hague Conference on Private International Law, 'Status Table: Convention of 25 October 1980 on the Civil Aspects of International Child Abduction', available at www.hcch.net/index_en.php?act=conventions.status&cid=24.

[56] P Beaumont and P McEleavy, *The Hague Convention on International Child Abduction* (Oxford, Oxford University Press, 1999) 4. At present, in terms of success, the Hague Abduction Convention is closely followed by the Hague Convention of 29 May 1993 on Protection of Children and Co-operation in Respect of Intercountry Adoption ('1993 Intercountry Adoption Convention'). As of September 2011, the 1993 Intercountry Adoption Convention boasts 84 Contracting States. See Hague Conference on Private International Law, 'Status Table: Convention of 29 May 1993 on Protection of Children and Co-operation in Respect of Intercountry Adoption', available at www.hcch.net/index_en.php?act=conventions.status&cid=69.

[57] Eg Judgment of May 14, 1971, HR [Highest Court], 1971 NJ, No 369 (the Netherlands) as cited by CD Van Boeschoten, 'Hague Conference Conventions and the United States: A European View' (1994) 57 *Law and Contemporary Problems* 47, fn 24.

[58] Nevertheless, as envisaged by the Convention itself, there are certainly cases where a non-return order is warranted by the circumstances of the particular case. Moreover, with an increasingly higher proportion of primary carer mothers as alleged abductors, due consideration should be given by judges in abductions motivated by spousal abuse.

[59] WA Stoffel, 'Enlightened Decision Making' (2001) 75 *Tulane Law Review* 1195, 1201.

responsible, as neither of these institutions manifested a compliance with their legal duty to examine the proposals submitted to them by the Commission for their consistency with subsidiarity.[60]

iii. Political Nature of Subsidiarity

The above analysis has shown that neither of the two elements of the subsidiarity test was carried out to a satisfactory standard. Despite this failure, however, the Commission was able to get away with ignoring dissenting voices and self-assuredly presenting the initiative as indispensable. It appears justified to ask how this was possible. It is suggested here that the answer lies in the fact that subsidiarity is by its very nature highly ambiguous. There is a general agreement that the principle of subsidiarity is a very elastic notion that does not give a clear answer to the question when the Union should legislate.[61] Indeed, many critics have expressed doubts about the functional utility of subsidiarity as a legal principle.[62] It has rightly been pointed out that often there is a large amount of political judgment involved, turning subsidiarity into more of a political than a legal doctrine.[63] This in practice means that where the Union has a strong political motivation and is determined to act in a particular area, it is very difficult, if not impossible,

60 Protocol No 30, provision 11.

61 See, eg, Toth, 'Legal Analysis of Subsidiarity' (n 12) 37; T Koopmans, 'Subsidiarity, Politics and the Judiciary' (2005) 1 *European Constitutional Law Review* 112; Steiner (n 12) 49; De Búrca (n 30) 9 (describing subsidiarity as a concept characterised by 'a high degree of fluidity and vagueness'); S Weatherill, 'Better Competence Monitoring' (2005) 30 *European Law Review* 23, 26 (suggesting that 'subsidiarity has little visible purchase in breaking an EC institutional culture loaded in favour of legislative centralisation'); KM Poo, 'Struggle for Democratic Legitimacy within the European Union' (2001) 19 *Boston University International Law Journal* 111, 119 (arguing that 'the meaning of subsidiarity remains unclear'); L Hoffman and J Shaw, 'Constitutionalism and Federalism in the "Future of Europe" Debate: The German Dimension', The Federal Trust, Online Paper No. 03/04, (February 2003), available at www.fedtrust.co.uk/uploads/constitution/03_04.pdf (rightly asserting that the principle of subsidiarity is 'both unclear and widely regarded as rather toothless'); J Schréré, 'Subsidiarity and Federalism in the European Union' (2000) 24 *Fletcher Forum of World Affairs* 175, 178 Estella (n 23) 80, 82 and 96 (stating that subsidiarity has 'an important degree of indeterminacy', that it constitutes 'a very elastic notion' and that it is 'diffuse and ambiguous, when not incoherent').

62 J Pelkmans, 'Testing for Subsidiarity', College of Europe, Bruges European Economic Policy Briefings, No 13 (February 2006), available at www.coleurope.eu/template.asp?pagename=ecopublic. See also A Tomkins, 'Legislative Comment: The Draft Constitution of the European Union' [2003] *Public Law* 571, 576 (describing the doctrine of subsidiarity as 'largely impotent'); NW Barber, 'The Limited Modesty of Subsidiarity' (2005) 11 *European Law Journal* 308, 325–6. Overall, Barber views the principle of subsidiarity favourably; nevertheless, acknowledges that as a legal principle subsidiarity 'has had little obvious effect'. See also Snell, 'European Constitutional Settlement' at 630 (asserting that 'the word that saved Maastricht has lost much of its practical utility').

63 J Peterson, 'Subsidiarity: A Definition to Suit Any Vision?' (1994) 47 *Parliamentary Affairs* 116, 118; F Kistenkas, 'European and Domestic Subsidiarity: An Althusian Conceptionalist View' (1999–2000) 8 *Tilburg Foreign Law Review* 247, 254, describing subsidiarity as 'a weathervane in ever-changing political wind-directions'. In a less stringent tone, G Bermann suggests that '[t]hough solemn in tone, and certainly solemn in origin, subsidiarity nevertheless speaks in unmistakably political terms'. Bermann (n 23) 339. See also P Syrpis, 'In Defence of Subsidiarity' (2004) 24 *Oxford Journal of Legal Studies* 323, 334. Syrpis acknowledges that subsidiarity is principally a political concept; however, maintains that this is true in 'technical terms' only. He believes that subsidiarity can be applied effectively by the Community institutions.

for the opponents of the proposed law to successfully invoke non-compliance with subsidiarity.[64] Subsidiarity is also subject to judicial review by the European Court of Justice (so called 'judicial or ex post monitoring of the principle').[65] The ECJ, however, shows great unwillingness to enter into a substantive review of subsidiarity,[66] and to date, no piece of legislation has been condemned by the ECJ for non-compliance with the principle.[67]

It is suggested that, in the case of the new child abduction regime, the ambiguity of the subsidiarity principle coupled with a strong political motivation allowed the political camp led by France and supported by the Commission to disregard requirements embodied in the necessity and efficiency test. This helped the group to achieve an underhand victory in the battle over the new intra-Union child abduction regime. Unfortunately, it appears that subsidiarity infringement in the instant case was not an isolated incident but part of a general lack of subsidiarity commitment in EU legislation, in particular in the area of family law.[68] Nevertheless, where future developments are concerned, there is a little hope that the situation will improve with the Treaty of Lisbon having entered into force. The Treaty of Lisbon guarantees a more effective application of the principle of subsidiarity as it accords to national parliaments the right to intervene whenever a subsidiarity infringement is suspected.[69] The role of national parliaments as 'watchdogs of the principle of subsidiarity'[70] was first introduced by the 2004

[64] It has rightly been suggested that due to its ambiguous character subsidiarity can be used 'to rebut criticism and manipulate debate'. Davies, 'Subsidiarity: The Wrong Idea' (n 15) 77.

[65] A Cygan, 'Democracy and Accountability in the European Union—The View from the House of Commons' (2003) 66 *Modern Law Review* 384, 400. Cygan distinguishes between *ex ante* monitoring of the principle of subsidiarity (ie monitoring of a political nature) and *ex post* monitoring of the principle of subsidiarity (ie monitoring of a judicial nature). Paul Craig refers to the ECJ's subsidiarity review as 'relatively light touch' and criticises the Court for not requiring 'more from the Commission in procedural terms'. See P Craig, 'Institutions, Power, and Institutional Balance' in P Craig and G De Búrca, *The Evolution of EU Law* 2nd edn (Oxford, Oxford University Press, 2011) 41, 60.

[66] Timmermans, 'Subsidiarity and Transparency' at S115.

[67] Snell (n 38) 629. The competence of the ECJ to review legislation was based on Art 230 of the EC Treaty (now Art 263 of the TFEU); see Estella (n 23) 137. The ECJ has been presented with a number of cases on the subject of subsidiarity. However, the number of cases in which the Court ruled directly on subsidiarity is relatively small. See, eg, C-84/94 *United Kingdom v Council* [1996] ECR I-05755; C-233/94 *Germany v Parliament and Council* [1997] ECR I-02405; and C-377/98 *Kingdom of the Netherlands v European Parliament and Council of the European Union* [2001] ECR I-07079. For a review of the ECJ case law on subsidiarity see F Sander, 'Subsidiarity Infringements before the European Court of Justice: Futile Interference with Politics or a Substantial Step towards EU Federalism?' (2005–2006) 12 *Columbia Journal of European Law* 517, 537–42.

[68] See P McEleavy, 'First Steps in the Communitarisation of Family Law' in K Boele-Woelki (ed), *Perspectives for the Unification and Harmonisation of Family Law in Europe* (Oxford, Intersentia, 2003) 513, fn 14.

[69] For an academic analysis of the new mechanism see Craig, 'The Treaty of Lisbon' at 149–50; Snell (n 38) at 635–6; G Barret, '"The King is Dead, Long Live the King": The Recasting by the Treaty of Lisbon of the Provisions of the Constitutional Treaty Concerning National Parliaments' (2008) 33 *European Law Review* 66; and R Visser, 'Observations on a Change: The European Union, the Treaty of Lisbon, and the Area of Freedom, Security and Justice' (2011) 32 *Statute Law Review* 77.

[70] Cooper, 'The Watchdogs of Subsidiarity' (n 22).

Constitutional Treaty.[71] In the context of the Constitutional Treaty, the scheme sparked off considerable debate.[72] Under the currently valid Protocol on the Application of the Principles of Subsidiarity and Proportionality,[73] drafts of all EU legislative acts are to be forwarded to national parliaments, which have eight weeks to scrutinise them for their compliance with the principle of subsidiarity.[74] If one third of all national parliaments signal non-compliance with subsidiarity, the draft must be reviewed.[75] Following the review a decision is taken as to whether the proposal will be maintained, amended or withdrawn.[76] Reasons for the decision must always be given.[77] Where a measure is made in accord with the ordinary legislative procedure, and the correct application of the principle of subsidiarity is contested by more than half of national parliaments, and the Commission nevertheless decides to maintain its proposal, the Commission must give a reasoned opinion on the issue and it is up to the Council and the European Parliament to decide.[78] Generally, the new subsidiarity monitoring mechanism has received widespread support. It is, however, submitted that the relevant provisions appear to be relatively weak. Nevertheless, it remains to be seen whether the scheme will make a real difference to the application of the principle of subsidiarity.

B. Proportionality[79]

The Union institutions involved in the legislative process must also ensure adherence to the principle of proportionality.

Proportionality applies to all areas of Union action, not only to those that fall within the shared competences.[80] The principle of proportionality was at the

[71] Treaty Establishing a Constitution for Europe, 29 October 2004 (an unratified international treaty later replaced by the Treaty of Lisbon) Art 6.

[72] See, eg, Tomkins, 'Legislative Comment' at 576; Dashwood, 'The Relationship' at 368–9; Cooper (n 22); G Davies, 'The Post-Laeken Division of Competences' (2003) 28 *European Law Review* 686; and NP Zalany, 'The European Union Constitution and Its Effects on Federalism in the EU' (2005) 66 *Ohio State Law Journal* 615, 623–5.

[73] Protocol No 2, annexed to the Treaty of Lisbon. This Protocol should be read in conjunction with the Protocol on the role of national parliaments in the European Union (Protocol No 1, annexed to the Treaty of Lisbon).

[74] Protocol No 2, annexed to the Treaty of Lisbon Art 6.

[75] *Ibid*, Art 7(2). This threshold is lowered to one-quarter in certain cases concerning the area of freedom, security and justice.

[76] *Ibid.*

[77] *Ibid.*

[78] *Ibid*, Art 7(3). These provisions do not apply to the principle of proportionality and therefore the national parliaments have no formal role in relation to that principle, see Craig, 'Institutions' (n 65) 77.

[79] Generally on proportionality see E Ellis (ed), *The Principle of Proportionality in the Laws of Europe* (Oxford, Hart Publishing, 1999); and P Craig and G De Búrca, *EU Law: Text, Cases and Materials* (Oxford, Oxford University Press, 2008) 544–51. For an in-depth analysis of the proportionality principle in EU law from a legal theoretical and constitutional perspective see T Harbo, 'The Function of the Proportionality Principle in EU Law' (2010) 16 *European Law Journal* 158.

[80] Emiliou, *The EU Principle of Proportionality* (n 16) 140. See also De Búrca (n 30) 24.

relevant time set out in the third clause of Article 5 of the EC Treaty.[81] It read as follows: 'Any action by the Community shall not go beyond what is necessary to achieve the objectives of this Treaty'.

Proportionality further limited the scope of the Community's competences the exercise of which is determined by the principle of subsidiarity.[82] To some extent, proportionality overlaps with the efficiency criterion of the subsidiarity principle, as it is unlikely that 'a Community intervention beyond what is necessary to achieve the objectives of the Treaty would be found to be efficient'.[83] However, an important difference between the two principles is that subsidiarity is linked to the 'objectives of the proposed action' whereas proportionality is related to the 'objectives of the Treaty'. The link to the 'objectives of the Treaty' is, nevertheless, a source of practical difficulties with the principle. These problems originate from the fact that the Treaty defines its objectives very broadly. Consequently, almost any action can be justified as necessary to achieve the objectives of the Treaty. In practice, therefore, it is extremely difficult to demarcate the actual objectives of the Community by reference to the Treaty.[84]

According to Article 2 of the then EC Treaty the Community aims at establishing a common market and an economic and monetary union. Article 14(2) further specifies that 'the internal market shall comprise an area without internal frontiers in which the free movement of goods, persons, services and capital is ensured'. Title IV of the Treaty (Articles 61–69) entitled 'Visas, Asylum, Immigration and Other Policies' described measures to be taken to establish the area of freedom, security and justice. Obviously, the objectives of the Treaty corresponded with the vision of the European Union as an economic and monetary union based on the free movement of goods, persons, services and capital.

At first sight, it is difficult to see how the objective of deterring child abduction can be subsumed under the above 'economic' objectives. Particularly, it is to be asked how deterring child abduction can contribute to the establishment and the proper functioning of the internal market.[85] It can be argued that tackling child abduction will increase the ease of family movement within the Union and thus pursue the objective of the free movement of persons. This interpretation is,

[81] Under the currently valid Treaty of Lisbon, the definition of proportionality is enshrined in Art 5 of the Treaty on European Union (consolidated version).

[82] F Goudappel, 'Subsidiarity under the Constitution for Europe' 1, available at www.repub.eur.nl/res/pub/7791/Subsidiarity%20under%20the%20Draft%20Constitution%20for%20Europe.pdf.

[83] Dehousse, *Europe After Maastricht* (n 54) 115. Also M Desomer and K Lenaerts, 'Bricks for a Constitutional Treaty of the European Union: Values, Objectives and Means' (2002) 27 *European Law Review* 377, 390; and Swaine, 'Subsidiarity and Self-Interest' (n 16) 56.

[84] De Búrca (n 30).

[85] In a more general sense, it has been questioned to what extent can measures in the area of family law be considered 'necessary for the proper functioning of the internal market'? McEleavy, 'The Brussels II Regulation' (n 30) 883.

however, not accepted here and it is submitted that one can hardly find any free movement advantage in tightening child abduction exceptions to return.[86]

The wide scope of the definition of the objectives of the Treaty gives the Union a free hand to classify virtually any action as being necessary to achieve the objectives of the Treaty. This enables the Commission to shape proportionality to suit any political agenda.[87] Consequently, like subsidiarity, proportionality is more a political than a legal concept. As a result, as manifested by the case of child abduction, the principle has very little practical effect on the law-making process in the Union.

Another aspect of proportionality is that it determines the means by which the Union's powers should be exercised after the decision to act has been taken.[88] In other words, it is intended to provide an answer to the question what is the most appropriate instrument for achieving the objectives of the Treaty.[89] The Union's 'better lawmaking' policy aims at less and better legislation. One of the means to achieve this objective is a more diversified governance system. In other words, more use should be made of non-legislative approaches or 'soft legislation' as a part of the broader European regulatory framework.[90] The roots of this strategy trace back to the 1992 Edinburgh European Council. The Council concluded that:

> The form of action should be *as simple as possible*, consistent with satisfactory achievement of the objective of the measure and the need for effective enforcement. The Community should legislate only *to the extent necessary*. Other things being equal, directives should be preferred to regulations and framework directives to detailed measures. *Non-binding measures* such as recommendations should be preferred where appropriate.[91] (Emphasis added.)

> Where appropriate under the Treaty, and provided this is sufficient to achieve its objectives, preference in choosing the type of Community action should be given *to encouraging cooperation between Member States*, coordinating national action or to complementing, supplementing or supporting such action.[92] (Emphasis added.)

[86] One commentator has even argued that the return mechanism as established by the Hague Abduction Convention hinders free movement. See JA Pontier, *Left Behind Children and Left Alone Mothers: Reconsidering the 1980 Hague Convention on International Child Abduction?*, Unpublished Conference Paper, Journal of Private International Law Conference 2007, Birmingham. Professor Pontier believes that the Convention summary return mechanism poses a threat to the right of free movement in particular in cases where young primary carer mothers seek to relocate with their children from one country to another.

[87] Peterson, 'Subsidiarity' (n 63) 132.

[88] De Búrca (n 30) 24.

[89] Committee of the Regions (EC), 'Implementation and monitoring of the principles of subsidiarity and proportionality: issues and prospects for the Committee of the Regions' (Report) May 2004, available at www.assemblealegislativa.regione.emilia-romagna.it/biblioteca/pubblicazioni/MonitorEuropa/2004/monitor_8/Regioni/CdR_CIG_Sussidiariet%C3%A0.pdf. See also Emiliou (n 16) 140. Emiliou suggests that proportionality provides a standard to measure the intensity of Community action.

[90] See De Búrca (n 30) 32–3.

[91] Edinburgh European Council: Presidency Conclusions (n 8) Annex 1 to Part A: Overall Approach to the Application by the Council of the Subsidiarity Principle and Article 3b of the Treaty on European Union, 9.

[92] *Ibid.*

Following the Edinburgh European Council, the preference for alternative means of regulation has been expressed in several Union instruments. In July 2001, a white paper on European governance stressed the need for a greater use of different policy tools including recommendations.[93] Similarly, the 2002 Commission action plan on simplifying and improving the regulatory environment encouraged the use of soft-law regulation methods.[94] Finally, the Interinstitutional agreement on better lawmaking adopted in December 2003 dealt with a wide range of governance instruments.

Soft law has been defined as 'rules of conduct that are laid down in instruments which have not been attributed legally binding force as such, but nevertheless may have certain—indirect—legal effects, and are aimed at and may produce practical effects'.[95]

Against this background, it is suggested that, instead of at once opting for the Regulation, the Commission could have considered other, less intrusive options for improving the operation of the 1980 Convention.[96] For example, in co-operation with the Hague Conference, efforts could have been made to encourage cross-border judicial co-operation. In this context, it could have been helpful to tackle problems posed by alleged conflicting interpretations of Article 13(1)(b) by frequent judicial conferences and bilateral meetings. Another option would be a recommendation on the interpretation of Article 13(1)(b) in the context of the 1980 Convention. Alternatively, a guide to good practice could have been developed with the aim of promoting consistent practices in relation to Article 13(1)(b) (additionally, other issues could have been added, for example timing, hearing of the child and the applicant, etc); and providing examples of good practice in this area.

If the alternative steps outlined above had not led to a significant improvement, then a formal, binding instrument such as a protocol to the 1980 Hague Abduction Convention that would be ratified by all EU Member States could have

[93] Commission (EC), 'European Governance' (White Paper) COM (2001) 428 final, 5, 25 July 2001.

[94] Action Plan on Simplifying and Improving the Regulatory Environment (n 4) 7. Following the Commission Action Plan, a recommendation for use of the alternative regulation mechanisms was incorporated into the Interinstitutional agreement on better lawmaking (2003/C 321/01) adopted on 16 December 2003. The importance of the alternative regulatory tools provision was reinforced by the Communication of the Commission to the European Parliament, Council, the European Economic and Social Committee and the Committee of Regions on implementing the Community Lisbon programme: A Strategy for the Simplification of the Regulatory Environment from 25 October 2005. Commission (EC), 'A Strategy for the simplification of the regulatory environment' (Communication) (COM (2005) 535 final, 25 October 2005.

[95] Senden (n 5) 9.

[96] It has rightly been pointed out that '[h]ad proportionality been central to the reformers' agenda, then the child abduction proposal would surely have focused on how to improve the practical operation of the existing global instrument within the EU'. P McEleavy, 'The New Child Abduction Regime in the European Union: Symbiotic Relationship or Forced Partnership?' (2005) 1 *Journal of Private International Law* 5, 16.

been considered.[97] The protocol would provide a worldwide legal framework for dealing with Article 13(1)(b) cases, including the related issue of undertakings and the measures to facilitate the safe return of the child and the protection of the child and the abducting parent upon return, especially in controversial cases of sexual abuse and other forms of domestic violence. In contrast to the guide to good practice and other soft-law instruments, the protocol would constitute a more binding and effective regulation of the disputed area of interpretation.[98]

II. The Consultation Policy

Under Protocol No 30 of the EC Treaty the Commission was obliged to consult widely on every piece of legislation prepared under the auspices of the Community.[99] In particular, provision 9 of the Protocol stated:

> Without prejudice to its right of initiative, the Commission should, except in cases of particular urgency and confidentiality, consult widely before proposing legislation and, wherever appropriate, publish consultation documents.

In 2001, the Commission declared its intention to develop a 'reinforced culture of consultation and dialogue in the EU'.[100] As a part of this movement, a call was made to flesh out the principle of mandatory consultation. It was suggested that this should be achieved through an establishment of minimum standards for consultation and guidelines on collection and use of expert evidence, and through an introduction of a two-stage impact assessment process.[101]

[97] The possibility of a Protocol to amend or supplement the Hague Abduction Convention was considered by the Permanent Bureau of the Hague Conference at the first part of the Sixth Special Commission to review the operation of the Convention in June 2011. See Permanent Bureau of the Hague Conference, 'Consultations on the Desirability and Feasibility of a Protocol to the Hague Convention of 25 October 1980 on the Civil Aspects of International Child Abduction: A Preliminary Report', Preliminary Document No 7 (2011) 7, available at www.hcch.net/upload/wop/abduct2011pd07e.pdf. It looks, however, as though the idea of a Protocol will not be pursued.

[98] For academic writings advocating a Protocol see P Beaumont, 'The Jurisprudence of the European Court of Human Rights and the European Court of Justice on the Hague Convention on International Child Abduction' (2008) 335 *Hague Recueil* 103; L Silberman, 'Patching Up the Abduction Convention: A Call for a New International Protocol and a Suggestion for Amendments to ICARA' (2003) 38 *Texas International Law Journal* 41; The Right Honourable Lord Justice Thorpe, 'The Hague Child Abduction Convention—24 Years On' (2006) 11 *Judges' Newsletter* 8; and P Ripley, 'A Defence of the Established Approach to the Grave Risk of Harm Exception in the Hague Child Abduction Convention' (2008) 4 *Journal of Private International Law* 443.

[99] Protocol No 30, provision 9. See also De Búrca (n 30) 33–4.

[100] European Governance (n 93).

[101] *Ibid.*

A. Consultation[102] and Expertise

In December 2002, the Commission set out principles and minimum standards for consulting interested parties.[103] The key objective of consultation of interested parties is to improve the quality of legislative proposals and to enhance the participation of external parties.[104] By fulfilling its obligation to consult, the Commission seeks to guarantee that its proposals are 'technically viable and practically workable', and that consultation processes are 'transparent and coherent'.[105]

The basis for the consultation relationship between the Commission and the interested parties is formed by five general principles: participation, openness, accountability, effectiveness and coherence.[106] The principle of participation reflects the Commission's commitment to consult 'as widely as possible on major policy initiatives'.[107] Openness and accountability express the belief that policy-making processes must 'be visible to the outside world if they are to be understood and have credibility'.[108] Effectiveness is based on the premise that in order to be effective, consultation must commence as early as possible. This will enable interested parties to participate at a stage where they can still influence 'the formulation of the main aims, methods of delivery, performance indicators and, where appropriate, the initial outlines of that policy'.[109] Finally, coherence refers to the requirement that consultation processes must be coherent and transparent.[110]

Together with the general principles and minimum standards for consultation, guidelines on the collection and use of expertise[111] were issued. The primary objective of the guidelines was to assist the Commission in the task of obtaining and using up-to-date expert knowledge in making policy choices.[112] The guidelines set out three core principles of collection and use of expert advice. These can be summarised as follows: 1) advice sought should always be of an appropriately high quality; 2) in seeking and acting on advice from experts the Commission must be open; and 3) the Commission must ensure that its methods for collecting and using expert evidence are efficient and impartial.[113]

102 Consultation *stricto sensu* as opposed to the obligation of mandatory consultation in its wider meaning as laid down by Protocol No 30 of the EC Treaty.

103 Commission (EC), 'Towards a reinforced culture of consultation and dialogue: general principles and minimum standards for consultation of interested parties by the Commission' (Communication) COM (2002) 704 final, 11 December 2002.

104 *Ibid*, 5.

105 *Ibid*.

106 *Ibid*, 15.

107 *Ibid*, 16.

108 *Ibid*, 17.

109 *Ibid*, 18.

110 *Ibid*.

111 Commission (EC), 'On the collection and use of expertise by the Commission: principles and guidelines' (Communication) COM (2002) 713 final, 11 December 2002.

112 *Ibid*, 4.

113 *Ibid*, 10.

Undoubtedly, the general principles and minimum standards for consultation together with the guidelines on the collection and use of expertise formed a clear basis for the Commission's conduct in the Union law-making processes. Unfortunately, however, primary sources indicate that the drafting procedure of the Brussels II bis Regulation fell short of the standards and principles established in the above documents. Indeed, there is no evidence of adherence to any of the general principles of consultation, or any of the core principles of collection and use of expert evidence. The non-compliance is, however, to some extent justifiable as it was only at the last stage of the preparation of the Brussels II bis Regulation when the principles were formulated and published. Moreover, the implementation of these principles must be regarded as an 'evolutionary process',[114] which means that good-quality results cannot be expected immediately. Nevertheless, it can be argued that, given the fact that the principles apply to all stages of the policy-making process,[115] once published, their application should have been considered regardless of the progress of negotiations. This course of action would have demonstrated not only the level of eagerness on the side of the Commission to implement the above documents, but also the level of commitment to the strategy of proactive communication embodied in the principle of openness (that is, the second principle of the use of expertise).[116]

The partly legitimate excuse for the non-adherence to the consultation principle as fleshed out by the general principles and minimum standards for consultation, and guidelines on the collection and use of expertise, however, did not exempt the Commission from the consultation obligation imposed by the protocol. Quite the contrary, a strong desirability of a wide consultation procedure was stressed on several occasions in the course of the negotiations on the Brussels II bis Regulation. For example, child abduction experts who participated at the Second UK Family Law Conference in London in October 2001 called upon the negotiators to seek 'response and advice of those whose responsibility it will be to implement the regulation in their professional lives'.[117] Despite both the binding nature of the protocol and numerous calls for expert consultations, the Commission showed obvious reluctance to consult. In particular, the following shortcomings have been observed. First, there were no experts from the area of child abduction (that is, leading scholars, Central Authorities' specialists and experienced practitioners) involved in the preparation of the early draft of the proposal for the new child abduction regime.[118] Second, no reports addressing the asserted need for the separate intra-EU child abduction rules were submitted by the experts.

[114] *Ibid*, 2.

[115] *Ibid*, 7; and Towards a Reinforced Culture of Consultation and Dialogue (n 103) 18.

[116] On the Collection and Use of Expertise by the Commission (n 111) 9.

[117] The Right Honourable Lord Justice Thorpe, 'The Second UK Family Law Conference: London, England' (2002) 4 *Judges' Newsletter* 32, 33.

[118] This was also recommended by judges and practitioners at the Third UK-German Conference on Family Law: 'The adequate opportunity should be given to judges and practitioners in family law to comment on and influence development of policy in relation to family law in the European Union and elsewhere'. 'The Third UK-German Conference on Family Law' (2000) 2 *Judges' Newsletter* 16, 16.

It is suggested that, as an inherent part of the pre-legislative consultations, the Commission should have requested the assistance of child abduction experts in conducting a thorough empirical research into the operation of the 1980 Hague Convention. Also, a detailed analysis of existing resources (the 1999 statistical survey in particular) should have been carried out. Following the necessary empirical, analytical and comparative research work, an extensive report on the topic should have been prepared; and only then the need for a legislative initiative in the area should have been considered.

The above analysis points to the conclusion that the obligation to consult widely on the proposed legislation was completely ignored by the Commission, remaining thus only a 'procedural nicety'.[119] No expert opinion whatsoever was sought by the drafters of the Regulation, who, although no doubt excellent jurists, could not have and indeed did not have sufficient knowledge and skills in the area of child abduction.[120]

B. Impact Assessment

Finally, it is to be noted that in June 2002, the Commission issued a Communication on impact assessment.[121] Impact assessment has been defined as 'a tool to improve the quality and coherence of the policy development process'[122] by means of assessing the potential economic, social and environmental consequences that they may have.[123] The aim of this process is to prepare evidence for political decision makers on the advantages and disadvantages of possible policy options by assessing their potential impact. Impact assessment also helps to explain why an action is necessary at the EU level and why the proposed response is an appropriate choice. It may of course also demonstrate why no action at the EU level should be taken.[124] The impact assessment initiative was launched in 2003, with the intention to gradually implement the programme from 2003 for all major initiatives.[125] This leads to the conclusion that the preparation of the new intra-Union return mechanism had preceded the implementation of the impact assessment initiative. Consequently, it would be unjustified to reproach the Commission for not having carried out an impact assessment on the Brussels II bis initiative.

[119] J Bercow MP, 'Subsidiarity and the Illusion of Democratic Control', the Bruges Group (2003), available at www.brugesgroup.com/mediacentre/index.live?article=192#introduction.

[120] The Commission itself has recognised that it is not feasible to cover internally the wide spectrum of specialisation that is needed in the Community law-making processes: 'As the expertise needed is quite wide and the knowledge required becomes increasingly technical and highly specialised, the Commission calls upon external specialists in different fields to provide advice'. See European Commission, 'Better Regulation: Expertise', available at www.ec.europa.eu/governance/better_regulation/expertise_en.htm.

[121] Commission (EC), 'On Impact Assessment' (Communication) COM (2002) 276 final, 5 June 2002.

[122] *Ibid*, 2.

[123] *Ibid*.

[124] European Commission, *Better Regulation—Simply Explained* (Luxembourg, Office for Official Publications of the European Communities, 2006) 7, available at www.ec.europa.eu/governance/better_regulation/documents/brochure/br_brochure_en.pdf.

[125] 'On Impact Assessment' (n 121) 2.

4

The Argument of the Misuse of Article 13(1)(b): Myth or Reality?

The previous Chapter examined to what extent the Union principles of good legislative drafting were put into practice during the preparations of the new intra-EU child abduction regime. Sadly, it was found that the Commission failed miserably to apply the EU standards of law making as the drafting procedure suffered from numerous legislative defects. The fatal flaw was a lack of research into the operation of the 1980 Hague Abduction Convention, particularly into the application of Article 13(1)(b) of the Convention. It is a matter of fact that the assumption of the misuse of Article 13(1)(b) was based only on one information source, the 1999 statistical survey. Beyond a rather superficial analysis of this empirical study, the Commission did not conduct any library-based and/or empirical research to actually justify the need for a separate intra-EU child abduction regime.

With the aim of challenging the Commission's assertion of the abuse of the Article 13(1)(b) 'grave risk' defence, this Chapter has undertaken the task of examining all available documents regarding the interpretation and the application of Article 13(1)(b) from the early 1990s until the adoption of the Brussels II bis Regulation. The analysed materials embrace a wide range of references, including the 1999 statistical survey, the Hague Conference Special Commission documents, conclusions of conferences and judicial seminars, and academic literature.

Overall, this Chapter aspires to review all available documents the Commission should have, at a minimum, evaluated as a part of the legislative preparation of the Brussels II bis Regulation. It aims to answer the question whether there was sufficient evidence to claim that the separate intra-EU child abduction regime was indispensable.

I. The Statistical Analysis of Applications made in 1999 under the Hague Convention on the Civil Aspects of International Child Abduction[1]

The 1999 statistical survey was the first comprehensive review of the practical operation of the 1980 Child Abduction Convention. This survey analysed all return (and access) applications received globally by the Central Authorities of the Contracting States in 1999. The findings of the 1999 statistical survey were presented at the fourth Special Commission to review the operation of the 1980 Hague Abduction Convention in March 2001.[2] The survey proved to be a vitally important piece of research and was recognised as an irreplaceable tool for the assessment of the practical functioning of the 1980 Hague Abduction Convention.[3]

A part of the findings of the 1999 statistical survey was used by the European Commission as a rationale for the plan to pursue the new intra-EU child abduction regime. In its working document on the mutual recognition of decisions on parental responsibility from March 2001, the Commission claimed a frequent abuse of Article 13(1)(b), allegedly evidenced by the 1999 statistical survey.[4]

The following analysis looks into the 1999 statistical survey, globally as well as separately at the EU Member States, with the aim to establish whether the allegations of the misuse of Article 13(1)(b) had a basis in fact. Its goal is to answer the following question: 'Could the 1999 statistical survey have given rise to the presupposition that, globally or at the European level, the Convention had not been working well (in particular, that Article 13(1)(b) had been misused)?'

[1] N Lowe, S Armstrong and A Mathias, 'A Statistical Analysis of Applications made in 1999 under the Hague Convention on the Civil Aspects of International Child Abduction', Preliminary Document No 3 (2001), available at www.hcch.net/upload/abd2001pd3e.pdf ('1999 statistical survey').

[2] For more information on the fourth Special Commission see section entitled 'The Fourth Special Commission Meeting: 22–28 March 2001' below.

[3] 'Any review of the practical operation of a Convention such as that of the Hague Convention of 25 October on the Civil Aspects of International Child Abduction should be conducted in the light of the best and most reliable information available.... In order to provide the Special Commission of 2001 with data concerning the operation of the 1980 Convention, the Permanent Bureau decided that it would be helpful to organise a detailed analysis of all return and access applications arising within the Contracting States in the year 1999.' See Deputy Secretary General of the Hague Conference, Professor William Duncan, in Lowe *et al* (n 1), Preface.

[4] Commission (EC), 'Mutual recognition of decisions on parental responsibility' (Working Document) COM (2001) 166 final, 8, 27 March 2001. For a more detailed analysis see Chapter 2.

A. Global Analysis

i. Outcomes

a. Overall Outcomes

The 1999 statistical survey analysed 945 return applications received by 34 Contracting States (38 Central Authorities).[5] Of these applications, only 107 (11%) were judicially refused; 304 (32%) resulted in a judicial order for return; and 173 (18%) ended in a voluntary return. Altogether, therefore, 50% of the applications resulted in the return of the child. Undoubtedly, at 11%, the proportion of judicial refusals was not high.

b. Outcomes of the Applications that Went to Court

Four hundred and eleven cases went to court. Of these, 74% resulted in a judicial return. Only 26% of the applications that went to court were judicially refused.

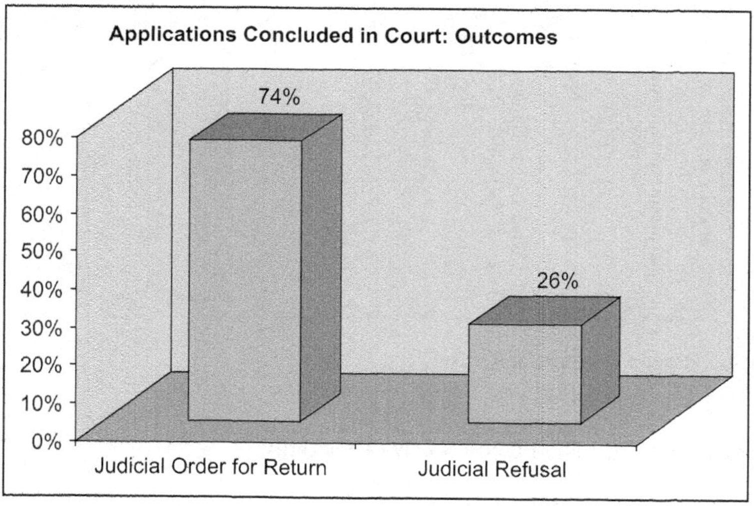

Figure 4.1: Applications concluded in court: Outcomes

[5] The United Kingdom, Canada and China Special Administrative Regions of Hong Kong and Macao were treated as single Contracting States. However, United Kingdom jurisdictions were analysed separately because of the high number of applications handled by England and Wales. Lowe *et al* (n 1), fn 1.

ii. Reason for Judicial Refusal

a. Article 13(1)(b) As a Sole Reason for Judicial Refusal

The reason for refusal was available in 99 of the 107 applications which were judicially refused. The highest number of refusals, 21, were based on Article 13(1)(b). Proportionally, however, Article 13(1)(b) accounted for only 21% of all refusals. The remaining 79% of refusals were evenly spread over a variety of reasons.

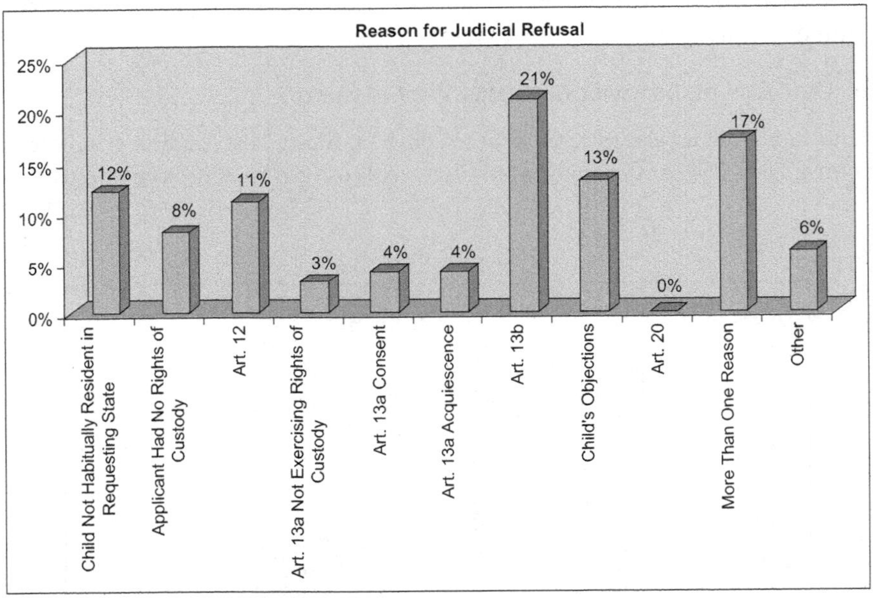

Figure 4.2: Reason for Judicial Refusal

b. Article 13(1)(b) Relied Upon Solely or Partially

As Figure 4.2 shows, 17% of refusals were based on more than one reason. Of these, Article 13(1)(b) as one of multiple reasons for refusal was cited in five applications. Altogether, therefore, Article 13(1)(b) was relied upon (either as a sole reason for refusing an application or with another reason) in 26 out of 99 (26%) judicial refusals (for which the reason for refusal was known).

B. Analysis of the Performance of the EU Member States[6]

No separate intra-EU analysis was done on the 1999 applications; nevertheless, the 1999 survey allows us to examine at least the global performance of the EU Member States. A special focus is on the application of Article 13(1)(b) in France. This aims at detecting whether the eager support for the new child abduction regime on the side of France could have been triggered by concrete evidence of an abuse of the Article 13(1)(b) 'grave risk' exception in this jurisdiction.

The section below attempts to answer the following questions: 'How were the return applications dealt with by the EU Member States' Central Authorities?' 'Was the refusal rate in these Contracting States alarmingly high?' 'What was the proportion of refusals based on Article 13(1)(b)?'

i. Number of Applications

Of the 945 return applications that were analysed in the survey, more than a half, 486, were made to the States that are now Members of the European Union. The highest number of applications, 149, was received by the United Kingdom jurisdiction of England and Wales. In contrast, Luxembourg did not receive any return applications in 1999.

Table 4.1: EU Member States: Number of received applications

Requested Contracting State	Number of applications
Austria	9
Belgium	9
Czech Republic	5
Finland	2
France	42
Germany	70
Hungary	8
Ireland	38
Italy	41
Luxembourg	0

(Continued)

[6] The analysis considers the European Union as it stands today (ie including the 'new' Member States that joined the European Union in May 2004 and in January 2007. It is, however, to be noted that only three of the 17 'new' Member States participated in the 1999 survey). Overall, of the Contracting States that participated in the 1999 statistical survey, the following countries are Members of the European Union: Austria, the Czech Republic, Belgium, Finland, France, Germany, Hungary, Ireland, Italy, Luxembourg, the Netherlands, Portugal, Romania, Spain, Sweden, and the United Kingdom (England and Wales, Northern Ireland and Scotland). Note: For the purposes of this analysis Denmark has been excluded.

Table 4.1: (Continued)

Requested Contracting State	Number of applications
Netherlands	26
Portugal	11
Romania	9
Spain	36
Sweden	14
UK—England & Wales	149
UK—Cayman Islands	1
UK—Northern Ireland	6
UK—Scotland	10
Total	**486**

ii. Outcomes

a. Overall Outcomes

Of the 486 applications that were received by the EU Member States, 65 (13%) were judicially refused. This compares with the global proportion of 11%.

Table 4.2: EU Member States: Overall outcomes

	Judicial refusal	Return (judicial/ voluntary)	Total number of applications
Austria	7	0	9
Belgium	0	7	9
Czech Republic	1	3	5
Finland	0	1	2
France	3	21	42
Germany	13	24	70
Hungary	3	4	8
Ireland	4	23	38
Italy	7	24	41
Luxembourg	0	0	0
Netherlands	2	15	26
Portugal	1	4	11

(Continued)

Table 4.2: (Continued)

	Judicial refusal	Return (judicial/ voluntary)	Total number of applications
Romania	0	3	9
Spain	4	18	36
Sweden	4	8	14
UK—England and Wales	14	84	149
UK—Cayman Islands	0	1	1
UK—Northern Ireland	2	3	6
UK—Scotland	0	9	10
Total	**65**	**252**	**486**

A very poor performance was produced by Austria, with the highest proportion of refused applications (78%, seven out of nine applications refused). Austria was followed by Hungary (38%), UK—Northern Ireland (33%) and Sweden (29%).

Interestingly, France, despite being a chief instigator of the reform, judicially refused only three out of 42 applications, recording a refusal rate well below the EU average (7% as opposed to 13%).

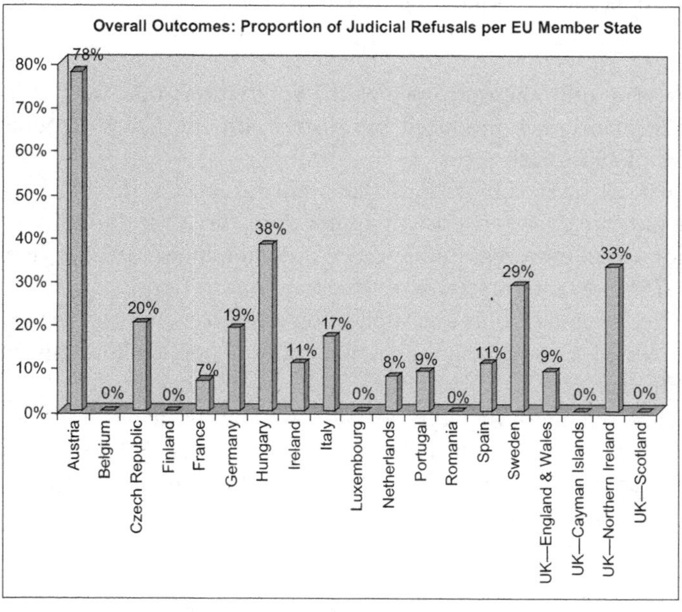

Figure 4.3: Overall outcomes: Proportion of judicial refusals per EU Member State

b. Outcomes of the Applications that Went to Court

Two hundred and thirty-six applications were concluded in court, 65 (28%) of which ended in a refusal to return, and 171 (72%) in a judicial return. At 28%, the proportion of judicial refusals in the EU Member States was by 2% higher than the global refusal rate (26%).

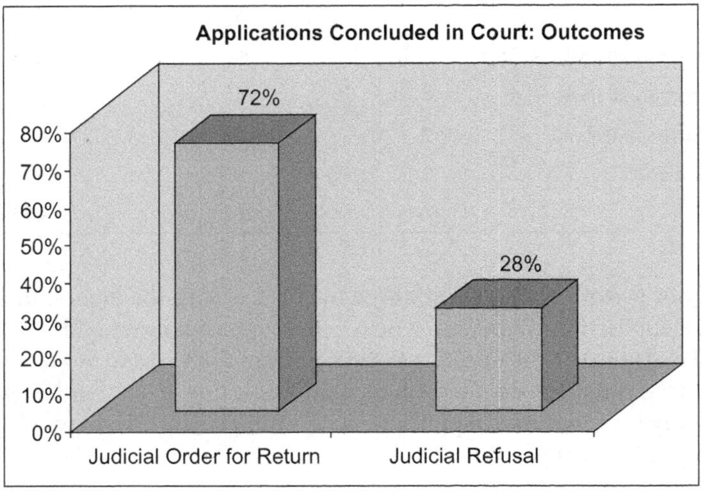

Figure 4.4: Applications concluded in court: Outcomes

When assessing only the outcomes of the applications that went to court, the worst performance was produced by Austria and the Czech Republic with a refusal rate of 100% each.

In Austria all seven applications that went to court were judicially refused. This may indicate a fairly consistent approach of the Austrian judiciary towards Convention cases; however, this approach does not appear to be in line with the doctrine of narrow interpretation of the exceptions to return.

In the Czech Republic only one application went to court and was subsequently judicially refused. Considering the small number of applications, this finding has little significance.

Austria and the Czech Republic were followed by Germany with a 50% refusal rate (13 out of 26 applications refused), Hungary with a 43% refusal rate (three out of seven applications refused) and Sweden with a refusal rate of 40% (four out of 10 applications refused). It is, however, to be noted that the smaller the number of applications going to court is, the less relevant the findings are (Hungary and Sweden).

Interestingly, as with the overall outcomes, against all expectations France recorded a lower proportion of judicial refusals than was the EU average, 23% as opposed to 28%.

Table 4.3: EU Member States: Applications concluded in court: Outcomes

	Judicial refusal	Judicial return	Number of applications that went to court
Austria	7	0	7
Belgium	0	3	3
Czech Republic	1	0	1
Finland	0	0	0
France	3	10	13
Germany	13	13	26
Hungary	3	4	7
Ireland	4	16	20
Italy	7	18	25
Luxembourg	0	0	0
Netherlands	2	10	12
Portugal	1	1	2
Romania	0	2	2
Spain	4	8	12
Sweden	4	6	10
UK—England and Wales	14	76	90
UK—Cayman Islands	0	1	1
UK—Northern Ireland	2	2	4
UK—Scotland	0	1	1
Total	**65**	**171**	**236**

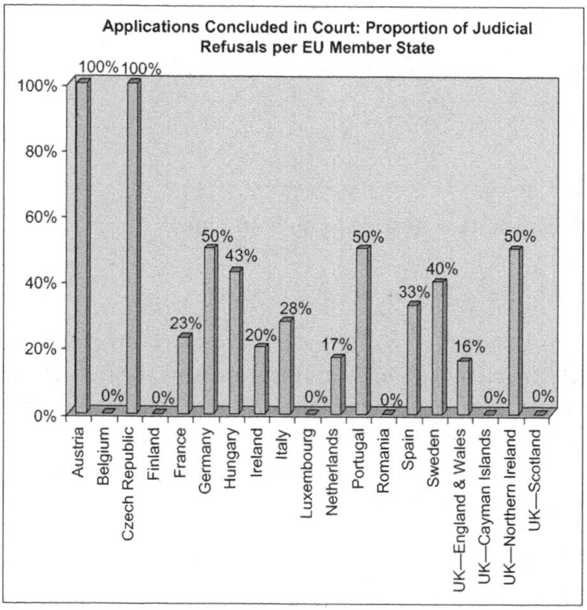

Figure 4.5: Applications concluded in court: Proportion of judicial refusals per EU Member State

iii. Reason for Judicial Refusal

a. Article 13b as a Sole Reason for Judicial Refusal

The reason for refusal was stated in 59 of the 65 applications that were judicially refused by the EU Member States. The highest number of refusals, 18, was based on Article 13(1)(b). Proportionally, Article 13(1)(b) accounted only for 31% of all refusals made by the EU Members that participated in the survey. This was 10% higher than the global rate of 21%. The remaining 69% of refusals were spread over a range of reasons.

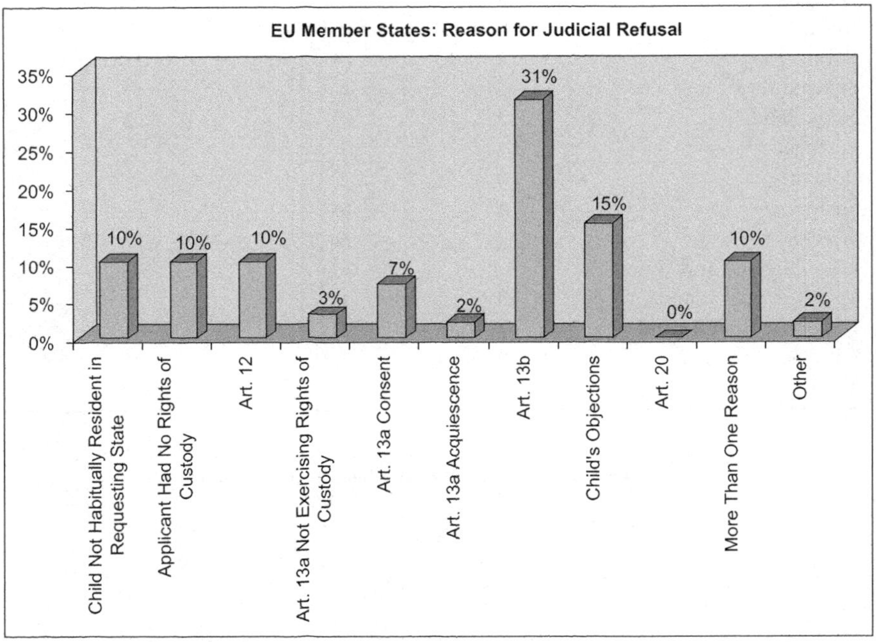

Figure 4.6: EU Member States: Reason for judicial refusal

b. Article 13(1)(b) Relied Upon Solely or Partially

As the above figure shows, 10% of refusals were based on more than one reason. Of these, Article 13(1)(b) as one of multiple reasons for refusal was cited in two applications. Altogether, therefore, Article 13(1)(b) was relied upon (either as a sole reason for refusing an application or with another reason) in 20 out of 59 (34%) judicial refusals (for which the reason for refusal was known). This was 8% higher than the global rate of 26%.

c. Reason for Judicial Refusal per Requested State

When looking at individual Contracting States, a legitimate concern is given by the performance of Sweden, where all refusals (four out of four, 100%) were based on Article 13(1)(b). Indeed, particular concentration of the reasons under one ground may be a cause for concern and therefore should give pause for thought.[7] Similarly, France and Austria recorded a high proportion of refusals based on Article 13(1)(b), 67% and 43% respectively. Although these figures may indicate a certain degree of an overuse of Article 13(1)(b), it must be pointed out that the situation in these jurisdictions was later rectified with the assistance of the Permanent Bureau of the Hague Conference.[8] Direct evidence is provided by the 2003 statistical survey.[9] According to the 2003 survey, there were no Article 13(1)(b) refusals either in Sweden or in Austria in 2003 (Sweden refused three altogether and Austria two applications). In France, one out of four refused applications (25%) was grounded on Article 13(1)(b). Undoubtedly, these figures demonstrate a significant improvement on the 1999 performance, dispelling all doubts about the correct application of the exception in these Member States.

Table 4.4: EU Member States: Reason for refusal: Article 13(1)(b)

	Article 13(1)(b)	Total number of refusals
Austria	3	7
Czech Republic	0	1
France	2	3
Germany	3	12
Ireland	0	1
Hungary	0	3
Italy	2	7
Netherlands	0	2
Spain	0	4
Sweden	4	4
UK—England & Wales	4	13
UK—Northern Ireland	0	2
Total	**18**	**59**

[7] Lowe et al (n 1) 19.

[8] Interview with Ms Aude Fiorini, Legal Consultant to INCADAT (Civil Law Editor) and Lecturer in Law at the University of Dundee, 12 June 2007.

[9] N Lowe, E Atkinson, K Horosova and S Patterson, 'A Statistical Analysis of Applications Made in 2003 under the Hague Convention of 25 October 1980 on the Civil Aspects of International Child Abduction' Preliminary Document No 3 (2006) 41, available at www.hcch.net/upload/wop/abd_pd03e2006.pdf ('2003 statistical survey').

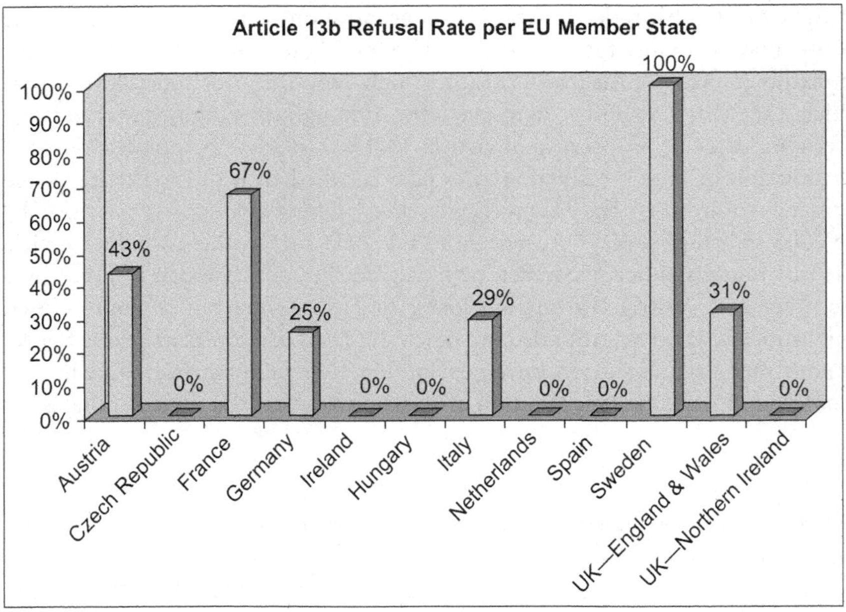

Figure 4.7: Article 13(1)(b) refusal rate per EU Member State

To sum up, the global analysis has revealed that, in terms of overall outcomes, only a small proportion of applications, 11%, were judicially refused. Of the applications that went to court, 74% resulted in a judicial return with only 26% ending in a judicial refusal. At the European level, the proportion of judicially refused applications was slightly higher in both categories, that is, the overall outcomes as well as the outcomes of applications that went to court. It is, however, submitted here that, at 2% for each of the categories, the difference was almost negligible. One may conclude that the refusal rate at the European level was in line with the global percentage, with both results indicating generally a very low proportion of refused applications.

Globally, as well as at the EU level, the most common reason for refusing an application was Article 13(1)(b). Moreover, the EU analysis showed that the percentage of judicial refusals based on Article 13(1)(b) was 10% higher in the EU than it was globally (8% when all the reasons, including multiple reasons for refusal, are analysed). Proportionally, however, Article 13(1)(b) accounted for only 21% of all refusals globally (26% when all the reasons, including multiple reasons for refusal, are analysed), and 31% of all refusals at the EU level (34% when all the reasons, including multiple reasons for refusal, are analysed). The remaining 79% (74% when all the reasons, including multiple reasons for refusal, are analysed), and 69% (66% when all the reasons, including multiple reasons for refusal, are analysed) of refusals respectively were evenly spread over a variety of reasons. It is therefore submitted here that Article 13(1)(b), despite being the most often relied-upon reason for refusal, was in no case being overused. Neither the global percentage of 21% nor the EU proportion of 31% suggests any abuse of the exception. In no case could these figures justify the general conclusion arrived at by the Commission that Article 13(1)(b) was being interpreted in a more liberal fashion than intended by its drafters.

It is, nevertheless, recognised that had the information about the increased use of the defence in Europe been at the Commission's disposal, it could have raised concerns about the proper application of the exception in the EU. It is, however, suggested here that the proportion of 31% (34% when all the reasons, including multiple reasons for refusal, are analysed) is anyway not high enough to give serious cause for alarm. Moreover, out of scientific curiosity, a further investigation into the application of Article 13(1)(b) in the EU beyond the 1999 statistical survey was conducted. In particular, a comparable analysis to the above study was performed on the 2003 statistical survey[10] to establish trends in the application of the Article in the EU between 1999 and 2003. The findings were as follows: in 1999, the reason for refusal was given in 59 out of 65 applications that were judicially refused by the EU Member States that participated in both surveys. Article 13(1)(b) was relied upon in 18 cases (31%). In 2003, the same EU Member States judicially refused altogether 70 applications. Of these, the reason for refusal was available in 64 cases. Refusals based on Article 13(1)(b) accounted for 17% of the decisions where the reason was available (11 cases). These findings revealed a 14% decrease in the proportion of refusals based on Article 13(1)(b), demonstrating a clearly downward trend in the successful invocation of the exception between 1999 and 2003.

The above analysis inevitably leads to the conclusion that the 1999 survey did not detect an overuse of Article 13(1)(b) that would justify a need for a separate intra-EU return mechanism. The question therefore is what could have led the Commission to believe that the grave risk of harm exception was being overused. Although it was not expressly stated in the Commission's preparatory documents, it is suggested that the argument of an alleged misuse of Article 13(1)(b) could have been founded on the remark that occurs in the survey itself. In particular, in the section 'reasons for judicial refusal', the authors commented: 'It is notable that the reason for refusal most frequently relied upon was Article 13(1)(b), as general jurisprudence requires extreme justification for the use of this defence'.[11] The above statement was, however, in no way intended to suggest a need for a new instrument regulating child abduction. This was made quite clear by Professor Lowe, the author of the 1999 statistical survey, at the fourth UK-German Family Law Conference, which took place in September 2002 in Trier in Germany. At this conference, Professor Lowe criticised the Commission's ambition to establish a separate child abduction regime within the EU. He described the proposed

[10] *Ibid*. It is, however, to be noted that the analysis concerned only the use of Art 13(1)(b) as a sole reason for judicial refusal.

[11] Lowe *et al* (n 1) 17.

intra-EU return mechanism as a system that would radically conflict 'with the Hague regime that has been operated by most Member States for many years'.[12]

II. Special Commission Meetings to Review the Operation of the Hague Convention of 25 October 1980 on the Civil Aspects of International Child Abduction

Prior to the adoption of the Brussels II bis Regulation, four Special Commission meetings were held in The Hague (in 1989, 1993, 1997, and 2001). Special Commissions are attended mainly by child abduction specialists based at the Central Authorities of the Contracting States, judges and government personnel.[13] Discussions held at the Special Commissions are based on a highly specialised approach to the problem of child abduction. Indeed, the participants at the Special Commissions assess potentially problematic aspects of this phenomenon and related provisions of the 1980 Hague Convention with a high degree of professionalism. This specialisation was lacking in the Union institutions.

A. The First Special Commission Meeting: 23–26 October 1989

The First Special Commission to review the operation of the 1980 Hague Abduction Convention was held in October 1989. The Commission recognised that the case law available at that time indicated that the Article 13(1)(b) defence was the most common exception relied upon. It was also pointed out that Article 13(1)(b) (as well as Article 13(1)(a)) may be used by defendants to delay the return proceedings. Nevertheless, the Commission acknowledged that the prevalent attitude adopted by the courts reflected a narrow interpretation of the words 'grave risk' and 'intolerable situation'. Consequently, the Commission concluded that '[i]n the great majority of cases from all countries the courts have interpreted Article 13(1)(b) strictly and have adhered closely to the spirit of the Convention'.[14]

Participating experts recommended a deeper involvement of Central Authorities in Article 13(1)(b) cases, particularly in the form of social assistance for abductors

[12] 'Reports on Judicial Conferences Concerning the International Protection of Children: Fourth UK-German Family Law Conference at Trier, Germany, September 2002' (2003) 5 *Judges' Newsletter* 3, 10.

[13] 'A Special Commission for Judges?' (1999) 1 *Judges' Newsletter* 5, 5.

[14] Permanent Bureau of the Hague Conference, 'Overall Conclusions of the Special Commission of October 1989 on the Operation of the Hague Convention of 25 October 1980 on the Civil Aspects of International Child Abduction' n 4, available at www.hcch.net/upload/abdrpt89e.pdf.

returning to the requesting State. In this context, reference was made to Article 7(h), which regulates obligations of the Central Authorities.[15] It is to be noted that the Central Authorities' involvement in facilitating the safe return of the child would further reduce the use of Article 13(1)(b).[16]

Overall, the operation of the Convention was considered effective and the Convention was seen as meeting its aims: 'There was a broad consensus that the Convention works well in the interests of children and meets the needs for which it was drafted'.[17] Only two major problems were cited in the report; none of them, however, related to the Article 13(1)(b) exception. The first difficulty was seen in the locating of the child in cases where the applicant does not know the exact address of the child in the requested State. The second problem was related to legal aid.[18]

One Contracting State, namely Spain, was chastised for serious problems of 'a structural, legal and procedural nature'[19] in handling incoming return applications. This criticism appears to target overall administrative and judicial deficiencies in processing the 1980 Convention cases in Spain (for example, personally and financially under-equipped Central Authority, insufficient judicial training, etc). There is no indication that the criticism of Spain had a direct link with the issue of a misuse of the exceptions to return. One must, nevertheless, acknowledge that the problems of a 'legal' nature might have led to an increased application of defences by Spanish judges, including the defence of Article 13(1)(b).

B. The Second Special Commission Meeting: 18–21 January 1993

The second Special Commission meeting was held in January 1993. The overall conclusion of the second Special Commission was that 'the Convention [the 1980 Hague Abduction Convention] works well in practice and the State Parties are generally happy with its operation'.[20] No concern was expressed regarding the Article 13(1)(b) exception. Quite the contrary, most participating child abduction specialists reported that in their countries the Article 13(1)(b) defence was construed narrowly by the courts and subsequently only a few applications where this provision was invoked were successful.[21]

[15] *Ibid*, para 29.

[16] See Chapter 6, section entitled 'Protection of the Abductor Parent and the Child upon the Return'.

[17] *Ibid*, conclusions of the main points discussed by the Special Commission para I.

[18] *Ibid*, para 59.

[19] *Ibid*, conclusions of the main points discussed by the Special Commission para III.

[20] Permanent Bureau of the Hague Conference, 'Report of the Second Special Commission Meeting to Review the Operation of the Hague Convention on the Civil Aspects of International Child Abduction, 18–21 January 1993' part II, conclusion I, available at www.hcch.net/upload/abdrpt93e.pdf.

[21] *Ibid*, response to question 22.

One of the participating experts initiated a discussion on the problem of sexual abuse of the child by the applicant parent. A question was raised whether the child should be returned in this case. It was suggested that the return should be ordered; nevertheless, the child should be protected from the applicant parent. The protection should be facilitated by allowing the child to stay in de facto care of the abductor or by placing the child in the care of a third party.

Another issue that was raised in the course of the discussions was the problem of domestic violence. No further debate was, however, held on this point, apart from brief information regarding one Irish case. In this case, the court refused to return the child, arguing that any domestic violence would expose the child to a great risk of psychological harm.[22]

It was suggested that Article 13(1)(b) should not be used to safeguard the protection of the child from the applicant parent, as the requesting State is in a better position to deal with this issue.[23]

It was questioned whether courts should seek social welfare reports in cases where Article 13 is invoked. It was concluded that the reports should not be sought, unless they are already available. The preparation of such a report may take up to three months and this would cause unwelcome delays in the proceedings.[24]

C. The Third Special Commission Meeting: 17–21 March 1997

The third Special Commission met in March 1997. The third Special Commission recognised that Article 13(1)(b) formed 'a sensitive part of the Convention' and that if it 'is misused, it could destroy the effectiveness of the Convention'.[25] Nevertheless, no claim of an actual 'misuse' of Article 13(1)(b) was made. It was stressed that the grave risk of harm exception must be interpreted in a very narrow fashion.

The Commission recognised that a child may face a risk upon return, especially where questions of alleged abuse and violence arise. This issue was highlighted by an increased proportion of abductions committed by mothers in the 1990s. To address this problem, the importance of the administrative co-operation between the Central Authorities upon the return of the child, pursuant to Article 7(h), was stressed. Following a proposal submitted by the Australian delegation, the Central Authorities were encouraged 'to adopt a flexible approach to their obligations under Article 7(h)'.[26] The Central Authorities' activities in this respect should

[22] *Ibid.*
[23] *Ibid.*
[24] *Ibid.*
[25] Permanent Bureau of the Hague Conference, 'Report on the Third Special Commission to Review the Operation of the Hague Convention of on the Civil Aspects of International Child Abduction, 17–21 March 1997' para 58, available at www.hcch.net/upload/abduc97e.pdf.
[26] *Ibid*, annex III: Synthetic revision of working document No 20 as drawn up by the Permanent Bureau in the light of the comments and suggestions made by experts.

involve 'providing returning parents with information on social, welfare and legal aid services in the country of habitual residence'[27] as well as establishing contact with such services on behalf of the parents. Also, a need for improved judicial co-operation was stressed, especially with regard to the enforcement of undertakings. It was suggested that undertakings should be enforceable by requesting States so as to ensure the protection of the child guaranteed by them. However, in some countries it is not possible to ensure a prompt enforcement of undertakings incorporated into the return order as additional proceedings to recognise the foreign order are needed. Therefore, it was suggested that undertakings be 'mere agreements between the parties that can be entered before a judge in the requesting State and thus be incorporated in a "safe harbour" order, which is more readily enforceable'.[28]

The above recommendations sought to prevent an increase in abuse- or violence-related Article 13(1)(b) refusals. It was rightly pointed out that a strengthened administrative and judicial co-operation would hinder an unwelcome increase in the number of refusals where alleged abuse and violence is involved.[29]

D. The Fourth Special Commission Meeting: 22–28 March 2001

The last Special Commission prior to the adoption of the Brussels II bis Regulation met in March 2001 (the fourth Special Commission). The fourth Special Commission was held after the 1999 statistical survey was conducted by the Centre for International Family Law Studies at the Cardiff Law School.

Like the preceding Special Commissions, the fourth Special Commission concluded that, in accordance with the objectives of the Convention, as supported by the Explanatory Report by Elisa Pérez-Vera, the 'Article 13(1)(b) exception to return had been given a very strict interpretation by the courts in the Contracting States' . Evidence to support this statement was drawn from the 1999 statistical survey:

> This is confirmed by the relatively small number of return applications which were refused on this basis according to the Statistical Analysis of Applications made in 1999 (Prel Doc No 3, March 2001).[30]

Interestingly, the above conclusion stands in complete contrast to the European Commission working document on the mutual recognition of decisions on

[27] *Ibid*, para 60.
[28] *Ibid*, para 64.
[29] *Ibid*, annex III: Synthetic revision of working document No 20 as drawn up by the Permanent Bureau in the light of the comments and suggestions made by experts.
[30] Permanent Bureau of the Hague Conference, 'Conclusions and Recommendations of the Fourth Meeting of the Special Commission to Review the Operation of the Hague Convention of 25 October 1980 on the Civil Aspects of International Child Abduction, 22–28 March 2001' part IV, para 4.3, available at www.hcch.net/upload/concl28sc4_e.pdf.

parental responsibility from March 2001 where the claim of an overuse of Article 13(1)(b), allegedly evidenced by the 1999 statistical survey, was first made.[31]

III. Conferences and Judicial Seminars

An analysis of available resources has revealed that five major relevant conferences/judicial seminars were held in parallel with the preparation of the Brussels II bis Regulation. First, it was the Common Law Judicial Conference on International Parental Abduction in September 2000; second, the International Judicial Seminar on the 1980 Hague Convention on the Civil Aspects of International Child Abduction in October 2001; third, the 2001 World Congress on Family Law and the Rights of Children; fourth, the Anglo/French Conference in June 2001; and fifth, the Fourth UK-German Family Law Conference in September 2002.

A. Common Law Judicial Conference on International Parental Abduction (17–21 September 2000, the Hosting Institution: the US Central Authority—US State Department's Office of Children Issues)

The judges present at the Common Law Judicial Conference on International Parental Abduction shared the view of the Special Commissions and concluded that the Article 13(1)(b) exception had generally been construed narrowly in the Contracting States. Undertakings (in some jurisdictions known as stipulations or conditions) were recognised as a useful instrument 'to facilitate arrangements for return and/or alleviate Article 13(1)(b) concerns'[32] until a court of the habitual residence takes control. Orders containing undertakings were acknowledged as being fully in accordance with the spirit of the Convention.

B. International Judicial Seminar on the 1980 Hague Convention on the Civil Aspects of International Child Abduction, De Ruwenberg Conference Centre, Netherlands, 20–23 October 2001

This judicial seminar, attended by 31 judges from seven jurisdictions (England and Wales, France (three), Germany, the Netherlands, Scotland, Sweden and the United States) unanimously agreed that the Article 13(1)(b) 'grave risk' defence

[31] Mutual Recognition of Decisions (n 4). See Chapter 2, section entitled 'March 2001: Commission Working Document: Mutual Recognition of Decisions on Parental Responsibility'.

[32] 'Common Law Judicial Conference on International Parental Child Abduction' (2000) 2 *Judges' Newsletter* 9, 11.

'has generally been narrowly construed'.[33] It also held that a return application based on Article 13(1)(b) should not be refused unless all the available means of protection of the child in the requesting State were found to be inadequate. Quite interestingly, despite the strong support for the child abduction regime on the side of France, none of the three French judges present at the seminar expressed concerns regarding the operation of the Convention. On the contrary, they shared the view of the participants from other jurisdictions and agreed that Article 13(1)(b) had been interpreted in a narrow fashion.

C. The 2001 World Congress on Family Law and the Rights of Children[34]

In September 2001, a third World Congress on Family Law and the Rights of Children 'International Co-operation and the Protection of Children in the Millennium' took place in Bath, England. The Congress was attended by about 600 specialists from a diverse range of jurisdictions. One of the workshops held was focused on the operation of the 1980 Hague Abduction Convention. The speakers were child abduction experts Professor William Duncan, Joseph Kay, Mr Adair Dyer and Professor Martha Bailey. They agreed that the Convention was working well; nevertheless, they accepted that a few issues needed further attention. Article 13(1)(b) was, however, not cited among these subjects. The areas considered to be in need of improvement were the co-operation between Central Authorities, maintaining uniformity of interpretation and Article 21 (access rights).

D. Anglo-French Conference at Dartington Hall in Devon

The first Francophone-Anglophone Family Law Judicial Conference was held in Devon, England in June 2001. One of the issues discussed at the conference was the return of abducted children under the 1980 Hague Abduction Convention. No particular note was made about Article 13(1)(b) of the Convention; nevertheless, a tension was felt between the pro-reform EU Members and those EU Member States that did not support the separate intra-EU child abduction initiative. Hinting at the proposal for the Brussels II bis Regulation, it was held that:

> [t]he most controversial topic was the development of future international conventions and regulations. The evident divide was between those who give primacy to our regional relationship as Europeans and those who advocate the wider bonds explored by the

[33] Permanent Bureau of the Hague Conference, 'International Judicial Seminar on the 1980 Hague Convention on the Civil Aspects of International Child Abduction, De Ruwenberg Conference Centre, the Netherlands, 20–23 October 2001: Conclusions and Recommendations' 2, available at www.hcch.net/upload/der2001e.pdf.

[34] The Honourable Dr P Nygh, 'The 2001 World Congress on Family Law and the Rights of Children' (2001) 3 *Judges' Newsletter* 19.

Permanent Bureau of the Hague Conference, particularly through the medium of the 1980 Abduction Convention.[35]

E. Fourth UK-German Family Law Conference at Trier, Germany, September 2002

The fourth UK-German Family Law Conference took place in Trier in Germany between 24 and 29 September 2002. Among the topics that were addressed by the participating experts was the progress on the Brussels II bis Regulation. On the one hand, it was recognised that some of the provisions of the draft Regulation, namely those on the recognition and enforcement of orders, were highly beneficial. On the other hand, however, the proposed Regulation was heavily criticised for its ambition to set up a separate intra-EU regime for tackling child abduction. Moreover, in the conclusions of the conference, the participating experts called for the reconsideration of the child abduction provisions from the draft Regulation. It was held: '[The conference] recommends that the Commission should reconsider Chapter III of its Proposal of May 2002 for a Council Regulation on Jurisdiction and the Recognition and Enforcement of Judgments in Matters of Parental Responsibility'.

In this context, the conference warned about the danger of the multiplication of competing international instruments. It was rightly pointed out that 'we should not complicate their [fractured families' as well as vulnerable children's and adults'] already complicated lives nor aggravate their distress by encumbering litigation processes with a battery of conventions, regulations and instruments (sometimes more competitive than complementary)'.[36] Strong support was expressed for the 1980 Hague Abduction Convention and a recommendation was made not to go beyond the Convention itself in case a need for the improvement of this instrument is established:

> The conference is satisfied that the 1980 Hague Convention on the Civil Aspects of International Child Abduction is generally working well in cases of wrongful removal and retention, both within and outside the Member States of the European Union. Accordingly it is of the firm opinion that where changes to the 1980 Convention prove necessary they should be made within the context of that global instrument.

IV. Academic Literature

As a part of the examination of all available resources regarding the application of Article 13(1)(b) prior to the adoption of the Brussels II bis Regulation, a detailed review of all academic literature on the topic was conducted. The analysis revealed that a few commentators did express their concerns regarding the application of

[35] The Right Honourable Lord Justice Thorpe, 'Anglo/French Conference at Dartington' (2001) 3 *Judges' Newsletter* 16, 17.

[36] Fourth UK-German Family Law Conference (n 12) 11–12.

the exception. These authors warned about frequent abuses of Article 13(1)(b),[37] the problem of inconsistent interpretation of Article 13 (including the Article 13(1)(b) 'grave risk' exception),[38] an unreasonably wide interpretation of Article 13(1)(b),[39] and the failure on the side of the courts to apply the exception in Article 13(1)(b) strictly, energetically and consistently.[40]

The harshest criticism of the application of Article 13(1)(b), especially by some European countries, came from a US specialist Thomas Johnson, attorney with the United States Department of State and a human rights activist. Johnson accused European civil law jurisdictions (particularly Sweden, Germany and Austria) of not complying with their international obligations under the Hague Abduction Convention. The author claimed that in many cases where Article 13(1)(b) had been invoked, the above jurisdictions conducted essentially custody proceedings under the label of Hague cases.[41]

Other critics pointed out that in Article 13(1)(b) cases the courts had often addressed the concept of the best interests of the child in return proceedings, instead of leaving this issue to be decided in custody proceedings. Using their own interpretation of the best interests of the child, the courts were frequently satisfied to refuse the return of the child, arguing that the return would put the child in danger.[42]

One commentator, although acknowledging that defences, including Article 13(1)(b), had in his view been used more often than necessary, feared that too narrow an interpretation of the exceptions would lead to an excessively rigorous application of the Convention.[43]

Nevertheless, the majority of commentators believed that the 'grave risk of harm' exception had been interpreted in a narrow fashion and had rarely been invoked successfully.[44] Notably, this view was shared also by Professor Paul

[37] T Johnson, 'The Hague Child Abduction Convention: Diminishing Returns and Little to Celebrate for Americans' (2000–2001) 33 *New York University Journal of International Law & Politics* 125.

[38] K Wolfe, 'A Tale of Two States: Successes and Failures of the 1980 Hague Convention on the Civil Aspects of International Child Abduction in the United States and Germany' (2000–2001) 33 *New York University Journal of International Law & Politics* 285.

[39] GF DeHart, 'The Relationship Between the 1980 Child Abduction Convention and the 1996 Protection Convention' (2000–2001) 33 *New York University Journal of International Law & Politics* 83.

[40] K Siehr, 'The 1980 Hague Convention on the Civil Aspects of International Child Abduction: Failures and Successes in German Practice' (2000–2001) 33 *New York University Journal of International Law & Politics* 207, 212.

[41] It is to be noted that the severe criticism of the application of the 'grave risk of harm' defence on the side of the author had its root causes in his personal experience. Mr Johnson's daughter was wrongfully retained in Sweden by her mother in 1995. Mr Johnson's application for return was refused by a Swedish court on the basis of Art 13(1)(b) and his daughter never returned to the United States. Johnson, 'The Hague Child Abduction Convention'.

[42] DeHart, 'The Relationship' (n 39) 83; and Siehr, 'The 1980 Hague Convention' (n 40) 207.

[43] W Duncan, 'Action in Support of the Hague Child Abduction Convention: A View from Permanent Bureau' (2000–2001) 33 *New York University Journal of International Law & Politics* 103.

[44] See, eg, P McEleavy, 'Brussels II bis: Matrimonial Matters, Parental Responsibility, Child Abduction and Mutual Recognition' [Notes] (2004) 53 *International and Comparative Law Quarterly* 503; M Britton, 'Undertakings: A Satisfactory Safeguard to Grave Risk?' [2003] *Cork Online Law Review*, available at www.corkonlinelawreview.com/editions/2003/2003xi.pdf; J Lewis, 'The Hague

Beaumont and Peter McEleavy, the authors of the leading monograph on the 1980 Convention *The Hague Convention on International Child Abduction*.[45] In this monograph, the authors commented:

> While Article 13(1)(b) may appear at first glance to allow the greatest scope to the abductor in attempting to oppose a return it is without doubt the most strictly regulated of all the exceptions and had been upheld in only a handful of cases[46] (citations omitted).

A high proportion of commentators even warned that Article 13(1)(b) was being interpreted too strictly and children were returned 'even in what appear to be genuine cases of grave risk'.[47] A particular focus was on cases involving domestic violence or child abuse. For example, Professor Bruch described judicial returns in cases of proven spousal abuse as 'cavalier judicial decisions'.[48] Similarly, Professor Kaye criticised 'an overriding concern by courts and researchers not to undermine the Convention' and warned of dangers inherent in the ignorance of the fact that 'circumstances surrounding abductions are inevitably gendered'.[49]

It was proposed that abductions committed against the background of domestic violence receive special treatment in the context of the 'grave risk of harm' defence. Several suggestions were made as to how to achieve it. For example, it was suggested that courts adopt a more flexible approach to the interpretation of Article 13(1)(b).[50] Another proposal was for domestic violence to be incorporated into the Article 13(1)(b) definition of a 'grave risk of harm'.[51] Yet another suggestion was that a defence for victims of domestic violence be incorporated into the Convention.[52] Finally, a recommendation was made to consider the option

Convention on the Civil Aspects of International Child Abduction: When Domestic Violence and Child Abuse Impact the Goal of Comity' (2000) 13 *Transnational Lawyer* 391, 411; M Bailey, 'Canada's Implementation of the 1980 Hague Convention on the Civil Aspects of International Child Abduction' (2000–2001) 33 New York University Journal of International Law & Politics 17; and N Lowe, 'Negotiating the Revised Brussels II Regulation' [2004] *International Family Law Journal* 205.

[45] P Beaumont and P McEleavy, *The Hague Convention on International Child Abduction* (Oxford, Oxford University Press, 1999).

[46] *Ibid*, 140.

[47] P Ward, 'Child Abduction: A Rare Refusal to Return' [2000] *Family Law Journal* 50.

[48] C Bruch, 'The Hague Child Abduction Convention: Past Accomplishments, Future Challenges' (1999) 1 *European Journal of Law Reform* 97, 105.

[49] M Kaye, 'The Hague Convention and the Flight from Domestic Violence: How Women and Children are Being Returned by Coach and Four' (1999) 13 *International Journal of Law, Policy and the Family* 191.

[50] See R Schuz, 'The Hague Child Abduction Convention and Children's Rights' (2002) 12 *Transnational Law & Contemporary Problems* 393; M Freeman, 'Primary Carers and the Hague Child Abduction Convention' [2001] *International Family Law Journal* 140; The Right Honourable Baroness Hale, 'The View From Court 45' [1999] CFLQ 377, 380, per J Caldwell, 'Child Welfare Defences in Child Abduction Cases—Some Recent Developments' [2001] *Child and Family Law Quarterly* 121; and S Shetty and JL Edleson, 'Adult Domestic Violence in Cases of International Parental Child Abduction' (2005) 11 *Violence Against Women* 115.

[51] EL Buckwalter, 'In the Best Interest of the Child' (2006) *The Berkeley Electronic Press*, Paper 1166, available at www.law.bepress.com/cgi/viewcontent.cgi?article=5555&context=expresso.

[52] See MH Weiner, 'International Child Abduction and the Escape from Domestic Violence' (2000–2001) 69 *Fordham Law Review* 593, 692; BE Lubin, 'International Parental Child Abduction: Conteptualizing New Remedies Through Application of the Hague Convention' (2005) 4 *Washington*

of subsuming domestic violence under the Article 20 exception of fundamental human rights.[53]

It is submitted here that in order to achieve an effective functioning of the Convention, it is inevitable that courts adhere to the requirement of the strict interpretation of Article 13(1)(b). At the same time, however, each case should be decided on its own facts, with the safety of the child and the returning parent being the first priority.

To conclude, from the above analysis it appears that there was no evidence to justify a claim for the indispensability of the separate intra-EU child abduction regime. In contrast, overall, the available resources point to a generally efficient functioning of the 1980 Convention, with a narrow interpretation of Article 13(1)(b).

University Global Studies Law Review 415, 444; MS Wills, 'Interpreting the Hague Convention on International Child Abduction: Why American Courts Need to Reconcile the Rights of Non-Custodial Parents, the Best Interests of Abducted Children, and the Underlying Objectives of the Hague Convention' (2006) 25 *Review of Litigation* 423, 457; R Hoegger, 'What If She Leaves? Domestic Violence Cases Under the Hague Convention and the Insufficiency of the Undertakings Remedy' (2003) 18 *Berkeley Women's Law Journal* 181; and Freeman, 'Primary Carers' (n 50) 140. This proposal was, however, strongly criticised by Professor Silberman in L Silberman, 'Patching Up the Abduction Convention: A Call for a New International Protocol and a Suggestion for Amendments to ICARA' (2003) 38 *Texas International Law Journal* 41, 45.

[53] MH Weiner, 'Using Article 20' (2004–2005) 38 *Family Law Quarterly* 583; MH Weiner 'Strengthening Article 20' [2005] *International Family Law Journal* 209; KS Mast, 'The Application of the Fundamental Principles Exception of the Hague Convention on the Civil Aspects of International Child Abduction' (2003) 17 *Emory International Law Review* 241, 262 and 265.

5

Operation of the Brussels II bis Regulation: Empirical Study

The previous Chapter showed that the Commission did not have a valid reason to pursue the new intra-EU child abduction regime. Indeed, in contrast to the Commission's allegation of the misuse of the Article 13(1)(b) exception, no evidence of any significant improper use of this provision was found. Despite this finding, the Brussels II bis Regulation was adopted. It is now for practice to show whether the instrument was a wise choice. This can only be revealed through thorough empirical research. Bearing this in mind, we have undertaken a statistical survey on the practical operation of the Regulation. The main objective of this empirical survey is to find out how 'effectively' the Brussels II bis Regulation is working and to what extent the instrument has fulfilled the expectations of its drafters. The analysis aims at identifying possible shortcomings in the operation of the Regulation. The term 'effectively' is used here to refer to the objective of the drafters of the Brussels II bis Regulation to achieve a reduction in judicial refusals to return, especially refusals based on Article 13(1)(b) of the Convention. Contrary to this understanding, it is, however, submitted that 'effectiveness' of child abduction law should not be measured solely by the criterion of a refusal rate. Instead, the objective of low refusal statistics should be placed on an equal footing with a concern for the safety of the child and the returning parent, in particular in cases where the defence of Article 13(1)(b) has been raised. 'Effective' law of child abduction should therefore combine concern for a rigorous interpretation of the Convention concepts with a highly sensitive approach to the need for protection of the child and the abducting parent upon their return to the requesting State. In order to achieve a uniform application of the Convention, it is important that child abduction law is interpreted in a consistent manner, both across the EU jurisdictions as well as globally. At the global level, the need for uniform interpretation of the Convention has recently been highlighted by the Supreme Court of the United States in the case of *Abbott v Abbott*.[1] In particular, the court quoted approvingly a general principle that 'in interpreting any treaty, the opinions of our sister signatories are entitled to considerable weight'[2] (references omitted). The court further held that in the area of child

[1] *Abbott v Abbott* 130 SCt 1983 (2010).
[2] *Ibid*, para 6.

abduction this principle applied with a special force as 'uniform international interpretation of the Convention is part of the Convention's framework'.[3] At the European level, however, the European Court of Human Rights has recently paid insufficient attention to the need for consistent interpretation in the area of child abduction.[4]

This Chapter contains brief information on the background of the survey as well as information on the scope, aim and methodology of the project. The most extensive part of the Chapter covers detailed analysis of the findings of the survey.

I. Background to the Empirical Study

The survey is a statistical and analytical study of the effectiveness of the new intra-EU child abduction regime. As far as the author is aware, this was the first comprehensive statistical survey into the operation of the Brussels II bis Regulation.[5]

[3] *Ibid.*

[4] See the judgment of the Grand Chamber of the European Court of Human Rights in the case of *Neulinger and Shuruk v Switzerland* App no 41615/07 (ECtHR, 6 July 2010), which does not adequately build on its own good case law on the Hague Child Abduction Convention; see P Beaumont, 'The Jurisprudence of the European Court of Human Rights and the European Court of Justice on the Hague Convention on International Child Abduction' (2008) 335 *Hague Recueil* 9, nor consider the interpretation of the Hague Convention by courts in other States. For an analysis of *Neulinger* see Chapter 6, section entitled 'Investigation of Allegations'. For a comprehensive analysis of the case law of the European Court of Human Rights concerning the provisions of the Hague Abduction Convention, including the *Neulinger* case, see L Walker, 'The Impact of the Hague Abduction Convention on the Rights of the Family in the Case-Law of the European Court of Human Rights and the UN Human Rights Committee: The Danger of *Neulinger*' (2010) 6 *Journal of Private International Law* 649. Serious misunderstandings of the Hague Abduction Convention by the ECtHR are apparent also in the European Court of Human Rights decision in *Raban v Romania* App no 25437/08 (ECtHR, 26 October 2010). See L Walker and P Beaumont, 'Shifting the Balance Achieved by the Abduction Convention: The Contrasting Approaches of the European Court of Human Rights and the European Court of Justice' (2011) 7 *Journal of Private International Law* 231.

[5] Additionally, a detailed quantitative and qualitative study into the problem of parental child abduction, including the operation of the child abduction provisions of the Brussels II bis Regulation, was carried out on 2007 and 2008 cases in Belgium by Thalia Kruger. Her study 'International Child Abduction by Parents to and from Belgium in 2007–2008' has been published as a book by Hart Publishing: T Kruger, *International Child Abduction: Inadequacies of the Law* (Oxford, Hart Publishing, 2011). The scope of this study and the methodology used, however, differed significantly from the present survey. Kruger's study in Belgium involved an analysis of the total of 667 files. Of these, only 31 cases were incoming Brussels II bis applications (ie cases in which the child was abducted from another EU Member State to Belgium). Consequently, the outcomes are not comparable with the outcomes of the present survey. Nevertheless, out of interest, a number of references have been made to the findings of this study throughout the analysis of the present survey. A similar study was conducted in Hungary by Kék Vonal, a Hungarian organisation working with children. Outcomes of this study have, however, not been published in their entirety because of privacy constraints. Kruger, *International Child Abduction*, 2, fn 2.

In the past, prior to the Brussels II bis Regulation, two large comprehensive empirical studies had been conducted on the operation of the 1980 Hague Abduction Convention. The aim of these surveys was to contribute to an effective monitoring of the functioning of the Convention, to reveal weaknesses in the implementation of the Convention in some of the Contracting States, to suggest solutions for improvement and thus to achieve a uniform interpretation and application of this treaty in all Contracting States. No less importantly, these studies aimed at exploring misconceptions about particular aspects of the application of the Convention, including the myth about the misuse of Article 13(1)(b).[6]

Both projects were carried out by the Centre of International Family Law Studies at Cardiff University Law School, under the directorship of Professor Nigel Lowe, in co-operation with the Permanent Bureau of the Hague Conference. The first survey was conducted in 2001 and concerned applications made worldwide under the 1980 Convention in 1999. Its findings were presented at the Fourth Special Commission in March 2001.[7] The second project involved applications made globally under the 1980 Convention in 2003 and was carried out in the years 2005/2006. A response was received from 58 Contracting States, including all European Union Member States. The findings of this statistical survey were presented at the fifth Special Commission held in October–November 2006.[8] The author was involved in this project as a research assistant of Professor Lowe.

Being aware of the need for a regular review of implementation of international instruments and drawing on her experience with the monitoring of the operation of the 1980 Convention, the author decided to carry out her personal research on the operation of the Brussels II bis Regulation within the European Union. This decision was reinforced when the author was provided unrestricted exclusive access to the 2003 database. This was by kind permission of the Centre for International Family Law Studies at Cardiff University Law School.[9] The access rights to the database provided the author with a set of extremely valuable information, enabling her to obtain data comparable with her empirical survey. Concretely, she was able to perform a 2003 analysis of the operation of the Convention exclusively within the European Union and consequently, to demonstrate whether the reform

[6] N Lowe and K Horosova, 'The Operation of the 1980 Hague Abduction Convention—A Global View' (2007) 41 *Family Law Quarterly* 59, 60.

[7] N Lowe, S Armstrong and A Mathias, 'A Statistical Analysis of Applications Made in 1999 under the Hague Convention on the Civil Aspects of International Child Abduction' Preliminary Document No 3 (2001), available at www.hcch.net/upload/abd2001pd3e.pdf.

[8] N Lowe, E Atkinson, K Horosova and S Patterson, 'A Statistical Analysis of Applications Made in 2003 under the Hague Convention of 25 October 1980 on the Civil Aspects of International Child Abduction' Preliminary Document No 3 (2006) 41, available at www.hcch.net/upload/wop/abd_pd03e2006.pdf.

[9] In this regard, the author thanks Professor Nigel Lowe for making the 2003 database accessible to her for the purposes of her research.

in the form of the Brussels II bis Regulation has improved the standard of the intra-EU child abduction regime.

Following the present study, a second comprehensive survey into the operation of the Brussels II bis Regulation in the area of child abduction was carried out on 2008 applications by the Centre for International Family Law of the Cardiff University.[10] The results were, however, not fully comparable with our survey due to differences in the Member States involved,[11] and partly also due to a differing cut-off period.[12] At the end, limited comparison was, nevertheless, made possible by the generous assistance of the Centre for International Family Law, which kindly agreed to perform a comparable analysis on its 2008 database to provide us with answers to specific questions related to outcomes, reasons for judicial refusal, and timing.[13] The data obtained have been referred to throughout the analysis of this survey.[14]

II. Scope, Aim and Methodology of the Empirical Study

The survey involved a detailed statistical analysis of return applications made within the European Union[15] under the Brussels II bis Regulation from 1 July 2005 to 30 June 2006. The reason for choosing the particular researched period was that 2005/06, being the first year of the operation of the Brussels II bis Regulation, had been the only year of the functioning of the separate intra-EU

[10] See N Lowe, 'A Statistical Analysis of Applications made in 2008 under the Hague Convention on the Civil Aspects of International Child Abduction: Part II—Regional Report', Preliminary Document No 8 (2011), available at www.hcch.net/upload/wop/abduct2011pd08be.pdf.

[11] In particular, Slovakia participated in the 2005/06 survey but did not take part in the 2008 survey; and Bulgaria, Greece, Netherlands, Romania and Spain participated in the 2008 survey but did not take part in the 2005/06 survey.

[12] For the 2008 survey the cut-off date for outcome was 18 months after the last possible application could have been made. In contrast, the cut-off period for the 2005/06 survey was eight months after the last possible application could have been made.

[13] In this respect, the author thanks Professor Nigel Lowe and Ms Victoria Stephens for their kind assistance.

[14] It must, however, be pointed out that the 2008 analysis still did not ensure complete comparability with the 2005/06 data, for the following two reasons. First, the analysis did not include Slovakia as Slovakia did not take part in the 2008 survey. Second, the cut-off period for the 2008 survey differed from the cut-off period for the 2005/06 survey (see n 12 above).

[15] The European Union as of 2005/06. Romania and Bulgaria were not included in the survey as they were not Members of the European Union in the researched period (July 2005—June 2006). Note: These two jurisdictions joined the Union in January 2007. Also, Denmark was excluded from the research as it, in accordance with Arts 1 and 2 of the Protocol on the position of Denmark annexed to the Treaty on European Union and the Treaty establishing the European Community, did not take part in the adoption and application of the Brussels II bis Regulation. Consequently, the following 24 EU Members were included in the research: Austria, Belgium, Cyprus, the Czech Republic, Estonia, Finland, France, Germany, Greece, Hungary, Ireland, Italy, Latvia, Lithuania, Luxembourg, Malta, the Netherlands, Poland, Portugal, Slovakia, Slovenia, Spain, Sweden, and the United Kingdom.

child abduction regime prior to the commencement of this research in November 2006. The primary objective of the survey was to assess the operation of this new Community instrument between 24 Member States of the European Union. To achieve this aim, a detailed questionnaire was created and sent to the relevant Central Authorities.[16] The questionnaire sought to obtain information on the number of return applications the Central Authority received within the researched period, information on the requesting State, information on the profile of the abductor (that is, mother or father of the child), the nationality of the abductor, and most importantly the outcome of the applications and the timing of the cases. Where the return was judicially refused, the reason for the refusal was sought. Also, a short description of the procedure under Articles 11(6) and 11(7) of the Regulation was asked for in cases of judicial refusals based on Article 13(1)(b).[17]

The questionnaire was designed in a way that followed the example of the 2003 survey, so as to achieve as high a comparability of results as possible. Nevertheless, although the questionnaire was modelled on that used in the 2003 project, it was less detailed than its predecessor. It only sought information considered relevant to the changes introduced to the return mechanism by the Regulation. The questionnaire, for example, did not seek information on the number of children involved in the application, on the age of the children, on the gender of the children, on the nationality of the applicant, and on the reason for rejection of the application by a Central Authority.

The questionnaire consisted of five questions. Additionally, one of the questions contained three sub-questions. Only one question was a simple tick box; the remaining four questions needed specific information in response.

The questionnaire was designed in English; however, a covering letter accompanying the questionnaire was written and sent out in four languages: in German to Austria and Germany, in Slovak to Slovakia, in Czech to the Czech Republic and in English to the remaining jurisdictions.

The survey included all applications received by the Central Authorities between 1 July 2005 and 30 June 2006, irrespective of when the application was resolved. The cut-off date for the survey was 28 February 2007, that is, eight months after the last possible day for the receipt of the application. Applications that were not resolved by the end of February 2007 were classified as 'pending'. Initially, the cut-off period proved problematic in relation to the comparability with the 2003 survey. The problem was that for the 2003 survey the cut-off date for outcome was 18 months after the last possible application could have been received. The period of 18 months was, however, considered

[16] As in the 2003 survey, United Kingdom jurisdictions (England and Wales, Northern Ireland, and Scotland) were treated separately because of the vast number of applications handled by the Central Authority of England and Wales.

[17] It is, however, to be noted that virtually no information was obtained in this respect as relevant data had not been made available to the Central Authorities.

too long for the purposes of this empirical survey. Therefore, in order to achieve full comparability with the 2003 survey, it was necessary to apply the eight-month cut-off period to the 2003 findings. Consequently, outcomes that were concluded after the eight-month deadline were re-classified and categorised as 'pending'. As a result, timing also had to be checked out and modified accordingly.

Altogether, 23 out of 26 requested Central Authorities responded positively to the request to participate in the research.[18] Of these, 22 Central Authorities kindly completed and returned the questionnaire either by post, email or fax. The Central Authority of England and Wales replied that they were overburdened and due to a lack of financial and personnel resources were unable to assist with the survey. Nevertheless, they generously invited the author to visit their office in London in person and granted her full access to their files in order to obtain the information required. The Spanish Central Authority and the Dutch Central Authority both acknowledged the receipt of the questionnaire; however, owing to limited resources, were not in a position to complete it. Finally, no response whatsoever was received from Greece.

III. Findings of the Empirical Study

A. The Number of Applications

The survey analysed 363 return applications received by the participating Central Authorities.[19] This compares with 301 return applications received by the participating Central Authorities in 2003.[20] However, at 536, the number of applications received by the participating Central Authorities was considerably higher in 2008. This clearly indicates that the volume of intra-EU child abduction cases continues to increase.

As Table 5.5 shows, the highest number of applications, 105, was made to England and Wales. On the other hand, no return application was sent to Latvia.[21]

[18] Austria, Belgium, Cyprus, the Czech Republic, Estonia, Finland, France, Germany, Hungary, Ireland, Italy, Latvia, Lithuania, Luxembourg, Malta, Poland, Portugal, Slovakia, Slovenia, Sweden, and UK-England and Wales, UK-Northern Ireland, and UK-Scotland.

[19] During the researched period Latvia did not receive any return application under the Brussels II bis Regulation.

[20] In 2003, five Central Authorities did not receive any incoming return applications from what are today Brussels II bis Member States (Latvia, Lithuania, Luxembourg, Slovenia, and UK-Northern Ireland).

[21] Although no incoming return application was made to Latvia, our database—based on the records of the participating Central Authorities—shows that, during the researched period, this jurisdiction made four outgoing return applications under the Brussels II bis Regulation.

Table 5.5: Number of applications: Requested States

	Number	Percent
UK–England & Wales	105	29%
France	69	19%
Germany	53	15%
Ireland	32	9%
Poland	24	7%
Belgium	18	5%
Czech Republic	13	4%
Austria	9	2%
Cyprus	4	1%
Finland	4	1%
Slovakia	4	1%
Sweden	4	1%
UK–Northern Ireland	4	1%
UK–Scotland	4	1%
Italy	3	1%
Portugal	3	1%
Slovenia	3	1%
Estonia	2	1%
Luxembourg	2	1%
Hungary	1	<1%
Lithuania	1	<1%
Malta	1	<1%
Total	**363**	**~100%**

The sharpest increase in the number of applications was recorded by France, Ireland and England and Wales, from 20 to 69 applications, from 21 to 32 applications and from 76 to 105 applications respectively. On the other hand, a significant fall in the number of applications was recorded by Sweden, Italy, Portugal and Hungary.[22]

[22] Despite the sharp drop in the number of incoming applications to Italy (from 21 in 2003 to three in 2005/06), this jurisdiction was the second busiest with regard to outgoing cases. Our records show that in 2005/06 Italy, preceded only by England and Wales with 43 outgoing applications, made 34 return applications.

Table 5.6: Number of applications

	Number of applications 2005/06	**Number of applications 2003**
UK–England & Wales	105	76
France	69	20
Germany	53	54
Ireland	32	21
Poland	24	17
Belgium	18	17
Czech Republic	13	9
Austria	9	8
Cyprus	4	7
Finland	4	4
Slovakia	4	7
Sweden	4	12
UK–Northern Ireland	4	0
UK–Scotland	4	5
Italy	3	21
Portugal	3	9
Slovenia	3	0
Estonia	2	1
Luxembourg	2	0
Hungary	1	10
Lithuania	1	0
Malta	1	3
Latvia	0	0
Total	**363**	**301**

The four busiest jurisdictions were England and Wales, France, Germany and Ireland. Surprisingly, in 2003, France took only fifth place, compared with second place in 2005/06. Italy, which held fourth place in 2003, was in 2005/06 replaced by Poland.

B. Relationship of the Alleged Abductor to the Child[23]

The survey revealed that 75% of alleged abductors were mothers.[24] Consequently, only a minority (22%) of the alleged abductions were perpetrated by fathers.

Table 5.7: Relationship of the alleged abductor

	Number	Percent
Mother	271	75%
Father	81	22%
Both Parents	3	1%
Grandparent	3	1%
Other Relative	3	1%
Other	2	1%
Total	**363**	**~100%**

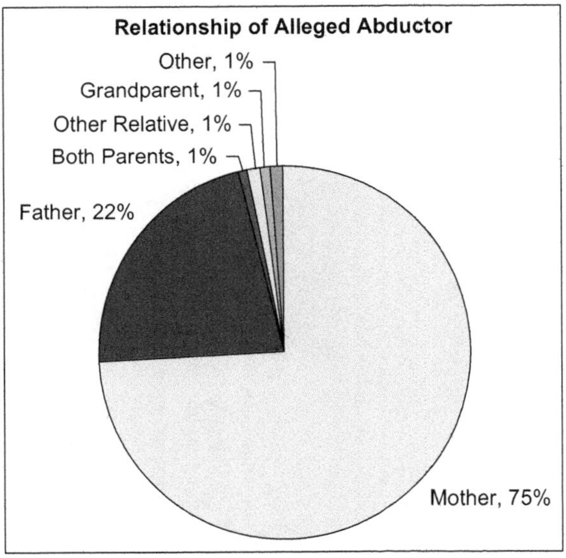

Figure 5.8: Relationship of alleged abductor

[23] The 2003 survey uses a slightly different terminology for the person who takes the child. Instead of referring to 'abductor', it uses the term 'taking person'. The 2005/06 survey uses the term 'alleged abductor'. However, sometimes the term 'respondent' is used instead. It is to be noted that all three expressions have essentially the same meaning.

[24] Kruger's study revealed that of the 31 abductions to Belgium, the mother was the abductor in 71.8% of the cases. Kruger, *International Child Abduction* (n 5) 79.

At 75%, the proportion of mothers as alleged abductors represents an increase on the 2003 percentage of 72%.[25]

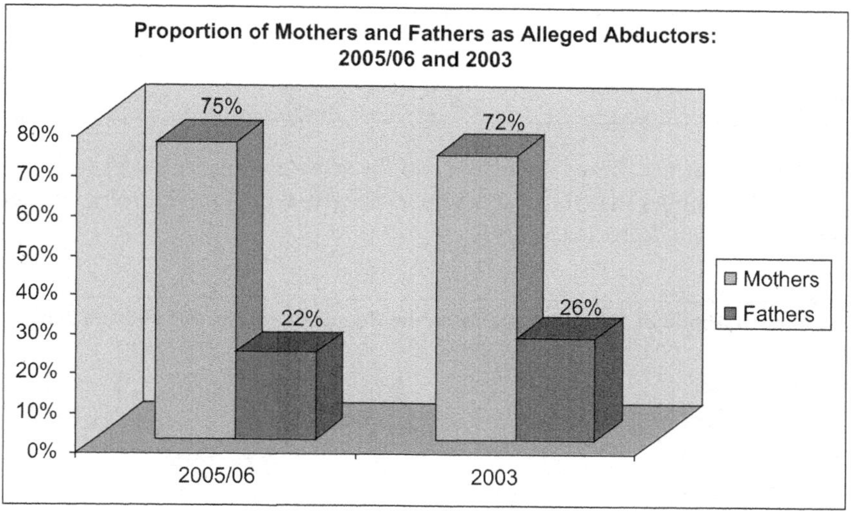

Figure 5.9: Proportion of Mothers and Fathers as Alleged Abductors: 2005/06 and 2003

C. Nationality of the Alleged Abductor[26]

Overall, 135 out of 238 of the alleged abductors, 57%, had the same nationality as the requested State. This fact indicates that over half of the abductors were returning to their country of origin (that is, 'going home').[27]

[25] In 2003, the information on the relationship of the alleged abductor to the child was unavailable in one out of the 301 applications.

[26] Germany and France were unable to provide information on the nationality of the alleged abductor. Altogether, the information on the nationality of the alleged abductor was available in relation to 238 applications.

[27] Interestingly, in 2007/2008 abductions to Belgium, the proportion of abducting parents 'going home' was only 45.6%: Kruger (n 5) 45. Kruger's study revealed that unhappiness and lack of integration into Belgian society on the part of the abducting parent (normally the mother) were the key contributory factors in these abductions. Kruger (n 5) 66–7.

Table 5.8: Alleged abductor same nationality as the requested State

	Number	Percent
Same Nationality	135	57%
Different Nationality	103	43%
Total	**238**	**100%**

In 2003, 61% of the alleged abductors had the same nationality as the requested State.[28] This implies that the proportion of alleged abductors returning to their country of origin decreased by 4%.

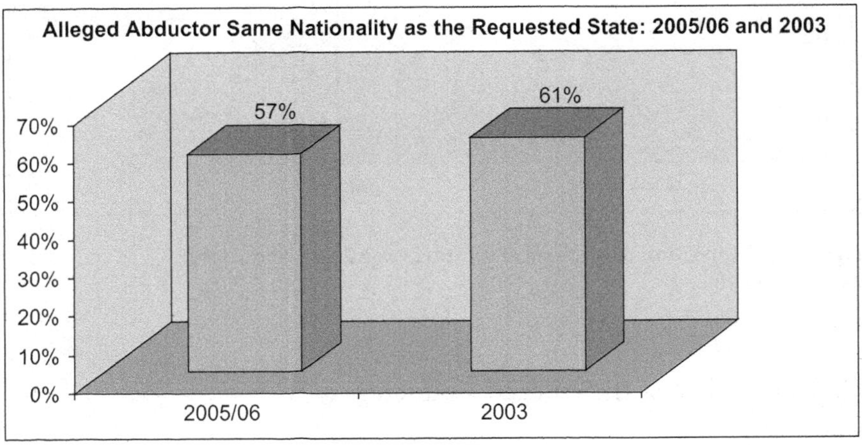

Figure 5.10: Alleged abductor same nationality as the requested state: 2005/06 and 2003

D. Relationship and Nationality of the Alleged Abductor

As Table 5.9 shows, 101 out of the 173 (58%) mothers as alleged abductors had the same nationality as the requested State. In relation to the fathers, 31 out of the 59 (53%) were nationals of the requested State. Surprisingly, the difference between the proportion of mothers and fathers 'going home' (5%) appears to be negligible.[29]

[28] In order to achieve better comparability, Germany and France, which were both unable to provide information on the nationality of the alleged abductor in 2005/06, were excluded from the 2003 analysis on the nationality of the alleged abductor.

[29] The finding is surprising given the general expectation that the proportion of mothers 'going home' is higher than the proportion of fathers 'going home'.

Table 5.9: Nationality and relationship of the alleged abductor to the child

	Relationship of Alleged Abductor to Child						Total
	Mother	Father	Both Parents	Grandparent	Other Relatives	Other	
Same Nationality	101	31	1	1	1	0	**135**
Different Nationality	72	28	0	1	1	1	**103**
Total	**173**	**59**	**1**	**2**	**2**	**1**	**238**

In 2003, 93 out of 155 (60%) respondent mothers were citizens of the requested State.[30] This shows a slight decrease (by 2%) in the proportion of mothers 'going home'.

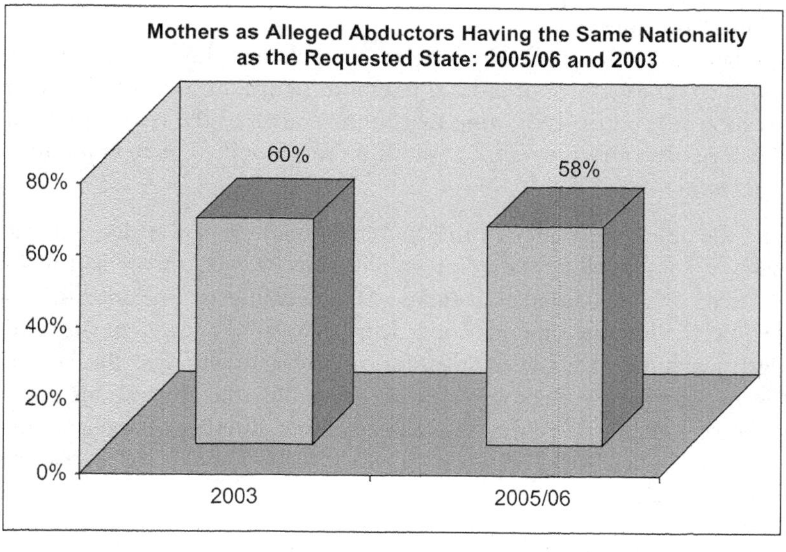

Figure 5.11: Mothers as alleged abductors having the same nationality as the requested State: 2005/06 and 2003

[30] In order to achieve better comparability, Germany and France, which were both unable to provide information on the nationality of the alleged abductor in 2005/06, were excluded from the 2003 analysis on the nationality and relationship of the alleged abductor to the child.

E. Outcomes

The 2003 statistical survey classified outcome categories as follows: 1. Rejection; 2. Voluntary return no court orders; 3. Judicial order for return by consent; 4. Judicial order for return not by consent; 5. Judicial refusal; 6. Access agreed or ordered; 7. Application pending; 8. Withdrawn; and 9. Other. The author of the 2005/06 survey, however, realised that the above classification was not entirely correct. In particular, it struck her that in the context of applications for return, the category 'access agreed or ordered' was not an outcome in the true sense of the word. Rather, it was one of the possible outcomes of an application for access under Article 21 of the Convention.[31] As a result, analysed in the context of return applications, these cases should have been re-classified as follows:

1. Where access was agreed, the outcome should have been classified as either 'withdrawn' application (indicating that in the course of the return proceedings the return application was modified to an application for access), or 'other' outcome; and
2. Where access was judicially ordered, the outcome should have been classified either as a form of judicial refusal to return, or as a withdrawn application for return (indicating that in the course of the return proceedings before the court, the return application was modified to an application for access).

Despite the above deficiency of the 2003 methodology, it was decided that for the sake of compatibility and comparability, the 2005/06 survey had to follow the pattern of the 2003 statistical survey. Moreover, it was concluded that, taken as a whole, the number of applications labelled as 'access agreed or ordered' was relatively insignificant and would therefore not substantially affect the overall outcomes. An exception was, however, made where only the applications that went to court were analysed.[32] Given the relatively small number of applications that were resolved judicially, the applications where 'access was ordered' were excluded from this analysis.

i. Outcomes: Overall Analysis

Table 5.10 and Figure 5.12 show the outcome of all applications in 2005/06. In addition to this there was one case in which the outcome was not available.

[31] 'An application to make arrangements for organising or securing the effective exercise of rights of access may be presented to the Central Authorities of the Contracting States in the same way as an application for the return of a child': Hague Abduction Convention Art 21. In contrast, return applications are based on Art 8 of the Convention: 'Any person, institution or other body claiming that a child has been removed or retained in breach of custody rights may apply either to the Central Authority of the child's habitual residence or to the Central Authority of any other Contracting State for assistance in securing the return of the child': Hague Abduction Convention Art 8.

[32] See section 'Outcomes: Applications That Went to Court' below.

Table 5.10: Outcome of the application

	Number	Percent
Rejection	23	6%
Voluntary Return No Court Orders	60	17%
Judicial Order for Return by Consent	41	11%
Judical Order for Return Not by Consent	63	17%
Judicial Refusal	28	8%
Access Agreed or Ordered[a]	19	5%
Application Pending	55	15%
Withdrawn	44	12%
Other[b]	29	8%
Total	**362**	**~100%**

[a] In 15 cases (4%) access was judicially granted and in 4 cases (1%) access was agreed.

[b] In 2 cases (1%) different outcomes were reached for different children (classified as 'other outcome').

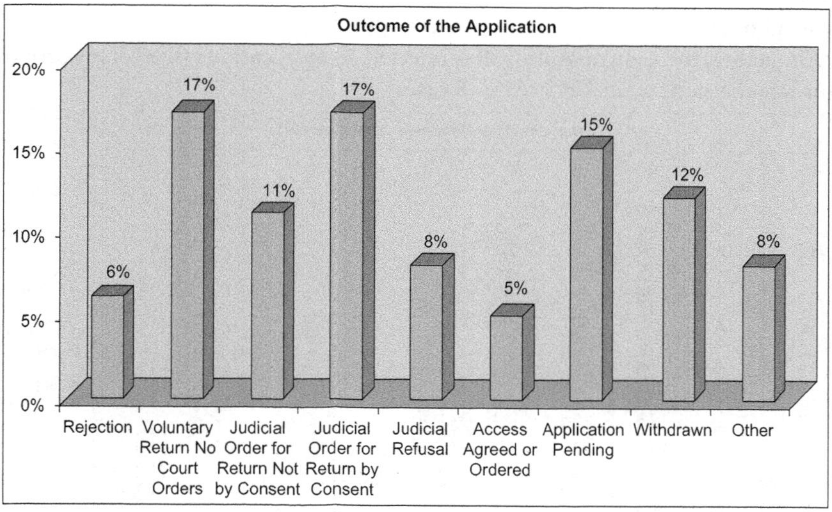

Figure 5.12: Outcome of the application

As Table 5.10 and Figure 5.12 demonstrate, 164 applications, 45%, ended in the child being returned.[33] Of these, 60 were resolved voluntarily and the remaining 104 were decided judicially. In 2003, the overall return rate was 55% (64 cases resolved voluntarily and 102 cases decided judicially). These figures reveal an alarming finding: the overall return rate dropped by 10%. Nevertheless, at 53%,

[33] In 2007/08 in Belgium, out of 31 incoming Brussels II bis cases that were analysed in the Kruger study, 17 (54.8%) resulted in the return of the child: Kruger (n 5) 117.

the 2008 overall return rate compared with the 2003 proportion of 55%, and was 8% higher than the 2005/06 return rate.

The proportion of judicial returns not by consent fell from 14% in 2003 to 11% in 2005/06. Similarly, the proportion of voluntary returns as well as judicial returns by consent decreased, by 4% and 3% respectively. In 2008, the proportion of both voluntary returns and judicial returns was higher than in 2005/06, by 5% and 3% respectively.

Twenty-eight return applications, 8%, were judicially refused.[34] This represents a decrease on the 2003 judicial refusal rate of 11%. Interestingly, the 2008 survey recorded a judicial refusal rate of 14%, which represented an increase by 6% on the 2005/06 findings and an increase by 3% on the 2003 findings.

Fifty-five applications (15%) were still pending as at the cut-off date for the survey (28 February 2007) and 44 applications (12%) were withdrawn. Interestingly, in 2003, the proportion of pending cases as at the cut-off date for the survey (31 August 2004) was only 6%. This shows that the percentage of pending cases rose sharply, by 9%. With regard to withdrawn applications, at 12%, the 2005/06 proportion represents a slight decrease on the 2003 findings (14%).

At 5%, the proportion of applications where access was agreed or ordered (instead of return) compares with the 2003 findings.

Altogether, the Central Authorities rejected 23 applications (6%). This proportion was the same as in 2003 (6%, 18 cases).[35]

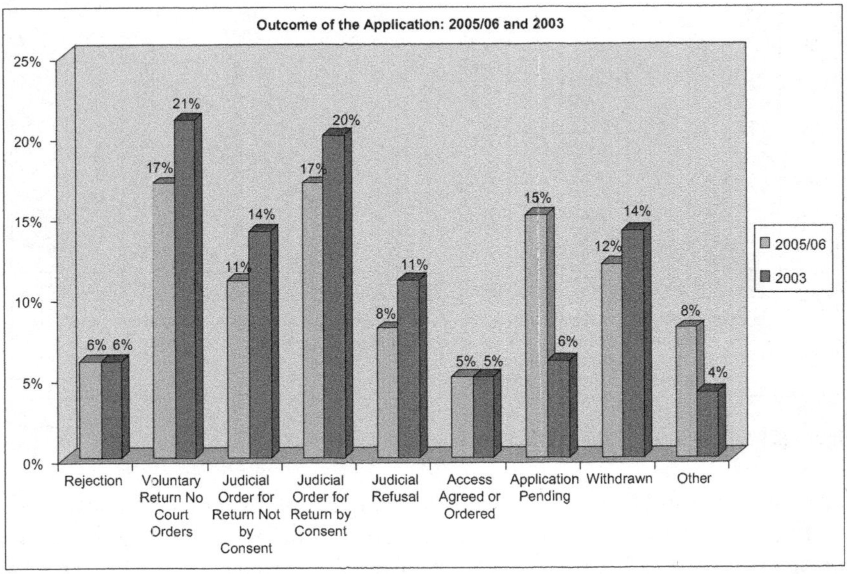

Figure 5.13: Outcome of the application: 2005/06 and 2003

[34] In 2007/08 in Belgium, out of 31 incoming Brussels II bis cases that were analysed in the Kruger study, 14 cases (45.2%) were judicially refused: Kruger (n 5) 117.

[35] Interestingly, in 2008, the rejection rate dropped to 3%.

ii. Outcomes: Applications that Went to Court[36]

One hundred and thirty-two applications went to court. Of these, 104, 79%, ended in a judicial return, and 28, 21%, were judicially refused.

In 2003, 135 applications went to court. Of these, 102, 76% were judicially returned, and 33, 24% ended in a judicial refusal.

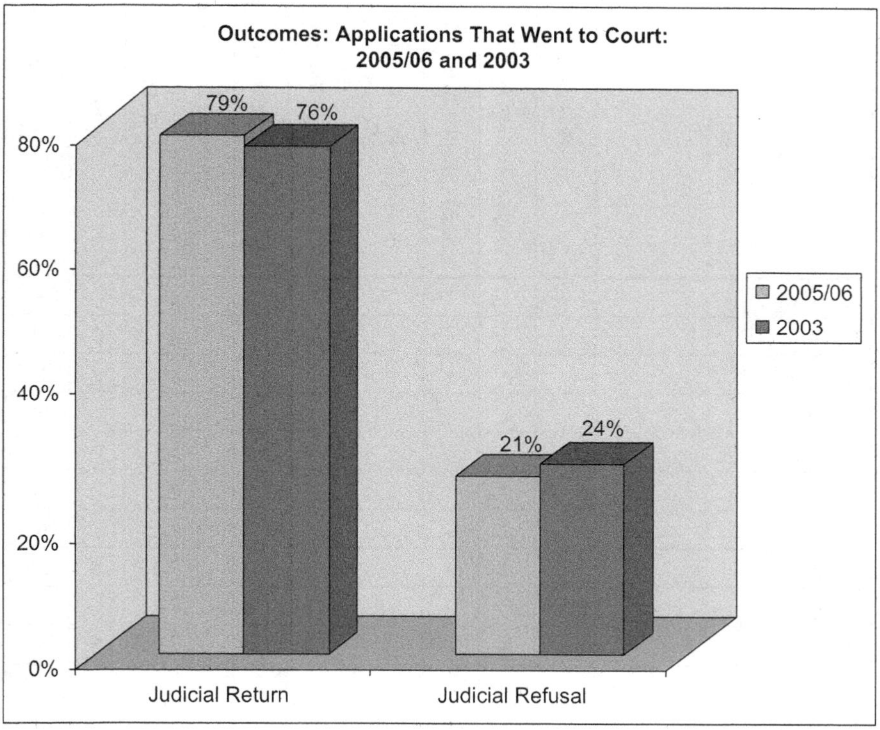

Figure 5.14: Outcomes: Applications that went to court: 2005/06 and 2003

As the above chart shows, the proportion of judicial returns increased from 76% in 2003 to 79% in 2005/06. The percentage of judicial refusals decreased from 24% in 2003 to 21% in 2005/06.

[36] For the purposes of this analysis, applications with the outcome labelled as 'access ordered' were excluded. For an explanation see introductory text to the section 'Outcomes' above.

iii. Outcomes: Analysis per Member State

Table 5.11: The outcomes by Contracting States which received the application

	Overall Outcome per Application									
	Rejection	Voluntary Return No Court Orders	Judicial Order for Return by Consent	Judicial Order for Return Not by Consent	Judicial Refusal	Access Agreed or Ordered	Application Pending	Withdrawn	Other	**Total**
Austria	2	1	1	1	4					**9**
Belgium	4	3	2		1	1	5		2	**18**
Czech Republic		3	1		1		4	2	2	**13**
Cyprus		1		1			1	1		**4**
Estonia			1				1			**2**
Finland		2		1	1					**4**
France	3	15	17	3	7		13	3	7	**68**
Germany	3	4	4	6	5	4	12	10	5	**53**
Hungary				1						**1**
Ireland	5	8		7	2		2	5	3	**32**
Italy		2			1					**3**
Lithuania		1								**1**
Luxembourg		1					1			**2**
Malta				1						**1**
Poland	1	2	5		2		8	6		**24**
Portugal							1		2	**3**
Slovakia		2					1	1		**4**
Slovenia							2	1		**3**
Sweden				1				2	1	**4**
UK–England & Wales	5	10	10	40	4	14	4	11	7	**105**
UK–Nth Ireland		4								**4**
UK–Scotland		1		1				2		**4**
Total	**23**	**60**	**41**	**63**	**28**	**19**	**55**	**44**	**29**	**362**

The above table shows the outcomes in relation to the Contracting States which received the applications. Given the relatively small number of applications handled by some of the Contracting States, a critical scrutiny of a particular State's performance and its comparison with another jurisdiction's performance would not be reasonable. Nevertheless, it appears balanced to examine the operation of the Regulation in the Member States after they had been categorised into groups, and then to compare the outcomes for each group with the percentage of applications which globally end in each different outcome. The classification standards included the type of legal system (that is, common law versus civil law), the geographic location (that is, Western Europe versus Eastern Europe), or the EU membership status (that is, the 'old' Member States versus the 'new' Member States).[37] Although it was not considered indispensable to include the full analyses based on each of the three criteria, it is regarded as vital to note that the use of the last criterion suggested a revealing finding: the Regulation operates far less effectively in the 'new' Member States than it operates in the 'old' Member States.[38]

F. Reason for Judicial Refusal[39]

i. Overall Reason for Judicial Refusal[40]

Table 5.12 and Figure 5.15 show the overall reason for judicial refusal in the intra-EU cases. As can be seen, the highest proportion of refusals (23%) was based on the lack of habitual residence of the child in the requesting State. Article 13(1)(b) was relied upon in five out of the 27 judicial refusals and thus accounted for 19% of all judicial refusals.[41] Three judicial refusals (11%) were based on the lack of rights of custody. The same proportion of refusals was based on Article 12 and

[37] The term 'new' Member States is used here to refer to the 10 countries that joined the European Union in May 2004. The expansion process continued further with the accession of Romania and Bulgaria to the European Union in January 2007. These two countries, however, were not included in the research for the reasons explained above (n 15). The term 'old' Member States is used here to describe the European Union prior to the 2004 enlargement.

[38] For a detailed analysis of and a commentary on this discovery see Chapter 6, section entitled 'Judicial and Administrative Qualities in the "New" Member States of the European Union'.

[39] The information on the reason for judicial refusal is particularly important so as to demonstrate whether the Regulation achieved its aim to minimise judicial refusals based on the Art 13(1)(b) objection.

[40] The reason for refusal was not available in one case.

[41] In 2008, the proportion of judicial refusals based on Art 13(1)(b) was significantly higher, 34%. This ground for refusal was followed by the lack of habitual residence of the child in the requesting State, 13%.

on more than one reason (3, 11% each). Only two cases (7%) were based on the child's objections.

Table 5.12: Overall reason for judicial refusal

	Number	Percent
Child Not Habitually Resident in Requesting State	6	23%
Applicant had No Rights of Custody	3	11%
Art 12	3	11%
Article 13 a Consent	2	7%
Art 13b	5	19%
Child's Objections	2	7%
Article 20	1	4%
More than one reason	3	11%
Other	2	7%
Total	**27**	**100%**

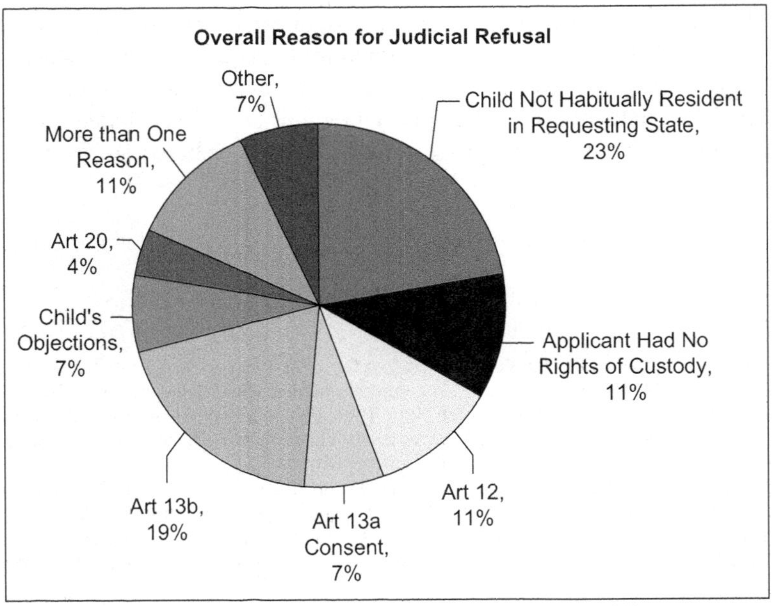

Figure 5.15: Overall reason for judicial refusal

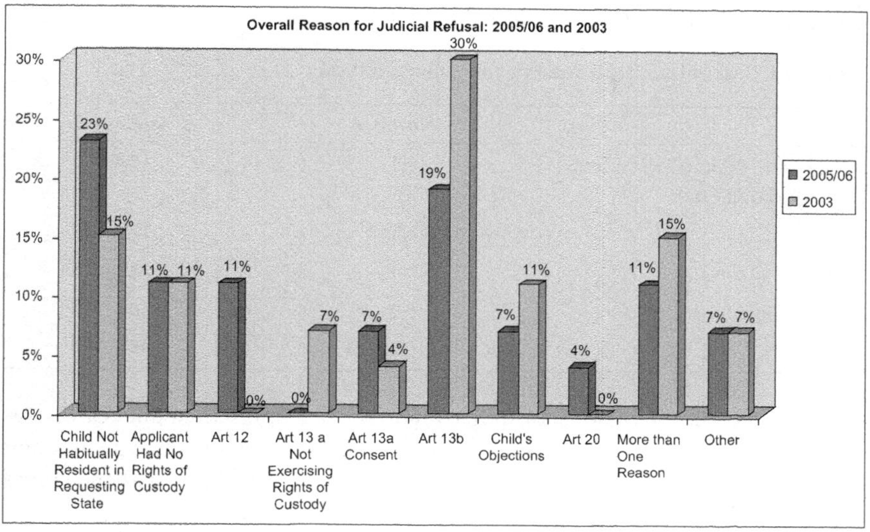

Figure 5.16: Overall reason for judicial refusal: 2005/06 and 2003

In 2003, the most commonly cited reason for judicial refusal (eight out of 27 applications, 30%) was Article 13(1)(b).[42] As the above chart shows, the proportion of refusals based on this reason fell significantly, from 30% in 2003 to only 19% in 2005/06.

The proportion of refusals based on the lack of exercise of the rights of custody also recorded a decrease, from 7% in 2003 to 0% in 2005/06. Similarly, the proportion of refusals based on the child's objections dropped from 11% in 2003 to only 7% in 2005/06.[43]

In contrast, the proportion of judicial refusals based on the lack of habitual residence, Article 12, the consent of the applicant (Article 13(1)(a)) and Article 20 increased from 15% in 2003 to 23% in 2005/06, 0% in 2003 to 11% in 2005/06, from 4% in 2003 to 7% in 2005/06, and from 0% in 2003 to 4% in 2005/06 respectively. At 11%, the proportion of judicial refusals based on the lack of the rights of custody remained the same as in 2003.

[42] The overall reason for judicial refusal was available in relation to 27 out of 33 judicial refusals made in 2003.

[43] This finding is surprising given the compulsory nature of the hearing of the child as a part of the return proceedings introduced by the Regulation. Indeed, unlike the 1980 Convention, the Regulation imposes on the courts the obligation to examine the child's wishes in the return proceedings (see Art 11(2) of the Regulation). Considering this change, an increase in the numbers of judicial refusals based on the child's objections rather than a decrease would be expected. Nevertheless, at 11%, the 2008 Cardiff Study recorded an increase in the proportion of refusals based on the child's objections.

ii. Bases of Multiple Reasons for Judicial Refusal

Table 5.13: Bases of multiple reasons for judicial refusal

	Number	Percent
Child Not Habitually Resident in Requesting State	1	17%
Art 12	1	17%
Art 13b	2	33%
Child's Objections	2	33%
Total	**6**	**100%**

Table 5.13 details the reasons for judicial refusal where more than one reason was stated. There were six reasons given in the three cases involving multiple reasons. As can be seen, the most frequently cited reasons were Article 13(1)(b) and child's objections (2, 33% each).

In 2003, eight reasons were given in the four cases involving multiple reasons. As in 2005/06, the most frequently cited reasons were Article 13(1)(b) and child's objections (2, 25% each).

iii. Reasons for Judicial Refusal Combined

Table 5.14: Reason for judicial refusal combined

	Number	Percent
Child Not Habitually Resident in Requesting State	7	23%
Applicant had No Rights of Custody	3	10%
Art 12	4	13%
Article 13 a Consent	2	7%
Art 13b	7	23%
Child's Objections	4	13%
Article 20	1	3%
Other	2	7%
Total	**30**	**~100%**

As Table 5.14 shows, when all the reasons are analysed, the exceptions most frequently relied upon when refusing a return were Article 13(1)(b) and the lack of habitual residence of the child in the requesting State (seven, 23% each).

In 2003, far more refusals were based on Article 13(1)(b) than on any other reason. Indeed, more than a third of all refusals (11, 35%) were either solely or partially based on this exception. Article 13(1)(b) was followed by the lack of the habitual residence of the child in the requesting State and the child's objections (five, 16% each).

In 2008, the two most 'popular' reasons for judicial refusals were the same as in 2003 and 2005/06: Article 13(1)(b) as the most common ground, followed by the lack of the habitual residence of the child in the requesting State. At 40% and 15% respectively, however, the findings are very similar to the 2003 proportions of 35% and 16%, differing significantly from the 2005/06 proportions of 23% for both grounds.

Table 5.15: Reason for judicial refusal combined: 2005/06 and 2003

Reason for judicial refusal	Number of judicial refusals 2005/06	Proportion of judicial refusals 2005/06	Number of judicial refusals 2003	Proportion of judicial refusals 2003
Child not habitually resident in requesting State	7	23%	5	16%
Applicant had no rights of custody	3	10%	4	13%
Art 13a Not exercising rights of custody	0	0%	3	10%
Art 12	4	13%	0	0%
Art 13a Consent	2	7%	1	3%
Art 13a Acquiescence	0	0%	0	0%
Art 13b	7	23%	11	35%
Child's objections	4	13%	5	16%
Art 20	1	3%	0	0%
Other	2	7%	2	6%
Total	**30**	**~100%**	**31**	**~100%**

A decrease was also recorded in the proportion of refusals based on the child's objections. This fall was, however, not as significant as it was in the case of judicial refusals based on Article 13(1)(b). Indeed, the proportion of judicial refusals based either solely or partially on the child's objections decreased by only 3%, from 16% in 2003 to 13% in 2005/06. In 2008, at 13%, the percentage of judicial refusals based on the child's objections was the same as in 2005/06.

Finally, a reduction of 3% and 10% was recorded in relation to judicial refusals based on the lack of the rights of custody and the lack of the actual exercise of the rights of custody (Article 13(1)(a)) respectively. Interestingly, in 2003, the latter reason was relied upon either solely or partially in three (10%) judicial refusals. In 2005/06, however, no judicial refusal was based on this exception.[44]

[44] In 2008, 3% of judicial refusals were based on the lack of the actual exercise of the rights of custody, and 11% of judicial refusals were based on the lack of the rights of custody. This compares with the 2005/06 proportions of 0% and 10% respectively.

In contrast, there was a rise in the proportion of judicial refusals based on the following four exceptions: the lack of the habitual residence of the child in the requesting State (by 7%), Article 12 (by 13%), the consent of the applicant (Article 13(1)(a)) (by 4%), and Article 20 (by 3%).[45]

Surprisingly, no judicial refusals were based on acquiescence (Article 13(1)(a)) either in 2005/06 or in 2003. Interestingly, in 2008, acquiescence accounted for 4% of all grounds for judicial refusals.

Table 5.16: Reason for judicial refusal per requested state

		Child Not Habitually Resident in Requesting State	Applicant had No Rights of Custody	Art 12	Article 13 a Consent	Art 13b	Child's Objections	Article 20	Other	**Total**
Requested State	Austria		1		1	1	1			**4**
	Belgium		1							**1**
	Czech Republic			1						**1**
	Finland			1						**1**
	France	2		1		2	1			**6**
	Germany	1	1			2	1		1	**6**
	Ireland	1						1		**2**
	Italy	1		1						**2**
	Poland	1				1				**2**
	UK–England & Wales	1			1	1	1		1	**5**
Total		**7**	**3**	**4**	**2**	**7**	**4**	**1**	**2**	**30**

[45] In 2008, the proportions of judicial refusals based on the lack of the habitual residence of the child, Art 12, Art 13(1)(a) consent and Art 20 were 15%, 9%, 1% and 0% respectively.

Table 5.16 shows the overall reason for judicial refusal by each of the EU Member States. As can be seen, the seven refusals based on Article 13(1)(b) were made by Austria, Poland and England and Wales (one each), and France and Germany (two each).[46]

Interestingly, in all but one of the seven refusals involving Article 13(1)(b) the alleged abductor was the mother of the child.

G. Timing[47]

i. Mean Number of Days to Settlement: General Analysis[48]

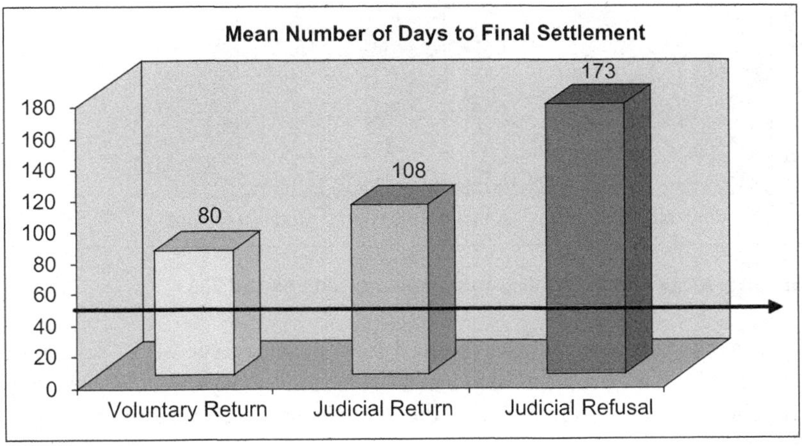

Figure 5.17: Mean number of days to final settlement

Figure 5.17 compares the mean number of days to voluntary return, judicial return and judicial refusal. The black arrow marks the six-week period within which applications have to be resolved under the Brussels II bis Regulation. As can be seen, none of the three categories of outcomes complied with the six-week rule. The voluntary returns took a mean average of 80 days (approximately 11 weeks) to be resolved; the judicial returns took a mean average of 108 days (approximately 15 weeks) to be decided and the judicial refusals were resolved in

[46] This finding does not show any disproportions; the five Art 13(1)(b) refusals were spread over five jurisdictions. The fact that both France and Germany refused two applications each on the basis of Art 13(1)(b) does not appear to be somehow 'suspicious' owing to the relatively high number of applications handled by these Member States.

[47] For the purposes of timing, judicial returns with consent and judicial returns without consent were analysed in a combined way under the heading 'judicial return order'.

[48] The timing was available in 52 out of the 60 voluntary returns, in 98 out of the 104 judicial returns and in 25 out of the 28 judicial refusals (see Table 5.17: 'Number of Days Taken to Reach Final Outcome'). In 2003, timing was available in 45 voluntary returns, 100 judicial returns and 29 judicial refusals.

an average of 173 days (approximately 25 weeks). Moreover, it must be taken into account that 15% of applications were still pending as at the cut-off period for the survey (28 February 2007). If the cut-off period had been put back, the mean averages would have been even longer.

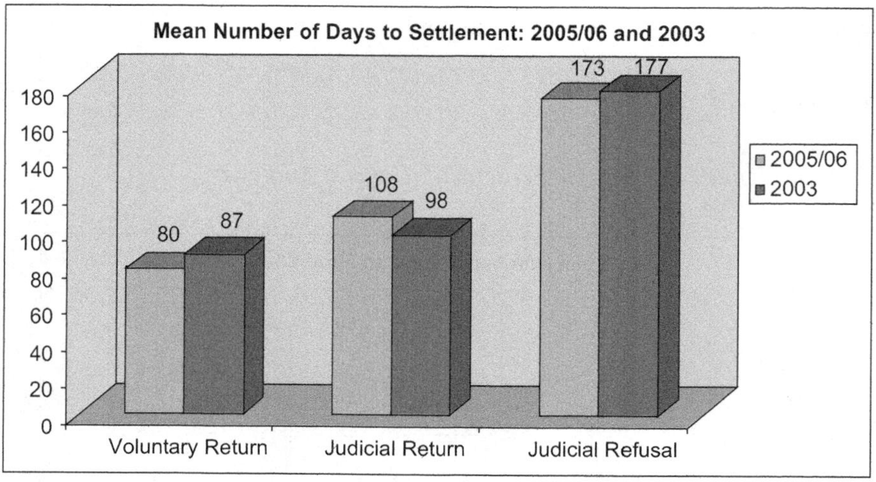

Figure 5.18: Mean number of days to settlement: 2005/06 and 2003

In 2003, voluntary returns were resolved in a mean average of 87 days. Judicial returns and judicial refusals took a mean average of 98 days and 177 days respectively. These findings compare with the 2005/06 mean averages of 80 days, 108 days and 173 days respectively.

The 2008 survey recorded a slightly better timing for voluntary returns (a mean average of 74 days); however, at 125 days and 217 days, the mean averages for judicial returns and judicial refusals were worse than those recorded in 2003 and 2005/06.[49]

Considering time taken purely in terms of the mean number of days can, however, be quite deceptive. Therefore, the minimum and the maximum numbers of days taken to reach the final outcome were also considered (see Table 5.17). As can be seen, the quickest voluntary agreement was reached in only one day, the quickest judicial return was resolved in six days and the quickest judicial refusal took 62 days to reach the final outcome. The slowest judicial decision, a judicial return order, was reached in almost 19 months![50] Moreover, it must be noted that these figures are in some way misleading as all cases still pending at the date of the cut-off of the survey were excluded from this analysis. The pending cases accounted

[49] It must, however, be borne in mind that the cut-off period for the 2008 survey was longer than the cut-off period for the 2005/06 survey so the figures are not fully comparable (see n 12 above).

[50] It is rather surprising that the slowest judicial decision was a return order rather than a judicial refusal.

for 15% of all applications. If pending cases were considered, the actual figures would be significantly higher.

Table 5.17: Number of days taken to reach final outcome

	Voluntary Return No Court Orders	Judicial Return Order	Judicial Refusal
Mean	80	108	173
Minimum	1	6	62
Maximum	455	527	491
Number of cases	**52**	**98**	**25**

ii. Mean Number of Days to Settlement: Analysis per Member State

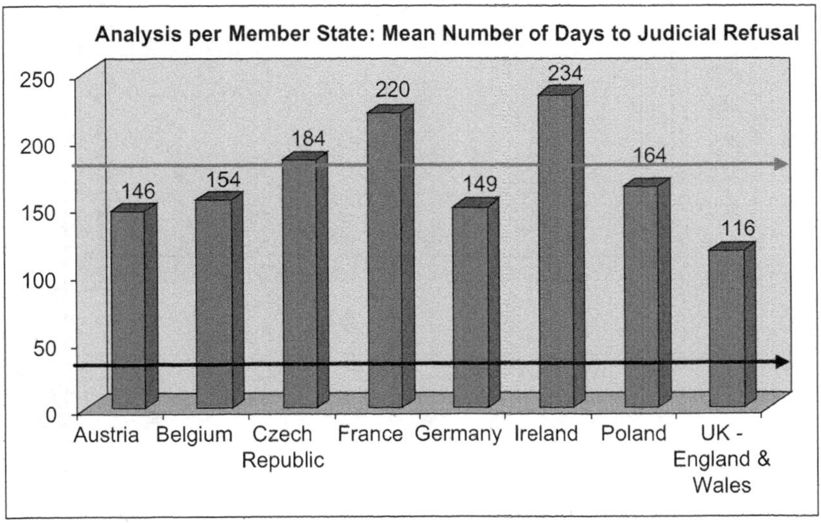

Figure 5.19: Analysis per Member State: Mean number of days to judicial refusal

The above chart shows the mean number of days to judicial refusal by each of the EU Member States. These findings can be compared with the 'EU mean average' of 173 days marked by the grey arrow. The black arrow marks the period of six weeks (42 days), the deadline for the resolution of applications prescribed by the Regulation. It must, however, be pointed out that findings regarding countries with a small number of judicial refusals (below three) cannot be given much weight.[51]

[51] The timing was available in all seven judicial refusals in France, all five judicial refusals in Germany, all four judicial refusals in UK-England and Wales, three out of the four judicial refusals in Austria, both judicial refusals in Ireland and Poland, and the one judicial refusal in Belgium and the Czech Republic. The timing was not available in the one judicial refusal in Finland and Italy.

The chart demonstrates that none of the EU Members where a return application was refused complied with the six-week rule prescribed by the Regulation. The best results were achieved by England and Wales with a mean average of 116 days. This figure was under the 'EU mean average' of 173 days. Four other countries were under the 'EU mean average': Austria, Belgium, Germany, and surprisingly also Poland. In contrast, at 184, 220 and 234, the mean averages of the Czech Republic, France and Ireland respectively were higher than the 'EU mean average'. The longest mean average for judicial refusals was recorded in Ireland (234 days). It is, however, to be stressed that Ireland refused only two applications. Hence, owing to the small number of applications, this finding cannot be considered as absolutely reliable.

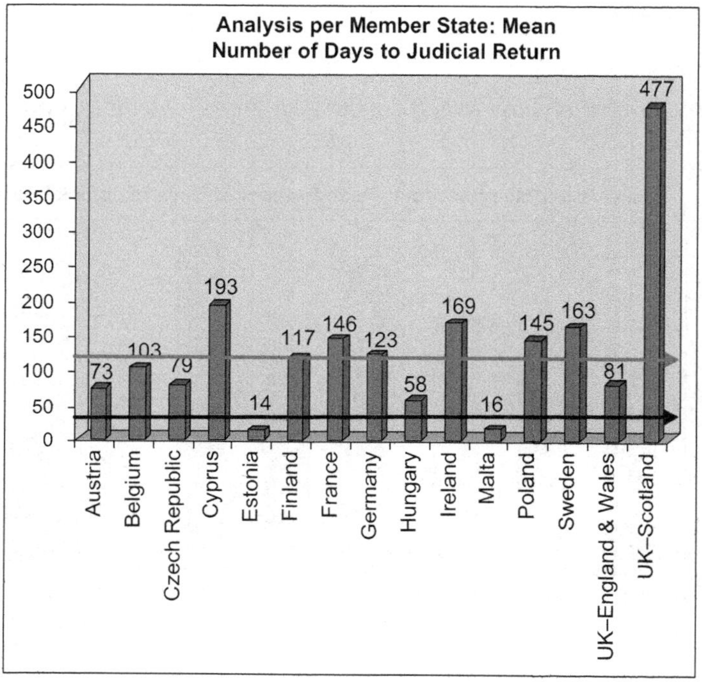

Figure 5.20: Analysis per Member State: Mean number of days to judicial return

Figure 5.20 shows the mean number of days to judicial returns by each of the EU Member States. These findings can be compared with the 'EU mean average' of 108 days marked by the grey arrow. As with the judicial returns, the black arrow marks the period of six weeks (42 days), the deadline for the resolution of applications prescribed by the Regulation. It must, however, be pointed out that findings regarding countries with a small number of judicial refusals (below three) do not carry much weight.[52]

[52] The timing was available in all 50 judicial returns from UK-England and Wales, all 15 judicial returns from France, all 10 judicial returns from Germany, six out of the seven judicial returns from

The chart demonstrates that only two EU Members, namely Estonia and Malta, complied with the six-week rule prescribed by the Regulation. Nevertheless, each of these jurisdictions recorded only one judicial return and therefore the finding cannot be given much relevance.

Taking account of the countries with a higher number of cases (three or more) only, the shortest mean average was recorded in England and Wales. At 81 days, this figure was under the 'EU mean average' of 108 days. In contrast, the mean averages recorded in the remaining four countries with a higher number of cases—Ireland, Poland, Germany and France—were all above the 'EU mean average' of 108 days. Of these four countries, the poorest results were achieved in Ireland, with a mean average of 169 days.

iii. Overall Time to Final Settlement: General Analysis

Table 5.18: Overall time to final judicial decision

	Number	Percent
0–6 weeks	24	20%
6–12 weeks	33	27%
3–6 months	37	30%
Over 6 months	29	24%
Total	**123**	**~100%**

Table 5.18 shows the overall time to a final judicial decision (judicial returns and judicial refusals combined). As can be seen, only 20% of all judicial decisions were made within the six-week deadline required by the Regulation. In 2003, 29% of all judicial decisions were reached between zero and six weeks.

Table 5.19: Overall time to judicial refusal

	Number	Percent
0–6 weeks	0	0%
6–12 weeks	2	8%
3–6 months	12	48%
Over 6 months	11	44%
Total	**25**	**100%**

Ireland, all five judicial returns from Poland, both judicial returns from Austria and Belgium, and the one judicial return from the Czech Republic, Cyprus, Estonia, Finland, Hungary, Malta, Sweden and UK-Scotland. Scotland's poor performance was due to a problem in locating the child.

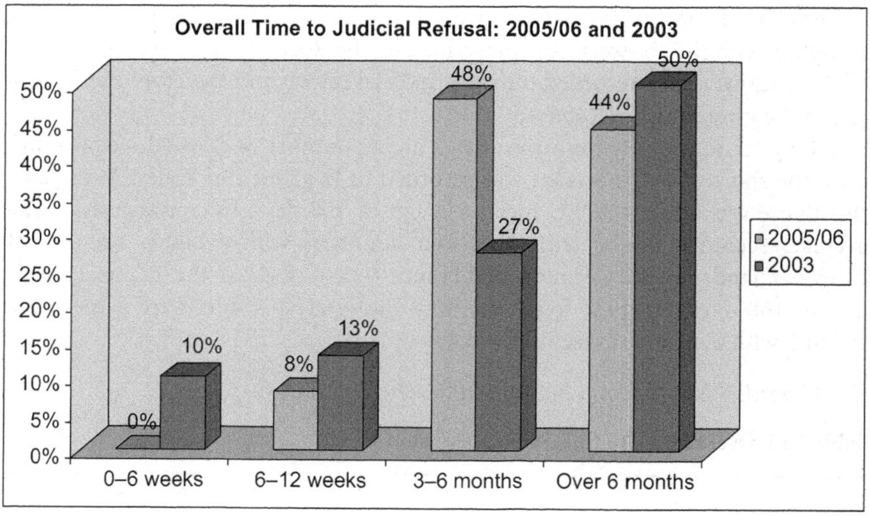

Figure 5.21: Overall time to judicial refusal: 2005/06 and 2003

Table 5.19 and Figure 5.21 show the overall time to a judicial refusal. As can be seen, no judicial refusals were made in less than six weeks. In 2003, 10% of judicial refusals were made within the six-week period.

The largest proportion of refusals, 48%, took between three and six months to decide. This represents a significant increase on the 2003 proportion of 27% and, at the same time, an improvement on the 2003 findings. In 2003, the largest percentage of judicial refusals, 50%, took over six months to resolve.

Table 5.20 and Figure 5.22 show the overall time to a judicial return order. As can be seen, the largest proportion of judicial returns, 32%, was concluded

Table 5.20: Overall time to judicial return order

	Number	Percent
0–6 weeks	24	24%
6–12 weeks	31	32%
3–6 months	25	26%
Over 6 months	18	18%
Total	**98**	**100%**

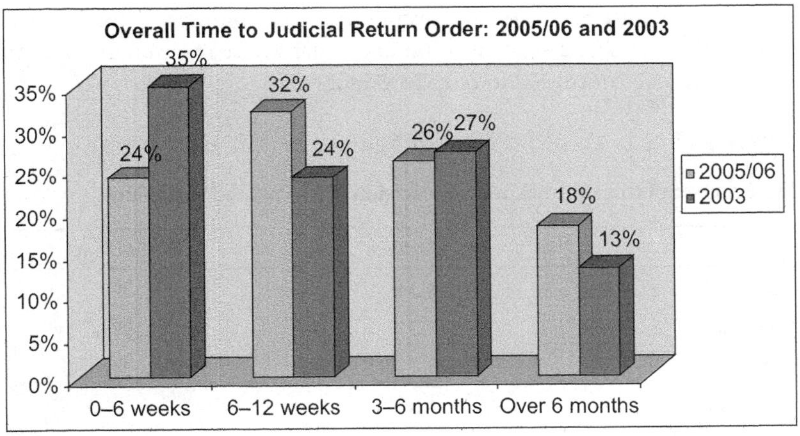

Figure 5.22: Overall time to judicial return order: 2005/06 and 2003

between six and 12 weeks. In 2003, the largest proportion of judicial returns, 35%, was made in less than six weeks. Only 24% of judicial return orders took less than six weeks to make. This represents a decrease of 11% on the 2003 findings.

Table 5.21: Overall time to voluntary return

	Number	Percent
0–6 weeks	27	52%
6–12 weeks	12	23%
3–6 months	6	12%
Over 6 months	7	13%
Total	**52**	**100%**

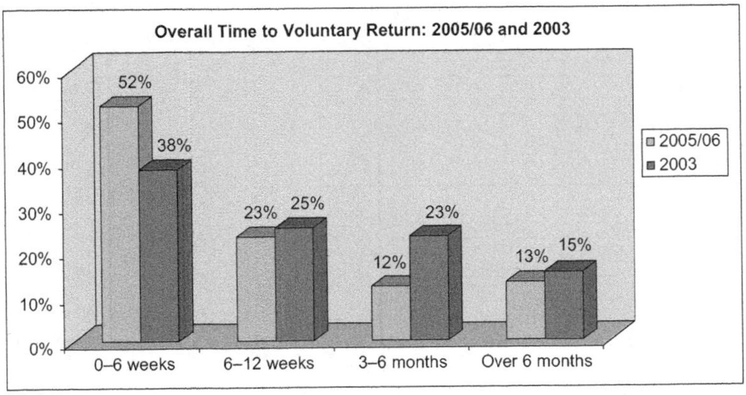

Figure 5.23: Overall time to voluntary return: 2005/06 and 2003

Table 5.21 and Figure 5.23 show the overall time to a voluntary return. As can be seen, more than a half, 52%, of all voluntary returns were resolved in less than six weeks. This can be contrasted to only 38% in 2003.

iv. Overall Time to Final Settlement: Analysis per Member State[53]

Table 5.22: Overall time to final judicial decision: UK–England and Wales

	Number	Percent
0–6 weeks	16	30%
6–12 weeks	21	39%
3–6 months	13	24%
Over 6 months	4	7%
Total	**54**	**100%**

Table 5.23: Overall time to final judicial decision: France

	Number	Percent
0–6 weeks	5	23%
6–12 weeks	1	5%
3–6 months	5	23%
Over 6 months	11	50%
Total	**22**	**~100%**

Table 5.24: Overall time to final judicial decision: Germany

	Number	Percent
0–6 weeks	1	7%
6–12 weeks	3	20%
3–6 months	7	47%
Over 6 months	4	27%
Total	**15**	**~100%**

[53] Given the relatively small numbers of judicial refusals, only a combined analysis of judicial returns and judicial refusals was conducted (section 'Overall Time to a Final Judicial Decision'). Moreover, only jurisdictions where more than five judicial decisions were made have been included in the analysis.

Table 5.25: Overall time to final judicial decision: Ireland

	Number	Percent
6–12 weeks	1	13%
3–6 months	3	38%
Over 6 months	4	50%
Total	**8**	**~100%**

Table 5.26: Overall time to final judicial decision: Poland

	Number	Percent
6–12 weeks	2	29%
3–6 months	3	43%
Over 6 months	2	29%
Total	**7**	**~100%**

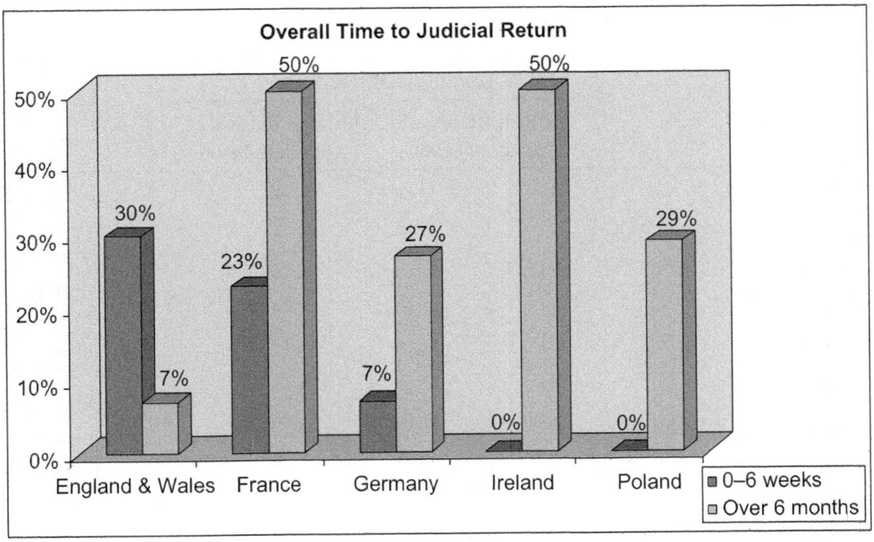

Figure 5.24: Overall time to judicial return

As can be seen, of the five analysed Central Authorities, England and Wales was the most successful jurisdiction in terms of compliance with the six-week rule. In England and Wales, 30% of all judicial decisions were made in less than six weeks. The largest proportion of applications, 39%, was judicially decided between six and 12 weeks. Only 7% of judicial decisions took more than six months to be made. In France and Germany, 23% and 7% of all judicial decisions respectively were made between zero and six weeks. However, no application was decided within the prescribed period either in Ireland or in Poland.

H. Appeals

Table 5.27: First instance decisions and appellate decisions

	Number	Percent
Judicial Return by Consent	36	29%
Judicial Return at First Instance	54	44%
Judicial Refusal at First Instance	18	15%
Judicial Return at Appellate Level	8	7%
Judicial Refusal at Appellate Level	7	6%
Total	**123**	**~100%**

Table 5.28: Appealed decisions per requested State

	Last Judicial Decision		Total
	Judicial Return at Appellate Level	Judicial Refusal at Appellate Level	
Austria	1	2	**3**
Finland	1		**1**
France	2	1	**3**
Germany	2	3	**5**
Poland		1	**1**
Sweden	1		**1**
UK–England & Wales	1		**1**
Total	**8**	**7**	**15**

As Tables 5.27 and 5.28 show, altogether 15 cases were appealed. This amounts to only 4% of all the cases analysed and 10% of all cases that went to court. The highest proportion of appealed cases (five out of the 15 judicial decisions, 33%) was in Germany. In contrast, out of the 54 judicial decisions made by England and Wales, only one (2%) was appealed.

Table 5.29: Appeals

		Appellate Final Judicial Decision		Total
		Return	**Refusal**	
First Judicial Decision	Information not available	2	1	**3**
	Return	4	1	**5**
	Refusal	1	4	**5**
	Total	**7**	**6**	**13**

Table 5.29 shows that the majority of decisions on appeal (four judicial returns and four judicial refusals) upheld the first instance decision.[54] Of the remaining two applications, one application was a judicial return at first instance but was refused on appeal and the other one was refused at first instance but ended in a return order on appeal.

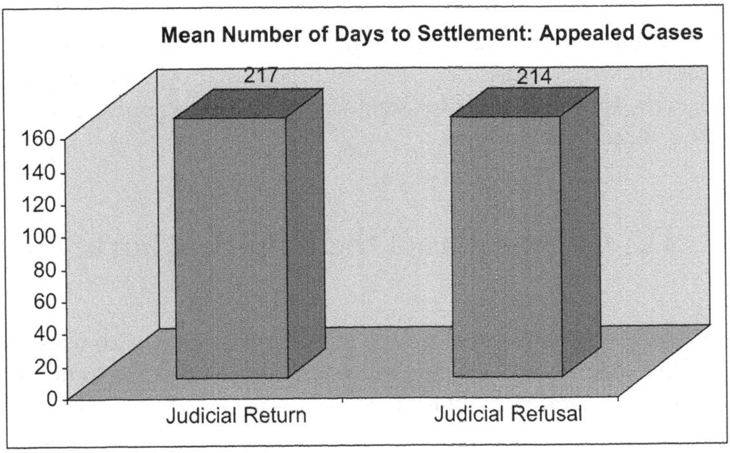

Figure 5.25: Mean number of days to settlement: Appealed cases

Figure 5.25 shows the mean number of days to conclude judicial returns and judicial refusals which ended on appeal.[55]

[54] It is, however, to be pointed out that, as Figure 5.25 shows, in three cases the information on the first instance decision was unavailable.

[55] The timing was available in relation to all 15 appealed cases.

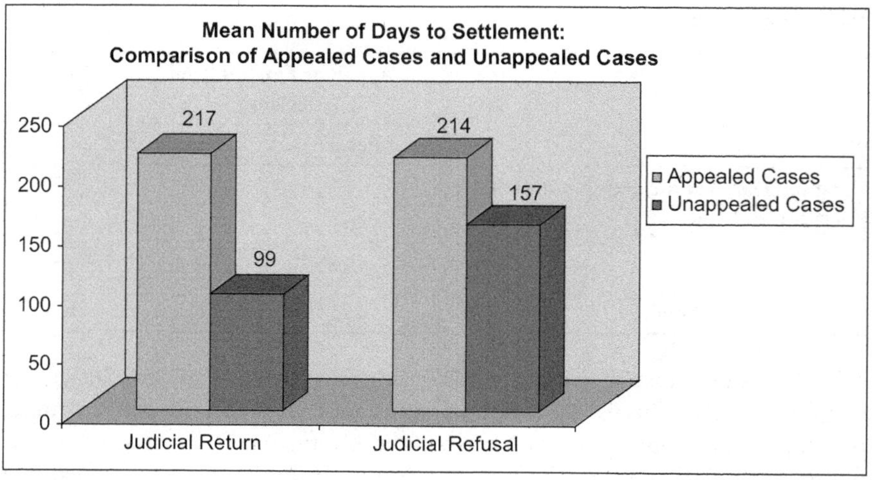

Figure 5.26: Mean number of days to settlement: Comparison of appealed cases and unappealed cases

Figure 5.26 compares the mean number of days to conclude judicial returns and judicial refusals which ended on appeal and those that were not appealed.[56] As can be seen, the appealed cases took significantly longer to resolve, particularly in relation to judicial return orders.

IV. Conclusions of the Empirical Survey

The empirical survey allows us to draw a number of numerical conclusions (that is, quantitative conclusions). Of these, a few are sufficiently clear to merit further analysis (that is, qualitative conclusions).

A. Quantitative Conclusions

1. Overall, in 2005/06 the Central Authorities received more return applications than in 2003, 363 as opposed to 301. This shows an upward trend in the number of intra-EU abductions. This trend is further evidenced by the 2008 survey, which recorded 536 applications.

[56] It must, however, be pointed out that there is a disproportion between the numbers of appealed cases and unappealed cases. In relation to unappealed cases, the timing was available in 90 judicial returns and 18 judicial refusals. However, the numbers of appealed cases were considerably lower, eight judicial returns and seven judicial refusals.

2. In 2005/06, mothers accounted for 75% of all alleged abductors, as opposed to 72% in 2003. This confirms the widely held view that mothers as taking persons are in the majority. Moreover, it shows that the proportion of mothers as alleged abductors increased slightly, by 3%.
3. Over a half of alleged abductors, 57%, had the nationality of the requested State. This represented a decrease on the 2003 proportion, by 4%. This indicates that fewer abductors were 'going home' than in 2003.
4. The proportion of mothers as alleged abductors having the same nationality as the requested State decreased from 60% in 2003 to 58% in 2005/06. This indicates that, in accordance with the general finding (see above), fewer mothers as alleged abductors were 'going home' than in 2003.
5. The overall return rate dropped by 10%. Nevertheless, in 2008, the overall return rate was almost back to the 2003 proportion (53% compared with 55%), being 8% higher than the 2005/06 overall return rate.
6. The overall refusal rate decreased by 3%. Interestingly, however, the 2008 survey recorded an increase by 6% on the 2005/06 refusal rate and an increase by 3% on the 2003 refusal rate.
7. The percentage of pending cases rose by 9%.
8. Of the applications that went to court, the proportion of judicial returns increased by 3% (79% in 2005/06 as opposed to 76% in 2003). The percentage of judicial refusals decreased by 3% (24% in 2003 as opposed to 21% in 2005/06).
9. Outcome analysis per Member States based on the criterion of the membership status revealed that the Regulation had operated far less effectively in the 'new' Member States than in the 'old' Member States.
10. The highest proportion of refusals (23%) was based on the lack of habitual residence of the child in the requesting State (Article 3). Article 13(1)(b) was relied upon in five out of the 27 judicial refusals and thus accounted for 19% of all judicial refusals. In 2003, the most commonly cited reason for judicial refusal, 30%, was Article 13(1)(b). The proportion of refusals based on this reason fell significantly, from 30% in 2003 to only 19% in 2005/06.
11. When all the reasons are analysed, the exceptions most frequently relied upon when refusing a return were Article 13(1)(b) and the lack of habitual residence of the child in the requesting State (Article 3) (7, 23% each). In 2003, far more refusals were based on Article 13(1)(b) than on any other reason (11, 35%). Consequently, the proportion of judicial refusals based on Article 13(1)(b) dropped significantly, by 12%, from 35% in 2003 to 23% in 2005/06. Interestingly, at 40%, the 2008 proportion of judicial refusals based on Article 13(1)(b) was even higher than the 2003 proportion of 35%.
12. In all seven refusals based on Article 13(1)(b), the alleged abductor was the mother of the child.
13. The proportion of refusals based on Article 13(1)(a) not exercising rights of custody, Article 13(1)(b), and Article 13(2) child's objections fell by 7%, 11% and 4% respectively, if the overall reason for judicial refusal is

considered; and by 10%, 12% and 3% respectively, if the reason for judicial refusal combined is considered.

14. The proportion of refusals based on Article 13(1)(a) consent, Article 12, Article 20, and Article 3 the lack of habitual residence of the child rose by 3%, 11%, 4% and 8% respectively, if the overall reason for judicial refusal is considered; and by 4%, 13%, 3% and 7%, if the reason for judicial refusal combined is considered.
15. In terms of mean number of days to settlement, none of the three categories of outcomes (voluntary returns, judicial returns or judicial refusals) complied with the six-week rule. The mean averages of both, voluntary returns as well as judicial returns, did not record any significant difference from the 2003 figures. The timing has slightly improved only in relation to voluntary returns and judicial refusals (a decrease in the mean average by seven days and four days respectively). The 2008 survey recorded a slightly improved timing for voluntary returns (a mean average of 74 days); however, the mean averages for judicial returns and judicial refusals were worse than those recorded in 2003 and 2005/06.
16. England and Wales had the best timing for both judicial refusals and judicial returns.
17. In terms of overall time to final judicial decision, only 20% of all judicial decisions were made within the six-week deadline. This represents a decrease by 9% on the 2003 findings.
18. No judicial refusals were made in less than six weeks. In 2003, 10% of judicial refusals were made within the six-week period.
19. 24% of judicial return orders took less than six weeks to make. This represents a decrease by 11% on the 2003 findings.
20. More than a half, 52%, of all voluntary returns were resolved in less than six weeks. This represents an increase by 14% on the 2003 findings.
21. Altogether 15 cases were appealed. This amounts to only 4% of all the cases analysed and 10% of all cases which went to court. The highest proportion of appealed cases (five out of the 15 judicial decisions, 33%) was in Germany. In contrast, out of the 54 judicial decisions made by England and Wales, only one (2%) was appealed.
22. The appealed cases took significantly longer to resolve, particularly in relation to judicial return orders.

B. Qualitative Conclusions

i. Small Improvement in Terms of Outcomes

The survey has revealed that the overall refusal rate decreased by 3%, from 11% in 2003 to 8% in 2005/06. Undoubtedly, this finding indicates an improvement in terms of outcomes. The scrutiny of outcomes solely from the perspective of the refusal rate may, however, be misleading for the reason that it does not question whether there has been a corresponding increase in the proportion of returned applications. In order to get an accurate picture, the outcome categories must be considered in their entirety. Simultaneous examination of all categories of outcomes then shows that the reduction in judicial refusals was accompanied by a 10% drop in the percentage of returns. This finding unfortunately goes against the conclusion that the Regulation has achieved an overall improvement in outcomes. Nevertheless, some evidence to the contrary can be found when only applications that went to court are considered. In particular, the refusal rate here fell also by 3%; however, unlike overall, the decrease was accompanied by a corresponding rise in the proportion of judicial returns (3%).

Unfortunately, the 2008 survey did not reiterate the 2005/06 finding of a small improvement in outcomes. On the contrary, alarmingly, in terms of the overall return rate and the overall refusal rate, the 2008 outcomes were even slightly worse than the 2003 outcomes as the overall return rate fell by 2% (55% in 2003 as opposed to 53% in 2008), and the overall refusal rate rose by 3% (11% in 2003 as opposed to 14% in 2008).

ii. Some Evidence of Avoidance of the Use of Article 13

The survey has shown that generally, there was a decrease in the number of judicial refusals based on the Article 13 defences (in particular, the lack of the exercise of the rights of custody; the grave risk of harm; and the child's objections). Interestingly, a concurrent increase was recorded in relation to judicial refusals grounded on the non-Article 13 defences (in particular, Article 12, Article 20, and Article 3 the lack of habitual residence of the child in the requesting State). Given the fact that the figures recorded (see above) appear to be more than marginal, this finding may indicate some evasion of Article 13. One of the possible explanations for such a development is the theory of the 'adverse effect of Articles 11(6)–11(8)', that is, a reaction of the judiciary to the provisions of Articles 11(6)–11(8) of the Brussels II bis Regulation. (For a detailed analysis see Chapter 6, section entitled 'More Liberal Interpretation of the Key Concepts of the Convention in Order to Avoid Judicial Refusals Based on Article 13'.) Meanwhile, it suffices to say that this finding suggests a highly undesirable trend. The findings of the 2008 survey neither confirm nor refute the above assumption.[57]

iii. Marked Decrease in the Use of Article 13(1)(b)

The survey has demonstrated that the proportion of refusals based on the Article 13(1)(b) grave risk of harm defence recorded a marked decrease (by 11% if the overall reason for judicial refusal is considered; and by 12% if the reason for judicial refusal combined is considered). This development suggests that the

[57] See Chapter 6, section entitled 'More Liberal Interpretation of the Key Concepts of the Convention in Order to Avoid Judicial Refusals Based on Article 13'.

Regulation has been successful in tackling the perceived problem of the overuse of Article 13(1)(b). Consequently, as intended by the drafters of the Regulation, more cases involving the grave risk of harm defence now result in a judicial return order. However, given the fact that the Regulation does not effectively address the problem of the safety of the child and the returning parent, the marked increase in the proportion of children returned despite allegations of a grave risk of harm causes particular concern.[58] Nevertheless, it must be noted that the development towards a decrease in the use of Article 13(1)(b) may only form a part of a more general trend of active avoidance of Article 13 defences (see above 'Evidence of Avoidance of the Use of Article 13'). If that was the case, the concern over the safety of the child and the abductor parent upon their return to the requesting State in the context of the Regulation would be slightly less pressing.

It must, however, be noted that the finding of a marked decrease in the use of Article 13(1)(b) is not supported by the 2008 survey. Interestingly, in 2008, the proportion of judicial refusals based on Article 13(1)(b) rocketed up to 40%, representing thus an increase not only on the 2005/06 findings (by 17%) but also on the 2003 findings (by 5%).

iv. Decrease in the Use of the Article 13(2) Defence of Child's Objections

Article 11(2) of the Brussels II bis Regulation imposes on the courts an obligation to give a child of sufficient age and maturity an opportunity to express his/her views in return proceedings. It would appear to be a natural consequence of the introduction of the principle of the mandatory inquiry into the child's views that the proportion of judicial refusals based on the defence of child's objections would increase. One could presume that the more children are heard, the more frequently returns will be refused on the ground of child's objections. Contrary to the legitimate expectations, however, the survey recorded a decrease in the use of the Article 13(2) exception. There is, nevertheless, an explanation for this development. In particular, the Regulation only requires the courts to respect the child's right to be heard in return proceedings; it does not obligate them to fulfil the child's wishes. This reasoning accords with the opinion of Baroness Hale of Richmond expressed in a House of Lords decision in *Re D (a child)*.[59] In this decision Baroness Hale highlighted the fact that there was a great difference between allowing children to express their views and actually granting their wishes.[60]

The findings of the 2008 survey support the above conclusion as, at 13%, the proportion of judicial refusals based on Article 13(2) exception recorded in 2008 was the same as in 2005/06.

[58] For a detailed analysis see Chapter 6, section entitled 'Protection of the Abductor Parent and the Child upon the Return'.

[59] *Re D (a child)* [2006] UKHL 51, [2007] 1 AC 619.

[60] To put it in the words of Baroness Hale: 'There is a large difference between taking account of a child's views and doing what he wants. Especially in Hague Convention cases. The relevance of the child's views to the issues in the case may be limited.'

v. Difficulties in Complying with the Six-week Timing Rule

The timing section of the survey points to an undisputable conclusion that it is at best difficult and at worst hardly attainable for the Member States to comply with the six-week rule imposed by Article 11(3) of the Brussels II bis Regulation. Even more alarmingly, the survey revealed that, at 15%, the proportion of pending cases increased by 9%. This suggests that Brussels II bis applications take longer to resolve than Convention cases.[61] Considerable difficulties in complying with the six-week timing rule were recorded also by the 2008 survey.

vi. Uneven Application of the Convention/Regulation

The survey has indicated a disparity in the effectiveness of the application of the Regulation in different groups of Member States. In particular, a marked difference was recorded between the 'old' Member States and the 'new' Member States, in terms of both outcomes and timing. Further analysis and discussion on this rather disturbing trend can be found in Chapter 6, section entitled 'Judicial and Administrative Qualities in the "New" Member States of the European Union'.

[61] For a detailed analysis see Chapter 6, section entitled 'Timing'.

6

Points of Concern

The statistical survey has indicated several points of concern with respect to the operation of the Brussels II bis Regulation. These can be outlined as follows. First, there is some evidence that, in order to avoid judicial refusals based on Article 13, courts might have adopted a more liberal interpretation of the key concepts of the Convention. Second, the proportion of judicial refusals based on Article 13(1)(b) decreased sharply, implying that the grave risk of harm defence might now be invoked less successfully than it was under the Convention. The main concern in this respect remains the protection of the child and the abductor parent upon their return to the requesting State. Third, the statistical survey revealed that the EU Member States are not able to comply with the six-week rule imposed by the Regulation. Finally, there are indications that the Convention and the Regulation operate less effectively in the 'new' Member States than they operate in the 'old' Member States, in terms of both outcomes and timing.

There is limited support for the first concern and substantial support for the third concern in the findings of the 2008 statistical survey. The 2008 survey, however, dispels entirely the second concern as it shows a marked increase in the acceptance of Article 13(1)(b) by the courts, suggesting that, contrary to the aim of the Regulation, the grave risk of harm defence is invoked even more frequently and successfully than it was under the Convention.

The final concern can neither be confirmed nor rejected as no comparable analysis was performed on the 2008 applications to expose differences in the application of the Convention/Regulation in the 'old' EU Member States and in the 'new' EU Member States.

I. More Liberal Interpretation of the Key Concepts of the Convention in Order to Avoid Judicial Refusals Based on Article 13

An area where the Brussels II bis Regulation entirely broke away from the Hague Convention is the position following a court refusal to return. According to Article 11(6) of the Regulation, if a court has issued an order on non-return pursuant to Article 13 of the Convention,[1] it must transmit a copy of the order and the relevant documents to the authorities of the requesting State. Unless the court of the requesting State has already been seized by one of the parties, the authorities that have received the information about the non-return order must notify the parties and invite them to make submissions to the court within three months.[2] If no submissions are made to the court within the time limit, the case will be closed.[3] If the submissions have been made, it is envisaged that they will be followed by a custody hearing.[4] Where these proceedings result in a judgment entailing the child's return, this judgment will automatically be enforceable in the State in which the child is present.[5] The judgment will be enforceable without the need for a declaration of enforceability and without any possibility of recognition being refused.[6] The only prerequisite for the enforcement is the certification of the decision by the judge of origin who delivered the judgment, according to Article 42(2) of the Regulation.

Thus far, only a few reported abduction cases were dealt with in England under this scheme.[7] In *Re A (Custody Decision After Maltese Non-Return Order)*, a Maltese non-return order was overturned by a decision of the English Court made in accordance with Art 11(7) of the Regulation. The child involved in this case was a 12-year-old boy, the youngest of three siblings. The boy was born in Malta. When he was 6½ years old, the family moved to England. However, in 2001 the parents separated and the father returned to Malta. From 2002 onwards the children visited Malta regularly to spend their summer holiday with their father. In 2002, the parents agreed that the eldest sibling, a boy then aged 16, would stay permanently in Malta because of drug and other problems he had in England. In summer 2004, the second sibling, a girl then aged 15, decided to remain in Malta. This decision was not opposed by the mother. In summer 2006, the youngest sibling did not return from his usual holiday in Malta. The decision to retain the boy in Malta was made by the father following the boy's confession that he had been in trouble with the police in England, had taken drugs and had witnessed drugs

[1] Such a non-return order can be based on any of the following exceptions to return: Art 13(1)(a) not exercising rights of custody, Art 13(1)(a) consent, Art 13(1)(a) acquiescence, Art 13(1)(b) grave risk of harm and Art 13(2) child's objections.

[2] Brussels II bis Regulation Art 11(7).

[3] *Ibid.*

[4] *Ibid.*

[5] *Ibid*, Art 11(8).

[6] *Ibid*, Art 42(1).

[7] *Re A (Custody Decision After Maltese Non-Return Order)* [2006] EWHC 3397 (Fam), [2007] 1 FLR 1923; *Re A (Custody); HA v MB* [2007] EWHC 2016 (Fam), [2008] 1 FLR 289; *Re H (a child) (abduction: jurisdiction)* [2009] EWHC 2280 (Fam), [2010] 1 FLR 598; *M v T (Abduction: Brussels II Revised, Art 11(7))* [2010] EWHC 1479 (Fam), [2010] 2 FLR 1685; *D v N* [2011] EWHC 471 (Fam), [2011] 2 FLR 464; and *AF (Father) v T (Mother)* [2011] EWHC 1315 (Fam), [2011] 2 FLR 891. Additionally, there were two cases where relief was sought under Art 11(7) of the Regulation but the applications were dismissed on the basis that the non-return had not been based upon a Hague Convention, Art 13 refusal: *Re RC and BC (Child Abduction); (Brussels II Revised: Article 11(7))* [2009] 1 FLR 574; and *Re RD (Child Abduction); (Brussels II Revised: Arts 11(7) and 19)* [2009] 1 FLR 586. The non-return orders were made under Art 3 and Art 12(2) respectively.

being taken by his maternal aunt in the family home. In August 2006, the mother initiated return proceedings. In September 2006, the relevant Maltese court found that the child had been retained wrongfully, but refused to make a return order. The court held that the threshold of Art 13(1)(b) had been made out and refused to make a return order. In September 2006, the mother initiated proceedings in England, pursuant to the Regulation, asking for the Maltese refusal to return to be reviewed. In these proceedings, the High Court in London ordered the return of the child to England, in accordance with Art 11(7) of the Regulation. The English judge reviewed the evidence and concluded that the situation upon the potential return of the child did not appear to him as risky as to the Maltese court.

Re A (Custody); HA v MB involved a French non-return order confirmed by an English order made pursuant to Art 11(7) of the Regulation. The application related to a two-year-old child. The child was born in England where his parents, a Palestinian father and a French mother, had married in 2001. The marriage enabled the father to gain the right of residence in the United Kingdom until 2008. Shortly after the child was born, the mother took him to France for two short visits. In summer 2005, during the second stay in France, the mother was alarmed by the father's behaviour and returned alone to England to inform the father that she wished to end the marriage. In September 2005, she initiated divorce proceedings in France. Subsequently, the father commenced return proceedings. In July 2006, the father's application was rejected on the basis of Art 13(1)(b) of the Convention. The father intended to appeal against the decision; however, due to delays between the French and English Central Authorities, he missed the time limit for appeal. Nevertheless, he brought proceedings in England pursuant to Art 11(7) of the Regulation. In these proceedings, the French refusal to return was upheld. The father's return application was dismissed. The refusal to return was upheld in the proceedings pursuant to Art 11(7) of the Regulation.

In *Re H (a child) (abduction: jurisdiction)* an Algerian/British father and a Spanish mother lived in England with their young daughter. When the child was 11 months old, the mother refused to return from Spain at the end of a holiday. The father issued proceedings in Spain for the child's return under the Convention. The mother evaded service and refused to participate in the proceedings. Following a delay of 18 months, the Spanish Court refused summary return on the grounds of Art 13(1)(b), noting that the child was settled in Spain. The father then sought order for return from the High Court, under Art 11(7) of the Regulation. The mother again evaded service. With the view of resolving this problem, international judicial co-operation was employed and contact was established with a senior judicial representative in Spain. Following this step, there was reason to believe that this would shortly lead to service on the mother and an effective hearing before the English Court. At an interim hearing, despite the mother's non-attendance, the father, being acutely aware of the delay, sought an order for reasonable direct contact with the child.

M v T (Abduction: Brussels II Revised, Art 11(7)) concerned a Lithuanian non-return order based on Art 13(1)(b) of the Convention. The child concerned was a 2½-year-old boy who had been wrongfully retained in Lithuania by the respondent mother. The father, who was Romanian, and the mother, who was Lithuanian, had met in England where the child was born and was habitually resident. During an agreed visit to Lithuania the mother informed the father that she did not intend to return to England. The father's application for a summary return of the child was refused by the Lithuanian Court. In exercising its jurisdiction under Art 11(7) of the Regulation, the High Court ordered the mother to return the child to England for a period of up to six weeks in which a regime of contact between the mother and the father would take place. At the end of that period the mother would be given permission to return to live permanently with the child in Lithuania and an ongoing contact order would be made by the High Court.

In *D v N* a Polish non-return order based on Art 13(1)(b) of the Convention was overturned by a decision of the High Court. The applicant father sought an order for the return of his daughter aged 4½ who had been wrongfully retained by her mother in Poland. The father, a British citizen, and the mother, a Polish citizen, had lived together with the child in England. After a family holiday in Poland, the mother refused to return with the child to England. The father issued return proceedings under the Convention but the Polish Court refused his application on the grounds of Art 13(1)(b), mother having alleged that the father's consumption of alcohol was excessive. In the proceedings under Art 11(7) of the Regulation, the High Court held that the child's welfare was best met by an order that she return to England. In order for the Court to undertake a full welfare inquiry to make arrangements for the long-term care of the child, it was inevitable that the father had an opportunity to spend some time with the child in England and was assessed by the guardian.

Finally, in *AF (Father) v T (Mother)* a non-return order of a German Court was confirmed by an order of the High Court. The case involved a seven-year-old boy born to a Jordanian/British father and an Eritrean/German mother in England. In May 2008, the mother wrongfully removed the child to Germany. The father petitioned for the child's return. His application was refused by a German Court on the basis of Art 13(1)(b) of the Convention and the decision was confirmed on appeal. It was held that the mother had been traumatised by the father's physical abuse and that the child's wellbeing would be considerably impaired because strains on the mother would also affect the child. In accordance with Art 11(7) of the Regulation, the applicant father then sought either an order for the child's return to England, or an order for contact with him. There was, however, a delay of three years between the abduction and the application under Art 11(7). This was because, following the non-return order, the German authorities refused to provide the father with information about the child's whereabouts, for fear (of the mother) that the father would abduct the child. During the Art 11(7) proceedings, the High Court found that the child was settled in Germany and on this ground refused to order the child's return. The court, however, ordered that the mother make the child available for supervised contact with the father.

Although certainly not anticipated by the drafters of the Regulation, the re-evaluation mechanism introduced by Articles 11(6)–11(8) of the Regulation might have an adverse effect on the interpretation of some of the key concepts of the Convention. Owing to the restrictions imposed on judicial refusals under Article 13, judges might seek to avoid refusing the return on the grounds of this Article. However, they may tend to find other grounds for a judicial refusal if they are convinced that the child's return is not in his/her best interests. Efforts to justify these refusals may in turn lead to a more liberal interpretation of the key concepts of the Convention that fall outside the scope of Article 13, that is, Article 12—child settled in the new environment; Article 3—the lack of rights of custody; Article 3—the lack of the habitual residence of the child in the requesting State; and Article 20.[8]

Unfortunately, the argument is not based solely on a theoretical assumption. Rather, it finds its base in the findings of the statistical survey. The survey has revealed that generally, there was a decrease in the number of judicial refusals based on Article 13 exceptions to return.[9] In particular, it was found that the proportion of refusals based on Article 13(1)(a) not exercising rights of custody, Article 13(1)(b) grave risk of harm, and Article 13(2) child's objections fell by 7%, 11% and 4% respectively, if the overall reason for judicial refusal is considered; and by 10%, 12% and 3% respectively, if the reason for judicial refusal combined is considered (see Table 6.30). The only Article 13 ground for refusal where an increase rather than a decrease was recorded was Article 13(1)(a) consent (a rise by 3% if the overall reason for judicial refusal is considered, and by 4% if reason for judicial refusal combined is considered.

Table 6.30: Article 13 Reasons for judicial refusal

	Overall reason for judicial refusal	**Reason for judicial refusal combined**
Art 13(1)(a) Not exercising rights of custody	↓ by 7%	↓ by 10%
Art 13(1)(a) Consent	↑ by 3%	↑ by 4%
Art 13(1)(b) Grave risk of harm	↓ by 11%	↓ by 12%
Art 13(2) Child's objections	↓ by 4%	↓ by 3%

In contrast, the survey recorded that there was a concurrent increase in the proportion of judicial refusals based on other than Article 13 grounds for refusal.

[8] In contrast, Ruth Lamont predicts that courts in the requested State might be more willing to refuse the return of the child under Art 13 defences, as under the Regulation the requesting State has, nevertheless, the final say over the child's future. This would in turn lead to a less restrictive approach to the interpretation of the Art 13 defences. See R Lamont, 'International Child Abduction and Domestic Violence in the European Union' in H Stalford *et al* (eds), *Gender and Migration in 21st Century Europe* (Aldershot, Ashgate Publishing Ltd, 2009) 27–43, 39.

[9] The Art 13(1)(a) acquiescence exception to return has not been included as there were no judicial refusals based on this ground either in 2003 or in 2005/06.

In particular, it revealed that the proportion of judicial refusals based on Article 12, Article 20, and the lack of habitual residence of the child in the requesting State rose by 11%, 4% and 8% respectively, if the overall reason for judicial refusal is considered; and by 13%, 3% and 7% respectively, if the reason for judicial refusal combined is considered (see Table 6.31). The only non-Article 13 ground for refusal where an increase was not recorded was the lack of the rights of custody. Here the proportion remained the same (at 11%), if the overall reason for judicial refusal is considered, and decreased by 3%, if the reason for judicial refusal combined is considered.

Table 6.31: Reasons for judicial refusal other than Article 13

	Overall reason for judicial refusal	Reason for judicial refusal combined
Art 12	↑ by 11%	↑ by 13%
Art 20	↑ by 4%	↑ by 3%
Applicant had no rights of custody	11% ↔ 11%	↓ by 3%
Child not habitually resident in requesting state	↑ by 8%	↑ by 7%

The 2008 survey provided some limited evidence in support of the above hypothesis. In particular, the survey recorded a decrease on the 2003 proportions of judicial refusals (reason for judicial refusal combined) in relation to all Article 13 exceptions, except from Article 13(1)(b) and Article 13(1)(a) acquiescence which, however, both showed only relatively small increases on the 2003 figures (by 5% and 4% respectively). The use of Article 13(1)(a) not exercising rights of custody fell by 7%, the use of Article 13(1)(a) consent and Article 13(2) child's objections decreased by 2% and 3% respectively. In contrast, an increase of 9% was recorded in the use of Article 12. The proportion of Article 20 refusals remained the same as in 2003 (0%) and although the proportion of Article 3 refusals based on the lack of the habitual residence of the child in the requesting State decreased, it was only by 1% (from 16% in 2003 to 15% in 2008).

As the 2008 survey neither confirmed nor rejected the assumption of the tendency towards a more liberal interpretation of the non-Article 13 grounds for judicial refusal, it was decided to examine those Brussels II bis refusals that appear to indicate an unwelcome shift towards a wider interpretation of non-Article 13 defences. A careful scrutiny of the interpretation of the non-Article 13 concepts given in these judgments was then performed. This analysis was carried out by way of comparison with a pre-Brussels II bis approach adopted towards the particular exception in the given jurisdiction. The aim of this analysis was to determine whether the Brussels II bis interpretation departed from the pre-Brussels II bis approach. If there were signs of a shift towards a more liberal approach, an additional exercise was then performed to assess the correctness of the hypothesis. This exercise consisted in a comparison of the interpretation of a particular non-Article 13 concept with an approach adopted towards this exception in major non-Brussels II bis jurisdictions since 2005 when the Regulation was adopted in Europe. The jurisdictions selected were Australia, Canada and the United States. The objective of this analysis was to determine whether dynamics in the interpretation of the non-Article 13 Convention concepts in Brussels II bis cases have not been a part of a global evolution rather than a deliberate reaction to the reality of the Regulation.

Admittedly, the above exercise has two major limitations. First, despite an in-depth research, only a small number of Brussels II bis judicial refusals based on provisions other than Article 13 were found to be publicly available. Second, the published case law was available from only a limited number of jurisdictions. In the end, the case law search resulted in two decisions being identified as potentially raising concerns of a trend towards a more liberal interpretation of the non-Article 13 defences. Both of these 'suspicious' decisions are from Ireland. The decisions analysed are the case of *Foyle Health and Social Services Trust v EC & Anor*[10] (judicial refusal based on Article 20), and the case of *B v G*[11] (judicial refusal based on the lack of the habitual residence of the child), both decided by the High Court of Ireland. For ease of reference, the analysis is broken down into two sections: Article 20 and Article 3—the lack of the habitual residence of the child in the requesting State.

A. Article 20

Article 20 provides that a return application may be refused if the return 'would not be permitted by the fundamental principles of the requested State relating to the protection of human rights and fundamental freedoms'. The Explanatory Report to the Convention emphasises the 'clearly exceptional nature of this provision's application'[12] and describes the high threshold required as follows:

> [t]o be able to refuse to return a child on the basis of the article, it will be necessary to show that the fundamental principles of the requested State concerning the subject matter of the Convention do not permit it; it will not be sufficient to show merely that its return would be incompatible, even manifestly incompatible, with these principles.[13]

Courts, adhering to the intention of the drafters, have used Article 20 very rarely.[14] Very surprisingly, however, a return order was refused on the basis of Article 20 in the Brussels II bis case of *Foyle Health and Social Services Trust v EC & Anor.*

[10] *Foyle Health and Social Services Trust v EC & Anor* [2006] IEHC 448, [2007] 4 IR 528.

[11] *B v G* [2009] IEHC 104.

[12] E Pérez-Vera, 'Explanatory Report on the 1980 Hague Child Abduction Convention' (1982) para 118, available at www.hcch.net/upload/expl28.pdf.

[13] *Ibid.*

[14] P Beaumont and P McEleavy, *The Hague Convention on International Child Abduction* (Oxford, Oxford University Press, 1999) 172; and N Lowe *et al*, *International Movement of Children: Law Practice and Procedure* (Bristol, Jordan Publishing, 2004) 369.

i. The Brussels II bis Case of Foyle Health and Social Services Trust v EC & Anor: Analysis[15]

Facts of the case: The child involved in this application was a boy, S, born in January 2005 in Northern Ireland. The applicant was Foyle Health and Social Service Trust, which claimed to be the corporate parent of S. The respondents were biological parents of the child. Both respondents had a criminal history; they suffered from alcohol abuse and had neglected their six children. The children were subsequently placed in the care of North Cork Community Services. Therefore, before S was born, it was decided that he would be at risk of significant harm and that an emergency order would be sought by the North Cork Community Services with a view to applying for a full care order thereafter. The mother did not agree with this decision and indicated that she would leave the jurisdiction of Ireland before the child was born in order to avoid the child being taken into care. Subsequently, she notified the Community Services that she was residing in Northern Ireland. The child was born in Northern Ireland on 15 January 2005. In February 2005, it was found by the relevant authorities of Northern Ireland that the mother had problems with alcohol abuse and that S lacked proper care. Therefore, interim orders were made in Northern Ireland and the child was placed with foster parents, the mother being granted access rights to the child. It was intended to place S for adoption. The mother, however, strongly opposed this option. During an access visit in February 2006, she removed the child and took him to Ireland. The Foyle Health and Social Service Trust subsequently initiated return proceedings.

Legal issues: Several objections against the return of the child were raised by the respondents. These included the issue of the habitual residence of the child; the issue of the rights of custody; the problem of acquiescence; the objection of Article 13(1)(b)—the grave risk of harm, and last but not least, Article 20. The judgment was based on the Article 20 exception to return.

Article 20: Counsel for the respondents argued that a return of the child to Northern Ireland would breach their constitutional rights as well as the constitutional rights of the child. It was against the purpose of the Convention to return the child solely for the purpose of cutting him off from his family. Counsel referred to the decision in the case of *ACW v Ireland*.[16] Having referred to that case, counsel argued that 'the proposal to adopt S does not accord with his rights as a member of the family'. Counsel also cited a judgment in the case of *London Borough of Sutton v RM and Others*[17] in which it was held that any arrangements regarding child care must be carried out 'with due regard for the natural and imprescriptible rights of the child'. Counsel stressed the impre-

[15] For a brief comment on this case see P Beaumont and E Johnston, 'Can Exequatur Be Abolished in Brussels I Whilst Retaining a Public Policy Defence?' (2010) 6 *Journal of Private International Law* 249, 275.

[16] *W v Ireland* [1994] ILRM 126, sub nom *ACW v Ireland* [1994] 3 IR 232.

[17] *London Borough of Sutton v RM and Others* [2002] 4 IR 488.

scriptible rights of the child and pointed out that Irish adoption law contains certain protections and guarantees that are not contained in the adoption law of Northern Ireland.

Ruling: The court, having assessed the submissions of counsel for the respondents, held:

> [b]efore an adoption can take place in this jurisdiction [Ireland], very stringent criteria must be met. I find it impossible to ignore the constitutional rights protected by Articles 41 and 42 of the Constitution in relation to the family. It seems to me that the possibility of adoption which are less favourable to the rights of the family including S in Northern Ireland are such that his return should not be permitted. In the circumstances I am refusing to make the order sought.[18]

Following *Foyle Health and Social Services Trust v EC & Anor*, the High Court of Ireland was presented with the Article 20 defence once more in another Brussels II bis case: *Nottingham County Council v KB and another*.[19] The facts of this case were similar to the facts of *Foyle Health and Social Services Trust*. The case involved two children who had been removed by their parents from England to Ireland. Following their arrival in Ireland, the children were placed in foster care. The applicant in the return proceedings was an English local authority with child protection responsibilities. This authority contended that the courts of England and Wales had rights of custody in relation to the children and that the children were removed from England in breach of those rights of custody. The respondents disputed this argument and also raised several objections to return, including Article 20 of the Convention. In particular, they argued that the return of the children was not permitted by the 'fundamental principles of [Ireland] relating to the protection of human rights and fundamental freedoms', having regard to the possibility of adoption of the children without their consent and the constitutional protection of family in Ireland. Before a decision on Article 20 was reached, *Foyle Health and Social Services Trust* was considered. Interestingly, the court found the *Foyle* judgment as having been decided *per incuriam* and therefore chose not to follow it as a precedent. Consequently, the Article 20 defence was not accepted in the present case. In particular, the court held:

> In reaching the conclusion set out above, I have obviously considered carefully and taken into account the judgment of Dunne J in *Foyle Health and Social Services Trust v EC & Anor*, referred to above. That judgment is distinguishable on the facts as there was in that case in place a care plan proposing adoption for the child. Further, it appears that the judgment in *Sanders v Mid-Western Health Board* [decision of the Supreme Court, unreported, 23 June 1987] was not opened to the Court in that case. Also, that on the construction and application of Article 20 of the Convention, the Court was not referred to the Australian decision, set out above [*The Director-General, Department of Families, Youth and Community Care v Rhonda May Bennet*, [2000] Fam CA 253—for analysis of

[18] *Foyle Health and Social Services Trust v EC & Anor* [2006] IEHC 448, [2007] 4 IR 528 at 552.
[19] *Nottingham County Council v KB and another* [2010] IEHC 9.

this case see section 'Recent Developments in Interpretation of Article 20 in Australia, Canada and the United States' below], nor the relevant provisions of the Perez-Vera Report [113 and 118]. Insofar as I differ on the application of Article 20, I do so for the reasons set out above.[20]

ii. Pre-Brussels II bis Interpretation of Article 20 in Ireland[21]

Article 20 was invoked under the Convention on two occasions only. First, it was used in the case of *W v Ireland*.[22] In this application, a child, aged three, habitually resident in the United Kingdom, was removed to Ireland by her mother. The mother claimed that the Hague Abduction Convention violated the Irish Constitution, particularly the following provisions: Article 40, section 3, which seeks to guarantee personal rights of the citizen, including the right of an Irish citizen to have access to Irish courts; and Article 42, section 1, which guarantees the right of a parent to invoke the protection of the Irish courts in respect of the welfare of his/her child.

The court held that personal rights of children were fully protected by the exceptions incorporated into the Convention, particularly Article 13 exceptions and the Article 20 exception. The court further concluded that the fact that the jurisdiction of the Irish courts was in the Convention cases ousted in favour of a foreign court was not in breach of the Constitution. This approach was found to be entirely in accordance with the Convention's policy. In this context, the court held that 'this is a common feature of conventions of this nature and is in accordance with well-established principles of private international law'.[23] A reference was made to Article 29, section 3 of the Irish Constitution providing that 'Ireland accepts the generally recognised principles of international law as its rule of conduct in relations with other States'.[24] Accordingly, the mother's application for a declaration that the Convention violated the Irish Constitution was dismissed and the return of the child was ordered.

The second application based on Article 20 in Ireland was the case of *CK v CK*.[25] In this case the applicant father argued that, where the issue of the welfare of the child is raised, the child has a constitutional right for a fair inquiry into his/her welfare. This inquiry should be a part of return proceedings. The court, rejecting the father's submission, held that there were no provisions either in the implementing legislation (the Child Abduction and Enforcement

[20] *Nottingham County Council v KB and another* para 76.

[21] It is to be noted that the cases considered below in the text of the book deal with the rights of the child whereas in the Brussels II bis case of *Foyle Health and Social Services Trust v EC & Anor* the issue was the fundamental rights of the child's parents. Nevertheless, in an Australian case of *A v GS* (2004) 187 FLR 240, it was held that the 'fundamental rights' are related to the child concerned or a custodial parent.

[22] *W v Ireland* [1994] ILRM 126, sub nom *ACW v Ireland* [1994] IR 232.

[23] *Ibid*, at 242.

[24] *Ibid*.

[25] *CK v CK* [1994] 1 IR 260, [1993] ILRM 534.

of Custody Orders Act 1991) or in the Irish Constitution that would demand such an inquiry. The court further concluded that the 1991 Act was presumed to be constitutional and did not deprive children of any constitutional rights. The court concluded that there was no evidence that a human right or a fundamental freedom or a constitutional right of the children involved in the case would be breached by their return to the country of their habitual residence (Australia). Similarly, there was no evidence that custody proceedings in Australia would breach a constitutional right of the children by not adequately inquiring into the welfare principle. Consequently, neither Article 20, nor the Irish Constitution, nor the facts of the instant case required that there should be an additional inquiry into the welfare of the children. Accordingly, the return of the children to Australia was ordered.

Against a background of both the general approach to Article 20 and the pre-Brussels II bis interpretation of the provision by the courts in Ireland, the acceptance of Article 20 as grounds for refusal in *Foyle Health and Social Services Trust v EC & Anor* is very surprising. Considering that prior to this refusal all pleas based on Article 20 in Ireland had failed, there is a clear indication that in *Foyle Health and Social Services Trust v EC & Anor* the court departed from the narrow interpretation of Article 20 evident from the Irish cases prior to Brussels II bis. Nevertheless, the *Nottingham County Council* case significantly reduces any fear of an abuse of Article 20 in Ireland.

iii. Recent Developments in Interpretation of Article 20 in Australia, Canada and the United States

The original aim of this analysis was to ascertain any developments in the interpretation of Article 20 in the three major non-Brussels II bis jurisdictions since 2005, that is, since the entry of the Regulation into force in Europe, and to compare them with the approach taken to Article 20 in *Foyle Health and Social Services Trust v EC & Anor.* In Australia, however, no 2005–2011 case law involving the Article 20 exception was available. Therefore, solely older cases were examined and a conclusion was drawn from this analysis. In Canada and the United States, only one 2005–2011 decision based on the Article 20 defence was found in each of the jurisdictions respectively. Therefore, in order to obtain a bigger picture, older cases were also included in the analysis.

In this context, it is to be pointed out that the lack of recent case law does not in any way affect the trustworthiness of the findings below. Indeed, if any major developments had lately taken place in relation to Article 20, the relevant case law would certainly have been published.

a. Australia

In Australia, Article 20 has generally been interpreted in a narrow fashion. Rules for the application of this exception in Australia were set in a 1994 decision in

McCall v State Central Authority.[26] In this case, the Full Court of the Family Court of Australia held that:

> To be able to refuse to return a child on the basis of this Article [Article 20], it would be necessary to show that the fundamental principles of the requested State concerning the subject matter of the Convention do not permit it; it will not be sufficient to show merely that its return would be incompatible, even manifestly incompatible with these principles.[27]

The court added that the application of Article 20 would only arise on the 'rare occasion that the return of the child would utterly shock the conscience of the court and offend all notions of due process'.[28]

The decision in *McCall v State Central Authority*[29] was referred to in other cases, for example *Emmett and Perry and Director-General*[30] and *A v GS*.[31] In the former case, it was found that a return of children to California, their move to India and possible betrothal there did not fall within Article 20. It was also held that if concluded otherwise, such a decision would be judgmental on lifestyles and cultural and religious beliefs. In the latter case, a 12-year-old step-sister of the child who was the subject of the return application argued that the return of the child would violate her [the step-sister's] human rights. This submission was rejected by the court on the basis that the Article 20 exception was concerned solely with the child to be returned or his/her custodial parents. The court also held that the importance of the right of the child involved in the return proceedings to have his future decided in the State of his habitual residence outweighed the consequences of the return order on the step-sister.

There was only one case in Australia where the exception of Article 20 formed a basis for judicial refusal to return. This refusal was made in a 1997 decision of the Family Court of Australia at Melbourne in the matter of *State Central Authority of Victoria v Ardito*.[32] Although in this case, Article 20 was not raised by the applicant, the court found that, alongside Article 13(1)(b), this provision was applicable to the instant case. The matter was that due to immigration issues, the respondent mother was unable to re-enter the requesting State (the United States). Consequently, she would not be able to appear before a US court during custody proceedings. The court therefore concluded that the return of the child would be contrary to the fundamental principles of Australia relating to the protection of human rights and fundamental freedoms. It was considered 'contrary to all concepts of fairness that the question of the custody of the child should be

[26] *McCall v State Central Authority* (1994) 121 FLR 45.
[27] *Ibid*, at 64. See also Explanatory Report to the 1980 Convention (n 12) para 118.
[28] *McCall v State Central Authority* (1994) 121 FLR 45 at 64.
[29] *McCall v State Central Authority* (1994) 121 FLR 45.
[30] *Emmett and Perry and Director-General* (1996) FLC 92-645.
[31] *A v GS* (2004) 187 FLR 240.
[32] *State Central Authority of Victoria v Ardito*, unreported, Family Court of Australia, 29 October 1997; INCADAT: HC/E/AU 283.

conducted in circumstances where the mother was denied the right to appear'.[33] Accordingly, the return of the child was refused partly on the basis of Article 20.

The decision in *State Central Authority of Victoria v Ardito* was later relied upon in the case of *The Director-General, Department of Families, Youth and Community Care v Rhonda May Bennet.*[34] In this case, however, the exception of Article 20 was not made out successfully. It was argued on behalf of the defendant mother that she was unable to return to the requesting State (the United Kingdom) for medical reasons. Consequently, she would be unable to participate in custody proceedings in the United Kingdom. Ultimately, this would mean that she would be denied the basic right of effective participation in proceedings concerned with the welfare of the child. The mother's submission was, however, rejected by the court. It was held that the mother was not unable to return to the United Kingdom for medical reasons. The court clearly distinguished between the terms 'unable' and 'unwilling'. Although it was accepted that the mother should not return, it was concluded that she was not unable to return, unlike the mother in the case of *State Central Authority of Victoria v Ardito.*

In the instant case, the defendant mother also argued that the child was of Torres Strait Islander origin and that this required an Australian court to consider the welfare of the child given the special significance of the child's culture and heritage. To support this submission, a reference was made to the Australian Family Law Act. The court, however, held that the child had only one great-great grandmother who was a Torres Strait Islander. The child herself was born in England and the factor of her heritage was not such a significant element in her life that only an Australian court could evaluate its importance in the child's life. The court found that there was no breach of a human right or a fundamental freedom inherent in the return of the child to England.

The court stressed the exceptional nature of Article 20, referring to the Explanatory Report to the Convention, the drafting history of Article 20 as well as to the decision in *McCall v State Central Authority.*[35]

b. Canada

Thus far, in Canada, the exception of Article 20 has never been invoked successfully. The first case where Article 20 was raised was a 1989 application of *Parsons v Stygger.*[36] In this case, the defendant mother argued that under section 6(1) of the Canadian Charter of Rights and Freedoms every citizen of Canada had the right to enter, remain in and leave Canada. Consequently, the child concerned as a Canadian citizen should have the right to stay in Canada. This submission

[33] *State Central Authority of Victoria v Ardito*, unreported, Family Court of Australia, 29 October 1997; INCADAT: HC/E/AU 283, INCADAT Summary, available at www.incadat.com/index.cfm?act=search.detail&cid=283&lng=1&sl=1.

[34] *The Director-General, Department of Families, Youth and Community Care v Rhonda May Bennet* [2000] Fam CA 253.

[35] *McCall v State Central Authority* (1994) 121 FLR 45.

[36] *Parsons v Styger* (1989) 67 OR (2d) 1 (Ont SCJ).

was rejected and the court held that the child did not have the right to remain in Canada in defiance of the Hague Convention. The defendant mother further argued that according to section 7 of the Charter of Rights and Freedoms, everyone has the right to life, liberty and security of the person and the right not to be deprived thereof except in accordance with the principles of fundamental justice. In response to this submission the court concluded that a return order would not mean a denial of fundamental justice. Consequently, the Hague Convention was found to be compatible with the Canadian Charter of Rights and Freedoms.

The decision in *Parsons v Styger* was followed in the 1996 case of *YD v JB*[37] and later in the 2001 case of *Struweg v Struweg*.[38] In the former case, the defendant, invoking section 6 of the Canadian Charter of Rights and Freedoms, argued that 'no Canadian citizen can be forced to leave our soil against his or her free will'. The court rejected this argument and noted that the provision of section 6(1) of the Charter related to the extradition of criminals—a situation which is diametrically different from the return of children who, under international and domestic law, have been wrongfully removed. Similarly, in the latter case, the defendant mother invoked the incompatibility of the Convention with section 6 of the Charter. The court, however, held that a return order would not impair any fundamental human rights which the child had as a Canadian citizen. It was concluded that:

> As a minor, a determination as to his custody must be made. If that determination is to be made in Pennsylvania [the requesting State] it does not in any way impair any fundamental human rights which the child may have as a Canadian citizen.[39]

Article 20 was again invoked in the 2001 case of *Moller v Despoja-Moller*.[40] In this case, the defendant mother submitted that German courts (courts of the requesting State) failed to guard her human rights and fundamental freedoms as well as the human rights and fundamental freedoms of her children. The presiding judge rejected the mother's allegations concluding that:

> It would be a strange finding indeed for me to make or to find in effect that Germany, a western industrialised democratic nation, was not protecting the respondent's rights or the rights of her children.[41]

Another Article 20 plea was made in 2003 in the case of *Jabbaz v Mouammar*.[42] In the return application, it was argued that due to the defendant mother's uncertain immigration status, the return of the child would be contrary to public policy. Though the facts of this case bore similarity to the Australian judicial refusal in *State Central Authority of Victoria v Ardito*, the Court of Appeal for Ontario rejected the defendant's reasoning and pointed out that 'courts should be very

[37] *YD v JB* [1996] RDF 753 (Que SCJ).
[38] *Struweg v Struweg* [2001] 9 WWR 581 (Sask Ct of Queen's Bench).
[39] *Ibid*, para 59.
[40] *Moller v Despoja-Moller* (2001) WL 598652 (Ont SCJ), [2002] WDFL 168.
[41] *Ibid*, para 16.
[42] *Jabbaz v Mouammar* (2003) 226 DLR (4th) 494 (Ont Court of Appeal).

wary of grafting new public policy exceptions on to the Convention in the face of the very clear public policy represented in the Convention itself'.[43]

Most recently, the Article 20 defence was raised in 2010 in the case of *Droit de la Famille—102375*.[44] This case involved the removal of a five-year-old girl by her lesbian mother from Mexico to Canada. The mother alleged discrimination in Mexico against homosexuals resulting in specific discrimination against herself as a lesbian parent. On this ground, upon her arrival in Canada, she claimed refugee status. She also alleged abusive treatment in Mexico from the child's father, that is, her ex-husband and an applicant in the return proceedings. The mother argued that due to homophobia faced by homosexuals in Mexico the return of the child would be contrary to the human rights and freedoms recognised in Quebec. When reaching its decision, the Quebec Supreme Court expressed an opinion that Articles 20 and 13(b) of the Convention were inextricably intertwined as 'the exceptions of Article 20 are in fact often englobed in Article 13(b)'.[45] It followed that, as the case was decided on the basis of Article 13(b), it was not necessary to conclude as to whether Article 20 applied.[46] The court, nevertheless, highlighted the fact that the exception of Article 20 was intended to be used in rare cases only and that there were almost no judgments invoking the defence.[47]

c. The United States

As in Australia and Canada, in the United States Article 20 has been subject to a very narrow interpretation. The US implementing legislation requires that Article 20 be established by 'clear and convincing evidence'.[48] Thus far, this exception has never been made out successfully in this jurisdiction.

Article 20 was relied upon in the 1996 application of *Caro v Sher*.[49] In this case, two children were wrongfully removed by their mother from Spain to the United States. The abduction took place in 1996. Prior to the removal, in November 1994, a Spanish court dismissed the mother's application to relocate with the children to the United States. The mother appealed against this decision; however, the appeal was not scheduled to be heard by the Spanish Court of Appeals until September

[43] *Ibid*, para 39.

[44] *Droit de la Famille—102375* (2010) CarswellQue 9711, (2010) QCCS 4390 (Que SCJ).

[45] *Ibid*, para 226.

[46] The court held that the return would expose the child to a grave risk of psychological harm or otherwise place her in an intolerable situation as the mother would risk further discriminatory treatment upon her return as well as imprisonment and this would be detrimental to the child's emotional wellbeing. *Ibid*, paras 218–21.

[47] *Ibid*, paras 224 and 225 respectively. Additionally, Art 20 was partially relied upon in the 2010 case of *Medina v Pallett* (2010) CarswellBC 449 (BC SC). Among other defences, the respondent mother relied on Art 20 arguing that owing to a coup d'état against the elected government of Honduras in June 2009, basic human rights in Honduras had been suspended; *ibid*, para 57. The British Columbia Supreme Court, however, rejected the argument on the basis that the mother had offered no admissible evidence to support her submission; *ibid*, para 58.

[48] International Child Abduction Remedies Act (1988) para 11603(e)(2)(A).

[49] *Caro v Sher* 687 A 2d 354 (Ch Div, 1996).

1998. Consequently, the application was still pending at the date of the wrongful removal of the children to the United States.

The mother argued that the delay by the Court of Appeals in hearing her application filed in September 1994 until September 1998 violated the United States' fundamental interest in procedural due process. The court, however, held that the mother had the burden of proving by 'clear and convincing' evidence that the return (not the delay) would violate the United States fundamental principles relating to the protection of human rights and fundamental freedoms under Article 20 of the Convention. As the mother failed so to prove, the court rejected her reasoning and concluded that there was no evidence that the Spanish courts would not address her present, specific custody issues in the best interests of the children.

With regard to the issue of delays in court proceedings the court concluded that this problem affected many litigants and was certainly not unique to Spain.

Another US application where the defence was based on Article 20 was *Ciotola v Fiocca*.[50] In this case, the defendant mother argued that the trial court failed to apply the 'best interests' test and that this was in breach of the child's constitutional rights to due process and equal protection. The mother further argued that Article 12 of the Convention was unconstitutional as 'it creates an arbitrary classification for children in the examination of habitual residency'.[51] Both arguments were, however, rejected by the court and it was held that examining the best interests of the child under traditional Ohio law would violate the spirit and aim of the Convention.

Article 20 was further invoked in the cases of *Janakakis-Kostun v Janakakis*[52] and *Hazbun Escaf v Rodriquez*.[53] In the former application, the defendant mother complained about the way she was treated by the police and court system of the requesting State (Greece). Similar allegations were made against the German judicial system in the Canadian case of *Moller v Despoja-Moller*.[54] As in *Moller v Despoja-Moller*, the court rejected the mother's submission and held that similar complaints were made many times by defendants in proceedings in the United States. No evidence was available to conclude that Greece was suspect in its treatment of the mother and/or the child.

In the latter case, the defendant father argued that he had been denied due process before Colombian courts when a custody agreement between him and the child's mother was decreed, and later when he was ordered increases in maintenance payments without notice. These arguments were, however, rejected outright as it was held that they had no effect on a determination under the Hague Convention. As for Article 20 itself the court held that this provision was 'seldom-cited

[50] *Ciotola v Fiocca* 684 NE 2d 763 (1997).
[51] *Ibid*, para 769.
[52] *Janakakis-Kostun v Janakakis* 6 SW 3d 843 (Ky Ct App 1999).
[53] *Hazbun Escaf v Rodriquez* 200 F Supp 2d 603, EDVa (2002).
[54] *Moller v Despoja-Moller* (2001) WL 598652 (Ont SCJ), [2002] WDFL 168.

and somewhat obscure',[55] and was intended to be 'restrictively interpreted and applied … on the rare occasion that return of a child would utterly shock the conscience of the court or offend all notions of due process'.[56]

At the time of writing, there was only one published judgment based on Article 20 that had been made in the United States since the Brussels II bis Regulation came into force in Europe, *McCubbin v McCubbin*.[57] In this case, the children involved were wrongfully retained by their father, a serviceman in the United States Navy, in the United States. The parties married in Australia in 1996. Shortly after the wedding, they moved to the United States where the father was transferred. Nevertheless, they planned to return to Australia eventually, after the father retired from the navy. In 2000, the couple's first child was born in the United States. In 2001, the father was re-stationed to Australia for two years. Whilst in Australia, the couple's second child was born. In 2003, the navy transferred the father back to the United States where he was to be stationed for his final three years in the navy. Consequently, the family moved back to the United States. In 2004, the father was assigned a six-month deployment in the Gulf of Mexico. The parents agreed that the mother would take the children to Australia to live there with her mother. During the period of separation, however, the relationship between the parents deteriorated. In late 2004, the father visited the mother and the children in Australia. At that time, it was obvious that the marriage was over. The father visited the children again in March 2005. The children remained with the mother as the father was still on active duty. The father was due to retire in November 2005. The mother agreed that the children would come to the United States to celebrate his retirement and to spend Christmas and New Year with their father. In January 2006, the father informed the mother that he would not be returning the children back to Australia. The mother initiated return proceedings. The father based his defence on the Article 20 exception to return, arguing that the principles contained in the Servicemembers Civil Relief Act, 50 USC, para 501 et seq would be violated if the mother was able to establish the habitual residence of the children in Australia while he was on active duty at sea.[58] Particularly, the father

[55] *Hazbun Escaf v Rodriquez* 200 F Supp 2d 603, EDVa (2002) at 614.

[56] *Ibid.*

[57] *McCubbin v McCubbin* (2006) WL 1797922 (WD Mo). Additionally, Art 20 was partially relied upon in a 2010 case, *Sullivan v Sullivan* (2010) WL 227924 (D Idaho), and in two 2011 cases, *Habrzyk v Habrzyk* 759 F Supp 2d 1014 and *Nelson v Petterle* 782 F Supp 2d 1081 (ED Cal, 2011). In *Sullivan v Sullivan* Art 20-related arguments were, however, so feeble that the court did not find it necessary to engage in a deeper analysis of the issue. Nevertheless, with a view to highlighting the exceptional nature of the Art 20 defence, the court reiterated the conclusion reached in *Hazbun Escaf v Rodriquez*: 'Article 20 was meant to be restrictively interpreted and applied … on the rare occasion that return of a child would utterly shock the conscience of the court or offend all notions of due process'; *Sullivan v Sullivan* para 37. The same quote from *Hazbun Escaf v Rodriquez* was reiterated in *Habrzyk v Habrzyk* and *Nelson v Petterle* before the Art 20 defence was rejected in both cases; *Habrzyk v Habrzyk* para 9 and *Nelson v Petterle* para 18.

[58] The aims of the Servicemembers Civil Relief Act are: '(1) to provide for, strengthen, and expedite the national defence through protection extended by this Act to servicemembers of the United States to enable such persons to devote their energy to the defence needs of the Nation; and (2) to provide

submitted that he was unable to seek the return of his children from Australia while he was still on active duty in the navy because he was permanently deployed at sea. Since a civil suit could not be held against him while he was absent, the period to establish habitual residence of the children in Australia should also be disregarded while he was on active duty. The court rejected the father's submission and held that the father had failed to establish the Article 20 exception by 'clear and convincing evidence' as required by the US implementing legislation, the International Child Abduction Remedies Act.[59] The court held:

> Even assuming that the Relief Act were the sort of 'fundamental principles ... relating to the protection of human rights and fundamental freedoms' contemplated by the Hague Convention, Michael McCubbin [the father] has not offered even a preponderance of evidence—much less clear and convincing evidence—that the return of the children in the present case would violate those principles.[60]

Accordingly, the court ordered the return of the children to Australia.

iv. Conclusions

As in the Irish cases prior to Brussels II bis, Article 20 has been interpreted in an extremely narrow fashion also in Australia, Canada and the United States. Consequently, the liberal interpretation of Article 20 in *Foyle Health and Social Services Trust v EC & Anor* contrasts sharply with the exceptional nature of this ground stressed by the courts in all three jurisdictions analysed.

The conclusion reached in the Canadian case of *Moller v Despoja-Moller*, 'It would be a strange finding indeed for me to make or to find in effect that Germany, a western industrialised democratic nation, was not protecting the respondent's rights or the rights of her children'[61] sharply contrasts with the attitude adopted by the Irish Court towards the legal system of Northern Ireland. Indeed, it is 'a strange finding that Northern Ireland, a western industrialised democratic nation, would not sufficiently protect the respondents' rights'. Against this background, one feels tempted to question the commitment of the Irish Court to the principle of the mutual trust between Contracting States, as one of the underlying concepts of the Convention and the Regulation. While it must be admitted that, in a general sense, mutual trust cannot be unlimited and Article 20 cannot mean nothing, it is submitted here that, in the given case, the non-adherence to mutual trust does not appear to be justified.

Finally, as a general observation, it has rightly been pointed out in relation to Article 20 that the fundamental principles of the requested State relating to the protection of human rights and fundamental freedoms are of such a primary

for the temporary suspension of judicial and administrative proceedings and transactions that may adversely affect the civil rights of servicemembers during their military service.'

[59] International Child Abduction Remedies Act (1988).
[60] *McCubbin v McCubbin* (2006) WL 1797922 (WD Mo) at 6.
[61] *Moller v Despoja-Moller* (2001) WL 598652 (Ont SCJ), [2002] WDFL 168.

nature that their violation may also give rise to a grave risk of harm and thereby fall within Article 13(1)(b).[62] In *Foyle Health and Social Services Trust v EC & Anor* the exception of Article 20 was invoked together with the Article 13(1)(b) defence of grave risk of harm. Surprisingly, despite the exceptional nature of the Article 20 objection, the court gave priority to this defence over Article 13(1)(b). It therefore appears justified to ask: 'Was the choice not made with the intention to avoid restrictions imposed on judicial refusals under Article 13 by the Regulation?' Nevertheless, hopefully, the *Nottingham County Council* case signifies a shift away from any risk of abusive use of Article 20 in Ireland.

B. Article 3—the Lack of the Habitual Residence of the Child in the Requesting State

Article 3 of the Hague Abduction Convention states that:

> The removal or the retention of a child is to be considered wrongful where—
>
> (a) it is in breach of rights of custody attributed to a person, an institution or any other body, either jointly or alone, under the law of the State in which the child was habitually resident immediately before the removal or retention; and
> (b) at the time of removal or retention those rights were actually exercised, either jointly or alone, or would have been so exercised but for the removal or retention.

Neither the Convention nor the Explanatory Report provides any definition of 'habitual residence'.[63] No guidance is given either by the Brussels II bis Regulation.[64] The notion has been left undefined so as to enable the courts to freely apply it to the facts of a particular case.[65] Case law in the Convention States indicates several approaches to this problem. Generally, four different models have been identified: the dependency model, the parental rights model, the child-centred model, and the fact-based model.[66] It is to be noted that a binding interpretation of 'habitual residence' for the purposes of parental responsibility cases under the Brussels II bis Regulation was given in 2009 by the European Court of Justice in the non-child abduction case of *Re A*.[67] *Re A* concerned an application for a care order to be overturned that had been made on the ground that the children involved had been abandoned. In 2005, the applicant mother, her three

[62] Beaumont and McEleavy, *The Hague Convention* (n 14) 173.
[63] For a detailed analysis of the concept of habitual residence in the context of the Hague Abduction Convention see R Schuz, 'Habitual Residence of Children under the Hague Child Abduction Convention? Theory and Practice' (2001) 13 *Child and Family Law Quarterly* 1.
[64] For a detailed analysis of habitual residence under the Brussels II bis Regulation see R Lamont, 'Habitual Residence and Brussels II bis: Developing Concepts for European Private International Law' (2007) 3 *Journal of Private International Law* 261. See also P Beaumont and P McEleavy, *Private International Law, Anton*, 3rd edn (Edinburgh, W Green & SULI, 2011) 196–209.
[65] Commission (EC), 'Practice guide for the application of the new Brussels II Regulation' 15, available at www.ec.europa.eu/civiljustice/publications/docs/guide_new_brussels_ii_en.pdf.
[66] Lowe *et al*, *International Movement of Children* (n 14).
[67] Case C-523/07 *A* [2009] ECR I-2805 (Third Chamber).

children and the children's stepfather moved to Finland. They lived in a camper van on campsites and with relatives. The children did not attend school. In October that year the children were taken into care in Finland and placed in a childcare unit, under the Finnish Law on the protection of children, on the ground that they had been abandoned, and in order to clarify their situation. On an application by the mother for the care order to be overturned, problems of jurisdiction arose and were referred to the European Court of Justice for preliminary ruling. One of the issues to be considered was the interpretation of 'habitual residence'. The court concluded that 'habitual residence' under Article 8(1) of the Regulation corresponded to the place which reflected some degree of integration by the child in a social and family environment. In particular, the following facts should be taken into consideration: the duration, regularity, conditions and reasons for the stay on the territory of a Member State and the family's move to that State, the child's nationality, the place and conditions of attendance at school, linguistic knowledge, and the family and social relationships of the child in that State. The court further held that it was for the national court to establish the habitual residence of the child, taking account of all circumstances specific to each individual case.

Habitual residence is essentially a factual concept, that is, a person must actually be resident in a jurisdiction for a certain period of time before he/she can acquire habitual residence there. This dimension of the concept is particularly important in child abduction cases as without a factual connection it would be inappropriate for the courts of the requesting State to assume jurisdiction over a custody dispute upon the return of the child.[68] Another aspect of habitual residence that cannot be underestimated in cases of child abduction is the intention of the parent.[69] This view appears to be justified on two grounds: first, it is unrealistic to separate the interests of a child from his/her primary carer's, especially when younger children are concerned; and second, taking account of intention alongside the factual aspect 'provides an element of flexibility to the application of the concept'.[70] Although the interpretation of habitual residence given by the European Court of Justice in *Re A* was not designed specifically for application in the context of child abduction, it appears to be sufficiently wide to encompass both factors, that is, the factual element as well as the importance of the intention of the parents in determining the residence of the child. The definition responds to the need to ensure the factual connection between the child and the place of habitual residence in referring to the following: a period of actual residence in the country ('duration'); and evidence of the child's integration into the environment ('linguistic knowledge', 'the place and conditions of attendance at school', and 'the family and social relationships of the child in that State'). The importance of the relationship between the child and his/her primary carer in establishing habitual residence of the child in child abduction cases is indirectly accounted for through the court's

[68] Beaumont and McEleavy (n 14) 90.
[69] R Lamont, 'Habitual Residence and Brussels II bis' (n 64) 267.
[70] *Ibid*, 267 and 268.

reference to 'reasons for the stay on the territory of a Member State and the family's move to that State'. More particularly, the significance of intention of the parents is highlighted in paragraph 40 of the judgment, which says:

> As the Advocate General pointed out in point 44 of her Opinion, the parents' intention to settle permanently with the child in another Member State, manifested by certain tangible steps such as the purchase or lease of a residence in the host Member State, may constitute an indicator of the transfer of the habitual residence. Another indicator may be constituted by lodging an application for social housing with the relevant services of that State.[71]

The matter was re-examined by the ECJ in 2010 in another non-child abduction case, *Mercredi v Chaffe*.[72] This case arose from proceedings in the United Kingdom between the father and the mother of a baby girl, concerning rights of custody in respect of that child. The girl was born in the UK and was taken by her mother to the island of Réunion when she was two months old. The court reiterated the principles articulated in *Re A*, emphasising the importance of the 'social and family environment of the child' for a determination of the habitual residence of the child.[73] The identifying factors of the 'social and family environment of the child' differ according to the age of the child.[74] In the case of a young child, the environment is basically a family environment determined by reference to the custodial parent.[75] This is particularly true in relation to an infant as 'an infant necessarily shares the social and family environment of the circle of people on whom he or she is dependent'.[76] The factors which should be taken into consideration include the duration, regularity, conditions and reasons for the stay, the custodial parent's geographic and family origins, and the family and social connections of the custodial parent and the child with the Member State.[77]

The following section turns to cases decided on habitual residence under the Brussels II bis Regulation. In particular, the Irish case of *B v G*[78] is examined.

i. The Brussels II bis case of B v G: *Analysis*

Facts of the case: The instant case involved a 12-year-old boy. The applicant, a Latvian national, was the father of the child. The respondent was the child's stepfather, a Romanian citizen living in Ireland. The respondent was married to the child's mother, a Latvian national. The applicant and the mother were never married. The mother came to Ireland in 2003 and was joined by the child in

[71] Case C-523/07 *A* [2009] ECR I-2805, para 40.

[72] Case C-497/10 PPU *Mercredi v Chaffe* [2010] ECR I-14309. For academic comment on the case see Beaumont and McEleavy, (n 64) 208–9. See also G Douglas, 'Jurisdiction: Brussels IIR—Habitual Residence' (2011) 41 *Family Law* 351.

[73] Case C-497/10 PPU *Mercredi v Chaffe*, judgment of 22 December 2010 [2011] OJ C55/30, para 53.

[74] *Ibid*.

[75] *Ibid*, para 54.

[76] *Ibid*, para 55.

[77] *Ibid*, para 56.

[78] *B v G* [2009] IEHC 104.

August 2007. In Ireland, the child lived with the mother and the respondent. On 8 May 2008, however, the mother died of cancer. The respondent travelled with the child to Latvia, for the purpose of the mother's funeral. After the funeral, on 28 May 2008, the respondent returned with the child to Ireland where the boy was attending school. The child returned with the consent of the applicant who, however, later contended that he had only agreed to the boy going back to Ireland until the end of the school year in Ireland on 15 June 2008. In September 2008, the applicant came to Ireland to bring the child back with him to Latvia. The boy, however, did not return, so the applicant initiated return proceedings under the Convention and the Regulation.

Legal issue: The sole issue in question before the court was the one of the habitual residence of the child.

The habitual residence of the child: It was agreed that prior to the death of the mother on 8 May 2008 the child had been habitually resident in Ireland. Counsel for the applicant, however, contended that, subsequent to 8 May 2008 but prior to 15 June 2008, the child ceased to be habitually resident in Ireland and acquired habitual residence in Latvia. Counsel for the applicant submitted that following the death of the mother, the applicant became the sole guardian of the child and therefore could make a unilateral decision as to where the child should live. His decision that the boy should reside in Latvia, even without it being implemented, then had the effect of changing the habitual residence of the child from Ireland to Latvia.

Ruling: The court, however, rejected the applicant's submission and concluded that following 8 May 2008 the child continued to be habitually resident in Ireland. There was no change in his place of residence. Without a change in his residence, the child could not have acquired a habitual residence in Latvia. Before reaching the judgment, the court reviewed key decisions on habitual residence made in Ireland. A reference was made to a statement by Fennelly J in a Supreme Court decision in *PAS v AFS*[79] emphasising that the issue of habitual residence was essentially one of fact. Fennelly J then cited a passage from the judgment of McGuinness J in *CM v Delegación Provincial de Malaga*:

> [h]abitual residence is not a term of art, but a matter of fact, to be decided on the evidence in this particular case. It is generally accepted that where a child is residing in the lawful custody of its parent …, its habitual residence will be that of the parent. However, the habitual residence of the child is not governed by the same rigid rules of dependency as apply under the law of domicile and that actual facts of the case must always be taken into account.[80]

The above approach was accepted by the court as a benchmark for determination of the instant case. Additionally, the court found the applicant's submission that his mere decision had changed the habitual residence of the child 'contrary to the

[79] *PAS v AFS* [2005] 1 ILRM 306, [2004] IESC 95.
[80] *CM v Delegación Provincial de Malaga* [1999] IEHC 138, [1999] 2 IR 363 para 63.

well-established view of the courts in this jurisdiction, and in England and Wales, that the terms "habitual residence" or "habitually resident" ... are not to be treated as terms of art with some special meaning, but rather, to be understood according to the ordinary and natural meaning of the two words they contain'.[81]

ii. Pre-Brussels II bis Interpretation of the Concept of Habitual Residence in Ireland[82]

In Ireland, the issue of habitual residence in the context of the 1980 Hague Abduction Convention was for the first time dealt with comprehensively by McGuinness J in the case of *CM v Delegación Provincial de Malaga*.[83] *CM v Delegación Provincial de Malaga* involved a child born in Spain in October 1995 and placed in a lawful custody of Delegación Provincial de Malaga (that is, a government body responsible for matters of child care and adoption in Spain). The biological mother of the child was an Irish citizen. She moved to Spain in May 1995 and stayed there until December 1995. Between October and December 1995, discussions were held between the mother and the above authority about a possibility of fostering or adoption of the child. The mother decided to sign a form consenting to a foster placement and the future adoption of the child, and handed the child over to the above authority. In December 1995, the mother moved back to Ireland, leaving the child in Spain. In February 1996, the child was placed for adoption. In the meantime, however, the mother contacted the above authority from Ireland and sought the return of the child. She submitted that she only intended to place the child in temporary care and did not wish her to be placed for adoption. The mother commenced proceedings before the Spanish courts seeking the custody and the return of the child. She also initiated proceedings before the Irish courts seeking a declaratory order pursuant to Section 15 of the 1991 Child Abduction and Enforcement of Custody Orders Act (a statute implementing the 1980 Hague Abduction Convention in Ireland; hereafter: the 1991 Act). Section 15 of the 1991 Act, giving force to Article 15 of the Convention,[84] states:

> The Court may, on an application made for the purposes of Article 15 of the Hague Convention by any person appearing to the Court to have an interest in the matter, make a declaration that the removal of any child from, or his retention outside, the State was wrongful within the meaning of Article 3 of that Convention.

[81] *B v G* [2009] IEHC 104 para 21.

[82] For analysis of the operation of the Convention in Ireland, see P Ward, 'In Practice—Family Law in Ireland: Child Abduction. A Rare Refusal to Return' (2000) 30 *Family Law* 59.

[83] *CM v Delegación Provincial de Malaga* [1999] IEHC 138, [1999] 2 IR 363.

[84] 'The judicial or administrative authorities of a Contracting State may, prior to the making of an order for the return of the child, request that the applicant obtain from the authorities of the State of the habitual residence of the child a decision or other determination that the removal or retention was wrongful within the meaning of Article 3 of the Convention, where such a decision or determination may be obtained in that State.'

One of the preliminary issues that had to be determined prior to making such a declaration was the question of where the child had been habitually resident prior to her alleged retention by Spanish authorities. The mother argued that the habitual residence of a child born to an unmarried woman is that of its mother and will follow the mother's habitual residence if she decides to move to another jurisdiction. Consequently, the mother's return to Ireland in December 1995 resulted in the child ceasing to be habitually resident in Spain and becoming habitually resident in Ireland. The respondent, however, submitted that there was no general rule that habitual residence of a child strictly followed that of its parent, as the concept of habitual residence was one of fact.

McGuinness J reviewed a number of authorities, including relevant decisions of English courts.[85] Reference was made also to an older Irish decision in the case of *CK v CK*.[86] Children involved in this case were born in Ireland and resided there until 1989 when their parents took them to live in Australia. The marriage, however, broke up and the father unilaterally decided to bring the children back to Ireland with the intention to remain there. The mother sought the return of the children to Australia. The father claimed that the children were habitually resident in Ireland. His contention was, however, rejected by Denham J, suggesting that habitual residence was a matter of fact, rather than a theoretical concept. Denham J also pointed out that the concept of habitual residence was entirely distinct from the concept of domicile.

In view of the facts of the given case, McGuinness J made the following findings:

> In the instant case the child C was born in Spain, was placed in the lawful custody of the first named Defendant in Spain, and has never left Spain. The mother has returned to Ireland and has sought the return of the child. I cannot accept that the mother's decision can of itself result in the change of the child's habitual residence to Ireland when the child has never, at any stage, been present in Ireland. As said by Stuart-White J such a decision would 'offend common sense'. I therefore hold that on the facts of this case, the habitual residence of the child C is Spain.[87]

Accordingly, McGuinness J concluded:

> It seems to me to be settled law in both England and Ireland that 'habitual residence' is not a term of art, but a matter of fact, to be decided on the evidence in this particular case. It is generally accepted that where a child is residing in the lawful custody of its parent (in the instant case the mother) its habitual residence will be that of the parent. However, the habitual residence of the child is not governed by the same rigid rules of dependency as apply under the laws of domicile and the actual facts of the case must always be taken into account. Finally, a person, whether a child or an adult must, for at

[85] *Re S: (Habitual Residence)* [1998] AC 750; *Re H (Minors) (Abduction: Custody Rights)* [1991] 2 AC 476; *C v S (a Minor) (Abduction)* [1990] 2 AC 562; *Re A (Abduction: Habitual Residence)* [1998] 1 FLR 497; and *Re M (Abduction: Habitual Residence)* [1996] 1 FLR 887.

[86] *CK v CK* [1994] 1 IR 260; [1993] ILRM 534.

[87] *CM v Delegación Provincial de Malaga* [1999] IEHC 138, [1999] 2 IR 363 para 64.

least some reasonable period of time, be actually present in a country before he or she can be held to be habitually resident there.[88]

The above conclusion was approvingly referred to in a High Court decision in the 2002 case of *Minister for Justice Equality and Law Reform v C (V)*.[89] Two years later, in 2004, the approach delineated by McGuinness J in *CM v Delegación Provincial de Malaga* was approved of by the Supreme Court in the case of *PAS v AFS*.[90] In this case, the respondent mother, an Irish citizen, moved to Canada in 1999 where she met the applicant, the father of the child. The respondent became pregnant and travelled to visit her parents in Ireland for two weeks. Whilst in Ireland, she was diagnosed with a brain tumour. Her treatment was postponed until after she had had the baby. The father visited her in Ireland on several occasions. One month after the birth of the child the mother underwent successful surgery. Following the operation, in February 2004, the parents returned with the child to Canada. The mother, however, shortly thereafter returned with the child to Ireland, contending that the parties had not intended to stay in Canada permanently. The father sought a return of the child, arguing that the child had been habitually resident in Canada immediately prior to the alleged wrongful removal.

The trial judge found that the parties' return to Canada in February 2004 was intended to be temporary, and therefore the child could not became habitually resident in Canada solely as a result of this visit. It followed that habitual residence in Canada had to be established by reference to prior events. Consequently, the central issue that arose was whether, for the purposes of the Convention, a child could be habitually resident in a country where he or she had never been physically present.

[88] *Ibid*, para 63.

[89] *Minister for Justice Equality and Law Reform v C (V)* [2002] IEHC 52. This case involved retention of an eight-year-old girl by her maternal aunt, the respondent, in Ireland. The respondent had been appointed by the mother as the testamentary guardian for the child. The applicant was the child's father who had been married to the mother until their divorce in 1985. Six years later the mother and the father reconciled and resumed living together for a period of three years in England at which time the child concerned was born in 1994. In February 2000, the mother was diagnosed with terminal cancer. She returned to her family in Ireland taking the minor with her with the consent of the father. Following the mother's death in December 2000, the child continued living in Ireland, staying with her aunt. The matter was heard by the High Court. The trial judge concluded that the move of the mother with the child to Ireland after she had been diagnosed with cancer, although with consent of the father, was for the purposes of her medical treatment only. Consequently, there was no change in habitual residence as a result of this arrangement, and the child did not cease to be habitually resident in England. The case was appealed to the Supreme Court who remitted the case to the High Court. The Supreme Court held that, in accordance with Art 3 of the Convention, the question of habitual residence must be *decided as a fact* at the time immediately before the removal or retention. This led the Supreme Court to the conclusion that prior to addressing the issue of habitual residence the High Court must determine the actual date of the wrongful removal or retention. The High Court, after having made the necessary findings, concluded that by the appointment of the aunt as the child's guardian, the mother had clearly indicated her intention for the child to remain habitually resident in Ireland, rather than in England. The court added: 'The mother was exercising rights of custody over the child. That custody was shared with the grandmother and the respondent. The mother in exercising rights of custody was entitled to determine the child's place of residence'.

[90] *PAS v AFS* [2005] 1 ILRM 306, [2004] IESC 95.

Fennelly J at the Supreme Court, referring to the opinion of McGuinness J in *CM v Delegación Provincial de Malaga*, pointed out that the issue of habitual residence was not 'a legal term of art' but a matter of fact. The learned judge held:

> The Convention deliberately left the notion of habitual residence undefined. It would be undesirable to lay down rigid criteria for the assessment of situations that were as variable as human nature.

The above analysis points to the conclusion that courts in Ireland have been very consistent in interpreting the notion of the habitual residence for the purposes of the 1980 Convention. The following principles have been accepted as general rules by the High Court of Ireland and the Irish Supreme Court:

1. The issue of habitual residence is essentially one of fact.
2. Habitual residence is not governed by the same rigid rules of dependency as applied under the law of domicile.
3. Generally, a person must, for at least some reasonable period of time, be actually present in a country before he/she could be held to be habitually resident there.[91]

The first two principles arose as relevant also in the above-analysed Brussels II bis case of *B v G*. As explicitly stated in the decision itself, both principles were applied in accordance with the established jurisprudence. This demonstrates that, contrary to the suggested hypothesis, the post-Brussels II bis interpretation of habitual residence has adhered to the traditional approach, without a tendency towards a more liberal attitude to the concept.

C. Conclusions

Overall, the above analysis has neither confirmed nor rejected the theory of the more liberal interpretation of the non-Article 13 grounds for judicial refusal. On the one hand, the Brussels II bis interpretation of Article 20 in *Foyle Health and Social Services Trust* in Ireland markedly departed from established jurisprudence (in Ireland as well as in Australia, Canada and the US), showing signs of evasion of Article 13(1)(b) in favour of Article 20. This unwelcome shift, however, appears to have been later corrected by *Nottingham County Council*. On the other hand, the interpretation of habitual residence in the Brussels II bis case of *B v G* strictly adhered to the traditional understanding of the concept in Ireland.

Given the outcomes, the case law analysis does not provide sufficient evidence to support the assumption of a shift towards a more liberal approach to the non-Article 13 concepts, as indicated by the statistical survey. It must, however, be emphasised that only a tiny fraction of all child abduction decisions become

[91] Most recently, the above principles were reaffirmed by the Irish Supreme Court in the case of *S v S* [2009] IESC 77.

publicly available and consequently, at two, the number of available 'suspicious' Brussels II bis refusals provides only a very small sample. In addition, the case law covers just one jurisdiction as both decisions come from Ireland. On the other hand, it must be borne in mind that the statistical survey represents merely a small sample of Brussels II bis return applications (applications made within the period of only one year), and might therefore not be reflecting overall long-term trends. Nevertheless, it should be pointed out that, like the outcomes of our survey, the 2008 findings were similarly inconclusive as they neither confirmed nor rejected the assumption of avoidance of Article 13 exceptions to return in favour of non-Article 13 defences.[92]

Despite the lack of conclusive evidence, it is nevertheless suggested that further research be undertaken into the area. The reason behind this recommendation is that if the presumption of a more liberal interpretation of non-Article 13 concepts is correct, then this undesirable development needs to be clearly identified, and addressed at the relevant level.

II. Protection of the Abductor Parent and the Child upon the Return

The statistical survey has revealed that the proportion of judicial refusals based on the Article 13(1)(b) exception decreased significantly from 35% in 2003 to 23% in 2005/06.[93] This implies that, as intended by the drafters of the Regulation, more cases involving the grave risk of harm defence resulted in a judicial return order. Undeniably, on the one hand, Article 11(4) deserves credit for the reinforcement of the Convention's return policy. On the other hand, however, there is a concern that, whilst sparing no effort to fulfil the ambitions of the Regulation, courts might in some cases compromise the safety of the child and/or the returning parent. It has rightly been pointed out that 'it is also dangerous, if the objective becomes high return statistics, rather than the safety of the child'.[94]

It must, nevertheless, be noted that the 2008 survey recorded a marked increase in the proportion of judicial refusals based on the Article 13(1)(b) exception. At 40%, the percentage was 17% higher than the 2005/06 proportion. It is very surprising that the figure was even higher than the 2003 proportion of 35%. How can this unexpected development be explained in the face of tighter requirements imposed by the Regulation? One possibility is that there are large fluctuations from year to year, pointing to the need to exercise caution when drawing conclusions

92 See Chapter 5, section entitled 'Reason for Judicial Refusal Combined'.

93 See Chapter 5, section entitled 'Reason for Judicial Refusal Combined'.

94 The Honourable Judge Shireen Fisher, 'How Far Did the Conclusions of the Fifth Meeting of the Special Commission Advance the Interpretation of Article 13(1)B, Grave Risk Defence?' (2007) 12 *Judges' Newsletter* 54, 55.

based solely on statistical data. Another possible explanation, however, is that avoidance of Article 13(1)(b) in the first year of operation of the Regulation was due to judges having been alerted to Article 11(4) and, in fear of not having their decisions 'trumped', opted rather for avoidance of Article 13(1)(b) (and other Article 13 exceptions).[95] This diversionary tactic in relation to Article 13(1)(b), could, however, have been only temporary as judges later realised that refusing reasons on the basis of Article 13(1)(b) would allow for at least a temporary protection of the child (if distrusting the requesting State), whilst it would lift the burden of the final word from their shoulders and 'throw the ball' into the hands of the requesting State. Judges could thus refuse a return safe in the knowledge that a welfare-based enquiry will be undertaken promptly in the Member State of origin with the full co-operation and assistance of the courts in the requested State (Articles 11(6)–11(8) of the Regulation). If this was the case, the ultimate effect of this strategy would be that, contrary to the intention of the drafters of the Regulation, the instrument has in effect widened the discretion not to return a child under the Hague Convention.

A. Article 11(4) Approach to the Grave Risk of Harm Defence

According to the rule set out by Article 13(1)(b) of the 1980 Hague Abduction Convention, the court is not obliged to order the return of the child if there is a grave risk that the return would expose the child to physical or psychological harm or otherwise place the child in an intolerable situation. In contrast, Article 11(4) of the Brussels II bis Regulation requires the court to order the return of the child even if it will put the child at risk, if it is established that the authorities in the requesting State have made arrangements to secure the child's protection after the return. Article 11(4) provides:

> A court cannot refuse to return a child on the basis of Article 13(1)(b) of the 1980 Hague Convention if it is established that adequate arrangements have been made to secure the protection of the child after his or her return.

Formally, Article 11(4) of the Brussels II bis Regulation goes a step further than Article 13(1)(b) of the 1980 Hague Abduction Convention.[96] Nevertheless, some academics have suggested that in terms of outcomes the provision was not likely to make much difference, at least not for common law jurisdictions.[97] Indeed,

[95] See section entitled 'More Liberal Interpretation of the Key Concepts of the Convention in Order to Avoid Judicial Refusals Based on Article 13' above.

[96] Commission Practice Guide (n 65) 40.

[97] Professor Lowe and Professor McEleavy believe that Art 13(1)(b) of the Convention has always been interpreted in a strict fashion, ie essentially identical with the wording of Art 11(4) of the Regulation. Similarly Andrea Schulz, although recognising that Art 11(4) may bring about some change for civil law judges, reckons that the provision will not make any difference to common law judges. See N Lowe, 'Negotiating the Revised Brussels II Regulation' [2004] *International Family Law Journal* 205; P McEleavy, 'The New Child Abduction Regime in the European Union: Symbiotic

available case law from major common law jurisdictions shows that, although the Convention does not require courts to perform ameliorative measures analysis, the strict Article 11(4) approach had been taken in a number of leading Convention cases.

The central characteristic of the Article 11(4) approach is that 'the child shall always be returned if he/she can be protected in the Member State of origin'.[98] The restrictive understanding of the grave risk of harm defence reflected in the Regulation is fully 'in line with the letter and the spirit of the Convention'.[99] On the other hand, however, it is submitted that Article 11(4) suffers from several defects that may in some cases prove fatal to the safety of the returning child and/or the safety of the returning parent.

B. Flaws of Article 11(4)

The first basic flaw of Article 11(4) is that the provision lacks clarity as to the question of where the burden of proof lies. Second, there is a lack of precise regulation of the responsibilities of the Central Authorities in facilitating a safe return in the Regulation as well as in the Convention. Third, Article 11(4) is based on an unrealistic presumption that all Member States are able to provide the same level of protection to the returning children. Fourth, Article 11(4) is silent on another important question—the extent of investigations that should be conducted where the grave risk of harm defence is raised. Finally, Article 11(4) ignores the reality that in many cases, especially those involving domestic violence, the risk of harm the child will be facing upon the return is interrelated to the risk of harm to the returning parent. Unfortunately, the provision gives no thought to the safety of the returning parent.

i. Burden of Proof

Article 11(4) has been welcomed by some academics as a guarantee of a higher degree of protection of children upon their return to the requesting State than it was under the Convention.[100] It was suggested that in Convention cases, it had only been presumed that children would be protected upon their return to the requesting State even if there was evidence of a grave risk of harm in the State of

Relationship or Forced Partnership?' (2005) 1 *Journal of Private International Law* 1, n 106; and A Schulz, 'The New Brussels II Regulation and the Hague Conventions of 1980 and 1996' [2004] *International Family Law Journal* 22.

[98] Commission Practice Guide (n 65) 40.

[99] EP Vera, 'On the 25th Anniversary of the Hague Convention on the Civil Aspects of International Child Abduction' (2006) 12 *Judges' Newsletter* 15, 17. See also Schulz, 'The New Brussels II Regulation', arguing that 'The exceptional nature of a refusal to return a child as a last resort is thus strengthened by Article 11(4) of Brussels II bis'.

[100] *McEleavy* (n 97) 5–34, 26.

origin.[101] There was no obligation to show that there were actually measures in place to protect the child upon his/her return to the requesting State. In contrast, under the Regulation it must be 'established' that adequate arrangements to protect the child have been made.

At first sight, the obligation to demonstrate the existence of protective measures in the requesting State may indeed seem to be a welcome development. The drawback, however, is that Article 11(4) is silent on the question of the allocation of the burden of proof as to the existence of 'adequate arrangements'. Indeed, the formulation 'if it is established' is rather vague; it does not indicate whether it is for the left-behind parent to demonstrate that protective measures are in place in the requesting State or whether it is to be assumed that adequate arrangements to protect the child have been made unless the alleged abductor shows otherwise.[102]

Under the Convention, the burden of proof as to the presence of a grave risk of harm to the child in the State of origin lies on the party which opposes the return of the child.[103] In most cases, this party will be the alleged abductor.[104] The Explanatory Report further clarifies why this particular approach has been chosen. It states that 'the solution adopted is indeed limited to stating the general legal maxim that he who avers a fact (or a right) must prove it'.[105]

In theory, the above statement could be useful in dealing with the problem of the burden of proof under Article 11(4). If the logic of the Convention is applied to Article 11(4), it is the applicant who is to prove the existence of protective

[101] See, eg, R Schuz, 'The Hague Child Abduction Convention and Children's Rights' (2002) 12 *Transnational Law & Contemporary Problems* 393, 448, expressing the view that '[t]he requested court's unquestioning faith in the ability of the authorities of the requesting state to protect the mother and the child is usually based on considerations of comity rather than on hard fact'. See also K Wolfe, 'A Tale of Two States: Successes and Failures of the 1980 Hague Convention on the Civil Aspects of International Child Abduction in the United States and Germany' (2000–2001) 33 *New York University Journal of International Law & Politics* 285. Wolfe states that the problem of availability of protective measures in the State of habitual residence requires the requested State to evaluate the sufficiency of child protective measures of the requesting State. Such attitude is, however, against the spirit of the Convention based on the concept of mutual trust between the Contracting States. The requested State must, therefore, have confidence in the willingness and in the ability of the State of habitual residence to protect the child upon the return.

[102] N Lowe *et al*, *The New Brussels II Regulation: A Supplement to International Movement of Children* (Bristol, Jordan Publishing Ltd, 2005) 28.

[103] Art 13 of the Hague Abduction Convention states: 'Notwithstanding the provisions of the preceding Article, the judicial or administrative authority of the requested State is not bound to order the return of the child if the person, institution or other body which opposes its return establishes that … (b) there is a grave risk of harm that his or her return would expose the child to physical or psychological harm or otherwise place the child in an intolerable situation'. See also *Re E (Children)* [2012] 1 AC 144, [2011] UKSC 27 para 32.

[104] The Explanatory Report explains that the party opposing the return of the child does not necessarily need to be the abductor. See Explanatory Report to the 1980 Convention (n 12) para 114. Nevertheless, in most cases, it will be the alleged abductor.

[105] Explanatory Report to the 1980 Convention (n 12) para 114.

measures in the requesting State.[106] This approach was adopted in a United States Convention case, *Simcox v Simcox*.[107] On appeal, the Sixth Circuit opined that the burden of establishing the 'appropriateness and efficacy' of the protective measures lay on the applicant.

Another possible alternative is that the omission of the question of burden of proof was deliberate by the drafters of the Regulation, allowing space for different jurisdictions to apply particularities of their legal system. In civil law jurisdictions, based on an inquisitional system, the adjudicating judge would be expected to seek relevant information from the Central Authorities or directly from his counterpart judge in the requesting State. In common law jurisdictions, conversely, it would be the litigants, rather than the judge, who would be expected to take the initiative to find and present evidence.

Any suggestion, however, is only conjecture. As no guidance is given in the Practice Guide, it remains unclear what the actual intention of the drafters of Article 11(4) was. Nevertheless, it is submitted here that the optimal approach would be the one adopted in *Simcox v Simcox*.[108] The imposition of the burden of proof on the applicant would work towards securing a higher degree of safety for the returning child. Admittedly, however, this scheme is not suitable for undertakings, albeit appropriate to all other types of protective measures.

ii. Co-operation of Central Authorities

Another source of concern with respect to the involvement of the Central Authorities in securing the safe return of the child is the lack of a precise regulation of such responsibilities in the existing instruments.

Article 55 of the Regulation lays down the rules for the co-operation of Central Authorities. Among other responsibilities, the provision imposes on the Member States a duty to 'provide information and assistance to holders of parental responsibility seeking recognition and enforcement of decisions on their territory, in particular concerning … the return of the child'.[109] There is, however, no specific provision that would require the Central Authorities to facilitate the safe return of the child.

At the global level, Article 7(h) of the Convention States that Central Authorities shall take all appropriate measures 'to provide such administrative arrangements as may be necessary and appropriate to secure the safe return of the child'. This provision, however, having attracted heavy criticism, is rightly described as

[106] Alfieri suggests shifting the burden of proof to the petitioner who then must 'prove, beyond reasonable doubt, that undertakings and other ameliorative measures will ensure the physical and psychological safety of the child'. J Alfieri, 'Trauma, Recovery, and Transnational Child Abduction: Posttraumatic Stress Disorder as Psychological Harm under the Hague Convention on Civil Aspects of International Child Abduction' (2003) 5 *Oregon Review of International Law* 40, 72.

[107] *Simcox v Simcox* 511 F Supp 3d 594 (6th Cir 2007) 605, 611.

[108] *Ibid.*

[109] Brussels II bis Regulation Art 55(b).

very vague and soft.[110] Partially in response to this criticism, the Fourth Special Commission attempted to translate Article 7(h) into a more detailed text. The conclusion adopted was then reaffirmed by the Fifth Special Commission.[111] The Commission held:

> To the extent permitted by the powers of their Central Authority and by the legal and social welfare systems of their country, Contracting States accept that Central Authorities have an obligation under Article 7 h) to ensure appropriate child protection agencies are alerted so they may act to protect the welfare of children upon return in certain cases where their safety is at issue until the jurisdiction of the appropriate court has been effectively invoked.
>
> ...
>
> The measures which may be taken in fulfilment of the obligation under Article 7 h) to take or cause to be taken an action to protect the welfare of children may include, for example:
>
> a) alerting the appropriate protection agencies or judicial authorities in the requesting State of the return of a child who may be in danger;
> b) advising the requested State, upon request, of the protective measures and services available in the requesting State to secure the safe return of a particular child.

The initiative of the Special Commissions, however, may be inadequate due to the non-binding nature of the Commissions' Recommendations. Professor Bucher, sharing a Swiss experience of a generally highly unsatisfactory co-operation between the Central Authorities in arranging the safe return of a child, called for a conversion of the conclusions of the Special Commissions into a more exact text that would form a basis for the co-operation between the Central Authorities and would be subject to regular monitoring.[112] Several suggestions have been made as to how this aim could be achieved.

First, it has been suggested that the 1996 Convention on Jurisdiction, Applicable Law, Recognition, Enforcement and Co-operation in Respect of Parental Responsibility and Measures for the Protection of Children[113] could be used to fill the gap in the Hague Abduction Convention as it contains rules on

[110] P Ripley, 'A Defence of the Established Approach to the Grave Risk of Harm Exception in the Hague Child Abduction Convention' (2008) 4 *Journal of Private International Law* 443, 463–4.

[111] Permanent Bureau of the Hague Conference, 'Report of the Fifth Special Commission Meeting to Review the Operation of the Hague Convention on the Civil Aspects of International Child Abduction and the Practical Implementation of the Hague Convention of 19 October 1996 on Jurisdiction, Applicable Law, Recognition, Enforcement and Co-operation in Respect of Parental Responsibility and Measures for the Protection of Children, 30 October—9 November 2006', available at www.hcch.net/upload/abduc97e.pdf.

[112] A Bucher, 'The Convention Should Be Revised!' (2006) 11 *Judges' Newsletter* 41, 42.

[113] Convention on Jurisdiction, Applicable Law, Recognition, Enforcement and Co-operation in Respect of Parental Responsibility and Measures for the Protection of Children (1996) (the 1996 Convention).

protective measures.[114] In particular, Article 11(1) of the 1996 Convention provides that:

> In all cases of urgency, the authorities of any Contracting State in whose territory the child or property belonging to the child is present have jurisdiction to take any necessary measures of protection.

The main provisions of the 1996 Convention have been incorporated into the Regulation.[115] The above rule on the emergency jurisdiction, however, does not appear to have been included into the Regulation. Nevertheless, Article 62 of the Regulation provides that the 1996 Convention shall continue to have effect in relation to matters not governed by the Regulation. This implies that the provision on the protective measures is applicable in the contracting parties to the 1996 Convention.

Another proposal was to supplement the Convention with a Protocol that would regulate in detail obligations and responsibilities of the Central Authorities in facilitating the safe return of a child.[116] The imposition of precise duties on the Central Authorities through the Protocol appears to be an attractive and reasonably realistic solution. The problem, however, is that parties to the Convention are not required to adopt a Protocol. Therefore, it is uncertain how many Member States would ratify or accede to it.[117] Nevertheless, it must be acknowledged that the added bonus of the Protocol is its potential of a global reach.

It is suggested here that, from the European perspective, a radical and effective reform could be achieved by an amendment to the Regulation itself. Article 11(4) should be revised and a provision listing specific duties of the Central Authorities

[114] See, eg, MH Weiner, 'International Child Abduction and the Escape from Domestic Violence' (2000–2001) 69 *Fordham Law Review* 593, 682. For detailed explanation of the inter-relationship between the 1980 and the 1996 Conventions see Permanent Bureau of the Hague Conference, 'Revised Draft Practical Handbook on the Operation of the Hague Convention of 19 October 1996 on Jurisdiction, Applicable Law, Recognition and Co-operation in Respect of Parental Responsibility and Measures for the Protection of Children', Preliminary Document No 4 (2011) 87–93, available at www.hcch.net/upload/wop/abduct2011pd04e.pdf.

[115] F Lortie, 'The Communitarisation of Family Law—The Hague Conventions and the New Brussels II Regulation' (2005) 10 *Judges' Newsletter* 47, 49.

[116] See The Right Honourable Lord Justice Thorpe, 'The Hague Child Abduction Convention—24 Years On' (2006) 11 *Judges' Newsletter* 8, 10; P Beaumont, 'The Jurisprudence of the European Court of Human Rights and the European Court of Justice on the Hague Convention on International Child Abduction' (2008) 335 *Hague Recueil* 103; A Bucher, 'The New Swiss Federal Act on International Child Abduction' (2008) 4 *Journal of Private International Law* 139, 145; L Silberman, 'Patching Up the Abduction Convention: A Call for a New International Protocol and a Suggestion for Amendments to ICARA' (2003) 38 *Texas International Law Journal* 41; and Ripley, 'A Defence of the Established Approach' (n 110) 465. Generally on the protocol initiative at the Hague Conference on Private International Law see Permanent Bureau of the Hague Conference, 'Consultations on the Desirability and Feasibility of a Protocol to the Hague Convention of 25 October 1980 on the Civil Aspects of International Child Abduction: A Preliminary Report', Preliminary Document No 7 (2011), available at www.hcch.net/upload/wop/abduct2011pd07e.pdf.

[117] It may also be argued that the adoption of the protocol could create a situation akin to the one that has arisen from the modification of the Convention return mechanism by the Regulation. In particular, it would mean that children returned to different jurisdictions could be treated differently. A child returned to a contracting party to the protocol would be guaranteed a higher level of protection than a child returned to a non-protocol country.

in facilitating a safe return should be included. The Central Authorities would be obliged to take responsibility for issues such as safe temporary accommodation for the returning parent and the child pending the custody proceedings or removal of criminal sanctions against the returning parent. The Central Authorities would also be under the duty to ensure that appropriate child welfare and child protection agencies are not only alerted but actively involved if the child and/or the abducting parent are in danger upon their return to the requesting State. No less importantly, the Central Authorities would be responsible for initiating substantive proceedings before an appropriate court, if no court had been seized with the matter prior to the abduction or pending the return proceedings. The involvement of the Central Authorities would, however, not end with the moment of a successful invocation of the jurisdiction of the appropriate court. It would exceed this point in the sense that the Central Authorities would have continuing responsibilities to ensure the safety of the child by monitoring the child's situation.[118] A compulsory progress report would then be prepared by the requesting Central Authority and sent to the Central Authority in the requested State. If the requested court expressed an interest in the progress of the case, the requested Central Authority would then be able to keep the judge informed of developments and/or forward him the progress report.[119]

iii. Variation in Standards

The Practice Guide states that it will be the Central Authority of the requesting State that will act as assessor of the existence and the adequacy of the arrangements to protect the child upon his/her return to the requesting jurisdiction. This information will then be passed on by the Central Authority to the adjudicating judge. The Practice Guide states:

> It will generally be difficult for the judge to assess the factual circumstances in the Member State of origin. The assistance of the central authorities of the Member State of origin will be vital to assess whether or not protective measures have been taken in that country and whether they will adequately secure the protection of the child upon his or her return.[120]

[118] There have been a number of voices advocating the importance of follow-up provisions within the framework of the Convention. See, eg, The Honourable Mr Justice Wall, 'International Child Abduction' (1996) 18 *Liverpool Law Review* 167, 172–3; A Bucher, 'The Convention Should Be Revised!' (2006) 11 *Judges' Newsletter* 41, 42; and EL Buckwalter, 'In the Best Interest of the Child' (2006) *The Berkeley Electronic Press*, Paper 1166, available at www.law.bepress.com/cgi/viewcontent.cgi?article=5555&context=expresso. Follow-up provisions have also been mentioned in the context of a possible protocol to the Hague Convention under the heading 'Providing for an Exchange of Information Following the Return of the Child'. See Consultations on the Desirability and Feasibility of a Protocol (n 116) 16.

[119] The Honourable Justice Wall in his article International Child Abduction, writing from the perspective of a requested judge, points out the importance of follow-up after the child's return. See Wall, 'International Child Abduction'.

[120] Commission Practice Guide (n 65) 40.

It is submitted here that the above recommendation has an inherent shortcoming. In particular, it is based on an unrealistic assumption that all Member States are able to provide the same level of protection to the returning child. It does not take into consideration that different Central Authorities may have different standards, depending especially on the financial resources available in the jurisdiction and the level of co-operation between authorities involved. There is no uniform definition of the 'adequacy' of the arrangements or any minimum requirements to consider the arrangements sufficient to protect the child. Consequently, what might appear sufficient to a Central Authority in one Member State might under the same circumstances appear insufficient to a Central Authority in another Member State. Although it is understandable that the adequacy of arrangements must first of all be assessed on the basis of the facts of an individual case, the matter of fact is that children returned to different jurisdictions will enjoy a different level of protection.

The danger of a lower degree of protection lies especially with the 'new' Member States.[121]

iv. Contradictory Statements

The Practice Guide brings confusion into another aspect of Article 11(4). The provision demands the return to be ordered only if it is shown that adequate arrangements to protect the child *have been made* in the requesting State. The Practice Guide, however, casts doubt on the required timing of the adoption of the protective measures. It indirectly raises a question of whether the adequate arrangements must already be in place at the time of the return order or whether it is sufficient that there is evidence that the authorities in the requesting State are prepared to make these arrangements. Contrary to the wording of Article 11(4), the Practice Guide states that it suffices for the purposes of the return order if there is willingness on the side of the authorities in the requesting State to ensure the protection of the child upon his/her return. Commenting on Article 11(4) the Practice Guide states:

> The Regulation … [extends] the obligation to order the return of the child to cases where a return could expose the child to [physical or psychological] harm, but it is nevertheless established that the authorities in the Member State of origin *have made or are prepared to make* adequate arrangements to secure the protection of the child after the return[122] (emphasis added).

In the following paragraph, however, the Practice Guide lays down that:

> [i]t is not sufficient that procedures exist in the Member State of origin for the protection of the child, but it must be established that the authorities in the Member State of origin have taken concrete measures to protect the child in question.[123]

[121] For a more detailed analysis of the problems with the application of the Brussels II bis Regulation in the 'new' Member States see section entitled 'Judicial and Administrative Qualities in the "New" Member States of the European Union' below.

[122] Commission Practice Guide (n 65) 40.

[123] *Ibid.*

There is no doubt that the Regulation takes precedence over the Practice Guide. Consequently, it is the wording of Article 11(4), rather than the Practice Guide's commentary, that is binding. Article 11(4) is clear: the existence of the protective measures (not just their potential) is an essential prerequisite for a return order. It is therefore not expected that the contradiction within the Practice Guide could cause practical difficulties. Nevertheless, the inconsistency shows that the document was drafted without sufficient consideration.

v. *Investigation of Allegations*

Article 11(4) instructs a court not to refuse the return of a child on the basis of the grave risk of harm defence, if it is established that adequate arrangements have been made to secure the protection of the child after his or her return. The provision of Article 11(4) raises an important procedural issue. In particular, it is the question to what extent investigations should be conducted in intra-EU abductions when dealing with the Article 13(1)(b) defence. Is it expected from the requested court to first establish whether 'grave risk' exists and then proceed to the examination of the availability of the protective measures, or should the requested court assess only the availability of the protective measures without investigating the presence of the 'grave risk'? Each of the two approaches has its pros and cons and these must be weighed up carefully. The former approach can be criticised on the basis that it may, contrary to the philosophy of the Convention, turn the 'grave risk' defence into a 'best interest' inquiry, usurping the task of custody proceedings. This would in turn significantly slow down the proceedings. On the other hand, however, a rigid adherence to the latter approach could prove dangerous to the safety of the returning children. Indeed, it is tricky to 'tailor' effective protective measures without first establishing the nature and the gravity of the harm.

The Practice Guide is silent on this issue and so it is uncertain what the authors of the Regulation had in mind when drafting Article 11(4). It may be suggested that guidance could be obtained from the Convention cases where the grave risk of harm defence was dealt with in accordance with the Article 11(4) approach. This recommendation, however, appears to be rather problematic as no homogenous view on the question of investigation of allegations was adopted by the courts adjudicating the Convention cases. For example, in a United States case, *Danaipour v McLarey*,[124] on appeal, the First Circuit held that the lower court had exceeded its authority in issuing undertakings before answering the grave risk question. The appellate court expressed the view that courts must first address the grave risk question and only then 'proceed intelligently down the next avenue of inquiry—whether the children can be returned safely to the country of habitual residence'.[125] In contrast, in another United States decision, *Blondin v Dubois*,[126]

[124] *Danaipour v McLarey* 286 F 3d 1 (1st Cir 2002).

[125] *Danaipour v McLarey* 286 F 3d 1 (1st Cir 2002) 15.

[126] *Blondin v Dubois* 189 F 3d 240 (2nd Cir 1999). The approach taken by the Second Circuit in *Blondin v Dubois* has been advocated by Professor Silberman, who recommended that courts 'fashion interim arrangements … to ensure the safety of the child'. Only 'if such alternatives are unavailable

the Second Circuit emphasised that before finding the grave risk of harm defence, the district court must consider whether 'any ameliorative measures' could be taken by the parties or by the authorities of the requesting State in order to eliminate the risk associated with the return of the child. Similarly, in an Australian case, *Cooper v Casey*,[127] the court refused to determine the factual issues of the case and instead focused only on the ability of the State of habitual residence to protect the children concerned. The court thus conveyed the view that 'grave risk' cannot be established if there is evidence that the requesting State has taken measures to secure the safety of the child upon his/her return.

Older Brussels II bis case law indicated a general tendency towards the first approach. In a High Court case, *Arvidsson v Harris*,[128] two children were removed by their mother from Sweden to England. The grave risk of harm defence was based on the abductor mother's mental health. It was submitted that if a return order was made, the mother would suffer deterioration in her mental state and this would impair her capacity as a parent or she would commit suicide. Prior to turning to the question of protective measures, the court decided to hear expert testimony to determine the truth of the submission. The court ordered an examination of the mother by a psychiatrist. The psychiatrist's report confirmed that the mother was suffering from a severe depressive disorder and that suicide was a real risk in her case. The court accepted that the mother was suffering from severe clinical depression and was at a considerable risk of self-harm if the children were returned to Sweden. In case she would not return with them, there would still be a very grave risk of suicide. The court held that 'the loss of their mother in this way would be enormously harmful to the children'. Consequently, it was concluded that the Article 13(1)(b) exception was made out in this case. Only after the finding of the grave risk of harm was made, the court considered the availability of adequate arrangements in accordance with Article 11(4) of the Regulation. The court, however, concluded that it was not possible to make any arrangements to eliminate the risk of suicide as it was in this case. Accordingly, the return was refused.

In *K v K*,[129] two children, aged 10 and 12, were wrongfully removed from Greece to England. The children spent most of their lives in the United Kingdom; however, they were habitually resident in Greece prior to their wrongful removal. In 2003, the family relocated to Greece, the father's native country, for professional reasons. While in Greece, the marriage broke down and there were

should the court proceed to a full scale hearing to determine whether the defence has been substantively established.' L Silberman, 'Hague Convention on International Child Abduction: A Brief Overview and Case Law Analysis' (1994) 28 *Family Law Quarterly* 32, 33. In another of her articles, Professor Silberman sums up this approach as follows: '[Where] [t]he habitual residence state can be trusted to take action to ensure the protection of the spouse and the child … there should generally be no "grave risk" of harm if the child is returned to that state for further proceedings'. L Silberman, 'The Hague Child Abduction Convention Turns Twenty: Gender Politics and Other Issues' (2000) 33 *New York University Journal of International Law & Politics* 221, 240.

[127] *Cooper v Casey* (1995) FLC 92-575.
[128] *Arvidsson v Harris* [2006] EWHC 688 (Fam).
[129] *K v K* [2007] EWCA Civ 533, [2007] 2 FLR 996.

incidents of domestic violence towards the mother and the children. At Christmas 2006, an adult daughter of the couple travelled from university in the United Kingdom to visit her parents. In January 2007, she removed her younger brother and sister to England. The following day, the mother also flew to England. The father swiftly initiated return proceedings before the Family Division of the High Court. The respondent mother argued that the return would expose the children to a grave risk of psychological harm. In accordance with Article 11(2) of the Regulation,[130] the judge ordered the children to be interviewed by a CAFCASS officer. The court found the CAFCASS officer's report to be 'manifestly a most exceptionally strong report'. The officer concluded that the return would be emotionally and psychologically damaging to the children and that even their mother accompanying them would not serve to ameliorate this. The trial judge held that, although the instant case was a wrongful removal of the children, he could not ignore the extraordinary strength of the evidence of the CAFCASS officer. The judge concluded that it was sufficient to meet the standard required under Article 13(1)(b).

Following the ruling on the grave risk of harm, the trial judge proceeded to the question of the availability of the protective measures under Article 11(4). The judge found that no adequate arrangements could have been made to secure the protection of the children upon their return to Greece and exercised his discretion in favour of the abductor mother. The applicant father appealed. The appeal was dismissed and the refusal to return confirmed.

K v K[131] shows that the inclination towards the first approach (the availability of protective measures is not assessed without first determining the truth of the 'grave risk' allegations) may well be influenced by other provisions of the Regulation, in particular Article 11(2). It cannot be ruled out that Article 11(5)[132] will cause the same effect. The obligation to hear the child and the left-behind parent during the return proceedings may indeed encourage the courts to investigate the 'grave risk' submissions before turning to the Article 11(4) requirement of the investigation of adequate arrangements. From the perspective of the safety of the returning child, this is considered as a welcome development. Indeed, it is hazardous to make a judgment about another country's ability to protect a child from harm without first determining the scope and the nature of the harm. The only undesirable side effect of this approach is the length of the proceedings. In *K v K*,[133] attention was drawn to the requirement in Article 11(3) of the Regulation requiring Convention proceedings to be dealt with within six weeks. The appellate judge (Thorpe LJ) held that this extended to appeal hearings. He did not criticise the approach of the investigation of the 'grave risk' allegations but suggested

[130] Art 11(2) provides that when applying Arts 12 and 13 of the Convention, the child concerned must be given the opportunity to be heard (unless this appears inappropriate having regard to his or her age or degree of maturity).

[131] *K v K* [2007] EWCA Civ 533, [2007] 2 FLR 996.

[132] Art 11(5) states that a court cannot refuse the return of a child unless the applicant has been given an opportunity to be heard.

[133] *K v K* [2007] EWCA Civ 533, [2007] 2 FLR 996.

another way round this problem. In particular, he recommended that applications for permission to appeal should be made directly to the trial judge and that the normal 21-day period for lodging a notice of appeal should be restricted.[134]

The most recent developments have been marked by some unexpected twists and turns. In 2009, in *Neulinger and Shuruk v Switzerland*,[135] the European Court of Human Rights sitting as a Grand Chamber expressed the view that domestic courts were expected to engage in:

> [a]n in-depth examination of the entire family situation and of a whole series of factors, in particular of a factual, emotional, psychological, material and medical nature, and make a balanced and reasonable assessment of the respective interests of each person, with constant concern for determining what the best solution would be for the abducted child in the context of an application for his return to his country of origin.[136]

The court appeared to say that Hague Convention orders cannot be granted automatically and that the best interests of the child must be considered.[137] A return order where the above procedure was not followed would conflict with the UNCRC Article 3(1) (best interests of the child a primary consideration) or violate the Article 8 ECHR rights (respect for family and private life) of the child or the abducting parent.[138]

By endorsing the 'full-blown examination' avenue the court appeared to advocate an extreme version of the first approach. Not surprisingly, the decision was greeted with concern as it might have been read 'as requiring national courts to abandon the swift, summary approach that the Hague Convention envisages, and to move away from a restrictive interpretation of the Article 13 exceptions to a thorough, free-standing assessment of the overall merits of the situation'.[139] This interpretation was, however, rejected on two important occasions: first, by the President of the European Court of Human Rights, extra-judicially,[140] and

[134] *K v K* [2007] EWCA Civ 533 paras 27–30. See section 'Timing' below.

[135] *Neulinger and Shuruk v Switzerland* (App no 41615/07) ECtHR 6 July 2010.

[136] *Ibid*, para 139.

[137] *Ibid*, para 138. The court said: 'The child's best interests, from a personal development perspective, will depend on a variety of individual circumstances, in particular his age and level of maturity; the presence or absence of his parents and his environment and experiences (see the UNHCR Guidelines, para 52 above). For that reason, *those best interests must be assessed in each individual case*' (emphasis added).

[138] The court was requested to address the question whether a decision of the Swiss Government to order a child to be returned to Israel under the Hague Convention was a violation of Arts 8 and 6 of the European Convention for the Protection of Human Rights and Fundamental Freedoms. The court decided that enforcement of the return order in that case would violate the Art 8 ECHR rights of the mother and the child. *Ibid*, para 151.

[139] Permanent Bureau of the Hague Conference, 'Conclusions and Recommendations of the Sixth Meeting of the Special Commission to Review the Operation of the Hague Convention of 25 October 1980 on the Civil Aspects of International Child Abduction, 01–10 June 2011' part I, para 48, available at www.hcch.net/upload/concl28sc6_e.pdf.

[140] 'Speech Given on 14 May 2011 by Mr Jean-Paul Costa, President of the European Court of Human Rights, at an Irish-British-French Symposium on Family Law' Information Document No 5 (2011), available at www.hcch.net/upload/wop/abduct2011info05_en.pdf.

second, by the UK Supreme Court in *Re E (Children)*.[141] The Supreme Court expressed strong support for the second approach, laying down the following guidelines:

> Where there are disputed allegations which can neither be tried nor objectively verified, the focus of the inquiry is bound to be on the sufficiency of any protective measures which can be put in place to reduce the risk. The clearer the need for protection, the more effective the measures will have to be.[142]

vi. No Consideration for the Safety of the Returning Parent

Article 11(4) obliges the adjudicating court to order the return of the child even where there is a grave risk that it will expose the child to physical or psychological harm or otherwise place him/her in an intolerable situation. The duty to order the return is conditional on the existence of measures taken in the requesting State to secure the protection of the child. This approach, although designed to protect the safety of the child, does not take into consideration the fact that often, it will be not only the child but also the abducting parent whose safety will be at risk upon the return to the requesting State. Indeed, frequently, the risk of harm the child will be facing upon the return is interrelated to the risk of harm to the returning parent.[143] This is particularly true for cases where the removal of the child was prompted by violent behaviour of the requesting party towards the abducting parent, typically the mother of the child. Bearing in mind abductions of this sort, it has been recognised that sometimes in order to protect the child it is necessary to take steps to protect the accompanying parent also.[144] This recommendation, however, was ignored by the drafters of the Regulation and not implemented into the wording of Article 11(4). It is suggested that the failure to give special thought to the safety of the returning parent is another serious flaw of Article 11(4).

141 *Re E (Children)* [2011] UKSC 27, [2012] 1 AC 144.

142 *Ibid*, para 52. More generally, the Supreme Court rejected the view that the Court in *Neulinger* had intended to introduce any revision to well-established Convention principles and refused to accept that abduction cases should now be approached differently at the domestic level. See *ibid*, paras 19–27.

143 See, eg, *Re W (Abduction: Domestic Violence)* [2004] EWCA Civ 1366, [2005] 1 FLR 727 and *Pollastro v Pollastro* [1999] OR (3rd) 485 (Ontario). In the former case, the English Court of Appeal acknowledged that, where domestic violence is involved, the situation of the child's mother will have a profound impact on the position of the child. The latter case also contained allegations of domestic violence. The Court of Appeal of Ontario opined that the '[t]he child's interests were inextricably tied to [the mother's] psychological and physical security' and therefore, in assessing the question of the grave risk of harm, it was necessary 'to take into account the serious possibility of physical and psychological harm coming to the parent on whom the child is totally dependent'.

144 Permanent Bureau of the Hague Conference, 'Report and Conclusions of the Special Commission Concerning the Hague Convention of 25 October 1980 on the Civil Aspects of International Child Abduction, 27 September—1 October 2002', available at www.hcch.net/upload/abd2002_rpt_e.pdf; and Fifth Special Commission Meeting (n 111). See also a decision of the ECtHR in the case of *Maumousseau and Washington v France* (App no 39388/05) ECtHR 6 December 2007.

a. Change in the Profile of the Abductor—Trend Towards an Increased Proportion of Abductor Mothers

The failure to give particular attention to abductions committed against the background of domestic violence is, however, not specific to the Brussels II bis Regulation only. The issue of spousal violence in the context of child abduction and the related problem of the safety of the returning parent escaped the notice of the Hague Abduction Convention.[145] The Convention, however, unlike the Regulation, had a reasonable excuse for this failure. First, at the time the Convention was drafted, in the late 1970s, domestic violence had not yet been identified as a serious social problem.[146] As a result, in the course of the preparatory work on the Convention, domestic violence attracted almost no attention, with the problem being excluded from the list of the primary motives for abduction.[147] At the Diplomatic Session which adopted the Convention, domestic violence was mentioned only on one occasion when one of the participating experts acknowledged that 'where one spouse was subject to threats and violence at the hands of the other and forced to flee the matrimonial home, it could be argued that the child … was exposed to an intolerable situation'.[148] It was only after the Convention was adopted that domestic violence was brought to prominent international attention and acknowledged as a serious problem.[149]

145 While this is a commonly accepted fact, one commentator has suggested that the Convention drafters, although having in mind the particular profile of the 'typical abductor', ie a non-custodial father, anticipated the possibility of abductor mothers escaping domestic violence. Evidence in support of this statement is found in the Explanatory Report to the 1980 Convention (n 12) para 29. It states: '[t]he interest of the child in not being removed from its habitual residence … gives way before the primary interest of any person in not being exposed to physical or psychological danger or being placed in an intolerable situation'. See also Fisher, 'How Far' (n 94) 56.

146 It was only in the 1990s that domestic violence was openly brought to international attention and acknowledged as a widespread problem. This process resulted in the adoption of the 1993 Declaration on the Elimination of Violence against Women (GA Res 48/104, UN GAOR, UN Doc A/RES/48/104 (1993). With the adoption of the Declaration the international community recognised that domestic violence hindered women's enjoyment of fundamental human rights.

Domestic violence is defined as 'a pattern of behaviour in any relationship that is used to gain or maintain power and control over an intimate partner'. J Kelly and M Johnson, 'Differentiating Among Types of Intimate Partner Violence: Research Update and Implications for Interventions' (2008) 46 *Family Court Review* 478.

147 Typical motives for abduction were identified as follows: 1. relationship between the parents has broken down or deteriorated; 2. existence of significant cultural differences between the parents; 3. exclusion of the non-custodial parent from access to the child; 4. where the issue of custody has not been decided, fear of the loss of the child, fear of the possible prejudice of the local courts of the other parent's country, fear of the other parent's superior financial resources, and fear of a concealment of the child by the other parent; 5. opportunity, ie end of the period of the exercise of access rights; 6. the abductor thinks that he/she has something to gain by the abduction, ie intention of 'forum shopping'; and 7. pressures from the child, ie child-motivated abduction. A Dyer, 'Report on International Child Abduction by One Parent ('Legal Kidnapping')' in Permanent Bureau of the Hague Conference (ed), *Actes et Documents 6–25 October 1980* (La Haye, Imprimerie Nationale, 1982) 20.

148 Procès-verbal No 8 in Permanent Bureau of the Hague Conference (ed), *Actes et Documents 6–25 October 1980* (La Haye, Imprimerie Nationale, 1982) 302.

149 This process resulted in the adoption of the 1993 Declaration on the Elimination of Violence against Women (GA Res 48/104, UN GAOR, UN Doc A/RES/48/104 (1993). With the adoption of the

The second and more pertinent reason for the omission of the issue of domestic violence in the Convention was the profile of the typical abductor. In the late 1970s and early 1980s, most abductors were non-custodial fathers.[150] The gender of the typical abductor has, however, changed over the years.[151] Nowadays, the majority of abductions are perpetrated by mothers.[152] Recent research shows that, globally, 69% of the abductors are mothers.[153] The statistical study in this book has indicated that, at the European level, this proportion is even higher and that there is a trend towards a larger percentage of mothers as abducting parents. In 2003, at the European level, mothers accounted for 72% of all alleged abductors whereas in 2005/06 it was already 75%.[154]

b. High Proportion of Abductor Mothers Fleeing Domestic Violence

Many of the abductor mothers claim to be fleeing domestic violence.[155] A study conducted by the International Child Abduction Centre, Reunite, revealed that domestic violence and/or child abuse were raised as the main concern relating to return in 67% of the representative sample of mother abductor cases.[156] This

Declaration the international community recognised that domestic violence hindered women's enjoyment of fundamental human rights.

[150] 'Summary of Findings on a Questionnaire Studied by International Social Service' in Permanent Bureau of the Hague Conference (ed), *Actes et Documents 6–25 October 1980* (La Haye, Imprimerie Nationale, 1982) 134 and 136.

[151] The change in the gender of the typical abductor has been widely acknowledged by child abduction specialists. See, eg, W Duncan, 'Action in Support of the Hague Child Abduction Convention: A View from Permanent Bureau' (2000–2001) 33 *New York University Journal of International Law & Politics* 103, 112; Silberman, 'The Hague Child Abduction Convention Turns Twenty' (n 126) 223–6; Weiner, 'International Child Abduction' (n 114) 609; and M Freeman, 'Primary Carers and the Hague Child Abduction Convention' [2001] *International Family Law Journal* 140.

[152] This new set of circumstances has brought about a strong criticism of the Convention's summary return mechanism. It has rightly been said that '... [w]hilst the carefully crafted scheme was workable in relation to the stereotypical situation in the mind of the drafters of a non-custodial father abducting the child from a custodial mother, it is much more difficult to apply in what has in practice become the stereotypical abduction situation where the abductor is the custodial mother.' Schuz, 'The Hague Child Abduction Convention' (n101) 443.

[153] N Lowe, 'A Statistical Analysis of Applications Made in 2008 under the Hague Convention of 25 October 1980 on the Civil Aspects of International Child Abduction', Preliminary Document No 8 (2011) para 42, available at www.hcch.net/upload/wop/abduct2011pd08ae.pdf.

[154] See Chapter 5, section entitled 'Relationship of the Alleged Abductor to the Child'.

[155] Lowe *et al* (n 14) 335. See also The Honourable Jacques Chamberland, 'Article 13(1)(b) and Domestic Violence: The Canadian Situation' (2003) 5 *Judges' Newsletter* 17, 17 describing the increasing occurrence of domestic violence within the scope of the grave risk of harm defence as follows: 'Over the last few years, the situation of domestic violence prevailing in the family before the child was abducted is raised more and more often to support a defence based on Article 13(1)(b) of the Convention.'

[156] See Report by the Reunite Research Unit, 'The Outcomes for Children Returned Following an Abduction' (September 2003) 29, available at www.reunite.org/edit/files/Library%20-%20reunite%20Publications/Outcomes%20Report.pdf. Another indication of the extent of the problem has been provided by answers given by Contracting States to the Hague Abduction Convention to the Hague Conference Questionnaire Concerning the Practical Operation of the Hague Convention of 25 October 1980 on the Civil Aspects of International Child Abduction. This questionnaire was prepared by the Permanent Bureau of the Hague Conference in April 2006 as a part of the preparations for the fifth meeting of the Special Commission to review the practical operation of the Hague Abduction

finding implies that if returned, over a half of the returning abductor mothers may potentially be at risk of re-victimisation at the hands of their violent ex-partners.[157] This concern appears to be substantiated by the widely recognised fact that spousal abuse does not necessarily end with separation.[158] In contrast, the period immediately following a woman's decision to leave her abusive partner is the time when the violence often culminates. The post-separation phase is frequently marked by a considerable increase in the risk to the safety of the domestic violence survivor and her children.[159] It is no exaggeration to maintain that often the woman has to live in a realistic fear that her ex-partner will discover her location and kill or harm her or her children.[160] It is well documented that there is a link between domestic violence and femicide and that the lethality of domestic violence tends to escalate after the woman decides to leave the relationship.[161] In the United Kingdom, for example, on average over two women per week are murdered by their partners or ex-partners.[162]

The Article 11(4) approach is based on the belief that responsibility for the safety of the returning parent is best left to the legal system of the requesting State. It is argued that, upon the return to the requesting State, the mother can seek protection through legal safeguards of a criminal and/or civil nature (that is, restraining orders). This argument, however, cannot stand on two grounds. First, not all signatory States have adequate protection laws. Professor Weiner argues

Convention, and was addressed to the Contracting States to the Convention. Question 25 concerned the issue of domestic violence. Fourteen EU jurisdictions expressly stated that domestic violence was raised often or increasingly frequently as an exception to return. See Permanent Bureau of the Hague Conference, 'Questionnaire Concerning the Practical Operation of the Hague Convention of 25 October 1980 on the Civil Aspects of International Child Abduction', available at www.hcch.net/upload/wop/abd_pd01e2006.pdf.

[157] See also The Honourable Justice Jacques Chamberland, 'Domestic Violence and International Child Abduction: Some Avenues of Reflection' (2005) 10 *Judges' Newsletter* 70, 70. Some resources, however, suggest an even higher proportion of abduction cases involving domestic violence. Ms Sandra De Silva, co-ordinator of the International Parental Child Abduction Service, International Social Service in Australia believes that, in Australia, abductions committed against the background of domestic violence account for 70–80% of all abduction cases. She points out that this figure is "in line with international findings". S De Silva, 'The International Parental Child Abduction Service of the International Social Service Australian Branch' (2006) 11 *Judges' Newsletter* 61, 63.

[158] See, eg, SM Buel, 'Fifty Obstacles to Leaving, AKA, Why Abuse Victims Stay' (1999) 28 *The Colorado Lawyer* 10, 28; P Jaffe, J Robinson, C Crooks and N Bala, 'Custody Disputes Involving Allegations of Domestic Violence: Toward a Differentiated Approach to Parenting Plans' (2008) 46 *Family Court Review* 500; and C Humphreys, 'Focusing on Safety—Domestic Violence and the Role of Child Contact Centres' (2003) 15 *Child and Family Law Quarterly* 237.

[159] Researchers have used the term 'separation assault' to describe the period following the domestic violence victim's decision to leave her abuser. See M Mahoney, 'Legal Images of Battered Women: Redefining the Issue of Separation' (1991–1992) 90 *Michigan Law Review* 1, 64–5.

[160] M Kaye, 'The Hague Convention and the Flight from Domestic Violence: How Women and Children are Being Returned by Coach and Four' (1999) 13 *International Journal of Law, Policy and the Family* 192.

[161] Jaffe *et al*, 'Custody Disputes' (n 158) 502.

[162] B Stanko, D Crisp, C Hale and H Lucraft, 'Counting the Costs: Estimating the Impact of Domestic Violence in the London Borough of Hackney', Children's Society and Hackney Safer Cities, 1997, per Humphreys, 'Focusing on Safety' (n 158) 237.

that in order to tackle domestic violence successfully, the entire panoply of legal remedies is necessary.[163] Availability of criminal law remedies without the possibility to obtain civil protection orders may make women reluctant to invoke the criminal law machinery, for example because they are financially dependent on the abuser.[164] Similarly, availability of civil protection orders without criminalising domestic violence makes the civil orders less authoritative. As a result, even if the civil protection orders are obtainable, they are practically ineffective against tactics such as stalking, harassment, physical violence or threats of violence. Indeed, such orders are commonly disregarded by abusers and the enforcement of these orders is rarely effective.[165] In practice, advocates often counsel domestic violence survivors that 'restraining orders are only pieces of paper that will not necessarily protect their physical safety'.[166] One can fully agree with Professor Kaye who suggests that 'the existence of legislation allowing women to apply for protection orders does not guarantee their safety'.[167]

It is, however, not only the ineffectiveness of protection orders that makes victims of domestic violence more vulnerable than other types of returning parents. The second problem, which cannot be underestimated, is that litigation incurs a high emotional and financial cost, especially for battered women already overwhelmed with the repercussions of an abusive relationship.[168] Moreover, it is unrealistic to expect that mothers who fled the country of habitual residence precisely because 'the courts and community have failed to take necessary steps to protect them from abuse or to hold the abuser accountable',[169] would have confidence in the protection system of the requesting State.

The lack of consideration for the safety of the returning parent in Article 11(4) of the Regulation makes women abducting to escape an abusive relationship a high-risk category of intra-EU abductors. Employing the Convention's strict return remedy to cases involving spousal violence poses a serious threat to the abductor mother's safety.[170] It is, therefore, suggested that Article 11(4) be

[163] Weiner (n 114) fn 139.

[164] *Ibid.*

[165] Honourable Judge Shireen Fisher put this truth in the following words: 'No court can protect against family violence.... I would suggest that family law judges have learned another sad lesson, if we are to be honest. That is, that no court can protect against domestic violence. Court orders are not bullet-proof. One court cannot always protect a child or her carer from domestic violence, regardless of the range of available protective measures at the judge's disposal.... [A]n ocean may be more effective protection than an order'. See Fisher (n 94) 58.

[166] R Hoegger, 'What If She Leaves? Domestic Violence Cases Under the Hague Convention and the Insufficiency of the Undertakings Remedy' (2003) 18 *Berkeley Women's Law Journal* 181, 198.

[167] Kaye, 'The Hague Convention' (n 160) 199.

[168] Jaffe opines that victims of domestic violence often suffer from 'anxiety, depression, [and] low self-esteem' and that return has a high potential to aggravate these problems. P Jaffe *et al*, *Child Custody and Domestic Violence: A Call for Safety and Accountability* (Thousand Oaks, CA, Sage Publications, 2003) 30.

[169] Kaye (n 160) 194–7.

[170] This worry appears to be substantiated by the findings of a research study into the outcomes for children returned following abduction, conducted by the International Child Abduction Centre (Reunite). This study demonstrated that concerns relating to the safety of the abducting parent upon

amended to take into consideration the need of protection and support that many returning mothers heavily depend on. The revised Article 11(4) would provide:

> A court cannot refuse to return a child on the basis of Article 13(1)(b) of the 1980 Hague Convention if it is established that adequate arrangements have been made to secure the protection of the child *and the returning parent* after *their* return (emphasis added).

Generally, survivors of abusive relationships are in desperate need of security and support. For the majority of domestic violence victims, separation from the abuser coupled with appropriate protection and support provides 'an opportunity for improvement in both general functioning and parenting capacities'.[171] Consequently, it would not only be the mother who would benefit from the inclusion of the reference to the returning parent into the wording of Article 11(4). The amended provision would indirectly promote the interests of the child as well. Indeed, if the returning mothers are given all the necessary support they need, there is a reasonable assumption that they will then be better able to protect their child.

Lately, at the global level, there have been some positive developments with regard to domestic and family violence in the context of the Hague Convention. In particular, the sixth Special Commission of the Hague Conference acknowledged that 'a large number of jurisdictions are addressing issues of domestic and family violence as a matter of high priority'.[172] The Permanent Bureau prepared a lengthy and very useful report on domestic violence and the Article 13 'grave risk' exception.[173] Discussions at the Commission meeting led to a conclusion that there was a need for greater consistency in dealing with domestic and family violence allegations when raised in return proceedings.[174] To this effect, three proposals for future work were considered:

1. To draft a Guide to Good Practice on the implementation of Article 13(1)(b).
2. To establish a working group, drawn primarily from the International Hague Network of Judges, to assess the possibility of developing an appropriate tool to assist in the consideration of the Article 13(1)(b) exception.
3. To form a group of experts (including judges, Central Authority experts and specialists in domestic violence) to develop principles or a Practice Guide

the return to the requesting State were very likely to be substantiated. Indeed, the fears proved to be well founded in 100% of cases. In one case, for example, the mother opposed the return on the grounds that if returned, she would face violence at the hands of the father and that the father would remove the children from her. Both of these concerns were substantiated upon the return. See Reunite Research Report (n 156).

171 Jaffe *et al* (n 158) 503.

172 Conclusions and Recommendations of the Sixth Meeting of the Special Commission (n 139) para 35.

173 Permanent Bureau of the Hague Conference, 'Domestic and Family Violence and the Article 13 "Grave Risk" Exception in the Operation of the *Hague Convention of 25 October 1980 on the Civil Aspects of International Child Abduction:* A Reflection Paper', Preliminary Document No 9 (2011), available at www.hcch.net/upload/wop/abduct2011pd09e.pdf.

174 *Ibid*, para 37.

on the management of domestic violence allegations in return proceedings under the Convention.[175]

No less importantly, the need to ensure a safe return of the accompanying parent, especially in cases involving domestic violence, was mentioned during preliminary discussions on the desirability and feasibility of a Protocol to the 1980 Convention as an issue that might be included in a potential protocol.[176] In the absence of a protocol, the problem could be dealt with by soft law. However, there is a risk that soft law instruments may prove insufficient to deal with the problem due to their non-binding nature.

c. Ineffectiveness of Undertakings

It has been suggested that, despite the lack of reference to the protection of the abducting parent in the Convention, there are remedies available to safeguard the abducting parent's safety when making a return order.[177] Called undertakings, these remedies are described as 'promises offered or in certain circumstances imposed upon an applicant to overcome obstacles which may stand in the way of the return of a wrongfully removed or retained child'.[178] Undertakings aim at ensuring a short-term welfare of the child and/or the returning parent, until the question of the child's welfare, custody and access comes before the court of the requesting State.[179]

The formal utility of undertakings within the framework of the Hague Abduction Convention was endorsed by the Fifth Special Commission to review the operation of the Convention. The Commission concluded that:

> Courts in many jurisdictions regard the use of ... undertakings as a useful tool to facilitate arrangements for return. Such orders, limited in scope and duration, addressing short term issues and remaining in effect only until such time as a court in the country to which the child is returned has taken the measures required by the situation, are in keeping with the spirit of the 1980 Convention.[180]

In the context of the Regulation, it has been rightly observed that Article 11(4) appears to 'approve of, if not encourage' the use of undertakings as a tool to facilitate the return.[181] A number of commentators, however, rightly pointed out that undertakings are generally largely ineffective as a means of protection

[175] *Ibid*, para 38.
[176] Consultations on the Desirability and Feasibility of a Protocol (n 116) 40.
[177] Silberman (n 126) 223–6 and 239. On the other hand, however, there have been voices opining that undertakings should primarily be used for the protection of the child, not the returning parent. See M Weiner, 'Half-Truths, Mistakes, and Embarrassments: The United States Go to the Fifth Meeting of the Special Commission to Review the Operation of the Hague Convention on the Civil Aspects of International Child Abduction' [2008] *Utah Law Review* 221, 295.
[178] Beaumont and McEleavy (n 14) 30.
[179] *In the matter of the Child Abduction and Enforcement of Custody Orders Act, 1991 and in the matter of R (a minor)* [1994] 3 IR 507 (per Denham J).
[180] Fifth Special Commission Meeting (n 111).
[181] Ripley (n 110) 471.

as their compliance depends only on the good faith of the left-behind parent.[182] Indeed, undertakings set a very low bar for applicants. In order for judges to order undertakings, the applicant only has to make oral assurances that the promises given by him will be kept.[183] This fact renders undertakings insufficient remedies, especially in cases involving family abuse. This harsh reality has accurately been described by Dr Rainer Hüßtege, the Presiding Judge of the Higher Appellate Court of Munich in Germany, in the following words: 'The danger of domestic violence is not reduced if the left-behind parent promises to desist from further acts of violence. Perpetrators behave reasonably and promise much in courtrooms.'[184]

Indeed, it has been demonstrated that individuals with the pattern of abusive and controlling behaviour often possess a high ability to manipulate, appearing before the courts as rational, co-operative and pleasant litigants.[185] It is therefore not surprising that it is only in some cases that undertakings given by the left-behind parent are actually honoured.[186] A research conducted by the International Child Abduction Centre Reunite revealed that non-molestation undertakings were broken in 100% of the representative sample of cases in which they were given.[187] The same study showed that left-behind parents were often instructed by their lawyers to agree to the undertakings that were sought in the return proceedings because the legislation in the requesting State was different and 'undertakings mean nothing'.[188] Looking into how the undertakings were viewed by the authorities in the requesting State, one abductor mother stated that undertakings given to a court in England were perceived 'as a joke' by the authorities in the State of habitual residence.[189] The most likely reason for the lenient attitude of the authorities towards the undertakings was the fact that undertakings as a legal concept are practically unknown to a majority of jurisdictions, in

[182] See, eg, R Hüßtege, 'Article 13(1) B) of the Hague Child Abduction Convention in the Light of Judicial Practice' (2006) 11 *Judges' Newsletter* 37; C Bruch, 'The Unmet Needs of Domestic Violence Victims and Their Children in Hague Child Abduction Convention Cases' (2004–2005) 38 *Family Law Quarterly* 529, 541, stating that undertakings are 'naïve at best' and 'at worst, they turn a blind eye to injustice'; Hoegger, 'What If She Leaves?' (n 166) 183; Alfieri, 'Trauma, Recovery, and Transnational Child Abduction' (n 106); and Freeman, 'Primary Carers' (n 152).

[183] The abducting mother, on the other hand, has to prove that the applicant will not comply with the undertakings—a task incomparably more difficult than that of the applicant. She can do this by invoking the applicant's disobedience of court orders, if this happened in the past. It has, however, been rightly said that 'obtaining past evidence may be difficult' for two main reasons. First, the evidence will most likely be located in the requesting State whilst the mother is in the requested State. Second, it is likely that no proof will be available as most domestic violence happens behind closed doors. See Hoegger (n 166) at 200.

[184] Hüßtege, 'Article 13(1) B)' (n 182) 38–9.

[185] K Waits, 'Battered Women and Their Children: Lessons from One Woman's Story' (1998) 35 *Houston Law Review* 29, 56.

[186] Even the Permanent Bureau has acknowledged that it was 'common' for the applicant parent to violate an undertaking once the child and the abducting parent were returned. See Fifth Special Commission Meeting (n 111).

[187] Reunite Research Report (n 156) 31.

[188] *Ibid*, 33.

[189] *Ibid*.

particular those operating a civil law system.[190] Consequently, even if a court of the requesting civil law country recognises a violation of undertakings, there is no existing remedy in the legal system of this jurisdiction.[191] It is only the common law countries that acknowledge the notion of undertakings and support their enforcement.[192] This unfortunately means that of the 27 EU Member States only three are potentially in the position to enforce undertakings: Cyprus, Ireland, and the United Kingdom.

A difficulty with the enforcement of undertakings is demonstrated by an Irish case, *P (L) v P (MN)*.[193] In this case, the High Court of Ireland ordered the return of the child to Italy, subject to various undertakings given both by the father and by the mother. The child and the mother then returned to Italy. In the following months, counsel for the mother informed the High Court about the near-absolute failure of the father to adhere to the undertakings given by him. It was also submitted by counsel that no legal mechanism existed in Italy for the enforcement of undertakings. As the undertakings had been given to the High Court, Mrs Justice McGuinness, who made the return order, concluded that it was permissible to bring a motion to enforce the father's undertakings before that court. In justification of her opinion, the learned judge stated:

> It appeared to me that the whole question of the giving and receiving of undertakings and their enforcement was one of very considerable importance in cases arising under the 1991 Act and the Hague Convention … The use of undertakings to cover an interim period could be of great practical advantage. Its use, however, depended on there being legal procedures for the recognition and enforcement of undertakings in the Courts of the country to which the child was returned.[194]

[190] See Permanent Bureau of the Hague Conference, 'Questionnaire Concerning the Practical Operation of the Hague Convention of 25 October 1980 on the Civil Aspects of International Child Abduction' (April 2006) Responses to Question 28, available at www.hcch.net/upload/wop/abd_pd02efs2006.pdf. See also Permanent Bureau of the Hague Conference, 'Checklist of Issues Raised and Recommendations Made in Response to the Questionnaire Concerning the Practical Operation of the Hague Convention of 25 October 1980 on the Civil Aspects of International Child Abduction', Preliminary Document No 1 (2001), available at www.hcch.net/upload/abd2001pd5e.pdf: '[t]he use of undertakings is confined largely to common law jurisdictions'. See also A Schulz, 'The New Brussels II Regulation and the Hague Conventions of 1980 and 1996' [2004] *International Family Law Journal* 22, discussing civil law countries: '[u]ndertakings are not known in that particular jurisdiction'. See also Lady Hale and Lord Wilson in *Re E (Children)* [2012] 1 AC 144, [2011] UKSC, acknowledging that '[t]he whole concept of undertakings is not generally understood outside the common law world'. *Ibid*, para 7.

[191] The honourable judge of the Australian Family Court, Kay J, in this respect rightly noted that 'there does not appear to be any existing mechanism by which the Court that extracts the undertaking can ensure that it is complied with'. *McOwan v McOwan* (1994) FLC 92-451.

[192] Beaumont and McEleavy (n 14) 157, stating that undertakings have mainly been recognised in 'jurisdictions of Anglo-American tradition'. See also M Britton, 'Undertakings: A Satisfactory Safeguard to Grave Risk?' [2003] *Cork Online Law Review*, available at www.corkonlinelawreview.com/editions/2003/2003xi.pdf.

[193] *P (L) v P (MN)* [1998] IEHC 151.

[194] *Ibid*, para 22.

Accordingly, the submission of counsel for the mother was accepted. The judge then requested the assistance of the Irish Central Authority in making enquiries of the Central Authority for Italy. A list of questions was then submitted to the latter Central Authority via the Irish Central Authority. Among these questions was an enquiry as to the availability of procedures for the enforcement of undertakings given to a foreign court in Italian law. The Central Authority for Italy provided, however, only a vague answer, stating that an enforcement of a foreign court order requires a prior recognition of the legal enforceability of the order in Italy. The response did not make it clear whether it is the foreign order itself which may be recognised as enforceable or whether the undertakings separate from the order may be recognised as enforceable. Following this enquiry the judge concluded that, under the given circumstances, there were no further steps available to the High Court to be taken in the matter.

Unable to pressure the enforcement of undertakings, the High Court must have realised how shaky these promises of security are.[195] It has rightly been noted that, in making a return order dependent on undertakings, courts 'engage in judicial fiction—simply because there is an appearance of solution, there is a solution'.[196] Regrettably, research shows that courts adjudicating child abduction cases engage in this judicial fiction extremely often.[197] Indeed, the type of complications that developed following the High Court return order in *P (L) v P (MN)* is far from being an isolated incident.[198]

Unrealistic reliance on the efficacy of undertakings makes these measures a dangerous basis for ordering return. Undertakings can only be relied on if an enforcement mechanism exists in the requesting country. Therefore, there has

[195] Freeman (n 151).

[196] *Ibid.* This judicial fiction, characterised by an unrealistic faith in the enforcement of undertakings, is well reflected in the view of The Honourable Mr Justice Wall: 'I would, however, hope and expect that the courts of a Contracting State would enforce an undertaking given by a party to the English High Court which, by its very nature, is an integral part of the English court's order'. Wall (n 118) 174. Similarly, Butler-Sloss LJ, quoting Waite LJ in a decision of the Court of Appeal in *Re M (Abduction: Non-Convention Country)* [1995] 1 FLR 1989, expressed a belief that: 'Judges in one country are entitled and bound to assume that the Courts and welfare services of the other country will all take the same serious view of a failure to honour undertakings given to a Court (of any jurisdiction) … It is to be assumed that the Courts in every country will not hesitate to intervene to enforce whatever Orders or to direct whatever enquiries are called for in the children's best interests. In that process every judge is bound to take into full and careful account what his or her colleagues have already ordered in antecedent proceedings in another jurisdiction'. *Re M (Minors) (Child Abduction: Undertakings)* [1995] 1 FLR 1021.

[197] See, eg, *McOwan v McOwan* (1994) FLC 92-451.

[198] The Reunite Research Report 'The Outcomes for Children Returned Following an Abduction' describes a case where, upon the return to the requesting State, an interviewee mother was constantly harassed by the applicant father. This harassment occurred in violation of non-molestation undertakings given to the English court in the return proceedings. The mother called the police, however, only to be told that she had to obtain a protection order as the undertakings had 'no real effect', despite having been registered in the local court in the requesting State. The mother pointed out that she had heard the same story 'time and again' from women who had been sent home subject to undertakings. Reunite Research Report (n 156) 33.

been a call for some official arrangement for the operation of undertakings.[199] Several suggestions have been made as to how to achieve this.

Professor Duncan believes that the use of 'safe harbour orders' or 'mirror orders', obtained from a court in a jurisdiction where the enforcement of undertakings is not possible, may provide a solution.[200] This means that the court of the requesting State would issue an order that would 'mirror' the undertakings order of the issuing court. Similarly, Professor Silberman suggests that carefully thought through and creatively implemented 'safe return orders' would maintain the return objective of the Convention whilst ensuring the safety of the child and the returning parent.[201]

Although 'safe harbour orders' and 'mirror orders' could theoretically serve as a potential remedy, the problem with them is that this practice is not common in Europe and has developed mainly in the United States.[202] Civil law jurisdictions are of the view that they are not authorised to make such an order.[203] Another shortcoming is that this procedure is quite lengthy as the case must be dealt with by judicial authorities in the State of refuge as well as by judicial authorities in the requesting State.[204]

In the English High Court case *Re O (Child Abduction: Undertakings)*[205] Singer J recommended that Central Authorities engage in bilateral discussions to explain their domestic courts' approach to undertakings. It is hoped that by such negotiations and exchange of opinions 'comity would be strengthened, and an understanding achieved that neither country wishes to cause offence to the courts of the other, nor to seek to interfere with or to influence what that court then does'.[206]

The proposal of Singer J, though noble in its reliance on the power of comity, has, however, a rather idealistic basis. In particular, it fails to take into consideration that comity cannot provide for the replacement of the missing statutory basis for the enforcement of undertakings.

In search of a remedy for the absent legislative foundation for the enforceability of undertakings, the commentators have offered two solutions. First, a suggestion was made by Professor Weiner that undertakings be authorised and made directly enforceable by the Convention.[207] She called for the signatory countries to the Convention to reconvene and negotiate an explicit provision authorising

199 One commentator expressed it as follows: 'The time has come to give these creatures of judicial activism a statutory basis, if not for the sake of certainty and cohesiveness, then at the very least for the sake of the children whose welfare and well-being may very well depend on their enforcement'. Britton, 'Undertakings' XI.

200 W Duncan, 'Hague Conference on Private International Law and the Children's Conventions' (1998) 2 *Irish Journal of Family Law* 3.

201 Silberman, 'Patching Up the Abduction Convention' (n 116) 55.

202 See Beaumont and McEleavy (n 14) 157.

203 Chamberland, 'Domestic Violence and International Child Abduction' (n 157) 72.

204 *Ibid.* See also Weiner (n 114) 679.

205 *Re O (Child Abduction: Undertakings)* [1994] 2 FLR 349.

206 *Ibid*, at 372.

207 *Weiner* (n 114) 678.

undertakings.[208] Second, an alternative proposition was made for the adoption of a Protocol to the Convention. The Protocol would provide for the enforceability of protective measures, including the enforceability of undertakings.[209]

The former proposal, although attractive in its potential to accomplish a reform of a global character, appears to be rather unattainable. The 'stone tablet' quality[210] of international conventions makes it extremely unlikely that the Contracting States to the Convention would come down in favour of a revision of the Convention.

The latter proposal is more pragmatic; however, it has other shortcomings. Most importantly, the fact that signatory States to the Convention are not bound to participate in a protocol initiative would mean that the enforceability of undertakings would be guaranteed at a restricted scope only. Unfortunately, this would significantly lessen the value of the protocol. Nevertheless, one can agree with Thorpe LJ that the protocol would 'at least enable like-minded States to strengthen the Convention *inter se*' and that 'a Protocol with a limited range of operation would be better than no Protocol at all'.[211]

At the European level, it has been suggested that Article 11(4) itself had the potential to solve problems surrounding the issue of the safe return.[212] The argument presented was that Article 11(4) might encourage judges from civil law jurisdictions to attach undertakings to return orders. This, in turn, would promote direct judicial communication between judges and might result in the practice of 'mirror orders' being developed in the EU Member States. Although it is possible that Article 11(4) may be conducive to the introduction of the practice of undertakings and 'mirror orders' in civil law jurisdictions, it is unlikely that a uniform alteration in the attitude will be accomplished. The surest way to achieve a consistent implementation of undertakings by the courts throughout the EU Member States is to amend the Regulation to provide for a direct enforcement of undertakings. It is, therefore, suggested that an extra provision be included into the Regulation. This provision would impose on the requesting States a duty to enforce undertakings that have been given by the applicant to the requested court and incorporated into the return order. The undertakings would stay in force until the court of the requesting State rules on the merits.

Simultaneously, an obligation would be imposed on the requesting Central Authority to oversee the compliance with undertakings. In case of a breach of the undertakings, the Central Authority will be required to initiate enforcement

[208] *Ibid.*

[209] Thorpe, 'The Hague Child Abduction Convention' (n 116) 10, and Ripley (n 110) 465. Both authors suggest that the protocol would provide for the enforceability of all types of protective measures, including undertakings. See also Silberman (n 116) 55. Professor Silberman proposes that the protocol establishes a mechanism to ensure that 'mirror orders' are made enforceable in the requesting State or establishes procedures for co-operation between the requested State and the requesting State in issuing 'mirror orders'.

[210] Thorpe (n 116) 10.

[211] *Ibid.*

[212] Lortie, 'The Communitarisation of Family Law' (n 115) 55.

proceedings on behalf of the abductor parent.[213] In the meantime, the Central Authority will be duty-bound to take all necessary steps to eliminate any risk to the child and/or the returning parent that might be associated with the breach of the undertakings.[214]

In conclusion, it has rightly been noted that the ineffectiveness of undertakings makes them a hazardous basis for ordering return.[215] Therefore, if undertakings are to serve as effective tools in the operation of Article 11(4), it must be guaranteed that they will be enforced in the requesting Member State.

III. Timing

Speedy resolution is crucial in any proceedings for the return of an abducted child. In recognition of this fact, Article 11 of the Hague Abduction Convention imposes on courts an obligation to 'act expeditiously' in return proceedings. In order to encourage authorities involved to 'accord maximum priority to dealing with the problems arising out of the international removal of children',[216] Article 11 further states that if a decision was not taken within six weeks, the court may be requested to give the reason for the delay.

The Brussels II bis Regulation appears to give the Convention requirement on timing an obligatory character.[217] In particular, Article 11(3) of the Regulation, second paragraph, states that the court must issue a decision within six weeks from being seized of the matter. This time limit may only be exceeded if exceptional circumstances make it impossible for the court to conclude the case within six weeks.[218] The first paragraph of Article 11(3) gives specific form to the Convention principle to act expeditiously, instructing the courts dealing with return applications to use 'the most expeditious procedures available in national law'.

The replacement of the soft provision of Article 11 of the Convention by the strict deadline imposed by the Regulation has generally been welcomed by commentators.[219] However, concerns have been expressed about the feasibility of the

213 The reason behind this suggestion is that, even where there is a legal basis for the enforcement of undertakings in the abducted-from country, their enforcement is often hindered by an emotional struggle on the side of the abducting parent. This struggle results from the abusive relationship and the forced return. The Reunite research revealed that most returning parents were feeling 'vulnerable and alone', 'totally isolated and impoverished' and 'terrified and distraught' upon the return, 'too busy just trying to survive to deal with the enforcement of the breached undertakings'. Report by Marilyn Freeman for the Reunite Research Unit, 'International Child Abductions—the Effects' (May 2006) 27–28 and 43, available at www.reunite.org/edit/files/Library%20-%20reunite%20Publications/Effects%20Of%20Abduction%20Report.pdf.

214 See section 'Co-operation of Central Authorities' above.

215 Kaye (n 160) 192.

216 Explanatory Report to the 1980 Convention (n 12) para 105.

217 Lowe *et al*, *The New Brussels II Regulation* (n 102) 30.

218 Brussels II bis Regulation Art 11(3) second paragraph.

219 Eg Lortie (n 115) 54.

time limit.[220] In this context, reference was made to the 2003 statistical survey, according to which in applications received by EU Member States, the average disposal time was 103 days for judicial returns and 205 days for judicial refusals.[221] It was rightly pointed out that these statistics were 'way outside the Regulation target of 42 days'.[222]

Unfortunately, our statistical survey only confirmed that the EU jurisdictions find the six-week time limit an exceedingly hard target.[223] In particular, the survey yielded the following results.

First, it was revealed that, as of 28 February 2007 (the cut-off date for the survey), 15% of applications were still pending. Disturbingly, this represents an increase by 9% on the proportion of pending cases in 2003.

Second, in terms of mean number of days to settlement, it was found that judicial refusals took a mean average of 173 days to be decided. A corresponding analysis per Member State revealed that none of the EU Members complied with the six-week rule when refusing return applications. The best results were achieved by England and Wales with the mean average of 116 days. This figure was under the 'EU mean average' of 173 days. Judicial returns were resolved in an average of 108 days. At 81 days, the shortest mean average was recorded in England and Wales.[224]

220 See, eg, N Lowe, 'The Current Experiences and Difficulties of Applying Brussels II Revised' [2007] *International Family Law Journal* 182; and His Honour Judge Ian Karsten QC, 'The State of International Family Law Issues: A View from London' (2009) *International Family Law Journal* 35. It is to be noted that the problem of attainability of the six-week period had long been discussed in the context of the Convention. See, eg, A Dyer, 'The Hague Convention on the Civil Aspects of International Child Abduction—Towards Global Cooperation' (1993) 1 *International Journal of Children's Rights* 273, 287–8; N Lowe, 'The 1980 Hague Convention on the Civil Aspects of International Child Abduction: An English Viewpoint' (1999) 48 *International and Comparative Law Quarterly* 179, 139–43; Duncan, 'Action in Support of the Hague Child Abduction Convention' (n 151) 103–23, 104; and M Bailey, 'Canada's Implementation of the 1980 Hague Convention on the Civil Aspects of International Child Abduction' (2000–2001) 33 *New York University Journal of International Law & Politics* 17, 27. Similarly, the Report on the fifth meeting of the Special Commission to review the operation of the Convention revealed the lack of speed as being one of the major concerns for Central Authorities. See Fifth Special Commission Meeting (n 111) 24. Last but not least, the failure to deal with the application for return speedily enough has been criticised on several occasions by the European Court of Human Rights. See, eg, *Maire v Portugal*, ECtHR, 26 June 2003, No 48206/99; *HN v Poland*, ECtHR, 13 September 2005, No 77710/01; *Karadzic v Croatia*, ECtHR, 15 December 2005, No 35030/04; *Bianchi v Switzerland*, ECtHR, 22 June 2006, No 7548/04; and *Iosub Caras v Romania*, ECtHR, 27 July 2006, No 7198/04. For a detailed analysis of the above cases see Beaumont, 'The Jurisprudence of the European Court of Human Rights' (n 116) 40–50.

221 Lowe, 'The Current Experiences and Difficulties of Applying Brussels II Revised' (n 220).

222 *Ibid*. The author acknowledged that the 2003 survey predated the implementation of the Regulation; nevertheless, pointed out the significance of these findings.

223 This finding was repeated by the 2008 Cardiff survey as, like in 2005/06, in 2008 'the large majority of applications were not resolved within the six-week timescale prescribed by the Brussels IIa Regulation'. N Lowe, 'A Statistical Analysis of Applications Made in 2008 under the Hague Convention of 25 October 1980 on the Civil Aspects of International Child Abduction, Part II—Regional Report', Preliminary Document No 8B (2011) para 22, available at www.hcch.net/upload/wop/abduct2011 pd08be. Alarmingly, the 2008 survey even recorded a deterioration in timing on the 2005/06 figures. For details see Chapter 5, section entitled 'Timing'.

224 This does not include countries with a small number of judicial return orders (ie fewer than three), as findings based on one or two cases only cannot be given much relevance. Nevertheless, if

Considering countries with a minimum number of cases (three or more) only, the shortest mean average was recorded in England and Wales.

Third, in terms of overall time to final judicial decision, it was revealed that only 20% of all judicial decisions were made within the six-week deadline. This finding undoubtedly gives cause for concern. The worrying character is exacerbated by the fact that it shows poorer results than the 2003 survey (a decrease by 9%).

No judicial refusals were made in less than six weeks. This result shows a decrease on the 2003 proportion of 10%. The largest proportion of refusals, 48%, took between three and six months to decide. This represents a significant increase on the 2003 proportion of 27% and, at the same time, an improvement on the 2003 findings. In 2003, the largest percentage of judicial refusals, 50%, took over six months to resolve. It is to be noted that from this point of view, the timing has improved (fewer refusals than in 2003 took over six months). Nevertheless, considering the 10% decrease on refusals made within the Regulation-prescribed period of six weeks, and the fact that the largest proportion of refusals fell within the 'three to six months' category, this result is far from being satisfactory. Indeed, in absolute terms, the timing of judicial refusals has deteriorated.

The largest proportion of judicial returns, 35%, was concluded between six and 12 weeks. In 2003, the largest proportion of judicial returns, 35%, was made in less than six weeks. In 2005/06, only 24% of judicial return orders took less than six weeks to make. In this context, it is to be noted that, as it was with judicial refusals and judicial decisions in general, the timing of judicial return orders has deteriorated. Indeed, given the 11% decrease in the 'zero to six weeks' category, the timing of judicial returns showed a poorer performance than was the performance produced in 2003.

Finally, the survey revealed that appealed cases took significantly longer to resolve than unappealed applications, 217 days as opposed to 99 days with respect to judicial returns and 214 days as opposed to 157 days with respect to judicial refusals.

The findings of the survey allow us to draw three general conclusions. First, the timing was better in 2003 than it was in 2005/2006; second, England and Wales is the most efficient EU jurisdiction in dealing with child abduction cases; and third, applications involving appeals took considerably longer to conclude than unappealed cases. The following section deals with each of the above conclusions.

A. Deterioration in Timing

The fact that the 2003 statistics showed better timing than the 2005/06 survey is disturbing on two accounts. First, it casts doubts on the general ability of the Member States to comply with the six-week rule. More alarmingly, however, it

these jurisdictions had been considered, the shortest mean averages would have been Estonia (14 days), Malta (16 days), Hungary (58 days), Austria (73 days) and the Czech Republic (79 days).

points to a general conclusion that Convention applications are disposed of faster than applications that fall within the Regulation regime. This, in turn, indicates that there might be factors within the Regulation itself that present obstacles to compliance with the six-week time limit. In particular, efforts to act expeditiously in Regulation cases may in some cases be hindered by procedural requirements of Articles 11(2) and 11(5) (the right of the child and the requesting party to have the opportunity to be heard). In other cases, delays may result from the application of Article 11(4) as courts await information on the availability of protective measures in the requesting State or negotiate undertakings or safe harbour/mirror orders.

Admittedly, the mere fact of deterioration in timing does not allow us to draw detailed inferences. Indeed, all efforts to reveal reasons behind the downward trend are no more than pure conjecture. It is therefore submitted that further research is needed into the topic. It is suggested that a study is undertaken in order to establish the causes of the delays and the means to reduce them.

B. England and Wales—the Most Efficient Jurisdiction

The survey showed that England and Wales had the best timing for both judicial refusals and judicial returns. This finding strongly suggests that England and Wales is the most efficient European jurisdiction when it comes to dealing with return applications under the Regulation. Indeed, even prior to the implementation of the Regulation, the English procedure had demonstrated a strong commitment to putting into effect the Convention's requirement for a speedy resolution of return applications. In this context, the courts of England and Wales have rightly been considered an example of speed and effectiveness.[225]

The resolution to fully comply with Article 11(3) of the Regulation can best be seen from efforts by the judges to 'prioritise and then strongly "manage" cases'.[226] For example, in the first case governed by the Regulation to reach the England and Wales Court of Appeal, *Vigreux v Michel*,[227] several re-listings of the case at the first instance led to a delay of five months in the proceedings. The Court of Appeal described this hold-up as 'shocking and unacceptable',[228] pointing out the importance of the compliance with the six-week time limit imposed by the Regulation. In particular, Wall LJ said:

> Failure to adhere to the timetables proposed will not only result in the English court being in breach of its international obligations; it will represent an unacceptable abnegation of the court's responsibility properly to address cases of international child abduction—a matter in which, in the past, we have taken legitimate pride.[229]

[225] Dyer, 'The Hague Convention' (n 220) 288. See also Wall (n 118) at 170; and Lowe (n 220).
[226] Lowe (n 220).
[227] *Vigreux v Michel* [2006] EWCA Civ 630, [2006] 2 FLR 1180.
[228] *Ibid*, para 86.
[229] *Ibid*, para 88.

Thorpe LJ added:

> [O]ur jurisdiction has acquired a reputation for high standards, administrative and judicial, in the application of the Hague Convention. It behoves us to be at or towards the top of the performance league when the Commission takes stock of the operation of the Regulation at its early stages.[230]

As practical advice to the courts, the Court of Appeal held that incoming cases from other Community Member States should be allowed to 'jump the queue', that is, prioritised, if necessary, even at the expense of previously listed domestic cases. Thorpe LJ accepted that 'opinions may differ as to whether that is acceptable'. Nevertheless, he concluded that 'that is not a debatable issue since the United Kingdom opted in to the negotiation of the Regulation and is bound by its stringent requirements'.

C. Effect of Appeals on Timing

Although it is not an express requirement of either Article 11 of the Convention or Article 11(3) of the Regulation, it has been suggested that the six-week time limit relates not only to the first instance proceedings but extends also to appeal procedures.[231] The Practice Guide for the application of the Brussels II bis Regulation goes even further when recommending that the six-week period cover also the enforcement stage of the return proceedings. The Practice Guide further states that it is a matter of national law to ensure that this goal is achieved. Two practical recommendations are then made:

(a) national law may preclude the possibility of an appeal against a decision entailing the return of the child; or
(b) national law may allow for the possibility for appeal, but provide that a decision entailing the return of the child is enforceable pending any appeal.[232]

Admittedly, this recommendation poses a serious problem for many jurisdictions. Indeed, most EU Members struggle to meet the target at the first instance, far less after appellate decisions and enforcement. Even though a particular jurisdiction has authorities such as an implementing legislation or opinions of judiciary endorsing the six-week time limit in place, the practical compliance with the obligation is still not guaranteed. In Germany, for example, the implementing law prescribes that return proceedings must be treated as a matter of priority at

230 *Ibid*, para 47.
231 See, eg, Permanent Bureau of the Hague Conference, 'Conclusions and Recommendations of the Fourth Meeting of the Special Commission to Review the Operation of the Hague Convention of 25 October 1980 on the Civil Aspects of International Child Abduction, 22–28 March 2001' para 3.3, available at www.hcch.net/upload/concl28sc4_e.pdf. The recommendation was reaffirmed by the fifth Special Commission to review the operation of the Convention. See Fifth Special Commission Meeting (n 111) para 1.4.1.
232 Commission Practice Guide (n 65) 41.

all instances.[233] Paragraph 15 of the statute, addressing the issue of preliminary injunctions, provides a basis for a court to declare an immediate enforceability of a return order (that is, a return order enforceable pending an appeal).[234] Nevertheless, it has been observed that, in practice, courts are unwilling to exercise this power.[235]

England and Wales, being 'something of a model jurisdiction'[236] (see above), has long been committed to a speedy adjudication of return applications, including appeals. In the 1999 case of *Re C (Abduction: Grave Risk of Physical or Psychological Harm)*[237] Thorpe LJ stated: 'The goal for which we should strive in this jurisdiction, both at first instance and on appeal, should be six weeks from invitation to conclusion'.[238] This aspiration was confirmed by the Court of Appeal in relation to applications made under the Brussels II bis Regulation. In the case of *K v K*[239] Thorpe LJ, having drawn attention to the requirement of Article 11(3) of the Regulation, held that the requirement to deal with Convention proceedings within six weeks extended to appeal hearings.[240] Thorpe LJ also recommended that applications for permission to appeal should be made directly to the trial judge and that the normal 21-day period for lodging a notice of appeal should be restricted.[241] This suggestion was reiterated in another Court of Appeal decision in the Brussels II bis case of *Re F (a child) (abduction: obligation to hear child)*.[242] Additionally, in this decision, Thorpe LJ gave detailed guidance on the issue:

> The specialist administrative and judicial resources in this court enable us to list an application or an appeal very quickly after issue but the application for permission should clearly be made to the trial judge. If it is refused by the trial judge, he should set the date by which the notice of appeal must be lodged. Although general rules of this court allow the applicant 21 days, that period may be either extended or reduced by the trial judge. I would suggest that 7 days rather than 21 should be the norm in any case in which an application for permission to appeal is made to a trial judge and refused by him

[233] Gesetz zur Aus- und Durchführung Bestimmter Rechtsinstrumente auf dem Gebiet des Internationalen Familienrechts (The Act on International Family Law), BGB1 I 2005, 162.

[234] Para 15 states: 'The court can ex officio or upon application issue preliminary injunctions in order to prevent the child from harm or to avoid damages to the interests of the parties concerned. In particular, it can order such injunctions to secure the location of the child during the proceedings or to prevent the frustration or complication of its return'. Per Working Party on European Parental Child Abduction, 'Review of the Implementation of Brussels II Regulation in Relation to Parental Abduction of Children: Information Note on Parental Child Abduction Cases within the EU' (Brussels, 31 October 2006) 13, available at www.jugendamt-wesel.com/PRESSE_POLITIQUE/ChildAbductionNotetoCommissionerFrattini2.pdf.

[235] *Ibid.*

[236] N Lowe, 'Regulating International Parental Child Abduction—Brussels Style' (2002/2003) 6 *Contemporary Issues in Law* 315.

[237] See *Re C (Abduction: Grave Risk of Physical or Psychological Harm)* [1999] 2 FLR 478.

[238] *Ibid*, 488.

[239] *K v K* [2007] EWCA Civ 533, [2007] 2 FLR 996.

[240] *Ibid*, para 27.

[241] *Ibid*, paras 27–30.

[242] *Re F (a child) (abduction: obligation to hear child)* [2007] EWCA Civ 468, [2007] 2 FLR 697.

> or her. That will enable this court to get onto the case that much more quickly and give us a better chance of concluding the litigation within the six-week period.[243]

Despite the concerted effort of the English judiciary to adhere to the ambitious timing rule, certain doubts have been expressed about the feasibility of the six-week time limit even in England and Wales.[244] In *Vigreux v Michel*, Thorpe LJ himself accepted that the six-week target may prove impractical and eventually might need to be reconsidered.[245]

In the light of the findings of our statistical survey, it appears that the time limit will indeed need to be reviewed and modified to set a more realistic target. Recital 29 of the Regulation obliges the Commission to keep the functioning of the Regulation under review. It is therefore recommended that for the purposes of the first review of the operation of the Regulation, a report on the effectiveness of the Regulation, where concerns related to the application of Article 11(3) are addressed in detail, is prepared. Consequently, appropriate steps should be taken towards the reconsideration of the six-week time limit.[246]

IV. Judicial and Administrative Qualities in the 'New' Member States of the European Union

On 1 May 2004 the European Union underwent a major change, a dramatic enlargement that increased the Community's membership from 15 to 25 Member States.[247] Eight Central and Eastern European countries: the Czech Republic, Estonia, Hungary, Latvia, Lithuania, Poland, the Slovak Republic and Slovenia, and two Mediterranean countries, Cyprus and Malta, completed their accession negotiations

243 *Ibid*, para 28.

244 Lowe (n 220).

245 *Vigreux v Michel* [2006] EWCA Civ 630, [2006] 2 FLR 1180 para 47.

246 There is a reasonable hope that the issue will indeed be assessed as part of the first review of the operation of the Regulation as the open invitation to tender for external evaluation of the Regulation has identified 'effectiveness' as one of the key evaluation questions of the review. Among other objectives, the evaluation of the effectiveness of the Regulation will seek to reveal 'to what extent have the core objectives of the Regulation' including 'the return without delay of children wrongfully removed or retained' been accomplished. European Commission, 'Open invitation to tender JUST/2011/JCIV/PR/0042/A4—External evaluation of Council Regulation (EC) No 2201/2003 of 27 November 2003 concerning jurisdiction and the recognition and enforcement of judgments in matrimonial matters and the matters of parental responsibility, repealing Regulation (EC) No 1347/2000' (Brussels, 30 October 2011) 12, available at www.ec.europa.eu/justice/newsroom/contracts/files/2011s188-306237/invitation_en.pdf.

247 The term 'new' Member States is used here to refer to the 10 countries that joined the European Union in this wave of enlargement (ie the May 2004 enlargement). The expansion process continued with the accession of Romania and Bulgaria to the European Union in January 2007. These two countries, however, were not included in the research for the reasons explained in Chapter 5, fn 15. To describe the European Union prior to the 2004 enlargement, the term 'old' Member States has been used.

with the EU and became full Members of the European Union.[248] As a result of this enlargement, the population of the European Union increased by 20% to 450 million citizens and the number of official languages went up from 11 to 20.[249]

Findings of our statistical survey have suggested that the 'new' EU Members operate the Regulation less successfully than the 'old' EU of 15 Members.[250] The aim of this sub-chapter therefore is to further investigate this indication and to explore potential causes of this imbalance. The methodology used to achieve these goals is a combination of empirical and library-based research.

The empirical part of this examination consists in a separate analysis of the operation of the Regulation in the 'new' Member States and in the 'old' Member States in 2005/2006, using the available 2003 and 2005/2006 databases. Results are presented in the form of a comparative study.[251] The statistical comparison has been complemented by follow-up interviews conducted with representatives of the Central Authorities of two of the 'new' Member States, Slovakia and the Czech Republic. These particular jurisdictions were selected primarily for linguistic reasons. The author, speaking both the Slovakian and Czech languages, was able to conduct the interviews in the native tongue of the interviewees, as opposed to English as the interviewees' second or third language. The main advantage of this approach was that by allowing the interviewees to express themselves in their native language they were able to give more comprehensive information and to provide a more genuine account of the situation. The responses were then translated by the author of the survey into English.

The primary aim of the follow-up interviews was to identify reasons behind the lack of effectiveness in the application of the Convention and the Regulation in the 'new' Member States. It was intended to pinpoint not only those reasons that occur at the practical level but also those that exist at a deeper ideological level. It is to be noted that the key objective of this exercise was not to seek solutions as to how the use of the Regulation in the 'new' Member States should be improved. Therefore, it was not considered vital to conduct comparable interviews in the 'old' Member States.

The interview with the Slovak Central Authority took place on 20 April 2007 at the Central Authority of the Slovak Republic in Bratislava. Altogether, three representatives of the Central Authority in the position of legal advisors were interviewed. The interview with the Czech Central Authority took place on 24 April 2007 at the Central Authority of the Czech Republic in Brno. The interview was

[248] See Final Act to the Treaty of Accession to the European Union 2003, 23 September 2003, OJ 2003 L 236. For a detailed description of the enlargement process see RJ Goebel, 'Joining the European Union: The Accession Procedures for the Central European and Mediterranean States' (2003–2004) 1 *Loyola University Chicago International Law Review* 15.

[249] JB Richardson, 'The Road to a Unified Peaceful Europe: Keynote Address' (2003–2004) *International Law Review* 1, 5–13 and 9.

[250] See Chapter 5, section entitled 'Outcomes: Analysis per Member State'.

[251] It is, however, to be noted that the data analysis cannot be fully relied upon as the number of return applications in the 'old' Member States was more than five times higher than the number of applications received by the 'new' Member States. Nevertheless, despite that, the analysis does carry a vital message and serves as an important and thought-provoking piece of information.

conducted with the Vice-Director of the Czech Central Authority. The interviews were semi-structured, with 12 questions having been prepared in advance and put to the interviewees. The questions covered various aspects of the application of the 1980 Convention and the Regulation. In particular, the following areas were targeted: the concentration of jurisdiction for child abduction cases, the implementing legislation, the quality of the judiciary and the training of judges, the use of undertakings and safe harbour/mirror orders, domestic violence, mediation, the hearing of the child pursuant to Article 11(2) of the Regulation, the hearing of the applicant pursuant to Article 11(5) of the Regulation, and the procedure following a non-return order pursuant to Articles 11(6)–11(8) of the Regulation.

A. Operation of the Brussels II bis Regulation in the 'New' EU Member States

i. The Number of Applications

Altogether, in 2005/2006 the Central Authorities of the EU Member States received 363 applications for return under the Brussels II bis Regulation.[252] Of these, 53 applications were received by the 'new' Member States (see Table 6.32). The remaining 310 applications were made to the 'old' EU Members.

Table 6.32: Requested States

	Number	Percent
Poland	24	45%
Czech Republic	13	25%
Cyprus	4	8%
Slovakia	4	8%
Slovenia	3	6%
Estonia	2	4%
Hungary	1	2%
Lithuania	1	2%
Malta	1	2%
Total	**53**	**~100%**

As Table 6.32 shows, the largest proportion of applications made to the new Member States was received by Poland (24, 45%). This was followed by the Czech Republic with 13 applications (25%).

252 See Chapter 5, section entitled 'The Number of Applications'.

Not only was Poland the busiest new Member State, but it must also be ranked first with regard to the increase in the number of received applications. Indeed, in 2005/2006 the Polish Central Authority handled 24 intra-EU abduction cases, as opposed to only 17 in 2003 (see Table 6.33). The rise in the number of incoming return applications to Poland is not surprising. This upward trend is most likely linked to the May 2004 accession of the country to the European Union. Following the membership of the Union, many Poles have left their home country and moved around Europe in search of job opportunities. Indeed, according to Franck Düvell from the Centre on Migration, Policy and Society at Oxford, of the 10 'new' EU countries, Poland has the most mobile population.[253] As a result, large Polish communities can be found in almost all 'old' EU Member States.[254] Undoubtedly, the increased mobility of Polish citizens within the EU has entailed a greater likelihood of their involvement in cross-border parental child abduction cases.

Table 6.33: The number of applications

	Number of applications 2005/06	**Number of applications 2003**
Poland	24	17
Czech Republic	13	9
Cyprus	4	7
Slovakia	4	7
Slovenia	3	0
Estonia	2	1
Hungary	1	10
Lithuania	1	0
Malta	1	3
Latvia	0	0
Total	**53**	**54**

The database indicates that the most popular destination of Polish citizens was neighbouring Germany, followed by England and Wales (see Table 6.34[255]). Indeed, the numbers of incoming return applications from Poland to these jurisdictions rose from five in 2003 to 14 in 2005/06 and from one in 2003 to six in 2005/06 respectively.

[253] F Düvell, 'Poles in Europe—From Illegal Immigrants to Members of the European Union', Talk at 'London's Polish Border's Conference, Polish Embassy, London (17 May 2006), available at www.surrey.ac.uk/cronem/files/Franck-Duvell.doc.

[254] *Ibid.*

[255] In 13 cases the precise information on the requesting State was not available. All of these applications were received by France. The French Central Authority stated that these applications were made by the United Kingdom, but did not specify the jurisdiction (England and Wales, Scotland or Northern Ireland).

Table 6.34: The number of applications

		Requesting State																							
		Austria	Belgium	Czech Republic	Cyprus	Estonia	Finland	France	Germany	Greece	Hungary	Ireland	Italy	Lativa	Lithuania	Luxembourg	Netherlands	Poland	Portugal	Slovakia	Spain	Sweden	UK—England & Wales	UK—Nth Ireland	UK—Scotland	**Total**
Requested	Austria			1					2	1			1				1	1					2			**9**
State	Belgium	1						3	3							1	3		2		3		2			**18**
	Czech Republic							1	5				5							1		1				**13**
	Cyprus									1		1											2			**4**
	Estonia						1															1				**2**
	Finland		1			1								1								1				**4**
	France		15		1				8	1		1	8	1		1	9	2	5		4					**56**
	Germany	2	5				1	4				2	10				4	14			4		7			**53**
	Hungary								1																	**1**
	Ireland				1			2	1		2							2	1	1			19	1	2	**32**
	Italy							1	2																	**3**
	Lithuania								1																	**1**

(Continued)

Table 6.34: (*Continued*)

	Requesting State																								
	Austria	Belgium	Czech Republic	Cyprus	Estonia	Finland	France	Germany	Greece	Hungary	Ireland	Italy	Lativa	Lithuania	Luxembourg	Netherlands	Poland	Portugal	Slovakia	Spain	Sweden	UK—England & Wales	UK—Nth Ireland	UK—Scotland	**Total**
Luxembourg								1										1							**2**
Malta																						1			**1**
Poland		1					2	4				6			2	1					1	7			**24**
Portugal							1															2			**3**
Slovakia			1									3													**4**
Slovenia							1	2																	**3**
Sweden						1				1										1		1			**4**
UK—England & Wales	1	1	4	2		1	13	10	2	3	13	9	2	2		5	6	9	4	15	3				**105**
UK—Nth Ireland											3		1												**4**
UK—Scotland								1								3									**4**
Total	**4**	**23**	**6**	**4**	**1**	**4**	**28**	**41**	**5**	**6**	**20**	**42**	**5**	**2**	**4**	**26**	**25**	**18**	**6**	**27**	**7**	**43**	**1**	**2**	**350**

However, Poland was not the only 'new' Member State that recorded a rise in the number of return applications. This upward trend was also reflected in the statistics provided by other 'new' EU Members. The Czech Republic, for example, recorded an increase in incoming as well as outgoing return applications; Slovenia, Estonia and Lithuania recorded an increase in incoming return applications; and Lithuania, Latvia and Slovakia recorded an increase in outgoing return applications.

ii. Relationship of the Alleged Abductor to the Child

Overall, 75% of all alleged abductors were mothers.[256] A separate analysis of the 'new' Member States and the 'old' Member States revealed a comparable proportion of respondent mothers in the latter Members. Indeed, in the 'old' Member States mothers accounted for 73% of alleged abductors. The 'new' Member States, however, recorded a considerably higher proportion of respondent mothers, 83% (see Figure 6.27).

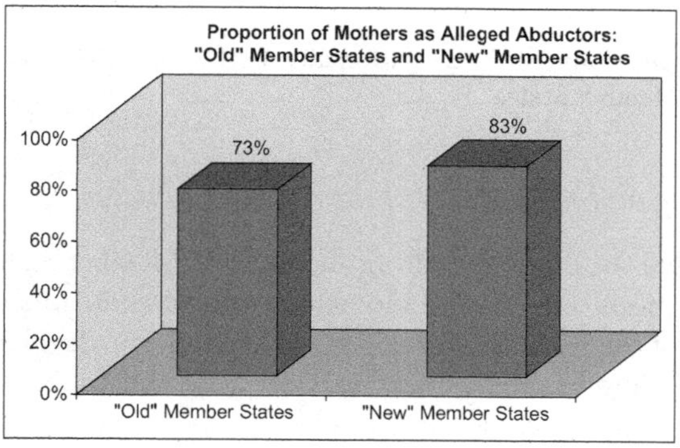

Figure 6.27: Proportion of mothers as alleged abductors: 'Old' Member States and 'new' Member States

iii. Nationality of the Alleged Abductor

The global analysis showed a general downward trend in the proportion of alleged abductors 'going home'.[257] This tendency was also recorded by the 'old' Members. In these EU Members, the percentage of alleged abductors who had the same nationality as the requested State fell by 7% (from 54% in 2003 to 47% in 2005/06) (see Figure 6.28).

In contrast, in the 'new' Member States, the proportion of alleged abductors 'going home' remained the same as in 2003 (83%) (see Figure 6.28). It is, however, to be pointed out that the percentage of 83% was noticeably high. Indeed,

[256] See Chapter 5, section entitled 'Relationship of the Alleged Abductor to the Child'.
[257] See Chapter 5, section entitled 'Nationality of the Alleged Abductor'.

it was almost double the proportion of 47% recorded in the 'old' Member States, and considerably higher (by 26%) than the global EU proportion of 57% (see Figure 6.28).

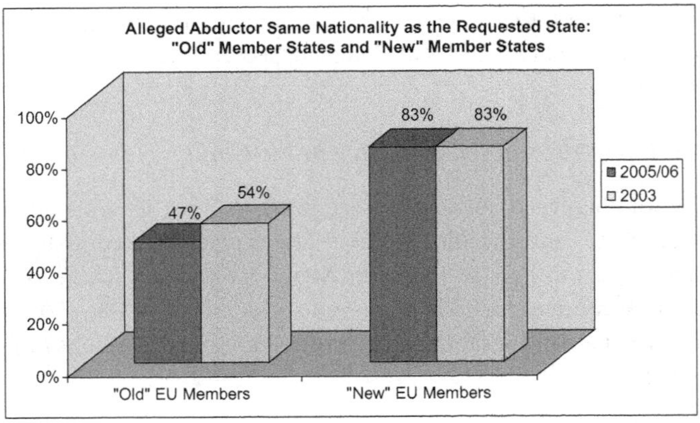

Figure 6.28: Alleged abductor same nationality as the requested State: 'Old' Member States and 'new' Member States

iv. Relationship and Nationality of the Alleged Abductor

A separate analysis of the records from the 'old' EU Member States revealed that in these jurisdictions only 49% of mothers as alleged abductors (63 out of 129) were nationals of the requested State. This was well below the global EU proportion of 58%.[258] However, in the 'new' EU Members, this proportion was almost double the percentage recorded in the 'old' Members (84%, 38 out of 45) (see Figure 6.29 below).

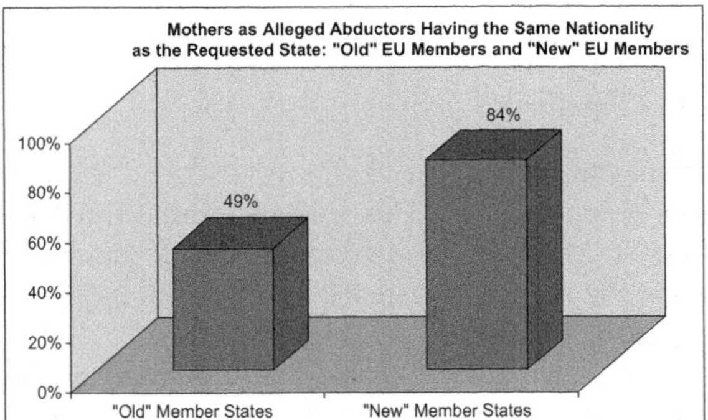

Figure 6.29: Mothers as alleged abductors having the same nationality as the requested State: 'Old' Member States and 'new' Member States

[258] See Chapter 5, section entitled 'Relationship and Nationality of the Alleged Abductor'.

Interestingly, almost no difference was found in the proportion of fathers having the same nationality as the requested State in the 'old' Member States and the 'new' Member States. Indeed, the analysis showed that 55% of respondent fathers (26 out of 51) in the 'old' Member States and 56% of respondent fathers in the 'new' Member States were nationals of the requested State.[259] Moreover, both figures were in line with the global EU proportion of 53% (see Figure 6.30).

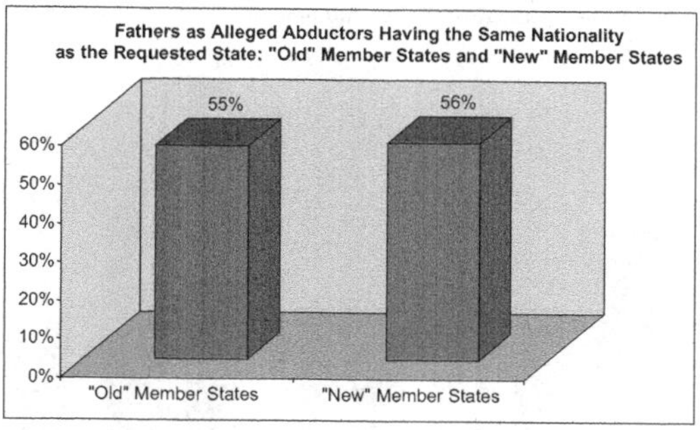

Figure 6.30: Fathers as alleged abductors having the same nationality as the requested State: 'Old' Member States and 'new' Member States

v. Outcomes and Timing

Overall, 45% of the return applications ended with the child being returned. In the 'new' Member States, however, only 38% of the applications (20) resulted in the return of the child. At 47%, the overall return rate in the 'old' Member States was 9% higher than the overall return rate in the 'new' Member States.

Of the 20 applications that ended with the return of the child, only three resulted in the return order not by consent. These accounted for 6% of all applications. This was significantly lower than the proportion of return orders not by consent recorded in the 'old' Member States (19%) (see Figure 6.31). On the other hand, however, the 'new' Member States recorded a higher proportion of judicial returns by consent than the 'old' EU Members (15% as opposed to 11%). Also, at 17%, the percentage of voluntary returns was the same as in the 'old' Member States.

Interestingly, the proportion of judicial refusals in the 'new' Member States was 2% lower than it was in the 'old' Member States (6% as opposed to 8%).

Interestingly, in the 'new' Member States, no application resulted in access being ordered or agreed. In the 'old' Member States, 6% of applications ended in an access agreement or an access order rather than a return order.

The figure below indicates very bad timing in the 'new' Member States. Indeed, the proportion of pending applications was almost three times higher in the

[259] However, it must be noted that the figures in relation to respondent fathers in the 'new' EU Member States were too low to enable an absolutely reliable conclusion to be drawn.

'new' Member States than it was in the 'old' Member States (32% as opposed to 12%).

Finally, the proportion of withdrawn applications in the 'new' Member States was 10% higher than it was in the 'old' Member States (21% as opposed to 11%).

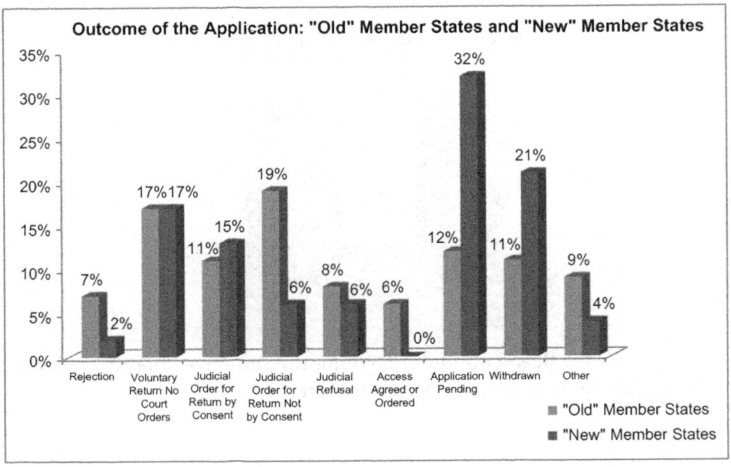

Figure 6.31: Outcome of the application: 'Old' Member States and 'new' Member States

B. Areas of Concern

The above analysis underlines two key areas of concern: outcomes and timing. In particular, the survey shows that the overall return rate in the 'new' Member States was 11% lower than it was in the 'old' Member States. Another worrying finding was the high proportion of pending cases. Indeed, at the cut-off date for the survey, in the 'new' Member States, the proportion of pending applications was almost three times higher than it was in the 'old' Member States. The poor timing had in turn an adverse effect on the withdrawal rate,[260] causing the proportion of withdrawn applications in the 'new' Member States to be 10% higher than it was in the 'old' Member States.

The findings of the survey were surprisingly closely reiterated by the follow-up interviews, with outcomes and timing being highlighted as the most worrying aspects. The follow-up interviews revealed that courts in the 'new' Member States often encountered serious difficulties when handling return applications. Many judges, when being presented with an application under the 1980 Convention or the Regulation, did not have sufficient knowledge about these international instruments and simply did not know how to proceed. Often, they investigated issues related to

[260] Generally, if the return proceedings take too long, applicants—frustrated with the lack of result—are more likely to withdraw their return applications.

custody in order to reach a conclusion on parental responsibilities. To make matters even worse, in one Czech application, for example, instead of returning the child or refusing the return the relevant Czech court decided to stay the return proceedings because 'it did not have jurisdiction to decide on the case as there was a foreign element involved'. With regard to the problem of timing, the follow-up interviews revealed that in most cases, judges were not aware of the six-week time limit to decide on the return application. Alarmingly, even where the judges were aware of the six-week time limit, they did not appear to take this obligation seriously.

C. Underlying Causes of Ineffective Operation of the Regulation in the 'New' Member States

One inevitably feels prompted to broach the question of the reasons behind the ineffective operation of the Convention and the Regulation in the 'new' Member States. In search of an answer, the follow-up interviews indicated several immediate causes: non-concentrated jurisdiction for adjudication of child abduction cases as a primary cause; and insufficient judicial training and overall condition of courts, that is, case backlog and overload, as secondary causes.

Additionally, in more general terms, the follow-up interviews suggested that central to the origins of the given problem were fundamental historical differences between the 'old' Member States and the 'new' Member States, in particular the communist history of the latter Members.

i. Non-Concentrated Jurisdiction, Insufficient Judicial Training and Overall Conditions of Courts

It has generally been recognised that concentrated jurisdiction and a good quality judicial training are the key elements to successful operation of the Convention.[261] It is in recognition of this truth that the Practice Guide for the application of the Brussels II bis Regulation notes that Member States which 'have centralised the application of cases under the 1980 Hague Convention to a limited number of courts ... show an increase in quality and efficiency'.[262] It also points out that 'the complexity of the various international instruments in the field of child abduction calls for specialised or well-trained judges'.[263]

Despite this recommendation, the majority of the 'new' Member States have failed to restrict the number of courts adjudicating child abduction

[261] See, eg, Lord Justice Thorpe: '[I]t is to be hoped that a keener appreciation of the requirements of the Convention will be achieved by restricting the number of judges exercising the jurisdiction and by offering them preparatory training'. The Right Honourable Lord Justice Thorpe, 'Interdisciplinary and Internationality in Modern Family Justice Systems' [2007] *International Family Law Journal* 165.

[262] Commission Practice Guide (n 65) 38.

[263] *Ibid.*

applications.[264] The non-concentrated jurisdiction, coupled with court systems lacking resources and sufficient knowledge of EU law, has been the key practical hurdle for effective application of the Convention and the Regulation.

In confirmation of this hypothesis, the follow-up interview with the Czech Central Authority, for example, revealed that due to the non-concentration of jurisdiction coupled with the lack of specialisation of judges, it was not possible to provide training on this very specific problem of private international law for all Czech judges who could potentially deal with child abduction cases. Consequently, if a return application was allocated to a judge who had not been trained in the 1980 Convention and the Regulation, this judge was very likely to fail in processing the application. The interview also highlighted the fact that the County Courts (which deal with return applications at first instance) were often extremely overloaded. Consequently, the judge who had never been trained in the area of child abduction did not have enough time for a quality self-study of the relevant international/European legislation on the problem in question.

ii. Fundamental Historical Differences Between the 'Old' Member States and the 'New' Member States

Prior to the 2004 enlargement, the Central and Eastern European countries (CEECs)[265] had been rather alienated from the rest of the European Community. Following the end of the Second World War, the CEECs came under the Soviet sphere of influence and were socialised according to the Soviet pattern. As a result, the satellite region was exposed to four decades of communist ideology, 'Soviet-type corruption'[266] and socialist propaganda. These penetrated deeply into the national administrations and judicial systems of the CEECs. It was only in the early 1990s when the fall of the Iron Curtain and the end of the Cold War made it possible for the CEECs to aspire to enter the liberal organisations of Europe, including the European Union.

The transformation from communist to democratic systems of governance was not an easy process. It involved a long battle where the communist-style governance had to be dismantled and 'institutions had to be rebuilt brick by brick'.[267] One of the core elements of the transformation was a judicial reform in the

[264] Permanent Bureau of the Hague Conference, 'Questionnaire Concerning the Practical Operation of the Hague Convention of 25 October 1980 on the Civil Aspects of International Child Abduction' (April 2006) Responses to Question 6, available at www.hcch.net/index_en.php?act=publications.details&pid=3765&dtid=3.

[265] The phrase 'Central and Eastern European countries' (CEECs) is used here to refer to eight of the 10 'new' Member States: Estonia, Latvia, Lithuania, Poland, the Czech Republic, Hungary, Slovakia and Slovenia. The expansion of the European Union that took place in 2004 also involved the accession of Malta and Cyprus. However, since this section is focused on the common history of the CEECs, the use of the expression 'the "new" Member States' does not refer to either Malta or Cyprus.

[266] C Varga, 'Transformation to Rule of Law From No Law: Societal Contexture of the Democratic Transition in Central and Eastern Europe' (1992–1993) 8 *Connecticut Journal of International Law* 487, 488.

[267] Richardson, 'The Road to a Unified Peaceful Europe' (n 249) 5 and 9.

sense of the 'purification' of the judiciary from the communist-era judges. It is in particular the mindset of judges that has been a primary concern in this respect.[268] It has rightly been pointed out that it would be unrealistic to expect the old judges, 'discredited by their service to the Communist regimes',[269] to be capable of mending their ways of thinking 'by a simple pronouncement or decision'.[270] Indeed, 'one simply cannot get rid of what became ingrained by nonchalantly throwing one's garment into the corner'.[271] Unfortunately, however, the process of intellectual reconstruction of judiciary remained incomplete at the enlargement,[272] having a damaging effect on the quality of judicial decision-making in the post-communist democracies.[273] The post-communist judiciary still suffers from numerous defects, including lack of experience with the application of international law, and the struggle to overcome methodological problems of post-communist legal reasoning such as extreme formalism and textual positivism.[274] The fatal impact of the imperfect purification of judiciary in the area of child abduction has been well captured by the follow-up interview with the Czech Central Authority. The Central Authority stated that, in 1984, the former Czechoslovakia was invited to become a Member State to the 1980 Convention. The then communist country, however, decided to reject the invitation. The underlying reason was that the communist ideology viewed the West as an 'enemy territory', untrustworthy of the protection of the best interests of the child, especially if a Czech child was involved. As a result, it seemed unacceptable to the communist judiciary to eventually order the return of a Czech child wrongfully removed to or retained in Czechoslovakia back to a 'capitalist' requesting State. Alarmingly, the interview revealed that this line of reasoning was still subtly present among part of the

[268] In this respect it has rightly been observed in general terms that 'fragments of old customs' as unwritten factors that exist between the 'written formula and the new law' have a profound effect on the mindset of jurists. R Sacco, 'One Hundred Years of Comparative Law' (2001) 75 *Tulane Law Review* 1159, 1169.

[269] Varga, 'Transformation to Rule of Law' (n 266) 504.

[270] *Ibid.*

[271] *Ibid.*

[272] G Pridham, 'The EU's Political Conditionality and Post-Accession Tendencies: Comparisons from Slovakia and Latvia' (2008) 46 *Journal of Common Market Studies* 365, 375. Of the Central and Eastern European countries, only the former East Germany has been able to recreate its entire judiciary by 'importing well-trained and impartial judges'. J Radon, 'Permitted Unless Prohibited: The Changed Soviet Mentality' (1996) 20 *Fordham International Law Journal* 365, per J Sitarz, 'Recent Changes to the Legal Professions of Central and Eastern Europe: The Case of Poland' (2008) 40 *Connecticut Law Review* 883, fn 80.

[273] G Falkner and O Treib, 'Three Worlds of Compliance or Four? The EU-15 Compared to New Member States' (2008) 46 *Journal of Common Market Studies* 293, 298. The Global Competitiveness Report 2004/2005 indicated judicial effectiveness estimate in the 'new' Member States far below the 'old' Member States. On a percentage scale, the judicial effectiveness estimate in Bulgaria, the Czech Republic and Slovakia, for example, was 22.4, 37.4 and 37.5 respectively. These figures contrasted sharply with, eg, Sweden and the United Kingdom, with judicial effectiveness estimate of 93.2 and 93.1 respectively. See the World Economic Forum, Global Competitiveness Report 2004/2005, per D Bozhilova, 'Measuring Successes and Failure of EU Europeanization in the Eastern Enlargement: Judicial Reform in Bulgaria' (2007) 9 *European Journal of Law Reform* 285, 296.

[274] Z Kühn, 'Worlds Apart: Western and Central European Judicial Culture at the Onset of the European Enlargement' (2004) 52 *American Journal of Comparative Law* 531, 532.

Czech judiciary, in particular among those judges who had started their judicial career prior to the 1989 Velvet Revolution, during the communist regime in the former Czechoslovakia. As a result, these judges are reluctant to defend the rule of law when it works against Czech citizens, posing a serious stumbling block in the successful application of the summary return mechanism. The gravity of this finding is exacerbated by the high proportion of alleged abductors 'going home' recorded in the 'new' Member States. At 83%, it was almost double the proportion recorded in the 'old' Member States (47%), and considerably higher than the global EU proportion (57%).

It is submitted here that the above-described situation is not specific to the Czech Republic only but, unfortunately, is very much the same in other post-communist European democracies. What comes to mind in this context is the principle of mutual trust among the EU Member States as one of the underlying principles of the Regulation.[275] As shown by the follow-up interview with the Czech Republic, regrettably, there is still a great deal of lack of trust on the side of the Central and Eastern European ex-communist Member States towards their Western European partners. This revelation highlights the urgency of the need for the completion of the judicial reform in the 'new' Member States. The total replacement of the old judiciary by a young generation of judges trained in the spirit of democratic values is the only way the 'new' Member States can become trustworthy Members of the European Union in the sense of progressing towards an effective application of the EU legislation, the child abduction provisions of the Brussels II bis Regulation included.

It may be argued that the care and justice orientations of judges in the 'old' Member States and the 'new' Member States differ rather radically. Judges in the 'old' Member States are more amenable to ordering return even in the face of ineffective legal protection of the returning parent compared to judges in the 'new' Member States who are more supportive of non-return orders when the interests of their own citizens are being threatened.[276] This line of argument is, however, not accepted here. It is submitted that when refusing a return, judges in the 'new' Member States are not motivated primarily by considerations for the safety of the returning parent. Rather, the tendency to place preference for their own society above objective considerations in return applications is a reflection of ideological considerations that still exist in judges' subconscious minds as a 'heritage' of the communist regime in the CEECs.

[275] Commission Practice Guide (n 65) 25.

[276] On the problem of the care and justice considerations of legal practitioners and scholars in contemporary culture see writings of the feminist legal critic Carrie Menkel-Meadow, eg C Menkel-Meadow, 'Peace and Justice: Notes on the Evolution and Purposes of Legal Processes [Comments] (2006) 94 *Georgetown Law Journal* 553; and C Menkel-Meadow, 'What's Gender Got to Do with it: The Politics and Morality of an Ethic of Care [Comments]' (1996) 22 *New York University Review of Law & Social Change* 265. The above argument appears to be of particular importance given the facts that in the 'new' Member States, a significantly higher proportion of mothers as alleged abductors were 'going home' than in the 'old' Member States (84% as opposed to 49%); the overall return rate in the 'new' Member States was markedly lower than in the 'old' Member States; and that in many cases the return objective is placed above the safety of the returning parent. (See section entitled 'No Consideration for the Safety of the Returning Parent' above.)

7

Added Value of the Brussels II bis Regulation: A More Child-Centred Approach as a Result of the Obligation to Hear the Child Introduced by Article 11(2) of the Regulation

The previous Chapter analysed issues indicated by the statistical survey as the main areas of concern with respect to the application and operation of the Brussels II bis Regulation. It highlighted a number of shortcomings. Despite the overall critical attitude of this book towards the Regulation, in order to remain objective and to offer a balanced picture it is considered equally important to acknowledge those aspects of the Regulation that represent an added value and to devote them some space. It is suggested that besides the general objective of the Regulation to reinforce the Convention policy, this instrument deserves praise for its focus on the voice of the child in the return proceedings.[1] Indeed, the

[1] An important argument in favour of hearing children in return proceedings is that in order to determine the child's maturity, a personal contact with the child may be inevitable. No less importantly, the information provided by the child may be important evidence of a situation which justifies a refusal to return on the grounds of Art 13(1)(b). See P Beaumont and P McEleavy, *The Hague Convention on International Child Abduction* (Oxford, Oxford University Press, 1999) 198. The right of the child to be heard in Convention proceedings has been given high importance also by the European Court of Human Rights in its case law on child abduction. For detailed analysis of ECtHR case law on child abduction see P Beaumont, 'The Jurisprudence of the European Court of Human Rights and the European Court of Justice on the Hague Convention on International Child Abduction' (2008) 335 *Hague Recueil* 98; and L Walker, 'The Impact of the Hague Abduction Convention on the Rights of the Family in the Case-Law of the European Court of Human Rights and the UN Human Rights Committee: The Danger of *Neulinger*' (2010) 6 *Journal of Private International Law* 649. A contrasting view has, however, been expressed by Sarah Vigers, who believes that many of the children that are now heard in Convention proceedings are too young and that this practice should be revisited; S Vigers, *Mediating International Child Abduction Cases* (Oxford, Hart Publishing, 2011) 84 and 91. According to Vigers, it is questionable whether hearing younger children is in their best interests as "their views in many cases will carry little or no weight" (*ibid*, 90). Similarly, Thalia Kruger suggests that young children should not be given the impression that they may decide the outcome of return proceedings. Children often perceive this as having to choose between their mother and father and it can place

Regulation places a high priority on the right of the child to be heard, recognising the importance of autonomous evaluation of the child's views and imposing on the courts the obligation to examine the child's wishes in the return proceedings. In particular, the Regulation states:

> When applying Articles 12 and 13 of the 1980 Hague Convention, it shall be ensured that the child is given the opportunity to be heard during the proceedings unless this appears inappropriate having regard to his or her age or degree of maturity. [2]

The principle of a mandatory hearing of the child of an appropriate age and a sufficient degree of maturity established by Article 11(2) represents an expansion on the Convention obligation to hear the child in those abduction cases where the defence of child's objections has been raised by the abducting parent (see Article 13(2) of the Hague Convention).[3] Importantly, the provision of Article 13(2) of the Convention must be seen in a wider context of the right of the child to have a say and be heard in matters affecting his/her life, as a part of the so-called participation rights. The right of the child to have his/her views respected has been incorporated into Article 12 of the 1989 United Nations Convention on the Rights of the Child (UNCRC)[4] and represents one of the four core principles of this Convention.[5]

on them 'a sense of responsibility which they are too young to assume'. T Kruger, *International Child Abduction: Inadequacies of the Law* (Oxford, Hart Publishing, 2011) 38.

[2] Brussels II bis Regulation Art 11(2). For a brief but very clear analysis of Art 13(2) of the Convention and Art 11(2) of the Regulation see P Beaumont and P McEleavy, *Private International Law, Anton*, 3rd edn (Edinburgh, W Green & SULI, 2011) 830–3. See also P McEleavy, 'Evaluating the Views of Abducted Children: Trends in Appellate Case Law' (2008) 20 *Child and Family Law Quarterly* 230. For an academic discussion of Art 11(2) of the Regulation see R Lamont, 'The EU: Protecting Children's Rights in Child Abduction' [2008] *International Family Law Journal* 126. Lamont acknowledges the European Union's increasing willingness to incorporate children's rights in the legislation that concerns children, but argues that in the case of the Brussels II bis Regulation only 'a blanket policy of incorporation' was pursued. Given the fact that the Regulation does not alter rules on the exercise of discretion, in order to give effect to the Convention return obligation reinforced by the Regulation, most children who would be heard would still need to be returned to the requesting State. Lamont in this context suggests that 'greater sensitivity to the legislative context may be required for the EU to understand the purpose of securing those [children's] rights'. It is, nevertheless, submitted that, even if the judge does not necessarily follow the child's wishes, the obligation to give the child an opportunity to be heard presents the court with a chance to explain to the child the underlying purpose of the Convention and the return mechanism. It is hoped that, despite being returned, such a child will not feel as a mere object of the return proceedings as he/she would have gained the understanding of the context within which the Convention/Regulation operate. This argument is of particular significance in abductions involving older children.

[3] The obligation to hear children in Convention proceedings is implied from the wording of Art 13(2) of the Convention: 'The judicial or administrative authority may also refuse to order the return of the child if it finds that the child objects to being returned and has attained an age and maturity at which it is appropriate to take account of its views.'

[4] The United Nations Convention on the Rights of the Child (the UNCRC) entered into force in September 1990 and as of January 2010 had been ratified or acceded to by 193 countries. See Status Table, available at www.treaties.un.org/Pages/ViewDetails.aspx?src=TREATY&mtdsg_no=IV-11&chapter=4&lang=en.

[5] Art 12 of the UNCRC states: '(1) States parties shall assure to the child who is capable of forming his or her own views the right to express those views freely in all matters affecting the child,

The analysis below looks into the practical operation of Article 11(2) of the Regulation by way of researching available case law, and aims at revealing what impact the provision has had on the treatment of the voice of the child in abduction cases. The analysis focuses on the EU jurisdictions of England and Wales, Scotland, Ireland and Northern Ireland. Other Member States have not been included because of the lack of available case law.

The analysis of EU case law is followed by the examination of current approaches toward the defence of child's objections in major non-EU jurisdictions (that is, Australia, Canada and the United States). The principal goal of this analysis is to explore how the current Australian, Canadian and US case law approaches the Article 13(2) defence of child's objections. It aims at concluding whether the recent EU authorities on child's objections show signs of a more child-centred approach than the case law from the major non-Brussels II bis jurisdictions. Ultimately, the analysis is intended to reveal whether, based on the comparison with the latest case law from non-EU jurisdictions, it is possible to conclude that the obligation of Article 11(2) of the Regulation has had a major impact on the treatment of the voice of the child in abduction cases in the European Union.

I. EU Jurisdictions: England and Wales, Scotland, Ireland and Northern Ireland

Given the complexity of the available case law, and for ease of reference, the analysis below has been broken into four interrelated categories:

1. Automatic inquiry into the views of the child.
2. Minimum age of the child.
3. The method of the examination of child's views.
4. Exercise of the discretion to return.

Within a particular category, the jurisdictions are dealt with separately, subject to availability of the relevant case law.

A. Automatic Inquiry into the Views of the Child

Article 11(2) of the Regulation mandates courts to adopt a proactive approach to investigation of the views of children involved in the return proceedings. In particular, all children of a sufficient age and degree of maturity involved in cases

the views of the child being given due weight in accordance with the age and maturity of the child. (2) For this purpose, the child shall in particular be provided the opportunity to be heard in any judicial and administrative proceedings affecting the child, either directly, or through a representative or an appropriate body, in a manner consistent with the procedural rules'.

where Articles 12 or 13 of the Hague Convention are raised must be given the opportunity to be heard.

i. England and Wales

a. *Re D (A Child)*[6]

Considering the geographic scope of the application of the Regulation, the obligation to examine the child's views arises *de lege* only in intra-EU child abduction cases. However, in the House of Lords decision in the case of *Re D (a child)*, Baroness Hale of Richmond expressed the view that 'the principle is of universal application and consistent with our international obligations under Article 12 of the UNCRC'. *Re D (a child)* involved a Romanian boy, aged eight, who had been removed from Romania and brought to England by his mother at the age of four, in December 2002. As the removal of the child took place prior to Romania's joining the European Union in January 2007 (and even prior to the Regulation's entry into force), this case did not fall within the new EU child abduction regime. In February 2003, proceedings were initiated by the father for the return of the child under the Hague Convention. A declaration pursuant to Article 15 of the Convention as to whether the removal of the child was 'wrongful' was sought from Romanian courts. The first instance court in Bucharest then took two years to provide the declaration. In 2004, the court finally ruled that the removal of the child had not been wrongful under Romanian law. The father appealed. In 2005, the ruling of the trial court was reaffirmed by the Court of Appeal of Bucharest. The father then requested the High Court in London that an independent expert in Romanian law would be allowed to prepare a report on the issue of 'wrongfulness' of the child's removal. The request was granted by the High Court. The opinion of the expert was contradictory to the ruling of the Romanian Court of Appeal. By the time the case came on for hearing in the English Court, the boy was already eight years old. In March 2006, the High Court ordered the return of the child. This decision was upheld by the Court of Appeal. The mother then appealed successfully to the House of Lords.

Before the trial court, there was no material available to the judge communicating the wishes of the child. The mother had applied for the examination of the child's views through a CAFCASS officer but her application had been refused. Following the first instance return order, the child spoke to a highly experienced solicitor in the area of child abduction. She signed an affidavit stating that the boy held strong objections to the return to Romania. The child then applied for leave to intervene in the appellate proceedings on the basis that at the first instance his mother had not raised his objections as a potential defence and he therefore needed to communicate his views directly to the court. The Appellate Court, however, refused the boy's application to intervene and ordered that the child be heard by a CAFCASS officer. Although a CAFCASS report was prepared, the

[6] *Re D (a child)* [2006] UKHL 51, [2007] 1 AC 619.

court did not give much weight to the child's objections as he was not separately represented and his objections did not form part of the mother's grounds for appeal. The boy subsequently sought leave to intervene in the appeal before the House of Lords. His petition was granted. This led to an unusual situation when the House of Lords was dealing with an issue that had not been considered either at first instance or in the Court of Appeal.

Although the issue of the child's objections was not determinative for the case,[7] Baroness Hale of Richmond gave consideration to the application of Article 13(2). In the beginning of her analysis, Baroness Hale pointed out that the present day was marked with 'a growing understanding' of the significance of listening to the children involved in family proceedings. At paragraph 57 she stated:

> It is the child, more than anyone else, who will have to live with what the court decides. Those who do listen to children understand that they often have a point of view which is quite distinct from that of the person looking after them. They are quite capable of being moral actors in their own right.[8]

Consequently, Baroness Hale expressed the view that children should be given the opportunity to be heard in return proceedings far more often than had previously been the practice. In particular, she emphasised that the principle set out in Article 11(2) of the Regulation should apply not only to abduction cases within the European Union but in every Hague Convention case. She also stated that the principle applies in all Convention cases, not just those in which a child's objections defence is raised.[9]

b. *Re F (A Child) (Abduction: Obligation to Hear Child)*[10]

The significance of the House of Lords decision in the case of *Re D (a child)* was emphasised by the Court of Appeal decision in the Brussels II bis case of *Re F (a child) (abduction: obligation to hear child)*.[11] In this case, the trial court failed to meet its obligation to give the child an opportunity to be heard during the return proceedings. This mistake was strongly criticised by Thorpe LJ at the Court of Appeal

[7] The father's return application was dismissed on the basis of Art 3 of the Convention. The House of Lords held that, as determined by the Romanian courts, the father lacked rights of custody for the purposes of the Convention and therefore the removal of the child was not wrongful.

[8] *Re D (a child)* [2006] UKHL 51, [2007] 1 AC 619 para 57.

[9] This proposal attracted severe criticism from Sir Nicholas Wilson. He argued that hearing children in abduction cases where defences unrelated to child's objections are involved (ie consent or acquiescence) would mislead the child into assuming that his/her views will determine the outcome of the case. Moreover, according to Sir Nicholas, hearing children in all abduction cases would lead to the waste of the resources of CAFCASS. This way Sir Nicholas targeted the principle of Art 11(2) of the Regulation itself. See Sir N Wilson, 'The Ears of the Child in Family Proceedings' (2007) 37 *Family Law Journal* 808. Baroness Hale accepted the argument that the child's wishes may not always be relevant to the issue of the case; however, she argued that the hearing of the child would offer an excellent opportunity to explain this to the child. See Baroness Hale of Richmond, 'The Voice of the Child' [2007] *International Family Law Journal* 171, fn 5.

[10] *Re F (a child) (abduction: obligation to hear child)* [2007] EWCA Civ 468, [2007] 2 FLR 697.

[11] *Ibid.*

and an indirect appeal was made to draw particular attention to the obligation imposed on the courts by Article 11(2) of the Regulation. Thorpe LJ said:

> I am surprised that the novel obligation imposed by Article 11, and highlighted by the relatively recent decision of the House of Lords in the case of *D (a child)* WLR [2006], UKHL 51 (51–71) decided in October 2006, has not focussed more attention on steps that need to be taken to ensure that in every case the Article 11 obligation is not overlooked.[12]

In the light of the speech of Baroness Hale in *Re D*, the Court of Appeal highlighted the importance of the instant case as precedent not only for future Brussels II bis cases but also for potential 'global abduction cases'.[13]

Facts of the case: The child involved in this application was a seven-year-old girl, habitually resident in Spain. The mother and the child came to England with the consent of the father to spend Christmas with maternal grandparents. They did not go back to Spain. The father initiated return proceedings nine months later. The mother argued that the father had acquiesced to the removal of the child and/or that the return would expose the child to a grave risk of harm. Her case was, however, rejected and the return of the child was ordered.

Legal issues: The mother appealed. She submitted that the trial judge had failed to fulfil the obligation of Article 11(2) of the Regulation to give the child an opportunity to be heard during the return proceedings. In its response, the Court of Appeal exhibited a highly child-focused attitude. Although no specific request regarding the hearing of the child was made at first instance, the mother's submission was accepted by the Appellate Court. The Court of Appeal concluded that it was a duty of the trial judge to hear the child, regardless of whether the parties made a reference to the obligation of Article 11(2) of the Regulation in their submissions or not, and more generally, regardless of the nature of the abducting parent's objections to return. Particularly, the court highlighted that the obligation to hear the child that arises from Article 11(2) of the Regulation was quite unrelated to the child's objections defence that is incorporated into Article 13(2) of the Convention:

> It was not a case in which the child's wishes and feelings had been projected into the centre of the stage by reliance on the child's objection to return. But a clear distinction has to be drawn between obligations that flow from a pleading of the child's objections and the court's obligation, quite apart from anything that may be pleaded, in all cases to hear the child, unless that necessity is excused by reference to the child's age and understanding.[14]

Moreover, it was rightly pointed out by counsel for the mother that a lack of reference to the court's obligation to hear the child in the parties' submissions may be

[12] *Ibid*, para 22.
[13] *Ibid*, para 25.
[14] *Ibid*, para 16.

motivated by tactical reasons, particularly by an effort to prevent the child from revealing certain facts of the case.

> Mr Setright reminds us that it can be something of a dangerous development in a Hague case since the child, when heard, may easily negate a defence that has been raised or developed by the abductor. So, it might be said that this was a strategic decision on the part of each of the parties: but the court is not concerned and certainly not ruled by the litigation strategy of either of the parties. It has an obligation, imposed by Article 11.2, to hear the child, whatever may be the consequences.[15]

Ruling: The court held that the trial judge had erred in not ensuring that the child was given an opportunity to be heard during the return proceedings as was her right granted by the Regulation. Accordingly, the appeal was allowed and the case was remitted for further consideration.

c. *M v M*[16]

The principle that in Brussels II bis child abduction cases, children of sufficient age and degree of maturity must be given an opportunity to express their views, regardless of whether the defence of child's objection has been raised or not, established by the Regulation and reaffirmed by the Court of Appeal in *Re F (a child) (abduction: obligation to hear child)* in March 2007, was followed in the proceedings in the case of *M v M*. This application was decided by the High Court in June 2007. The instant case involved two boys, born in England in 1996 and 2000 respectively. In 2002, the family moved to Greece. While in Greece, the relationship between the parents deteriorated and the mother suggested that she would return to England with the boys. The father agreed and in January 2007, the mother went to England alone with the children. The father was in phone contact with the sons and never made a request for return. Upon their arrival in England the mother initiated divorce proceedings. As soon as the father became aware of it, he commenced return proceedings. The father argued that he had not consented to the divorce and that it was planned that he would join the family later. The court, however, did not accept his submission and concluded that, at the time when the mother was leaving Greece, the father was aware of her intention to initiate divorce proceedings and agreed to the divorce. Consequently, the court found that the father consented to the removal of the children and dismissed his return application.

Although the mother's defence was based solely on Article 13(1)(a) consent and no recourse was made to the exception of Article 13(2) child's objections, the High Court ordered the hearing of the children. The boys were interviewed by a CAFCASS officer and their views were attached weight by the trial judge when assessing available evidence and reaching the decision.

[15] *Ibid*, para 17.

[16] *M v M* [2007] EWHC 1404 (Fam), [2007] 2 FLR 1010.

d. *K v K (Formerly P)*[17]

The importance of the Article 11(2) obligation in the context of the child's objections defence was also recognised in the High Court decision in the case of *K v K (formerly P)*. In particular, the court pointed out that the obligation to hear the child had been reinforced by the Brussels II bis Regulation:

> There are two important provisions within Article 11 [of the Regulation] relevant to this application. Under Article 11.2 and 11.3. – '2. When applying Article 12 and 13 of the 1980 Hague Convention it shall be ensured that the child is given the opportunity to be heard during the proceedings unless this appears inappropriate having regard to his or her age or degree of maturity'.[18]

ii. Ireland

The available case law indicates that, like English courts, the courts in Ireland have also given due weight to the obligation imposed by Article 11(2) of the Brussels II bis Regulation. It appears that children are routinely heard in all Brussels II bis cases involving the exceptions of Article 12 and 13 of the Convention, irrespective of the precise nature of the abducting parent's defence. In *VG applicant and P McD respondent*,[19] for example, the defence was based exclusively on Article 13(a) acquiescence. Nevertheless, the High Court highlighted the Article 11(2) duty to give the children involved the opportunity to express their views and feelings, even though in the end none of the three minors concerned, aged seven, four and three respectively, was found to be of sufficient age that his/her views could be taken into account. The court stated:

> Article 11.2 of Council Regulation 2201/2003 which applies to these proceedings obliges the Court to ensure that a child is given the opportunity to be heard in proceedings when applying Articles 12 and 13 of the Hague Convention 'unless this appears inappropriate having regard to his or her age or degree of maturity'. Having regard to the age of each of the children to which these proceedings relate it appeared inappropriate that the Court should hear the children.[20]

Similarly, in the case of *FL v CL*[21] the obligation of Article 11(2) of the Regulation received considerable attention from the High Court. Despite the fact that the defence was based solely on Article 13(1)(a) consent/acquiescence, the court examined the views of the eldest child (aged nine). The court stated:

> Article 11.2 of Regulation 2201/2003 obliges this Court to ensure that a child is given the opportunity to be heard during the proceedings 'unless this appears inappropriate having regard to his or her age or degree of maturity'. Having regard to the age of each of the children I am satisfied that it was only appropriate that O [the eldest child] should

[17] *K v K (formerly P)* [2006] EWHC 2685 (Fam), [2007] 1 FCR 355.
[18] *Ibid*, para 5.
[19] *VG applicant and P McD respondent* [2006] IEHC 69.
[20] *Ibid*, transcript, last paragraph.
[21] *FL v CL* [2006] IEHC 66, [2007] 2 IR 630.

> be interviewed in relation to the order for return sought. Further, having regard both to the age and to the degree of maturity of O I am satisfied that it was appropriate that she be heard in the proceedings by the assessment conducted by Dr Byrne [consultant child psychiatrist] and his report to the Court.[22]

The child objected to the return to Northern Ireland; however, the application for return had been refused on the ground of acquiescence and therefore it was unnecessary for the court to consider the issue of the child's objections.

B. Minimum Age of the Child

The Brussels II bis Regulation does not set a minimum age when the child must be given the opportunity to be heard. Neither does the Convention describe what age is considered 'appropriate' for the child's views 'to be taken into account'. It is left to the discretion of the court to judge the appropriateness of the child's age in each particular case.[23]

i. England and Wales

Although the English courts have not laid down any lower limit for the age of the child, the case law prior to 2005 indicated that the age range of 9–10 would generally be considered as the minimum 'appropriate' age.[24] In *Re D (a child)*,[25] however, Baroness Hale indicated that the youngest age at which a court should regard it as appropriate to take account of a child's views should be lowered to the age of 7½. Commenting on the circumstances of the case in question, Baroness Hale suggested that at the time of the commencement of the first instance proceedings, it would have been inappropriate to hear the child's views, as then he was only seven years old. However, once the proceedings went beyond then, the child 'had reached an age where it could no longer be taken for granted that it was inappropriate for him to be given the opportunity of being heard'. In more general terms, Baroness Hale expressed a view that 'children should be heard far more frequently in Hague Convention cases than has been the practice before'.[26]

[22] *Ibid*, para 41.

[23] The 'margin of appreciation' given to national courts to decide on how to interpret Art 13(2) of the Convention was emphasised by the European Court of Human Rights in *Maumousseau and Washington v France*, ECtHR, 6 December 2007, No 39388/05. P Beaumont, 'The Jurisprudence of the European Court of Human Rights and the European Court of Justice on the Hague Convention on International Child Abduction' (2008) 335 *Hague Recueil* 64. It appears that the court would defend the right of any school-aged child to be given the opportunity to express his/her views in return proceedings. *Ibid*, 98. Interestingly, in Belgium and the Netherlands, children below the age of 12 are not heard in return proceedings. See Kruger, *International Child Abduction* (n 1) 35.

[24] Although in a few decisions, objections of children as young as seven years old were held to justify a refusal to return, it is to be pointed out that these cases are just exceptions to the rule. See, eg, *B v K (Child Abduction)* [1993] 1 FCR 382 and *Re B (Abduction: Children's Objections)* [1998] 1 FLR 667.

[25] *Re D (a child)* [2006] UKHL 51, [2007] 1 AC 619.

[26] *Ibid*, para 59.

The innovative approach to the threshold age adopted by Baroness Hale in *Re D (a child)* was followed by Thorpe LJ in the Brussels II bis case of *Re F (a child) (abduction: obligation to hear child)*.[27] Indeed, in spite of the young age of the child concerned (seven years), the Court of Appeal held that the Regulation granted the child the right to be listened to in the return proceedings. The court recognised that, as the girl concerned was only seven years old, it was entirely up to the consideration of the trial judge to make the decision whether to hear her views or not. Nevertheless, it concluded that the child's age did not discharge the first instance court from the Article 11(2) obligation.

> The child is only just within the chronological range where the obligation is transparent. This is clearly an area in which the judge had had discretion … That submission does not begin to convince me that the deficiency emphasised by Mr Setright [counsel for the appellant mother] can be ignored. It is a fundamental deficiency and it cannot be shored up or papered over.[28]

Consequently, the trial judge was held to have erred in not ensuring that the child of seven years of age was given the opportunity to be heard in the return proceedings.

The recommendation of Baroness Hale in *Re D (a child)* to lower the minimum 'appropriate' age was fully embraced and even taken a step further by the High Court in the Brussels II bis case of *Re W (Abduction: Acquiescence: Children's Objections)*[29]. The court found that a child as young as six, together with her sibling, aged eight, had genuinely objected to a return and had reached an age and degree of maturity at which it was appropriate to take account of their views, and refused to order their return. The court observed that following *Re D (a child)* the views on the minimum requisite age have evolved and concluded that there was 'no absolute threshold age below which a child cannot be sufficiently mature for the purposes of the child's objections defence'.[30]

> There is no absolute threshold age below which a child cannot be sufficiently mature for the purposes of the child's objections defence, nor are there even any presumptions … In any given case, one can only determine whether a child has the requisite age and degree of maturity by looking at the attributes of the particular child, the circumstances in which he finds himself, and the nature of the objections.[31]

The respondent father sought permission to appeal arguing that, among other shortcomings in the first instance proceedings, the views of the six-year-old child should not have been taken into account. The Court of Appeal refused leave to appeal but granted leave to cite the judgments.[32] Sedley LJ acknowledged that

[27] *Re F (a child) (abduction: obligation to hear child)* [2007] EWCA Civ 468, [2007] 2 FLR 697.
[28] *Ibid*, para 17.
[29] *Re W (Abduction: Acquiescence: Children's Objections)* [2010] EWHC 332 (Fam), [2010] 2 FLR 1150.
[30] *Ibid*, para 37.
[31] *Ibid*.
[32] *Re W (Minors)* [2010] EWCA Civ 520, [2010] 2 FLR 1165.

both children were very young. Nevertheless, referring to Article 12 of the UN Convention on the Rights of the Child and Article 11(2) of the Brussels II bis Regulation, he pointed out that 'over the last 30 years the need to take decisions about much younger children not necessarily in *accordance* with their wishes but at any rate in the *light* of their wishes has taken hold'.[33] Sedley LJ was satisfied that Article 13(2) of the Hague Abduction Convention had been drafted in adequately flexible terms to accommodate this trend.[34] Nevertheless, he acknowledged that there was a danger that the lowering of the age at which a child's objections could be taken into consideration might 'gradually erode' the success the Convention had achieved over the years in securing the return of abducted children. This risk, however, can be alleviated through the widely accepted expectation that in the exercise of discretion whether to order the return of an objecting child, the objections of an older child will merit greater weight than those of a younger child.[35]

ii. Scotland

In Scotland, the minimum age at which a child must be given the opportunity to be heard appears to be higher than it is currently in England and Wales. In particular, in the Brussels II bis case of *Re WT*,[36] a child aged eight was considered 'too young for his views to be weighed in the balance' and therefore his views remained 'unknown'. Similarly, in *C v C*,[37] a nine-year-old younger sibling was not given the opportunity to express her views.

C. The Method of the Examination of Child's Views

The Brussels II bis Regulation does not specify how the hearing of the child should be conducted. Consequently, practices vary from one jurisdiction to another.[38]

i. England and Wales

a. Judges Seeing Children

The standard practice in the Convention proceedings has been for the child to be interviewed by a CAFCASS officer (formerly a court welfare officer). In *Re M (A Minor) (Child Abduction)*[39] Butler-Sloss LJ observed that the court welfare

33 *Ibid*, para 17.
34 *Ibid*.
35 *Ibid*, para 18 (citing *Re R (Child Abduction: Acquiescence)* [1995] 1 FLR 716).
36 *Re WT* [2007] CSOH 72.
37 *C v C* 2008 SCLR 329, upheld by the Inner House, 2008 SC 571.
38 For a detailed information on particular jurisdictions see Permanent Bureau of the Hague Conference, 'Questionnaire Concerning the Practical Operation of the Hague Convention of 25 October 1980 on the Civil Aspects of International Child Abduction' (April 2006) Responses to Question 9, available at www.hcch.net/index_en.php?act=publications.details&pid=3870&dtid=33.
39 *Re M (A Minor) (Child Abduction)* [1994] 1 FRL 390.

officer was the most suitable person to assist the court in cases where the issue of child's objections was involved. She said:

> In this case the obvious person to assist the court in an assessment of the degree of maturity of each child is the court welfare officer. He is also able to provide the court with the views of the child he has interviewed.

English judges have generally been reluctant to interview the child in private in the return proceedings. Indeed, in *S v S (Child Abduction)*[40] Ewbank J expressed the view that it would be 'an inappropriate step for a judge to take' to allow the child to address him directly.

Recent developments, however, indicate that, contrary to the established practice, a shift towards a more active involvement of the judiciary in interviewing (especially older) children in abduction cases may be expected. In particular, in *Re D (a child)*[41] Baroness Hale expressed the view that, if requested so by the child, he/she should be given the opportunity to speak directly to the judge.[42] At paragraph 51 of the judgment Baroness Hale said:

> There are three possible ways of doing this [interviewing the child]. They range from full scale legal representation of the child, through the report of an independent CAFCASS officer or other professional, to a face to face interview with the judge. In some European countries, notably Germany, it is taken for granted that the judge will see the child. In this country, this used to be the practice under the old wardship system, but fell into disuse with the advent of professional court welfare officers who are more used to communicating with children than are many judges. The most common method is therefore an interview with a CAFCASS officer, who is not only skilled and experienced in talking with children but also, if practising in the High Court, aware of the limited compass within which the child's views are relevant in Hague Convention cases. In most cases, this should be enough. In other cases, and especially where the child has asked to see the judge, it may also be necessary for the judge to hear the child.[43]

Baroness Hale did not address any practicalities of the hearing of the child directly by the judge. Nevertheless, one could agree with the suggestion that the judge should interview the child in private, as opposed to 'the intimidating atmosphere of the court room'.[44]

The suggestion that children should be allowed to directly address judges more frequently than the standard practice received a fairly neutral treatment by the Court of Appeal in the case of *Re F (a child) (abduction: obligation to hear child)*.[45] The opinion of Baroness Hale was neither followed nor expressly rejected by Thorpe LJ. Nevertheless, it appears that Baroness Hale's comment

[40] *S v S (Child Abduction)* [1991] 2 FLR 31.

[41] *Re D (a child)* [2006] UKHL 51, [2007] 1 AC 619.

[42] For an academic debate see Wilson, 'The Ears of the Child' (n 9) and Hale (n 9), 'The Voice of the Child'.

[43] *Re D (a child)* [2006] UKHL 51, [2007] 1 AC 619 para 51.

[44] R Harrison, 'Child Abduction after In Re D (A Child)' *Family Law Week* (4 June 2007), available at www.familylawweek.co.uk/site.aspx?i=ed573.

[45] *Re F (a child) (abduction: obligation to hear child)* [2007] EWCA Civ 468, [2007] 2 FLR 697.

prompted Thorpe LJ to make a suggestion that details of practical application of Article 11(2) should be regulated by amendments to the family proceedings rules. According to Thorpe LJ, several matters should be addressed, including the compliance with the six-week time limit when hearing the child and the issues related to the interviewer. In particular, he touched directly on the question whether in Brussels II bis cases the child should be interviewed by a CAFCASS officer or, given the European character of the instrument, the judge should hear the child in person.

The Court of Appeal maintained its positive stance on the problem of judges seeing children in a non-Brussels II bis case, *G (Children) (Abduction: Children's Objections)*.[46] In this case the court went a step further by fully endorsing the practice. Thorpe LJ remarked critically about the failure of a trial judge to meet a 13-year-old girl who had written him a letter and sought to communicate her views directly to him, and decided to meet the child himself. Thorpe LJ noted:

> In this jurisdiction, judges in the High Court have not traditionally in modern times heard the voice of the child directly but through the officer of the court, the CAFCASS Officer. That tradition is now under scrutiny, debate and revision.... [i]t is perhaps with hindsight a pity that HHJ Barnett did not have the opportunity of meeting her and hearing from her own lips.[47]

Although it was 'highly unusual' for the Court of Appeal to meet a child before deciding an appeal, Thorpe LJ was of the view that it was reasonable and indispensable in this case, given the fact that the trial judge had not himself met the girl and did not attach much weight to the letter she had written to him.[48]

Available Brussels II bis case law from the High Court indicates that this method of interviewing may indeed become a standard practice in abduction cases. For example, in *C v W*,[49] the examination of the wishes and feelings of the child was conducted directly by the judge (Sir Mark Potter), by way of talking to the child in the privacy of the judge's office. Sir Mark described the method employed as follows:

> In addition to reading her [the child's] evidence and hearing the submissions of counsel on her behalf, I saw her in my room for some 15 to 20 minutes in accordance with Article 11.2 of Brussels II Revised.[50]

Similarly, in *De L v H*,[51] Sir Mark 'had a lengthy conversation' with the child, following the child's wish to see the judge expressed before a CAFCASS officer. During the meeting, the boy, aged 13½, had the relevant law explained to him—that is, the philosophy of the Convention and the Regulation (in particular, the possibility of the procedure under Articles 11(6)–11(8) of the Regulation)—and

[46] *G (Children) (Abduction: Children's Objections)* [2010] EWCA Civ 1232, [2011] 1 FLR 1645.
[47] *Ibid*, para 15.
[48] *Ibid*, para 21.
[49] *C v W* [2007] EWHC 1349 (Fam), [2007] 2 FLR 900.
[50] *Ibid*, para 47.
[51] *De L v H* [2009] EWHC 3074 (Fam), [2010] 1 FLR 1229.

was assured that full evidence as to the nature and force of his objections had been received by the court.

b. Separate Representation and Party Status

The leading authority on the issue of separate representation in Hague Convention proceedings was for many years the decision of Wall J in *Re S (Abduction: Children: Separate Representation)*.[52] The underlying principle established by this judgment and followed in a number of decisions was the 'exceptionality' principle. In accordance with this standard, successful applications for party status in Convention proceedings were very rare. The established approach, however, came under attack in July 2006 when the Court of Appeal heard the case of *Re H*.[53] The applicant challenged the approach of the courts in Hague Convention cases to separate representation and called for a more active role of children in return proceedings. The request, however, provoked an adverse reaction as Thorpe LJ suggested that the bar had been raised by the Brussels II bis Regulation insofar as applications for separate representation were concerned. Despite the negative response, this decision has been of significant importance as it triggered an intense judicial discussion. In particular, Thorpe LJ's conclusion was rejected by Baroness Hale in *Re D (a child)*.[54] For all Convention cases, Baroness Hale advocated the established practice that the separate representation of the child in return proceedings would be allowed only where strictly necessary.[55] According to her, these cases would involve situations when the child's views may not be correctly presented to the court, in particular because there are legal arguments that are not being put forward by the adult parties. In the Brussels II bis case of *Re F (Abduction: Joinder of Child as Party)*[56] Thorpe LJ accepted that the bar had not been raised, but disapproved the suggestion of the House of Lords in *Re D* that it had been lowered, and concluded that 'the bar essentially remains where it was'.[57]

[52] *Re S (Abduction: Children: Separate Representation)* [1997] 1 FLR 486.

[53] *Re H* [2006] EWCA Civ 1247, [2007] 1 FLR 242.

[54] *Re D (a child)* [2006] UKHL 51, [2007] 1 AC 619.

[55] See *Re M (A Minor) (Child Abduction)* [1994] 1 FLR 390 and *In the matter of H (A Child)* [2006] EWCA Civ 1247, [2007] 1 FLR 242 for examples of decisions where separate representation was not permitted; and *Re M (A Minor) (Abduction: Child's Objections)* [1994] 2 FLR 126; *Re S (Abduction) (Children: Separate Representation)* [1997] 1 FLR 486; *Re HB (Abduction: Children's Objections)* [1998] 1 FLR 422; and *Re T* [1999] 2 FLR 796, *Vigreux v Michel* [2006] EWCA Civ 630, [2006] 2 FLR 1180 and *Nyachowe v Fielder* [2007] EWCA Civ 1129 for examples of the rare cases where due to the exceptional circumstances of the case, full-scale representation of the child was granted.

[56] *Re F (Abduction: Joinder of Child as Party)* [2007] EWCA Civ 393, [2007] 2 FLR 313.

[57] *Ibid*, para 60. The child involved in *Re F (Abduction: Joinder of Child as Party)* was a seven-year-old girl who had been wrongfully retained in England by her mother. The father initiated return proceedings. An application was made on behalf of the child for leave to intervene in the appeal. The Court of Appeal, however, refused the application, noting that there was a long line of Court of Appeal case law which emphasised how exceptional was a grant of permission to intervene. A particular reference was made to a recent Court of Appeal decision in the case of *Re H (A Child)* [2006] EWCA Civ 1247, [2007] 1 FLR 242. In this case, an application was made for a 15-year-old girl to be joined as an additional party to the Hague proceedings. The court, however, came to the conclusion that there was no circumstance that could be considered sufficiently exceptional to justify her intervention with the

The court also reaffirmed that there was a long line of authority that made clear it was an exceptional step to take to allow separate representation.

The 'exceptionality test' for the joinder of children in Hague Convention proceedings reiterated by the Court of Appeal in *Re F* was, however, later reconsidered and restated by the House of Lords in *Re M*.[58] In particular, Baroness Hale suggested that, when faced with an application for separate representation, a judge should consider whether separate representation would 'add enough to the Court's understanding of the issues to justify the resultant intrusion, delay and expense which would follow'.[59] This test has recently been accepted by the High Court as 'the proper test' for party status in Hague Convention proceedings. In particular, in its judgment in the Brussels II bis case of *C v C*,[60] the court refused to 're-interpret *Re M* by reference to previous decisions'.[61] The court further concluded that the test as formulated by Baroness Hale in *Re M* should be applied 'without gloss'.[62] Finally, with the view to backing up the legacy of the *Re M* approach, the court listed a number of secondary resources that support the test enunciated by Baroness Hale. These included: the Explanatory Report to the Hague Convention (paragraphs 78 and 24);[63] the speech of the President of

status of a party. Having reviewed the existing case law, the court pointed out that generally separate representation had been granted only in cases where there was an element of public law such as state involvement. In addition, neither the fact that it was a 'child-inspired' retention nor the age of the child persuaded the court that there was a justification for the grant of party status. The court held that if the child in this case had been granted representation, it would have been very difficult to refuse separate representation for any other 14- or 15-year-old child involved in Convention proceedings. The court was satisfied that the child's position would be clearly put before the judge through a report of a CAFCASS officer.

58 *Re M* [2007] UKHL 55, [2008] 1 AC 1288. *Re M* was a non-Brussels II bis application that concerned the removal of two girls aged 13 and 10 from Zimbabwe to the jurisdiction of England and Wales. Following the separation of the parents in 2001, the mother moved abroad and left the children in the care of the father. In 2004, the mother returned, re-established contact with the children, and in March 2005 removed them to England where she claimed asylum. The father learnt of his rights under the Hague Convention in late 2006, and instigated return proceedings. In June 2007, the High Court ordered the return of the children (*Re M* [2007] EWHC 1820 (Fam), [2007] Fam Law 888). The court accepted that the girls were of a sufficient age and maturity for their views to be taken into account, and that they were settled in the new environment; nevertheless, the trial judge exercised his discretion in favour of the applicant father. The mother appealed. The appeal was, however, dismissed (*Re M (Children)* [2007] EWCA Civ 992, [2007] 3 FCR 564). In October 2007, the mother was granted leave to appeal to the House of Lords. The appeal was allowed and return order refused. The court ruled that the children had become settled in their new environment and objected to a return, and exercised its discretion not to make a return order.

59 *Re M* [2007] UKHL 55, [2008] 1 AC 1288 para 57.

60 *C v C* [2008] EWHC 517 (Fam), [2008] 2 FLR 6. The case involved four children, aged 16, 13, 11 and nine. The applicant children applied to be joined as parties to return proceedings initiated by the applicant father following their removal from France to the jurisdiction of England and Wales by the respondent mother.

61 *Ibid*, para 33.

62 *Ibid*, para 35.

63 E Pérez-Vera, 'Explanatory Report on the 1980 Hague Child Abduction Convention' (1982), available at www.hcch.net/upload/expl28.pdf. Para 78: '[C]hildren under sixteen who have the right to choose their own place of residence … [T]his rule leaves it open to judicial and administrative authorities, whenever they are faced with the possibility of returning a minor legally entitled to decide on his

the Family Division to the 17th World Congress of the International Association of Youth and Family Judges and Magistrates on 28 August 2006 (at paragraph 3 page 5),[64] and the speech of Wilson LJ on the occasion of the Hershman/ Levy Memorial Lecture on 28 June 2007 entitled 'The Ears of the Child in Family Proceedings';[65] and Baroness Hale's extensive review of the problem of representation of children in an article entitled 'The Voice of the Child' derived from an address to the International Society of Family Law in July 2007.[66]

Not long after *C v C*, the High Court was confronted with a question related to the problem whether a child who is subject to the return proceedings should be joined to Hague Convention proceedings, namely, whether to join a child's sibling who is not a subject of the return proceedings. In particular, in a non-Brussels II bis case, *W v W (Abduction: Joinder as Party)*,[67] the question arose whether a 17-year-old sibling should be joined as a party to abduction proceedings that concerned her 11-year-old brother. The 17-year-old girl applied to be joined as a party to the proceedings on the grounds that she was extremely concerned about the welfare of her younger brother and her mother due to her father's violent behaviour. The judge was asked to decide whether the girl was entitled to join the proceedings as a mandatory defendant under rule 6.5(e) of the Family Proceedings Rules.[68] Having referred to 'the substantial step forward in judicial attitudes marked by … the decisions of the House of Lords in *Re D* and *Re M*',[69] the judge concluded that the girl fell within rule 6.5(e) as she was directly concerned in her brother's welfare as she sought to provide him with care and protection.[70]

D. Exercise of the Discretion to Return

Article 11(2) only obligates courts to give children the opportunity to be heard; it does not contain rules on the use of evidence obtained through such a hearing. Mandating judges to hear a child in return proceedings is far from ordering them to inevitably follow the child's wishes when reaching their decision. As a result, it is not

place of residence, to take the view that the opinion of the child should always be the decisive factor'. Para 24: 'Children must no longer be regarded as their parents' property but must be recognised as individuals with their own rights and needs.'

[64] The Right Honourable Sir M Potter, 'The Family in the 21st Century', paper given at the 17th World Congress of the International Association of Youth and Family Judges and Magistrates, 28 August 2006, Belfast.

[65] Wilson (n 9).

[66] Hale (n 9).

[67] *W v W (Abduction: Joinder as Party)* [2009] EWHC 3288 (Fam), [2010] 1 FLR 1342.

[68] Family Proceedings Rules 1991, SI 1991/1247). In order to be entitled to join as a mandatory defendant under rule 6.5(e), an applicant must establish that he or she is directly concerned with the welfare of the subject child in the sense that they have (1) provided care for the child and/or (2) have a continuing or potential interest in the provision of care for the child, or (3) have some legal or practical responsibility for the child's welfare.

[69] *W v W (Abduction: Joinder as Party)* [2009] EWHC 3288 (Fam), [2010] 1 FLR 1342, para 29.

[70] *Ibid*, para 30.

expected that Article 11(2) would have had a direct effect on the problem of exercise of discretion. Nevertheless, given the possibility of indirect influence, and for the sake of comprehensiveness exercise of discretion has been included in the analysis.

i. England and Wales

a. The Exceptional Circumstances Test

For a long time, the leading principle in exercise of discretion to return in the context of child's objections was the exceptional circumstances test. The exceptional circumstances test can be traced back to a Court of Appeal decision in the case of *Re S (A Minor) (Abduction: Custody Rights)*[71] where Balcombe LJ held that a court should order the return of the child unless there were exceptional circumstances for ordering otherwise. The court's discretion to refuse the return of a child had to be exercised in the context of the overall approach of the Convention.

> The scheme of the Hague Convention is that in normal circumstances it is considered to be in the best interests of children generally that they should be promptly returned to the country whence they have been wrongfully removed, and that it is only in exceptional cases that the court should have a discretion to refuse to order an immediate return. That discretion must be exercised in the context of the approach of the Convention.[72]

In *Re R (Child Abduction: Acquiescence)*[73] different approaches were supported as to the way in which discretion should be exercised and the pertinent factors that should be taken into account. Balcombe LJ held that in exercising discretion, the policy of the Convention should be a 'very weighty factor';[74] nevertheless, the importance attached to the objections of a particular child would differ with the child's age and maturity. In contrast, Millet LJ expressed the opinion that, in accordance with the provisions of the Convention, a child of sufficient age and maturity should not be returned against his/her wishes. The discretion in favour of the return should only be exercised if there are 'countervailing factors which require [the child's] wishes to be overridden'.[75]

In *Re T (Abduction: Child's Objections to Return)*[76] Ward LJ accepted the interpretation of Millet LJ. At the same time he specified that the 'countervailing factors' would be represented especially by the policy and purpose of the Convention.

The reasoning of Ward LJ in *Re T (Abduction: Child's Objections to Return)* was implicitly followed by the Court of Appeal in *Re J (Children) (Abduction: Child's Objections to Return)*.[77] However, it was rejected by the same court in a decision in the case of *Zaffino v Zaffino*,[78] which was later labelled as a 'restatement

[71] *Re S (A Minor) (Abduction: Custody Rights)* [1993] 2 WLR 775, [1993] Fam 242.
[72] *Ibid*, 251.
[73] *Re R (Child Abduction: Acquiescence)* [1995] 1 FLR 716.
[74] *Ibid*, 731.
[75] *Ibid*, 734.
[76] *Re T (Abduction: Child's Objections to Return)* [2000] 2 FLR 192.
[77] *Re J (Children) (Abduction: Child's Objections to Return)* [2004] EWCA Civ 428, [2004] 2 FLR 64.
[78] *Zaffino v Zaffino* [2005] EWCA Civ 1012, [2006] 1 FLR 410.

of well-established principles, and a demonstration of their application to a given set of facts'.[79] In *Zaffino v Zaffino*, the court accepted the exceptionality principle as well as the interpretation of Balcombe LJ in *Re R (Child Abduction: Acquiescence)*.[80] In particular, Thorpe LJ rejected the formulation of Millet LJ in *Re R (Child Abduction: Acquiescence)* that the child 'will not be returned against his wishes unless there are countervailing factors which require his wishes to be overridden'.[81] Thorpe LJ held:

> Let me then first express my conclusions on the law and the principles. I would unhesitatingly endorse the approach expressed by Balcombe LJ in *Re S (A Minor) (Abduction: Custody Rights)* [1993] Fam 242 and in *Re R (Child Abduction: Acquiescence)* [1995] 1 FLR 716. Millet LJ's formulation (also in *Re R*) does not, in my view, sufficiently mark the weight and importance of Convention factors in the exercise of the proportionate judgment. Second, since the point undoubtedly demands decision in the present appeal, I am persuaded that, in the exercise of discretion arising under Art 13 (possibly fortified by Art 18), the court must balance the nature and strength of the child's objections against both the Convention considerations (obviously including comity and respect for the judicial processes in the requesting state) and also general welfare considerations. To suggest otherwise seems to me to risk artificiality in judgments in future cases.[82]

Wall LJ supported the exceptionality test established by Balcombe LJ in *Re S (A Minor) (Abduction: Custody Rights)*. He said:

> Nothing we have said in this judgment should detract from the view, which has frequently been expressed and which we repeat, that it is only in exceptional cases under the Hague Convention that the court should refuse to order the immediate return of a child who has been wrongfully removed.[83]

In this case, the Court of Appeal also held that in the exercise of discretion the court must weigh the nature and strength of the child's objections against both the Convention policy and welfare considerations.

The exceptionality principle, established in *Re S (A Minor) (Abduction: Custody Rights)*, was accepted in the Court of Appeal decision in the case of *Re M (A Child) (Abduction: Child's Objections to Return)*.[84] The court also accepted the opinion given in *Zaffino v Zaffino* that in exercise of discretion regard should be paid also to welfare considerations. Before reaching its decision, the court posed a question:

> That leaves only the question whether the objection of M is such that this is one of the 'exceptional' cases justifying the court in using its discretion to refuse to order an immediate return. That involves balancing the nature and strength of M's objections against

[79] *Vigreux v Michel* [2006] EWCA Civ 630, [2006] 2 FLR 1180, per Wall LJ.
[80] *Re R (Child Abduction: Acquiescence)* [1995] 1 FLR 716.
[81] *Ibid*, 734.
[82] *Zaffino v Zaffino* [2005] EWCA Civ 1012, [2006] 1 FLR 410, para 19.
[83] *Re S (A Minor) (Abduction: Custody Rights)* [1993] 2 WLR 775, [1993] Fam 242, 251.
[84] *Re M (A Child) (Abduction: Child's Objections to Return)* [2007] EWCA Civ 260, [2007] 2 FLR 72.

> both the Convention considerations (including comity and respect for the judicial process in Serbia as well, of course, as the policy behind the Convention) and general welfare considerations.[85]

In the instant case, the court came to the conclusion that the child's objections had been exceptional in view of the unusual circumstances underlying them, namely an attempt by the applicant father to plant drugs on the mother to secure her arrest, prosecution and imprisonment. In deciding not to order the return of the child, the court paid regard to welfare considerations.

The principle of exceptionality was raised also in the case of *Nyachowe v Fielder*.[86] Wall LJ held that the need for exceptional circumstances was well established. He accepted that whilst the strength of objection could be sufficient to make the circumstances exceptional this was not so in the present case.

Brussels II bis Cases The entry into force of the Brussels II bis Regulation in March 2005 did not bring about any radical change in the established principles behind the exercise of discretion in the context of child's objections. Nevertheless, it was concluded that in Brussels II bis cases, the aims and policy of the Regulation had to be considered in addition to the policy of the Convention.

The first Brussels II bis case that reached the Court of Appeal, *Vigreux v Michel*,[87] reaffirmed the decision reached in *Zaffino v Zaffino*. Referring to the judgment of Balcombe LJ in the decision of *Re S (A Minor) (Abduction: Custody Rights)* Wall LJ reiterated that a discretion to refuse to order a return could only arise in exceptional cases. Wall LJ agreed with the opinion of Thorpe LJ expressed in *Zaffino v Zaffino* where he rejected the interpretation of Millet LJ in *Re R (Child Abduction: Acquiescence)* that the child 'will not be returned against his wishes unless there are countervailing factors which require his wishes to be overridden'.[88] Thereby he implicitly accepted the interpretation of Balcombe LJ. In addition, he reaffirmed his own opinion expressed in *Zaffino v Zaffino* where he accepted the exceptionality principle. He said:

> Nothing in the instant case causes me to change my mind on this point. It follows, in my judgment, that the test laid down by Balcombe LJ giving the judgment of this court in *Re S* remains good law, and that there is no statement of principle in *Re T* which would prevent this court refusing to exercise its discretion in the child's favour and ordering his return to France.[89]

The appeal in *Vigreux v Michel* was launched by the mother of a 14-year-old boy who had been removed by his father from France to England. The parents never married but had a long relationship before they separated. Custody over the child was regulated by a consented decision of the French court that granted

[85] *Ibid*, para 80.
[86] *Nyachowe v Fielder* [2007] EWCA Civ 1129.
[87] *Vigreux v Michel* [2006] EWCA Civ 630, [2006] 2 FLR 1180.
[88] *Re R (Child Abduction: Acquiescence)* [1995] 1 FLR 716, 734.
[89] *Vigreux v Michel* [2006] EWCA Civ 630, [2006] 2 FLR 1180, para 62.

the parents joint parental responsibility, with residence to the mother and access to the father. Neither of the parents was allowed to leave France with the child without the other's consent. In violation of the order, on 14 August 2005, the father and the son travelled to England. In the same month, the mother contacted the French Central Authority and her return application was issued in the Family Division of the High Court on 23 September 2005. The proceedings were delayed and the Convention application did not come to trial until February 2006. In the meantime, on 7 December 2005 the mother was awarded sole custody by the Cour d'Appel at Versailles. On 15 February the High Court found that the child objected to a return and that he was of sufficient age and maturity for his views to be taken into account. The trial judge then exercised his discretion in favour of a non-return order. On 4 April the mother was granted leave to appeal to the Court of Appeal.

The central question on appeal was whether the trial judge erred in his exercise of discretion. The Court of Appeal also considered how discretion should be exercised in a case governed by the Brussels II bis Regulation. Thorpe LJ held that the trial judge had placed too much weight on the child's concern that he would not receive a fair hearing in any subsequent proceedings in France, as well as on marginal welfare considerations. Although his Lordship rejected the submission that 'technically the new Community regime had imposed a heavier burden on abductors seeking to invoke one of the exceptions', it was accepted that in exercising discretion in Brussels II bis cases, the provisions of the Regulation had to be taken into account in addition to the policy of the Convention.[90] Thorpe LJ held that, in the instant case, the trial judge failed to weigh the child's objections against the policy of the Brussels II bis Regulation. The trial judge incorrectly placed welfare considerations above the policy of the Regulation. Consequently, the Appeal Court concluded that the trial judge did err in his discretion and ordered the return of the child.

In the matter of V (a child)[91] The judgment in *Vigreux v Michel* was followed in another Court of Appeal Brussels II bis decision: a decision of Neuberger LJ in the case *In the matter of V (a child)*. This case involved a boy wrongfully removed from Hungary to England by his father. As it was in the case of *Vigreux v Michel*, the boy was of a sufficient age and maturity for his views to be taken into account and strongly objected to his return to the requesting State. At the first instance, the defence of child's objections was rejected as Coleridge J concluded that the policy of the Brussels II bis Regulation had to prevail over the child's wishes. In

[90] This argument may explain why contrary to legitimate expectations our statistical survey recorded a decrease rather than an increase in the proportion of judicial refusals based on the child's objections. In particular, according to our findings, in 2005/06, 7% of all judicial refusals were based solely on the child's objections. This represents a decrease by 4% on the proportion of 11% recorded in 2003. When all the reasons are analysed, the exception of child's objections was relied upon in 13% of all judicial refusals. In contrast, in 2003, 16% of all judicial refusals were either solely or partially based on this exception.

[91] *In the matter of V (a child)* [2006] EWCA Civ 836.

reaching his decision, he referred to the Court of Appeal decision in *Vigreux v Michel.*

> Given the terms of the 1985 Act and Brussels II, as explained very recently in the judgment of Thorpe and Wall LLJ in *Vigreux v Michel* there was, as the judge accepted, and indeed as counsel for Mr V [the father] accepted, a strong presumption that the child would be returned to Hungary ... The judge considered all the issues, and reached the decision that M's desire to stay, and his reasons for that desire, were insufficient in all the circumstances to overcome the strong presumption in Brussels II that he should be returned to Hungary.[92]

The conclusion reached at the first instance was accepted and reaffirmed by the Court of Appeal. Coleridge J and Neuberger LJ also based their conclusion on the policy behind the Brussels II bis Regulation:

> In light of the guidance given by this court in *Vigreux*, it seems to me that the judge certainly reached a decision he was entitled to reach, and it may well be, in the light of the clear terms of Brussels II, as explained by Wall LJ in paragraph 78 to 83 of his judgment in *Vigreux*, that the decision reached by Coleridge J was, sadly for Mr V, the only right decision on the facts of this case.[93]

C v W[94] Finally, the last Brussels II bis application where the exceptionality principle was adopted appears in the case of *C v W.* The application involved a 14-year-old girl who had been removed from Ireland by her father in violation of the mother's rights of custody. Several defences were raised in the proceedings, namely consent and/or acquiescence, child's objection to return and the grave risk of harm objection. None of the exceptions was, however, accepted by the court and the return of the child was ordered. In relation to the defence of child's objections the court based its conclusion on the policy behind the Brussels II bis Regulation. Although the court was satisfied that the exception was established, it exercised its discretion in favour of the child's return. Potter LJ concluded:

> In my view, despite the clarity of S's objections and the consideration to which they are entitled, and despite the fact that it may well be that ordinary welfare considerations militate in favour of her being permitted to stay with her father in England, this is a case where I should exercise my discretion in favour of an order for her return, in order to enable the Irish Court to examine and deal with those welfare issues in accordance with the plain intention of the Hague Convention, as reinforced by Brussels II Revised.... [The discretion] involves balancing the nature and strength of S's objections against both the Convention consideration (including comity and respect for judicial process in Ireland as well as policy behind the Convention and Brussels II Revised) and general welfare considerations.[95]

92 *Ibid*, paras 2 and 3.
93 *Ibid*, para 5.
94 *C v W* [2007] EWHC 1349 (Fam), [2007] 2 FLR 900.
95 *Ibid*, para 49.

The above analysis demonstrates that, in early Brussels II bis decisions (that is, those reached between 2005 and 2006) the exceptionality test was applied as the proper principle of the exercise of discretion. It was accepted in these decisions that the provisions of the Regulation had to be taken into account in addition to the policy of the Convention. One may suggest that as a result, a more stringent test applied to Regulation cases than to Convention applications. Consequently, a reduction in cases where the defence of child's objections was made out successfully would rightly be expected. In accordance with these expectations, in 2005/06, 7% of all judicial refusals were based solely on the child's objections. This represented a decrease by 4% on the proportion of 11% recorded in 2003. When all the reasons were analysed, the exception of child's objections was relied upon in 13% of all judicial refusals. In contrast, in 2003, 16% of all judicial refusals were either solely or partially based on this exception.

b. *Re M*—A New Beginning?

The long line of authorities advocating the 'exceptionality test' in the exercise of court's discretion seems to have come to an end in 2007. The turning point was a recent decision of the House of Lords in a non-European Hague Convention case of *Re M*.[96] In this decision, Baroness Hale expressly rejected exceptionality. Analysing existing case law and considering how discretion should be exercised in all cases of child abduction, Baroness Hale on behalf of the full court concluded that it was not correct to import an extra test of exceptionality into the exercise of a court's discretion under the Convention. She held:

> The circumstances in which a return may be refused were themselves exceptions to the general rule. That in itself was sufficient exceptionality. It was neither necessary nor desirable to import an additional gloss into the Convention.[97]

Baroness Hale continued that where discretion arose from the terms of the Convention itself, the discretion was at large. A court would have the right to take account of the elements of the Convention policy, alongside the circumstances which gave the court discretion in the first place and the wider welfare considerations. In some cases, Convention objectives would be given more weight than the other considerations and in other cases they would not. Consequently, it would depend on the circumstances of the particular case, how much weight would be given to Convention considerations and to the considerations of the child's rights and welfare.

Baroness Hale then turned to consider the operation of discretion in relation to each of the exceptions separately. With respect to child's objections cases, she held that there the spectrum of considerations might be even broader than those in other defences. In particular, the court should consider the nature and strength of the child's objections, the degree to which these objections were genuinely the child's own or the result of parental influence, and the degree to which these objections

[96] *Re M* [2007] UKHL 55, [2008] 1 AC 1288. For a summary see above n 58.
[97] *Ibid*, para 40.

corresponded with other considerations of the child's welfare. Generally, the older the child, the greater importance should be attached to his/her views. However, Baroness Hale stressed that this was 'far from saying that the child's objections should only prevail in the most exceptional of circumstances'.[98]

The first post-*Re M* Brussels II bis decision involving the Article 13(2) defence of child's objections was a High Court judgment in the case of *Re F (children) (abduction)*.[99] This application involved two children, boys aged 13 and 11 respectively. The parents, both Polish nationals, were divorced. In December 2006, the boys were brought by their mother to England. Eleven months later, in November 2007, the father initiated return proceedings. The mother raised three defences: the lack of custody rights, the Article 13(1)(a) defence of acquiescence and the defence of child's objections. The former two exceptions were not made out successfully. Nevertheless, the mother succeeded in establishing the third defence, the child's objections. The boys were heard by a CAFCASS officer. During the interview, they strongly objected to the return and expressed anger at the father's application and fear from a possible return order. First, they said that the father had been informed about their intended move to England and never protested the relocation. Second, the children communicated that they were afraid of their father on the ground that his behaviour was unpredictable and at times aggressive. Third, the boys submitted that the father showed little interest in them when they were still living in Poland. Neither did he make any effort to contact them in England. The court found that the boys were of a sufficient age and degree of maturity for their views to be taken into account, and that their objections were genuine, based on the boys' own experience. Following these findings, the court turned to the exercise of discretion. The court accepted the innovative approach taken by Baroness Hale in *Re M* in which the exceptionality test was rejected. In paragraph 52 of the judgment, the trial judge held:

> In exercising my discretion, I propose to approach the matter on the basis of recent observations of Baroness Hale in the House of Lords in *Re M (FC) and Another (FC) (Children) (FC)* [2007] UKHL 55 at paragraphs 36 to 46 in which a corrective was applied to the views previously expressed by the Court of Appeal in cases such as *Zaffino v Zaffino* [2006] 1 FLR 410, *Vigreux v Michel* [2006] 2 FLR 1180, and *Klentzeris v Klentzeris* [2007] 2 FLR 996 that, in relation to the exercise of discretion under the Hague Convention in a child's objections case an additional test or requirement of 'exceptionality' is appropriate when the Court comes to weigh the policy considerations underlying the Convention against the general welfare considerations affecting the child in the individual case.[100]

In making its decision, the court focused primarily on the welfare of the children. In particular, account was taken of the fact that unlike in Poland the children were thriving in England. No less importantly, the court gave considerable weight

[98] *Ibid*, para 46.
[99] *Re F (children) (abduction)* [2008] EWHC 272 (Fam), [2008] 3 WLR 527.
[100] *Ibid*, para 52.

to the impact of the father's delay in pursuing the return application on the children's feeling of stability in their new environment.

The conclusion reached by the High Court reflects a highly child-focused approach in the sense that the judge treated the children's views with great respect. In the final paragraph of his judgment, the judge said:

> However, as I have made clear, my decision is based upon my conclusion that for these intelligent children, whose views must carry increasing weight with their increasing age, matters have significantly changed for the better since the matter was last before the Polish court and there are strong welfare grounds not to order their return.[101]

Owing to the fact that *Re M* was a non-European case, the court addressed a related problem of the applicability of the *Re M* approach to Brussels II bis cases. The judge came to the conclusion that the observations of Baroness Hale in *Re M* were applicable to all Convention cases, including those governed by the Brussels II bis Regulation. This conclusion was based on the finding that none of the provisions of the Regulation related to the exercise of discretion or directly acted 'to reduce or qualify the "at large" discretion in respect of child's objections under Article 13'.[102]

Finally, the court noted that in the exercise of discretion in Brussels II bis cases, courts should bear in mind the possibility of a non-return order being overturned by an order entailing the return of the child made by the requesting State under Article 11(8) of the Regulation and be aware of the negative impact of such a development on the welfare of the child. Nevertheless, the court came to the conclusion that the overall character of the exercise of discretion in European and non-European cases would remain fundamentally the same, as in both cases the primary task of the court would be a search for the balance between the Convention policy and welfare considerations.

> However, as it seems to me, the overall nature of the Court's task in performing its balancing exercise as between welfare and other Convention considerations remains the same whether or not the Convention is governed by Brussels 2 Revised.[103]

The new trend set by *Re M* was further followed in the Court of Appeal judgment in the Brussels II bis case of *Re F (A Child)*.[104] This application involved a Polish boy aged 9½. The parents, both Polish, were divorced in 2006. In August 2007, the mother unilaterally removed the child from Poland to Wales. Return proceedings were initiated by the father in early summer of 2008. The trial judge found that the removal was wrongful, but concluded that the child was sufficiently mature to have his objections to return considered. In the exercise of his discretion, the judge pointed out that the child was Polish, that Polish remained his first language, and that both his parental families were entirely Polish. He also noted that until the age of eight the boy had always lived in Poland. The trial judge acknowledged that it

101 *Ibid*, para 77.
102 *Ibid*, para 64.
103 *Ibid*, para 65.
104 *Re F (A Child)* [2009] EWCA Civ 416, [2009] 2 FLR 1023.

was not the purpose of the return proceedings to decide on the longer term best interests of the child; nevertheless, he held that insofar as the child's short-term welfare was concerned, the objections raised by the boy accorded with his short-term best interests. In particular, at the time of the proceedings, the boy had lived in Wales for 18 months; was well settled in school and had many friends there; and his whole maternal family had settled in Wales. Given these facts, the trial judge held that a return 'forthwith', as required by the Convention, would not be in the best interests of the child, as it would constitute a 'massive and damaging upheaval' in his life. The trial judge made it clear that the guiding principle of the exercise of discretion was no longer the principle of exceptionality, pointing out that 'the House of Lords have made plain that there is no super-added test of exceptionality within Article 13'.[105]

The reasoning of the trial judge was fully accepted at the appellate level. The Court of Appeal did not find any basis on which to challenge the first instance decision.

Clearly, this case demonstrates a marked shift from the focus on the policy of the Convention/Regulation to primary considerations being given to the welfare of the child. Given the relatively young age of the child, the nature of his objections as well as the background facts (especially the nearly complete lack of connection with England and Wales), the decision demonstrates that exceptionality is indeed no longer the governing principle. It accurately reflects the current movement towards a deeper understanding of the voice of the child in general as well as specifically in return proceedings, as instigated by *Re M*. Nevertheless, it might be questioned whether given the background facts of *Re F (A Child)* (in particular the young age of the child and the lack of significant connection with England), the courts in this case did not go too far in placing the wishes of the child above the policy of the Convention/Regulation.

Following *Re F (A Child)*,[106] the '*Re-M* approach' was applied in other first and second instance decisions. These included *De L v H*,[107] *M v B*,[108] and *BF (Children) (Abduction: Child's Objections), Re WF v RJ*.[109]

De L v H involved a 13-year-old boy who, following an access visit to his father in England, refused to return to his mother's care in Portugal. Shortly before he was due to return, the boy burned both his British and Portuguese passports, manifesting the strength of his objections to return. The High Court held that for the purposes of ascertaining the 'soundness and validity' of the child's strongly and clearly expressed objections, it was appropriate to consider:

1. the child's own perspective of what was in his own short, medium and long term interests;

[105] *Ibid*, para 5.
[106] *Re F (A Child)* [2009] EWCA Civ 416, [2009] 2 FLR 1023.
[107] *De L v H* [2009] EWHC 3074 (Fam), [2010] 1 FLR 1229.
[108] *M v B* [2009] EWHC 3477 (Fam), [2010] EWCA Civ 178.
[109] *BF (Children) (Abduction: Child's Objections), Re WF v RJ* [2010] EWHC 2909 (Fam), [2011] 1 FLR 1153.

2. the extent to which the reasons for objection are rooted in reality or might reasonably appear to be so grounded;
3. the extent to which those views have been shaped or coloured by undue parental pressure, direct or indirect;
4. the extent to which the objections would be modified on return and/or the child's removal from the pernicious influence of the abducting parent.[110]

On being so satisfied, the matter involved a wide range of considerations in relation to the exercise of discretion, as suggested by Baroness Hale in *Re M*.[111] The child was found to be 'domestically happy, settled and educationally secure'[112] in England, whereas his return to Portugal would result in a 'stressful and quarrelsome situation'.[113] His views were not shaped by pressure from the father[114] and there was no real likelihood that his views would be modified on return.[115] In those circumstances, the court exercised its discretion and rejected the return application.

In *M v B*[116] the applicant father, who was the custodial parent, sought the return to Italy of his two daughters, aged 12 and nine, who had been wrongfully retained in England by the respondent mother following an access visit. The children strongly objected to being returned as they wanted to stay with their mother and their half-sister and half-brothers. The High Court was satisfied that the children were of a sufficient age and maturity for their views to be taken into account and that those views were not the result of parental influence.[117] Having 'borne in mind Baroness Hale's observations in Re M'[118] the court concluded that despite the children having lived in Italy for most of their lives, with the father as their primary carer since 2004, and their school activities and friends being there,[119] it would not be appropriate to make a return order.[120] On appeal, the first instance decision was upheld. Thorpe LJ rejected the submission raised on behalf of the father that, in exercising discretion, the judge 'misconducted the balancing exercise'.[121] Thorpe LJ held that all relevant factors were considered by the judge and that the judgment was 'full and careful'.[122]

[110] *De L v H* [2009] EWHC 3074 (Fam), [2010] 1 FLR 1229, para 66.
[111] *Ibid*, para 63.
[112] *Ibid*, para 67.
[113] *Ibid*.
[114] *Ibid*, para 69.
[115] *Ibid*, para 70.
[116] *M v B* [2009] EWHC 3477 (Fam), [2010] EWCA Civ 178.
[117] *M v B* [2009] EWHC 3477 (Fam) para 57.
[118] *Ibid*, para 68.
[119] *Ibid*, para 61.
[120] *Ibid*, para 79.
[121] *M v B* [2010] EWCA Civ 178 para 8.
[122] *Ibid*, para 9.

BF (Children) (Abduction: Child's Objections), Re WF v RJ[123] concerned two children aged 13 and 12 respectively. The younger child was, however, suffering from a disorder called attention deficit hyperactivity disorder (ADHD) as a result of which his mental functioning was 12 to 18 months below his chronological age. The children were removed from Germany to England by their mother, who had divorced the applicant father and remarried. The mother was the victim of domestic violence from her second husband in Germany. The return was opposed by both children. The older child expressed 'strong, clear, considered and consistent'[124] objections that were considered by the court as 'congruent with many of her welfare interests and authentically her own'.[125] Accordingly, it was appropriate for the court to exercise its discretion. Justice Baker made it clear that in doing so he would adhere to 'the approach to the exercise of discretion identified by Baroness Hale in *Re M (Abduction: Zimbabwe)*'[126] as this was now 'the leading case from which all analysis must flow'.[127] The court concluded that a preponderance of the elements identified by Baroness Hale in *Re M* pointed in favour of refusing the return of the older child to Germany.

The younger child's objections were deemed as 'less clear, less strong and less authentically his own';[128] however, the court concluded that separating the siblings would place them in an intolerable situation and thus the gateway under Article 13(1)(b) had also been crossed. Accordingly, the return application was refused.

ii. Scotland[129]

Decisions reached by the House of Lords when it sits as an English Appellate Court are highly persuasive on future Scottish cases. It is therefore expected that the current case law in Scotland is likely to reflect the recent English developments, in particular the rejection of the exceptionality principle in the exercise of discretion. An examination of available case law has revealed that, in accordance with the above expectation, Scottish cases concluded prior to the House of Lords decision in *Re M* exhibited a rigid adherence to the principle of exceptionality. Two relevant first instance decisions have been made publicly available, *M, Petitioner*[130] and *Re WT*.[131]

In *M, Petitioner*, exceptionality was accepted as a guiding principle of the exercise of discretion. The case concerned a 14-year-old girl, habitually resident

[123] *BF (Children) (Abduction: Child's Objections), Re WF v RJ* [2010] EWHC 2909 (Fam), [2011] 1 FLR 1153.

[124] *Ibid*, para 74.

[125] *Ibid*.

[126] *Ibid*, para 70.

[127] *Ibid*, para 34.

[128] *Ibid*, para 76.

[129] For a detailed academic analysis see P Beaumont and P McEleavy, *Private International Law, Anton*, 3rd edn (Edinburgh, W Green & SULI, 2011) 830–3.

[130] *M, Petitioner* [2007] CSOH 66, 2007 SLT 433.

[131] *Re WT* [2007] CSOH 72.

in Australia. Following the separation of her parents, the girl spent alternate weeks with her mother and father. In January 2007, the mother, who was Scottish, decided to return to live in Scotland. The girl chose to join her mother. The father initiated return proceedings. In the course of the proceedings, it was acknowledged that the child had attained an age and degree of maturity for her views to be taken into account. The Court, however, noted that 'even a relatively mature abducted child does not have a veto over return',[132] and that 'the child's objection is to be upheld only in exceptional circumstances'.[133] It was held that this, however, was not such a case. Accordingly, the return of the child to Australia was ordered.

Similarly, discretion was exercised in accordance with the principle of exceptionality in *Re WT*. The case involved an application for the return of two children, a girl aged 14 and a boy aged eight, to Poland. Both parents were Polish nationals. The children were brought to Scotland by their mother where the mother's extended family had settled. The father applied for their return. Counsel for the mother argued that the older child, aged 14, objected to being returned to Poland. The court accepted that the child was old and mature enough to have her views considered, but held that it was only in cases of an exceptional nature where the child's objections could outweigh the purpose of the Convention, and that this was not such a case. In particular, the court noted:

> There is nothing special or of sufficient weight in the reasons for KT's objection, nor in the surrounding circumstances, as would justify a refusal to implement the purpose of the Convention, namely that it should be a Polish court that weighs KT's views in the balance when determining the arrangements for her and her brother's care.[134]

Accordingly, the submission that the child's objections to a return should be upheld was rejected, and the father's return application was granted.

Two post-*Re M* decisions were found to have been made publicly available, an appellate decision in the case of *C v C*[135] and a first instance decision in the case of *A, Petitioner*.[136] As for the former case, it is not clear from the decision which principle was used as the basic principle of the exercise of discretion. Nevertheless, the factual circumstances of this case were unusual, making it difficult, if not impossible, to apply a general principle in a straightforward manner. The application concerned four children, aged 15, 12, eight and six. The parents had married in the UK in 1989. In 1994, they left the country and moved to Mexico where they spent two years. Afterwards, they spent two years travelling in the US. In 1998, they returned to the UK for several months before moving to Spain. Whilst living in Spain, the parents separated. Following the breakdown of the marriage, in 2001, the mother moved to France. The father moved to the same area. Custody

[132] *M, Petitioner* [2007] CSOH 66, 2007 SLT 433, para 10.
[133] *Ibid.*
[134] *Re WT* [2007] CSOH para 16.
[135] *C v C* [2008] SCLR 329.
[136] *A, Petitioner* [2011] CSOH 215.

proceedings were initiated in France, resulting in the mother being designated as the primary carer and the father being allocated access rights. During a period of contact in July 2005, the father removed the children to South-East Asia. After six months of travelling, they settled, undetected, in the Philippines. They remained there until November 2006 whereupon they moved to Scotland. In the autumn of 2007, the mother discovered the location of the children and initiated return proceedings. The father argued that the children had settled in the new environment, and that the older children objected to being returned to France. At the first instance, the Outer House of the Court of Session (Lord Turnbull) rejected the father's submission and ordered the return of the children. The decision of Lord Turnbull was upheld on appeal.[137]

The facts of the second case, *A, Petitioner*,[138] were relatively straightforward: two children, a boy aged 11 and a girl aged five, had been brought to Scotland from Spain by their mother. The father initiated return proceedings. The judge's exercise of discretion in relation to the objections of the older child was clearly guided by the principles established by *Re M*. Having quoted Baroness Hale's speech in *Re M* at some length,[139] the judge concluded that the 11-year-old boy's objections were 'entitled to carry great weight'[140] and decided to refuse the return application.[141]

iii. Ireland

In *N v N*,[142] a six-year-old boy was given the opportunity to express his views, and was found to have attained an age and a degree of maturity at which it was appropriate to take account of his views. The child objected to being returned to Lithuania and expressed a desire to stay in Ireland with his mother. The court, however, cautioned that given his young age, the boy might not be able to fully appreciate the role of a father in a child's upbringing. On this ground it was concluded that the child's views could not be determinative and discretion was exercised in favour of the applicant father.

[137] See *C v C* [2008] SC 571. He was aware of Baroness Hale's comments in *Re M* about how the discretion to return should be exercised after a ground for non-return had been made out. He decided to order the return of the children against their wishes to remain in Scotland although they were aged 14 and 11. He concluded: 'In taking this approach I do not see myself as causing the children concerned to suffer for the sake of general deterrence of the evil of child abduction. I have taken account of the policy of the Convention in considering the arguments advanced under this head, but only as one of a number of other factors'. Lord Turnbull's conclusion was upheld by the Inner House at para 46 of the court's opinion delivered by Lord Osborne but with no analysis of the appropriate standard to apply when exercising discretion not to return a child who is old and mature enough to have his or her objections taken account of.

[138] *A, Petitioner* [2011] CSOH 215.

[139] *Ibid*, para 45.

[140] *Ibid*, para 46.

[141] The refusal was, however, not made solely on the grounds of Art 13(2) but in conjunction with Art 13(1)(a) consent. *Ibid*, para 47.

[142] *N v N* [2009] IEHC 213.

iv. Northern Ireland

KR and SR[143] This case, although having resulted in the return of the children involved, exhibited a highly child-centred approach to the issue of child's objections, particularly to the problem of influence of the abducting parent over the child's views. This case involved two children, born in 1996 and 1997 respectively, both habitually resident in Slovakia. The children were wrongfully removed by their mother from Slovakia to Northern Ireland. Following the wrongful removal, return proceedings were initiated by the father. Two objections were raised on behalf of the mother. First, that the return would expose the children to a risk of grave harm and second, that the children objected to being returned to Slovakia. The grave risk of harm exception was rejected fairly straightforwardly. With respect to the issue of child's objections, the court acknowledged that the children's views must be given full weight; nevertheless, it did not accept this defence either. The main factor set against the children's views was the underlying purpose of the Convention to return wrongfully removed children to the country of their habitual residence:

> The underlying purpose and the integrity of the Convention itself would be seriously compromised if the refusal to order a return was not confined to the wholly exceptional case. This is not such a case.[144]

It was found in the instant case that, to a certain extent, the views of the children resulted from the manipulation by the abductor mother. Nevertheless, despite that, the court did not disregard these opinions. In contrast, it was accepted that those views must be given full weight. The court held:

> We consider that the children's desire to remain living here is genuine. This may—to some extent—be the product of manipulation by the mother but we do not believe that this is a factor that should weigh heavily to discount the importance of their views.... We consider that full weight must be given to the children's views. They are of sufficient maturity to hold those views strongly.... Therefore, in reaching the conclusion that we do, we have not discounted their views in any way.[145]

Given the fact that decisions of the House of Lords are followed by courts in Northern Ireland, it would be a legitimate expectation for *KR and SR* to reject the exceptionality principle as an 'old law', and to endorse the approach adopted by Baroness Hale in *Re M*. There is, however, a satisfactory explanation for this 'failure'. In particular, the decision in *KR and SR* was taken two days before the judgment in *Re M* was reached by the House of Lords. Consequently, *KR and SR* was 'good law' at the time when the case was adjudicated; however, it could not be considered so now.

[143] *KR and SR* [2007] NICA 50.
[144] *Ibid*, para 19.
[145] *Ibid*, para 17.

E. Conclusions

The above analysis points to the conclusion that recently, there has been a massive movement towards a 'softer' and a more child-centred approach in child abduction cases. Admittedly, to some extent, this development is due to an increased understanding of the significance of the voice of the child in family proceedings generally, which had been slowly and gradually developing since the ratification of the UNCRC by the United Kingdom in 1991.[146] Nevertheless, the effect of Article 11(2) of the Brussels II bis Regulation can also be observed. The provision has clearly been working towards a reinforcement of the general trend, especially where automatic inquiry into the views of the child is concerned. In particular, in England and Wales, the obligation of Article 11(2) to give a child an opportunity to express his/her views in return proceedings has become a principle of 'universal application'. Through *Re D (a child)*,[147] the principle was declared as being applicable to all Convention proceedings, that is, including those that are not governed by the Brussels II bis Regulation. *Re D* also introduced a rule under which the

[146] Such evolution was rightly predicted by Paul Beaumont and Peter McEleavy in their monograph 'The Hague Convention on International Child Abduction' published in 1999. To put it in the words of the authors: 'Taking into consideration the creation of children's rights under international law, it is now time for Article 13(2) to be re-evaluated and for greater emphasis to be attached to discovering and, where possible, acting in accordance with the opinions of wrongfully removed and retained children ... Procedures should be put in place to ensure that ... views of any child capable of forming a cogent and coherent view are taken into account in Convention proceedings. Any other solution is in breach of the UNCRC'. Beaumont and McEleavy, *The Hague Convention* (n 1) 180 and 182. Indeed, in both England and Ireland, an indication of a more child-centred approach can be observed already in older (particularly post-1999) case law. In England, for example, in a 2000 decision of the Court of Appeal in the case of *Re T (Abduction: Child's Objections to Return)* [2000] 2 FLR 192, [2000] 2 FCR 159 the court held that, as a general rule, it would be indispensable for the judge to investigate why the child objects to being returned. Similarly, in the case of *Re J (Children) (Abduction: Child's Objections to Return)* [2004] EWCA Civ 428, [2004] 2 FLR 64, decided in 2004, a conclusion was reached that where there was a sincere matter as to a child's objections, deliberate attempts should be made to put such objections forward to the judge. Notably, the post-1999 case law stands in a marked contrast to older cases. See, eg, *Re M (A Minor) (Child Abduction)* [1994] 1 FLR 390. In this case Butler-Sloss LJ expressed the view that '[t]here is nothing in Article 13 or the Child Abduction and Custody Act 1985 which provides for automatic enquiry into the views of older children'. See also *P v P (Minors) (Child Abduction)* [1992] 1 FLR 155, where the court rejected the submission that there was an obligatory requirement for the examination of child's views when the defence of child's objections had been raised by the abducting parent. The court also held that '[n]o advantage would be gained and much valuable time in the lives of the children would be lost if there were to be any investigation by a court welfare officer into the child's views and/or her maturity'.

In Ireland, even prior to the adoption of the Regulation, the hearing of the child was considered an important part of return proceedings. The leading decision on the issue of child's objections was a judgment of the Irish Supreme Court in the case of *RMM v MD*, Denham J, No 162/99M of 9 December 1999. The Supreme Court in this case pointed out that it was the intention of the Hague Convention to secure the abducted child's right to have his/her views taken into account, if the condition of the sufficient age and a degree of maturity of the child was met. The Supreme Court concluded that the trial judge had the right to rely on the child's views, but had to make it clear that they accorded with other findings the trial judge had made in the case. The Supreme Court stressed that to take the child's feelings and wishes seriously was crucial so as to protect the child's long-term psychology.

[147] *Re D (a child)* [2006] UKHL 51, [2007] 1 AC 619.

obligation of Article 11(2) must be complied with in all Convention cases, not just those in which the defence of child's objection is raised. This interpretation appears to be even wider than the wording of Article 11(2) itself, as it suggests automatic hearings of children not only in cases where Articles 12 and 13 of the Convention are raised but also in applications where other issues are invoked (such as the lack of habitual residence of the child in the requesting State prior to the removal/retention under Article 3 of the Convention).

The principle of automatic hearing of children regardless of the nature of the exception raised was reinforced by the Court of Appeal decision in the Brussels II bis case of *Re F (a child) (abduction: obligation to hear child)*.[148] The decision also clarified that, when applying Article 11(2), judges were expected to act on their own initiative, that is, regardless of whether parties made a reference to Article 11(2) in their submissions. In the light of *Re D*, this principle was recommended to be applied universally, that is, beyond the scope of intra-EU abduction cases.

As in England and Wales, the obligation of Article 11(2) to give children of sufficient age and maturity the opportunity to be heard has been taken seriously by Irish courts (see cases *VG applicant and P McD respondent*[149] and *FL v CL*,[150] both governed by the Regulation). Available case law, however, does not reveal whether the principle of automatic hearing of children has also been accepted as applicable to global abduction cases. It remains to be seen whether judicial developments in this jurisdiction will follow the path of the English courts.

The minimum 'appropriate' age for hearing a child in return proceedings was reduced from 9–10 to 7½ by the non-Brussels II bis case of *Re D*. This trend was followed by the Regulation case of *Re F (a child) (abduction: obligation to hear child)*, which lowered the bar even further, to seven years. It was taken even a step further in the Brussels II bis case of *Re W (Abduction: Acquiescence: Children's Objections)* where a child as young as six was given the opportunity to be heard. Given the fact that the initial impulse came from a case not governed by the Regulation, it is not possible to conclude that Brussels II bis instigated the movement towards younger children being heard in return proceedings. Nevertheless, the Regulation has undoubtedly reinforced this trend.

Changes can also be observed in the method of examination of child's views, especially where older children are concerned. These innovations concern two interrelated areas: judges seeing children, and separate representation. The tendency towards a personal contact between a judge and a child in return proceedings was set in motion by *Re D*. In particular, it was held that if so requested by the child, he/she should be given the opportunity to be heard directly by the judge.

[148] *Re F (a child) (abduction: obligation to hear child)* [2007] EWCA Civ 468, [2007] 2 FLR 697.
[149] *VG applicant and P McD respondent* [2006] IEHC 69.
[150] *FL v CL* [2006] IEHC 66, [2007] 2 IR 630.

This approach seems to have been fully embraced by Brussels II bis case law (see cases *C v W*[151] and *De L v H*[152]).

In the area of separate representation, a new test was enunciated by the non-Brussels II bis decision of the House of Lords in the case of *Re M*.[153] The test replaced the old 'exceptionality test' and requires judges dealing with applications of children for a party status in return proceedings to consider whether separate representation would 'add enough to the Court's understanding of the issues to justify the resultant intrusion, delay and expense which would follow'. The principle was fully accepted and applied 'without gloss' in the Brussels II bis decision in *C v C*,[154] and extended to a non-subject child sibling in *W v W (Abduction: Joinder as Party)*.[155]

Although the innovative developments in both areas, judges seeing children and separate representation, have received a friendly welcome from Brussels II bis jurisprudence, there is no justification for asserting that the Regulation actually set off these developments. Rather, the trend towards a more child-centred approach in these areas appears to be a natural evolutionary development with a direct link to the overall climate of a deeper understanding of the importance of the voice of the child in family proceedings.

In accordance with our expectations, the Brussels II bis Regulation has had no direct impact on the established principles of the exercise of discretion. In England and Wales, the exceptional circumstances test introduced in the early 1990s by *Re S (A Minor) (Abduction: Custody Rights)*[156] and followed by a long line of authorities was not challenged by Brussels II bis jurisprudence. Quite the contrary, early intra-EU abduction decisions fully embraced the principle. In the first child abduction case governed by the Regulation that reached the Court of Appeal, *Vigreux v Michel*,[157] the court reiterated that discretion to refuse a return order can only arise in exceptional cases. Additionally, the court held that in exercising discretion in Brussels II bis cases, the policy of the Regulation had to be taken into account in addition to the provisions of the Convention. Accordingly, the court concluded that the trial judge had failed to weigh the child's objections against the policy of the Regulation and incorrectly placed welfare considerations above this policy. As the underlying aim of the Regulation is to reinforce the philosophy of the Convention, the above rule resulted in a very stringent test being applied in early Brussels II bis cases. The rule for exercise of discretion in Brussels II

[151] *C v W* [2007] EWHC 1349 (Fam), [2007] 2 FLR 900.

[152] *De L v H* [2009] EWHC 3074 (Fam), [2010] 1 FLR 1229.

[153] *Re M* [2007] UKHL 55, [2008] 1 AC 1288.

[154] *C v C* [2008] EWHC 517 (Fam), [2008] 2 FLR 6. The case involved four children, aged 16, 13, 11 and nine. The applicant children applied to be joined as parties to return proceedings initiated by the applicant father following their removal from France to the jurisdiction of England and Wales by the respondent mother.

[155] *W v W (Abduction: Joinder as Party)* [2009] EWHC 3288 (Fam), [2010] 1 FLR 1342.

[156] *Re S (A Minor) (Abduction: Custody Rights)* [1993] Fam 242.

[157] *Vigreux v Michel* [2006] EWCA Civ 630, [2006] 2 FLR 1180.

bis cases established by *Vigreux v Michel* was reaffirmed by another Court of Appeal decision, *In the matter of V (a child)*,[158] and followed by *C v W*.[159]

A turning point in the exercise of discretion in Article 13(2) cases came with a non-Brussels II bis decision in the case of *Re M*.[160] The House of Lords in *Re M* held that it was not correct to import an extra test of exceptionality into the exercise of discretion. Consequently, child objections should not succeed in exceptional circumstances only. The innovative approach adopted by *Re M* was readily accepted by Brussels II bis jurisprudence. In particular, the High Court in *Re F (children) (abduction)*[161] declared the new principle as applicable to all Convention cases, including those governed by the Regulation. In this context, the court pointed out that although in Brussels II bis cases courts should bear in mind the possibility of a non-return order being overturned by an order entailing the return under Articles 11(6)–11(8) of the Regulation, the exercise of discretion should nevertheless remain the same. In practice, the fresh direction resulted in a more relaxed attitude, with a particular focus on the welfare of the child (as opposed to the policy of the Convention/Regulation under the exceptional circumstances test). With a view to offering practical guidance, the court held that the primary task was now to search for the balance between the Convention policy and welfare considerations. The new trend in the exercise of discretion in Brussels II bis cases was reaffirmed by the Court of Appeal in *Re F (A Child)*.[162] Following this judgment, the '*Re M*' approach was applied in other first and second instance decisions such as *De L v H*,[163] *M v B*,[164] and *BF (Children) (Abduction: Child's Objections), Re WF v RJ*.[165]

II. Current Approaches Toward the Defence of Child's Objections in Major Non-EU Jurisdictions: Australia, Canada and the United States: Post-2005 Case Law Analysis

A. Australia

In Australia, the main statute governing family law is the Family Law Act 1975. By authority given under section 111B of the 1975 Act, Australia has implemented

[158] *In the matter of V (a child)* [2006] EWCA Civ 836.
[159] *C v W* [2007] EWHC 1349 (Fam), [2007] 2 FLR 900.
[160] *Re M* [2007] UKHL 55, [2008] 1 AC 1288.
[161] *Re F (children) (abduction)* [2008] EWHC 272 (Fam), [2008] 3 WLR 527.
[162] *Re F (A Child)* [2009] EWCA Civ 416, [2009] 2 FLR 1023.
[163] *De L v H* [2009] EWHC 3074 (Fam), [2010] 1 FLR 1229.
[164] *M v B* [2009] EWHC 3477 (Fam), [2010] EWCA Civ 178.
[165] *BF (Children) (Abduction: Child's Objections), Re WF v RJ* [2010] EWHC 2909 (Fam), [2011] 1 FLR 1153.

the Hague Convention into domestic law through Regulations (although not in identical terms) known as the Family Law (Child Abduction Convention) Regulations 1986 (the Regulations). Section 111B enables the Regulations to make such provisions as are necessary or convenient to enable Australia to perform its obligations, or obtain any advantage or benefit, under the Convention. Section 111B was last amended by the Family Law Amendment Act 2000 and recent amendments were made to the Regulations by the Family Law Amendment Regulations 2004. The Regulations effectively redraft the Convention, and as such can be amended to take account of judicial decisions.

The defence of child's objections set out in Article 13(2) of the Hague Convention can be found in reg 16(3)(c) of the Regulations. It states that the court may refuse to order the return if:

(i) the child objects to being returned;
(ii) the child's objection shows a strength of feeling beyond the mere expression of a preference or of ordinary wishes;
(iii) the child has attained an age, and a degree of maturity, at which it is appropriate to take account of his or her views.

Regulation 16(5) gives the court the right to exercise its discretion and to order the return of the child even if one of the exceptions to return is established:

> The court to which an application for the return of a child is made is not precluded from making an order for return of a child to the country in which he or she habitually resided immediately before his or her removal or retention only because a matter mentioned in subregulation (3) is established by a party opposing return.

i. Automatic Inquiry into the Views of the Child

Available Australian jurisprudence exhibits a diametrically opposed approach to the one envisaged by Article 11(2) of the Brussels II bis Regulation, and demonstrated by English and Irish case law. The Article 11(2) approach is not even contemplated by the Australian courts as there is no ongoing judicial discussion concerning the issue.

Unlike in England and Wales and Ireland, children involved in Convention proceedings in Australia are not heard routinely. Children's views are examined solely in those cases where the defence of Article 13(2) has been raised by the respondent (either as a sole exception or in conjunction with other defences); subject to the child's age being accepted by the judge as meeting the minimum threshold for testifying.[166]

[166] See section 'Minimum Age of the Child' below.

ii. Minimum Age of the Child

The recent jurisprudence indicates that the minimum age at which a child can be heard in Convention proceedings is seven years.[167]

iii. The Method of the Examination of Child's Views

In Australia, it is not an accepted practice among judges to interview children personally in Convention proceedings.[168] Rather, where the defence of child's objections is raised, and the judge considers it appropriate, an independent assessment of the child is ordered by the court.[169] This allows for the child to be interviewed by a court counsellor, that is, a qualified and experienced social worker/psychologist, known also as a family consultant.[170] The court counsellor is required to prepare a report, known as the 'Family Report', containing information on why the child objects and what the child's views are. The report is then relied upon by the court.[171]

Exceptionally, an Independent Children's Lawyer may be appointed in Convention proceedings to represent the child's interests.[172] The role of the Independent Children's Lawyer is to present an independent view, based on available evidence, of what is in the best interests of the child.[173] Importantly, the Independent Children's Lawyer is not a legal representative of the child and cannot be bound by the child's instructions.[174] This feature distinguishes the representation of the child by the Independent Children's Lawyer from the 'separate representation' of older children under English law. The appointment of the Independent Children's Lawyer is possible only if there are exceptional circumstances to justify it.[175] In *Director-General, Department of Community Services &*

[167] *HZ v State Central Authority* [2006] FamCA 466. It is, however, to be pointed out that although the child was given the opportunity to express her views, the court made it clear that objections of a child aged under eight could in no case stand the test of Art 13(2).

[168] Questionnaire (n 38).

[169] Permanent Bureau of the Hague Conference, 'Questionnaire Concerning the Practical Operation of the Hague Convention of 25 October 1980 on the Civil Aspects of International Child Abduction' (April 2006) Individual Reponses: Australia, Response to Question 9, available at www.hcch.net/index_en.php?act=publications.details&pid=3870&dtid=33.

[170] *Ibid.* Family consultants in Australia are an equivalent of CAFCASS officers in England and Wales. See *State Central Authority & Quang* [2009] FamCA 1038 para 24.

[171] See, eg, *Director-General, Department of Community Services NSW & Marshall* [2007] FamCA 1116; *Director-General, Department of Community Services & Wenceslas* [2006] FamCA 1493; *Richards & Director-General, Department of Child Safety* [2007] FamCA 65; *Department of Child Safety & Baker* [2008] FamCA 171; *Director-General, Department of Community Services & Heybridge* [2009] FamCA 937; and *State Central Authority & Litchfield* [2009] FamCA 317.

[172] *State Central Authority & Quang* [2009] FamCA 1038; *State Central Authority & Truman* [2009] FamCA 1175; *Director-General, Department of Community Services & Gamble* [2007] FamCA 1061; *State Central Authority & Hajjar* [2010] FamCA 648; and *State Central Authority v Hotzner (No 2)* [2010] FamCA 1041.

[173] Family Law Act 1975 (Cth), s 68LA(2).

[174] *Ibid*, s 68LA(4).

[175] *Ibid*, s 68LA(3).

Gamble,[176] for example, the exceptionality standard was met following strong expressions of the child and his demands to have a direct contact with the judge.

Despite the traditionally exceptional nature of the Independent Children's Lawyer, recent developments indicate a shift towards a wider acceptance of this form of representation in Convention proceedings. Interestingly, it appears that this trend in Australia is partially associated with the recent English developments in the area of separate representation. In particular, on two separate occasions, both successful applications for an appointment of the Independent Children's Lawyer, the court noted:

> [In *Re D (Abduction: Rights of Custody)* [2006] UKHL 51], Baroness Hale of Richmond observed that courts in the United Kingdom were moving away from a restrictive approach to separate representation of children towards the presumption from within the European Union that a child will be heard unless it appears inappropriate to do so.[177]

iv. Exercise of the Discretion to Return

Recent case law indicates that the threshold for the Article 13 child's objections defence is set very high in Australia. It appears to be difficult, if not impossible, to conclude that Australian courts attach particular importance to wishes and feelings of children in return proceedings. Indeed, between 2005 and 2009, the defence of child's objections, although raised in a number of applications, was made out successfully in only four cases. In addition, the circumstances of all four cases were to some extent controversial. Indeed, in one of these cases, *Re F (Hague Convention: Child's Objections)*,[178] the child concerned resisted an attempt to enforce a first instance return order. In another two cases, *Director-General, Department of Community Services & Gamble*,[179] and *Director-General, Department of Community Services & Heybridge*,[180] the child involved threatened to physically protest the return. In the fourth case, *Director-General, Department of Community Services NSW & Marshall*,[181] the child's objections were invoked in combination with the Article 13(1)(b) grave risk of harm defence and the non-return order was based on the grave risk of harm rather than on the child's objections.

[176] *Director-General, Department of Community Services & Gamble* [2007] FamCA 1061.

[177] State Central Authority & Quang [2009] FamCA 1038 para 25; and State Central Authority & Truman [2009] FamCA 1175 para 26. It is, however, to be pointed out that the Family Court of Australia manifestly misinterpreted the Brussels II bis Regulation as there is no direct link between the issue of separate representation and the right of the child to be heard as formulated by Art 11(2) of the Regulation.

[178] *Re F (Hague Convention: Child's Objections)* [2006] FamCA 685, (2006) FLC 93–277.

[179] *Director-General, Department of Community Services & Gamble* [2007] FamCA 1061.

[180] *Director-General, Department of Community Services & Heybridge* [2009] FamCA 937.

[181] *Director-General, Department of Community Services NSW & Marshall* [2007] FamCA 1116.

In *Re F (Hague Convention: Child's Objections)*,[182] the child involved was brought to Australia from the United States in 2003, when he was nine years old. The boy was wrongfully retained in Australia by his mother. In early 2004, the father initiated return proceedings. On 24 August 2004, a consent order was made before a Judicial Registrar for the return of the child to the United States. The child, however, was not returned.[183] The reason was that neither of the parents had sufficient funds to facilitate the return of the child. In February 2006, the mother sought to set aside the 2004 order made by the Judicial Registrar. The mother relied on the fact that the boy objected to being returned to the United States. The trial judge ordered a hearing of the child. During the interview the boy clearly indicated that he wanted to stay in Australia and threatened to protest if he was taken away. Despite that, the trial judge ordered the return of the child. He found that the child, though objecting to being returned to his father, did not object to being returned to the United States. The judge also concluded that the boy's objections did not 'show strength of feeling beyond the mere expression of a preference or of ordinary wishes'. The decision to order the return of the child was partly based on discussions by the delegation from the Commonwealth of Australia at the International Child Custody Convention in Washington in September 2000 under the heading 'Problems of Enforcement Arising from the Actions of the Child'. The trial judge placed a particular reliance on the conclusion arrived at by the delegation: 'The Convention should not be rendered ineffective by threats of misbehaviour by a child who would prefer not to go'.

It is submitted here that the conclusion of the delegation contrasts sharply with the increasingly child-centred approach exhibited in the above analysis of the European case law (English case law in particular). Indeed, the statement shows a complete lack of consideration for, if not an ignorance of the feelings of the child, demeaning the child to a mere object of the return proceedings.

Subsequent to the trial judge's order, the child twice refused to board a plane to the United States. On the second occasion, the child was accompanied to the airport by the Australian Federal Police. The police used a mild physical force on the child in an attempt to make him board the plane but refused to use stronger force when the boy resisted. Following these incidents, counselling of the child was ordered and an Independent Children's Lawyer was appointed. The principal aims of the counselling were to improve the boy's relationship with his father and to encourage him to return to the United States. These aims were, however, not achieved and the counsellor concluded that the child had become estranged from his father and retained strong objections to going back to the United States. According to the counsellor, the return would have negative psychological effects on the child. The counsellor further concluded that the child's objections showed

[182] *Re F (Hague Convention: Child's Objections)* (2006) FLC 93–277, [2006] FamCA 685.

[183] Obligations imposed by Judicial Registrars in their decisions become binding only if neither party seeks a review by the court. Therefore, the consent order made before the Judicial Registrar could not be formally enforced.

strength of feeling beyond mere expression of preference or ordinary wishes and that the child had demonstrated a sufficient degree of maturity.

The return order was appealed by the mother. The Appellate Court found that there was overwhelming evidence that the child objected to being returned and held that it was not possible to ignore the reality of the situation. The court concluded:

> It is difficult to see how almost three years after the wrongful retention has taken place it would be appropriate to return a most reluctant 12-year-old child in circumstances where the return might require the use of force and where the return would separate the child from his primary caregiver.... The evidence before us inextricably draws us to the conclusion that the requirements of Regulation 16(3) have been met and that the mother has clearly established that F objects to being returned to the United States, his objection shows strength of feeling beyond a mere expression of a preference or an ordinary wish and that he has attained an age and degree of maturity at which it is appropriate to take account of his views.[184]

Accordingly, the appeal was allowed and the application for the return of the child was dismissed.

Director-General, Department of Community Services & Gamble[185] involved an 11-year-old boy who had been wrongfully retained by his mother in Australia. The parents of the child married and lived in South Africa. The boy concerned was the youngest of three children born to the parents. At the time of the litigation, the older two were already adults. In February 2005, the parents separated. Thereafter, custody proceedings concerning the youngest child were initiated in South Africa. Pending the proceedings, in January 2006, the mother brought the child to Australia to visit his maternal grandmother. The trip was supposed to last three weeks. At the end of that period, however, the mother did not return the child to South Africa and remained in Australia. The mother, recognising that there had been a wrongful retention of the child, argued that the child would be exposed to a grave risk of harm if returned to South Africa. She further argued that the child objected to being returned.

The trial judge rejected both defences and on 29 August 2006 ordered the return of the child. In September 2006, the father came to Australia to collect the child. On 19 September 2006, the mother brought the boy to the Department of Community Services where attempts were made to return him to the father. The child, however, clearly indicated that he did not wish to be returned. The boy became deeply distressed and demanded to talk to the judge. He said: 'Let me talk to the Judge, I'll talk to the Judge. The Judge did not talk to me'.[186] The father then left Australia without the child and returned to South Africa.

The mother appealed. The Appellate Court dismissed the appeal but ordered that the matter be reconsidered by the trial judge. The trial judge was to decide whether, in the light of the events that occurred after the return order was made;

[184] In *Re F (Hague Convention: Child's Objections)* [2006] FamCA 685 para 68.
[185] *Director-General, Department of Community Services & Gamble* [2007] FamCA 1061.
[186] *Ibid*, para 26.

the order should be discharged or varied. On the recommendation of the Court of Appeal and due to the exceptional circumstances of the case, an Independent Children's Lawyer was appointed to assist in the proceedings. In addition, it was ordered that an up-to-date Family Report, based on interviews with both parents and the child, be prepared by a child psychiatrist.

The trial judge began his analysis with questions of law. He cited several cases[187] and summarised the relevant general principles as follows:

1. The Regulations do not specify the matters to be taken into account in the exercise of the discretion by reg 16(5).
2. The matters that may be considered will depend on the circumstances of the case.
3. However, although the discretion is at large, the relevant matters must relate to the welfare of the child.
4. The scope and purpose of the Regulations, namely a desire to protect children internationally from harmful effects of their wrongful removal or retention and to establish procedures to ensure their prompt return to the State of their habitual residence may make a particular matter extraneous. This has been expressed in some cases to mean that depending on the circumstances significant weight may be given to the scope and purpose of the Regulation. In considering the welfare of the child the discretion is not governed by the principle that the welfare of the child or best interests of the child is the paramount consideration.[188]

Next, the judge identified cases with facts similar to those of the instant case, that is, where an order for the return of a child was made but subsequent behaviour of the child frustrated the enforcement of the order. Among other cases, a reference was made to the recent decision of the Australian Court of Appeal in the case of *Re F (Hague Conventions: Child's Objections)*.[189] Particularly, the judge highlighted a section where the Appellate Court concluded that it could not ignore the reality that the child was highly resistant to return.[190] This paragraph of the decision in *Re F (Hague Conventions: Child's Objections)* was relied upon by counsel for the mother. Commenting on the analysed case law, the Independent Children's Lawyer concluded:

> Whilst the circumstances whereby the child came to be in a particular jurisdiction are a relevant consideration, it appears that Courts in various jurisdictions administering

[187] *DL v Director General, NSW Department of Community Services and Anor* (1996) 187 CLR 640; *Agee and Agee* (2000) FLC 93-055; *Rhyan v Director-General, Department of Child Safety* [2007] FamCa 65; and *Re F (Hague Conventions: Child's Objections)* (2006) FLC 93-277 [2006] FamCA 685.

[188] *Ibid*, para 41.

[189] *Re F (Hague Conventions: Child's Objections)* (2006) FLC 93-277 [2006] FamCA 685.

[190] In this section, the court concluded: 'It is difficult to see how almost three years after the wrongful retention has taken place it would be appropriate to return a most reluctant 12-year-old child in circumstances where return might require the use of force and where the return would separate the child from his primary caregiver'. See *ibid*, para 68.

> the Hague Convention have invariably placed the immediate physical welfare of the child over all other considerations. In particular, there appears to have been a consistent refusal to return a child (notwithstanding any other considerations) in circumstances where the child's return can only be achieved through the use of inappropriate force.[191]

The case law analysis was followed by an examination of the facts of the case. The trial judge concluded that under the given circumstances (especially the fact that the mother would not return to South Africa with the child) it was evident that the child's return could only be achieved through the use of inappropriate force. Given this reality and given the fact that the father did not wish to expose the child to a forced return, the judge decided to discharge the order for the return of the child. Nevertheless, he expressed his dissatisfaction with this decision, as it enabled the mother 'to effectively drive a carriage and four through the Convention'.[192] The trial judge concluded:

> In summary, I take into account that the child is 11 years of age, that the child has been in Australia since January 2006, that the child appears to be settled in Australia and that the child is primarily attached to the mother who does not intend to return to South Africa. However, if these were the only matters relied upon by the mother and the independent child lawyer, I would have no hesitation in making an order for the return of the child to South Africa. This is, in my opinion, a border line decision. The matters that ultimately resolve the case are the opinion of Dr R [the child's psychologist] as to what would have to be done to ensure the return of the child without mother, namely the child may have to be sedated and what Dr R recorded the father said, namely: '[The father] said he could not take up the doc's suggestion to get the Federal Police involved as it would have been too much for the child to handle.' … In the result I propose to discharge the orders for the return of the child. In doing so I record that this is a very unsatisfactory outcome …[193]

It is submitted here that given the extreme circumstances of the instant case, the non-return order cannot be considered as evidence of a trend towards a more child-focused approach in Australia. In contrast, the discontent of the judge over the decision clearly showed that the conclusion reached was nothing more than a mere exception.

Similar considerations as in *Director-General, Department of Community Services & Gamble*[194] also led to a judicial refusal to return in *Director-General, Department of Community Services & Heybridge*.[195] The application involved an objection of a 13-year-old boy who threatened to resist boarding an aeroplane if forced to return to the requesting State. The court in *Heybridge* criticised *Re F (Hague Convention: Child's Objections)* for failing to envisage the likelihood of the child's strong physical resistance to return, suggesting that in cases of this kind a

[191] *Director-General, Department of Community Services & Gamble* [2007] FamCA 1061 para 50.
[192] *Ibid*, para 79.
[193] *Ibid*, para 80.
[194] *Director-General, Department of Community Services & Gamble* [2007] FamCA 1061.
[195] *Director-General, Department of Community Services & Heybridge* [2009] FamCA 937.

refusal to return should be considered rather than a return order. Accordingly, the court concluded that given the child's age and capacity to resist an order for return, the application had to be dismissed.

Finally, *Director-General, Department of Community Services NSW & Marshall*[196] concerned an 11-year-old boy who had been wrongfully removed by his mother from Italy to Australia. The father commenced return proceedings. The mother raised two defences: the Article 13(1)(b) grave risk of harm defence and the Article 13(2) defence of child's objections. In the course of the return proceedings, the child was interviewed by a family consultant whose report was later relied upon by the court. Although the report specifically addressed issues related to the defence of child's objections, it was written predominantly with the view to provide insight into the question of grave risk of harm. In particular, the report elaborated in detail allegations made by the child that he had been a victim of physical violence at the hands of his father.

The court was satisfied that the child objected to being returned to Italy, that his objections showed a strength of feeling beyond the mere expression of a preference or ordinary wishes, and that the child was of an age and maturity at which it was appropriate to take account of his wishes. On the available evidence, the court decided to dismiss the father's application. However, considerations related to the defence of child's objections did not play a significant role in making the non-return order. The rationale behind the decision was the judge's finding that the child would be exposed to a grave risk of psychological harm if returned to Italy. The judge concluded:

> Consistent with my finding that the child would be traumatised by an order for return, it must follow that the child's interests would be adversely affected by such an order.[197]

As concluded with respect to *Re F (Hague Convention: Child's Objections)* and *Director-General, Department of Community Services & Gamble*, neither *Director-General, Department of Community Services NSW & Marshall* can be considered as an indication of a shift towards a more child-centred approach. This is for the reason that the child's objections were interconnected with the grave risk of harm, and the non-return order was made on the basis of Article 13(1)(b) rather than on the ground of the child's objections.

Director-General, Department of Community Services NSW & Marshall bears some resemblance to another Article 13(2) case, *HZ v State Central Authority*.[198] The similarity is in defences' parallel reliance on both exceptions, Article 13(2) and Article 13(1)(b). Unlike in *Director-General, Department of Community Services NSW & Marshall*, however, in *HZ v State Central Authority* the defence of Article 13(2) received intensive consideration and played a central role in reaching a

[196] *Director-General, Department of Community Services NSW & Marshall* [2007] FamCA 1116.
[197] *Ibid*, para 96.
[198] *HZ v State Central Authority* [2006] FamCA 466.

decision.[199] Moreover, in contrast to *Director-General, Department of Community Services NSW & Marshall*, the latter case resulted in a refusal to return, with the court conveying the message that objections of a child younger than eight years of age would in no circumstances be considered eligible to stand the test of Article 13(2). The trial judge accepted that the child's objection to return was 'beyond the mere expression of preference or of ordinary wishes', but reached the conclusion that having regard to her age (below eight) and degree of maturity it would not be appropriate to take account of her views. The judge further held that even if her conclusion with regard to the child's objections was not correct, she would still exercise her discretion in favour of the applicant. In other words, even if the defence of child's objections was made out successfully, the child would still be returned. In the view of the judge, it would have been against the purpose and underlying philosophy of the Convention, if the return order had been refused in the wrongful retention of such a 'blatant kind'. The first instance decision was upheld on appeal.[200]

A similar position with respect to the exercise of discretion was also taken in the cases of *Department of Child Safety & Pelt*[201] and *Director-General, Department of Community Services & Wenceslas*.[202] In the former case, the court held that the standard of Article 13(2) had not been met as the child did not object in a relevant sense, that is, rather than opposing being returned to a particular country, the child objected to living with a particular parent. Nevertheless, the court held that even if Article 13(2) had been established, discretion would have been exercised in favour of the applicant parent. In the latter case, Article 13(2) was not made

[199] The case involved three children, one girl and two boys, aged seven, five and three respectively. The children were brought to Australia from Greece by their mother and wrongfully retained. The father initiated return proceedings. The mother made allegations of domestic violence towards the father and submitted that the return to Greece would expose the children to a grave risk of physical or psychological harm. She claimed further that the eldest child objected to being returned to Greece and that she had attained an age and degree of maturity at which it was appropriate to take account of her views within the meaning of reg 16(3)(c) of the Regulations. At the first instance, a hearing of the child by a psychologist was ordered by the court. The views of the child were to be used as one of the factors to resolve the grave risk of harm defence. The child strongly objected to being returned to Greece and expressed a strong preference to live in Australia with her mother, her brothers and the mother's extended family. The rationale behind the child's objections to return was her father's violent, aggressive and unpredictable behaviour towards the mother, the children and paternal grandparents. On the prospect of returning to Greece, the child became evidently distressed and tearful. In her report, the psychologist described the girl's maturity as beyond the maturity expected at her age, with the ability to distinguish her views from those of others. Nevertheless, the psychologist accepted the possibility of parental influence and concluded that given her young age, the child was not fully capable of assessing the long-term implications of her expressed views.

[200] The appellate court concluded: 'Given that the child was less than eight years of age at the time of the hearing before her Honour [the trial judge], it is difficult to see how her Honour's conclusion could be the subject of a successful attack'.

[201] *Department of Child Safety & Pelt* [2009] FamCA 412.

[202] *Director-General, Department of Community Services & Wenceslas* [2006] FamCA 1493. This case involved a 10-year-old boy who had been wrongfully removed by his mother from New Zealand to Australia. The father commenced return proceedings. The mother raised several defences, among them the defence of child's objections.

out due to parental influence and the lack of maturity on the side of the child. In particular, the court recognised that the child had expressed a desire not to be returned to New Zealand; however, it found that his objections were significantly affected by his mother's views. Moreover, the court was not satisfied that the child had attained an age or degree of maturity at which it was appropriate to take into account his views. Nevertheless, it was noted in the judgment that even if the exception of child's objections had been established, the court would not have been prepared to exercise its discretion against the child's return.[203] The court explained that this was so as to give effect to the Convention's policy that the merits of the case should be decided by a court of the habitual residence of the child prior to his/her removal or retention.[204]

The primacy of the Convention's policy in exercising discretion was reiterated in *Richards & Director-General, Department of Child Safety*.[205] Being confronted with the issue of the exercise of discretion, the trial judge held that the objectives of the Convention required a return order being made and that, generally, there had to be 'clear and compelling' evidence to uphold an exception raised. The trial judge concluded that due to the lack of the 'clear and compelling' evidence the instant case was not exceptional and made a return order. On appeal, the principle of 'clear and compelling' evidence formulated by the trial judge was rejected. The Appellate Court held that, when exercising discretion, the relevant factors would vary from case to case; however, they would always include giving considerable importance to the objectives of the Convention. Given the error of the trial judge, the Appellate Court re-exercised the discretion. Nevertheless, it reached the same

[203] In particular, the court stated: 'Even if I am wrong about that, I would not in the exercise of my discretion refuse to order his return on that basis.'

[204] 'It must be remembered, of course, that the purpose of this application is not to have this Court determine whether the Child should live with the Father or the Mother or in New Zealand or in Australia, but simply to return the Child to New Zealand where the New Zealand Courts will be able to determine, inter alia, whether the Mother should be permitted to bring the Child to live in Australia.'

[205] *Richards & Director-General, Department of Child Safety* [2007] FamCA 65. The application related to two girls, born in the United States in 1994 and 1996 respectively. The children's parents separated in 2002. Following the separation, the girls remained in the care of their mother in Michigan. In January 2004, a Michigan Court ordered that the parents have joint legal custody, with the mother having physical care of the children and the father having access. At this time, the mother commenced a relationship with Ms A, an Australian resident. In February 2004, the father moved to Florida, but flew to Michigan regularly to have contact with the children. The mother filed an application with the Michigan Court seeking permission to relocate with the children to Australia. This application was, however, refused by the court. As the mother had decided to move to Australia, she agreed that the children would live with their father in Michigan. In summer 2006, the children visited the mother in Australia. At the end of this visit, the girls were not returned to the United States and the father therefore initiated return proceedings. The mother argued that both girls objected to being returned, that their objections showed strength of feeling beyond the mere expression of a preference or of ordinary wishes and that the children had attained an age and maturity which made it appropriate to take account of their views. A family consultant was appointed to hear the children and to prepare a report. The report showed that the children had a strong preference to live with their mother. This preference was, however, not an objection to being returned to the United States. Nevertheless, the trial judge found that the exception had been established and considered the exercise of discretion.

conclusion as the first instance court and held that after balancing the relevant considerations,[206] the children should be returned.

A factually similar situation as in *Richards & Director-General, Department of Child Safety*, that is, a child-inspired abduction, arose later in the case of *Department of Child Safety & Baker*.[207] In this case, however, the court did not face the question of exercise of discretion but dealt only with the issue of whether the standard of Article 13(2) was met. The latter application involved the objection of a 13-year-old boy who opposed his return from Australia to the United States.[208] The boy had lived with his father in the United States for seven years prior to refusing to return from an access visit to his mother in Australia. The child expressed a clear preference to remain in Australia and to live with his mother.[209] Nevertheless, he reiterated that he loved his father and desired regular contact with him. The boy showed a high degree of maturity in the sense that his objections were far from being a result of parental influence. In a letter addressed to his father, he stated: 'I spent seven long happy years living with you … I would like to spend the rest of my teen years with my mum … This is my decision.'[210]

The court recognised that the child had a strong preference to live in Australia and was of an age and degree of maturity at which it was appropriate to take account of his views. Nevertheless, it was concluded that his objections had not showed the strength of feeling necessary to meet the standard required by Article 13(2) of the Convention. Consequently, an order for the return of the child was made.

A similar conclusion was reached in *State Central Authority & Wolfe*[211] where a boy aged 15 years and nine months objected to being returned to New Zealand in return proceedings instigated by his father. The objections to return were based primarily on the fear of the abductor mother's ex-partner, who was described as a very dangerous man affiliated with drug dealing and violent motorcycle gangs. Despite the teenager being only three months short of attaining the age when the Convention would no longer apply to him, the court held that the objection 'does

[206] The considerations included: the children's strong objections; the objectives of the Convention; the American origin of the children and parents; the prior adjudication by American courts; the fact the children's difficulties arose from the mother's decision to relocate and the father's offer to allow the mother to retain care and have a guardian represent the children's interests.

[207] *Department of Child Safety & Baker* [2008] FamCA 171.

[208] The child was born in Australia. His parents separated in 2001. Following the separation, the parties entered into a parental agreement according to which the child was to reside with the father. The father remarried and in early 2004, the father, his new wife and the child moved to the United States with the mother's consent. An agreement was made between the parents regarding contact between the child and the mother. In accordance with this agreement, the boy visited his mother in Australia in June 2007.

[209] In particular, the child raised objections to his living and schooling arrangements with his father. Particularly, he was resistant to the prospect of moving and changing his school. He also identified some problems between him and his stepmother and stepsister.

[210] *Department of Child Safety & Baker* [2008] FamCA 171 para 27.

[211] *State Central Authority & Wolfe* [2010] FamCA 1226.

not go beyond the mere expression of a preference or of ordinary wishes'.[212] This conclusion was upheld on appeal.[213]

B. Canada

i. Automatic Inquiry into the Views of the Child

It appears from the recent case law that in Canada, as in Australia, children are heard in Convention proceedings strictly in cases where Article 13(2) has been raised by the respondent.

ii. Minimum Age of the Child

Available recent case law suggests that the minimum age at which a child can be given the opportunity to express his/her views in return proceedings is nine years.[214] The rules are, however, different in each Province, resulting in the minimum threshold being much higher in some Canadian jurisdictions. As an example, Nova Scotia can be mentioned where children under 14 will not be heard in Convention proceedings.[215]

iii. The Method of the Examination of Child's Views

The method of examination of child's views in Canada differs widely from one Province to another. For example, in Manitoba, children's views are conveyed to the court by social service professionals; in Alberta, it is up to the discretion of the judge whether and how the children are to be heard; and in Nova Scotia, there are no set rules with respect to the methods that are used in order for children to be heard in return proceedings.[216]

iv. Exercise of the Discretion to Return

In Canada, only one current published case exhibited a child-focused approach in the sense that the return was refused exclusively on the basis of a child's objections.[217] This application was a decision of British Columbia Supreme Court in the case of *Innes v Innes*.[218] The child involved in this case was a 12-year-old

[212] *Ibid*, para 50.

[213] *Wolfe & Director-General, Department of Human Services* [2011] FamCAFC 42.

[214] *Garelli v Rahma* [2006] WDFL 2524, 28 RFL (6th) 455 (Ont SCJ).

[215] Permanent Bureau of the Hague Conference, 'Questionnaire Concerning the Practical Operation of the Hague Convention of 25 October 1980 on the Civil Aspects of International Child Abduction' (April 2006) Individual Reponses: Canada, 13, available at www.hcch.net/upload/abd_2006_cae.pdf.

[216] *Ibid*.

[217] Additionally, there was one case where return was refused partly on the basis of the child's objections. The defence was made out successfully in conjunction with the fact that the abducting parent who had been the sole primary carer of the child was unable to return to the requesting State (United States) as she had been issued a deportation order by the United States' Immigration authorities. *SJ v JB* [2011] QCCS 4266 (Que SC).

[218] *Innes v Innes* [2005] WDFL 3282, 2005 CarswellBC 1296 (British Col SC).

boy who had been wrongfully removed by his mother from the United States to Canada. The father initiated return proceedings. The boy, although not despising his father, objected to being returned to the United States. He wanted to remain in Canada with his mother and his 19-year-old brother, who also resided there. His objections did not show any signs of parental influence and the main reason behind his wish not to be returned to the United States was that he felt settled in Canada. The boy expressed a desire to maintain regular contact with his father and was open to travelling to his father's home in the United States once regular access arrangements have been made. The court concluded that the boy had reached a level of maturity at which his views should be taken into account. Moreover, the views expressed were authentically his alone and were not a result of pressure from either of the parents. The court found the child's views sufficient reason to dismiss the father's application and decided to exercise its discretion against the return of the child.

The issue of the exercise of discretion further arose in the cases of *Garelli v Rahma*[219] and *Den Ouden v Laframboise*.[220] Although the factual circumstances of these applications differed from those of *Innes v Innes*, both cases displayed a much more restrictive attitude when confronted with the exercise of discretion.[221] *Garelli v Rahma* concerned two children, boys, aged nine and 14 respectively.[222] Both children were held to be of an age and maturity where their views should be considered. The older boy expressed a strong preference to stay in the requested State (Canada) as a result of his links to his new community there. On the other hand, the reason behind the younger boy's objections against being returned was his preference as to custodial parent. He wanted to stay with his mother and did not mind going back to the requesting State (Italy) if she went too. The court found that the children loved both parents and that their views did not show any signs of parental influence. Moreover, it was concluded that the age of the older boy spoke strongly against his return to Italy. Nevertheless, the court reached the conclusion that the interest of keeping the siblings together outweighed the objections of the older boy. For this reason, the return of both children was ordered.

Similar considerations as in *Garelli v Rahma* led the Alberta Court of Queen's Bench to the decision to order the return of three children aged five, 11 and 14 respectively in *Den Ouden v Laframboise*. In this case, the eldest child objected to being returned to the Netherlands. Although it was found that the child had not

219 *Garelli v Rahma* [2006] WDFL 2524, 28 RFL (6th) 455 (Ont SCJ).

220 *Den Ouden v Laframboise* 2006 CarswellAlta 1693 (Alberta CA), 2006 ABCA 403, [2007] WDFL 1835.

221 A restrictive approach to the exercise of discretion in Art 13(2) cases was taken also in the recent cases of *Beatty v Schatz* [2009] BCCA 310 (CanLII); and *Mitchell v Mitchell* [2009] 66 RFL (6th) 189 (Ont SCJ).

222 The children were wrongfully retained by their mother in Ontario. The mother travelled with the children from Italy to Canada for the purpose of visiting her family; however, she did not return and informed the father of her intention to stay in Ontario. The father initiated return proceedings. Several objections to return were raised by the mother, including the Art 13(2) defence of child's objections.

attained a degree of maturity which was appropriate to take account of her views, the trial court concluded that even if there was evidence of the sufficient degree from the eldest child, the court would not be prepared to exercise its discretion against her return, as it would be contrary to the interests of the family to separate the children. The decision of the first instance court was appealed by the respondent mother. In her appeal, she argued that the trial judge erred in failing to find that the eldest child had attained a sufficient degree of maturity to have her views considered. The Alberta Court of Appeal accepted this submission, but concluded that the 'error was not fatal'.[223] The trial judge was correct in his decision, as to give effect to the views of the child in this case would undermine the fundamental objective of the Convention.

The review of the Canadian case law is to be concluded with two cases that stand quite separate from the above authorities. First, the case of *England v England*[224] dealt with child objections in the context of the grave risk of harm defence. The children involved objected that they would suffer a grave risk of psychological harm, or otherwise be placed in an intolerable situation if returned. The court, however, concluded that the children had grossly exaggerated their concerns and ordered their return.[225] The second case, *Riedel v Thomopoulos-Danilov*,[226] concerned the problem of parental influence. It involved an 11-year-old boy who objected to being returned to California to the care of his father. The boy was retained by his mother in Canada during an access visit. Prior to the retention the child had lived with his father in California. The father had sole custody of the child. Although the boy expressed strong objections to being returned to California, the Ontario Superior Court of Justice did not find these objections genuine in the sense that they were a result of a strong influence of the mother on the child. The son loved his mother and would say anything to please her for fear of losing her. The boy's fear of losing his mother was based on the fact that she made him believe that he would not see her again if he returned to California. The court further concluded that the boy had not attained an age and degree of maturity at which it would be appropriate to take account of his wishes. In particular, he was not able to assess the degree to

[223] *Den Ouden v Laframboise* 2006 CarswellAlta 1693 (Alberta CA), 2006 ABCA 403, [2007] WDFL 1835, para 17.

[224] *England v England* [2005] WDFL 3012, [2005] WDFL 3430, 20 RFL (6th) 266, 2005 CarswellOnt 2763 (Ont CJ).

[225] The children were unilaterally and wrongfully retained in Ontario by their father. The court ordered the return of the children to their mother in England. The return order was, however, not issued as cross-motions were brought to consider additional evidence. The issue was whether new evidence was enough to trigger the amendment of the return order. The court found that the reason for the children's resistance to being returned to England appeared to be based solely on their wishes, not on any serious facts upon which their fears could be based. Nevertheless, the court decided to refer the matter to the local children's aid society and to request a review of the new evidence. The results of the review, however, did not change the course of the proceedings.

[226] *Riedel v Thomopoulos-Danilov* [2006] WDFL 272, 21 RFL (6th) 167, 2005 CarswellOnt 6448 (Ont SCJ).

which he was entangled in his mother's psyche. Consequently, the father's return application was granted.

C. The United States

Pursuant to the US implementing legislation, the party asserting the child's objection defence has the burden of establishing the child's maturity by a preponderance of evidence.[227]

i. Automatic Inquiry into the Views of the Child

It appears from available US case law that the approach adopted by US courts follows that identified in the two other non-EU jurisdictions, Australia and Canada. As in these jurisdictions, children involved in return proceedings in the United States are given the opportunity to express their views only where the Article 13(2) defence of child's objections has been raised by the respondent, provided that the judge considers the child to be old and mature enough to be heard.[228]

ii. Minimum Age of the Child

Early post-2005 case law shows a rather restrictive approach, with strictly no children under the age of 10 years being given the opportunity to express their views in return proceedings. The issue arose and was discussed in *Garcia v Angarita*[229] where it was concluded that a nine-year-old child could not be of a sufficient age and maturity to testify. The case involved three boys, aged 11, nine and seven. The children had been wrongfully removed from Colombia to the United States. The respondent mother relied on multiple defences, including Article 13(2), arguing that all three children objected to being returned to Colombia. The district judge, however, having automatically excluded the two younger children, decided that only the eldest boy could arguably be of a sufficient age and maturity to be allowed to express his views in the proceedings. It is to be noted that the denial of the two younger boys' opportunity to express their views contrasts strikingly with the English approach suggested by Baroness Hale in *Re D* that a child as young as 7½ should be given the opportunity to be heard. In the same way, it markedly differs from the approach taken by Thorpe LJ in the Brussels II bis case of *Re F*

[227] 42 USC § 11603(e) (2)(A).

[228] Nevertheless, in one case the court implicitly suggested that a child would be allowed to contact the court by letter or otherwise, to express his/her wishes, even if neither parent wanted the child to testify. See *Avedano v Smith*, Slip Copy, 2011 WL 3702401 (DNM, 2011). The court, however, made it clear that it would not be prepared to examine the views of the child on its own motion. In particular, it was noted that as the children (aged 11 and six) had not attempted to contact the court, by letter or otherwise, to express their wishes, this suggested that 'neither girl was sufficiently mature to make an objection that the Court should recognise'. *Ibid*, 23.

[229] *Garcia v Angarita* 440 F Supp 2d 1364 (SD Fla, 2006).

(a child) (abduction: obligation to hear child),[230] where this threshold was by implication lowered to seven years.

More recent case law, however, demonstrates that there has been a change for the better as to the approach to establishing minimum age. In particular, the case law departed from the 'rigid rule' method, and suggested that the considerations surrounding the problem of minimum age should be treated as a matter of factual determination. This resulted in children as young as eight being given the opportunity to testify, with the courts reserving the right to determine the child's maturity on the basis of the interview. In particular, in an appellate decision in the case of *Yang v Tsui*,[231] the court held that the determination of the age at which a child should be given the opportunity to express his/her views in return proceedings should be made on a case-by-case basis. The approach adopted by *Yang v Tsui* was followed in *Falk v Sinclaire*,[232] where the court held that it was 'unwilling to rule as a matter of law that an eight-year-old child is too immature to prevent him or her from testifying at all'. Similarly, in *Simcox v Simcox*,[233] *Dalsgaard v Montoya*[234] and *Dionyspoulou v Papadoulis*[235] testimony was taken from an eight-year-old child. In *Khalip v Khalip*[236] and *Rivera Rivas v Segovia*[237] the court even agreed to interview a child as young as 7.[238]

iii. The Method of the Examination of Child's Views

It appears to be a general rule in the US that children in Convention proceedings are heard by judges in chambers.[239] *In camera* examination of child's views is normally conducted through a private conversation with the judge in the presence of

[230] *Re F (a child) (abduction: obligation to hear child)* [2007] EWCA Civ 468, [2007] 2 FLR 697.
[231] *Yang v Tsui* 499 F 3d 259 (3d Cir 2007).
[232] *Falk v Sinclaire*, Slip Copy, 2009 WL 4110757 (D Me).
[233] *Simcox v Simcox* 511 F 3d 594 (6th Cir 2007).
[234] *Dalsgaard v Montoya*, Slip Copy, 2011 WL 5037223 (MD Fla, 2011).
[235] *Dionyspoulou v Papadoulis*, Slip Copy, 2010 WL 5439758 (MD Fla, 2010).
[236] *Khalip v Khalip*, Slip Copy, 2011 WL 1882514 (ED Mich, 2011).
[237] *Rivera Rivas v Segovia*, Slip Copy, 2011 WL 5394778 (WD Ark, 2010).
[238] Nevertheless, for an unknown reason, in *Nelson v Petterle*, 782 F Supp 2d 108 (ED Cal, 2011) a testimony was not taken from an 11-year-old boy despite the Art 13(2) defence having been raised by the respondent father. The child's views were made known to the court only through a testimony of the father.
[239] See, eg, *De Silva v Pitts*, 481 F 3d 1279 (10th Cir 2007); *Wasniewski v Grzelak-Johannsen*, Slip Copy, 2007 WL 2344760 (ND Ohio); *Leites v Mendiburu*, Slip copy, 2008 WL 114954 (MD Fla, 2008); *Man v Cummings*, Slip copy, 2008 WL 803005 (D Or, 2008); *Di Giuseppe v Di Giuseppe*, Slip Copy, 2008 WL 1743079 (ED Mich, 2008); *Matovski v Matovski*, Slip Copy, 2007 WL 2600862 (SDNY); *Kofler v Kofler*, Slip Copy, 2007 WL 2081712 (WD Ark) (children aged 15, 13 and 11 interviewed twice and additionally, given the opportunity to express their feelings in letters addressed to the court); *Yang v Tsui*, 499 F 3d 259 (3d Cir 2007); *Ago v Odu*, Slip Copy, 2009 WL 2169857 (MD Fla); *Falk v Sinclaire*, Slip Copy, 2009 WL 4110757 (D Me); *Andreopoulos v Nickolaos Koutroulos*, Slip Copy, 2009 WL 1850928 (D Colo); *Gatica v Martinez*, Slip Copy, 2010 WL 6744790 (SD Fla, 2010); *Haro v Woltz*, Slip Copy, 2010 WL 3279381 (ED Wis, 2010); *Khalip v Khalip*, Slip Copy, 2011 WL 1882514 (ED Mich, 2011); *Dalsgaard v Montoya*, Slip Copy, 2011 WL 5037223 (MD Fla, 2011); *Walker v Walker*, Slip Copy, 2011 WL 5008533 (ND Ill, 2011); and *Lockhart v Smith*, Slip Copy, 2011 WL 4402361 (D Me, 2011).

only one or two other persons (that is, a law clerk and a court reporter), so as to minimise any distress that might be caused by taking of the testimony.[240]

In two recent cases,[241] however, rather than being heard *in camera*, the children involved were appointed a law guardian to act as an attorney for them. In one case,[242] the law guardian (referred to as 'attorney ad litem') was appointed in addition to the child being questioned by the court *in camera*. The task of the guardian is to prepare a report for the court, recommending, among other things, what role the children should play in the proceedings. Nevertheless, this method of examination of child's views does not appear to be a new trend; rather these three cases seem to be a mere exception to the rule.

iv Exercise of the Discretion to Return

The relevant statutory provision[243] as well as older line of authority on the Article 13(2) child's objections exception indicates a narrow application of the defence by the US courts.[244] A conservative attitude is exhibited also in early post-2005 cases. For example, in the case of *Re Skrodzki*,[245] the court qualified a child's resistance to return from the United States to Poland only as a 'preference for the luxuries of living in New York, not an objection to returning to Poland'[246] within the meaning of Article 13(2) of the Hague Convention.[247] Consequently, the defence of child's objections was rejected and the return was ordered.

A turning point in approaching the defence of child's objections in the US, however, came in 2007 with the Court of Appeal decision in the case of *De Silva*

240 *Falk v Sinclaire*, Slip Copy, 2009 WL 4110757 (D Me).

241 *Kufner v Kufner*, 519 F 3d 33 (CA 1 (RI), 2008), involved two boys aged eight and nine; and *Smyth v Blatt*, Slip Copy, 2009 WL 3786244 (EDNY), involved three children aged 15, 13 and 11.

242 *De Vasconcelos v De Paula Batista*, Slip Copy, 2011 WL 806096 (ED Tex, 2011).

243 42 USC § 11601(a)(4) provides that 'children who are wrongfully removed or retained within the meaning of the Convention are to be promptly returned unless one of the narrow exceptions set forth in the Convention applies'.

244 Eg *England v England*, 234 F 3d 268, 272 (5th Cir 2000); *Locicero v Lurhasi*, 321 F Supp 2d 295, 298 (DPR2004); *Hazbun Escaf v Rodriquez*, 200 F Supp2d 603, 615 (ED Va 2002); *Friedrich v Thompson*, 1999 WL 33954819 (MDNC Nov 26, 1999) 6; and *Nicholson v Nicholson*, 1997 WL 446432 (DKan July 7, 1997) 3.

245 *Re Skrodzki*, 642 F Supp 2d 108 (2007). This case involved two children, a boy and a girl, aged 13 and five respectively. The children had been wrongfully removed by their mother to the United States. Their father petitioned for their return to Poland. The mother argued that, at the time of the removal of the children, the father did not have rights of custody. She further asserted that the children were settled in their new environment and that the older child, the boy, objected to being returned to Poland. In support of the latter defence, the mother submitted a declaration by the child, translated from Polish. The declaration was taken when the boy was 12 years old. In this declaration, the child described his life in New York and compared its quality with his life in Poland, expressing a clear preference to live in the United States.

246 *Ibid*, para 10.

247 The court quoted a paragraph from a decision in the case of *Friedrich v Friedrich*. In this decision it was concluded: '[E]ven if the home [of the petitioner] were a grim place to raise a child in comparison to the pretty peaceful streets of Ironton, Ohio, the fact would be irrelevant to a federal court's obligation under the Convention' (*Friedrich*, 78 F 3d at 1068).

v Pitts.[248] The decision, having given more weight to the child's desire to stay in the United States than to the policy of the Convention,[249] departed from the line of authorities that generally showed reluctance to place a child's wishes above the philosophy of the Convention. The case involved a 14-year-old boy who was born in the United States to a Sri Lankan mother and an American father. The parents were not married. In July 1994, the mother unilaterally removed the boy to Sri Lanka. In January 2003, the mother moved to Canada with the child, where she was accepted as a refugee. In 2005, the boy travelled to the United States to spend a summer holiday with his father. At the end of the visit period, he did not return, expressing a wish to live with his father in the United States. The mother initiated return proceedings. The child was interviewed *in camera* by a magistrate judge. He expressed a desire to remain in the United States. The boy stated that he had discussed the relocation with his father during a prior visit to the United States; however, at that time he was uncertain about staying permanently. By 2005, however, he felt more at home in the United States and desired to stay. He considered his father's house luxurious and very comfortable and found the local school better than the one he attended in Canada. The magistrate judge did not find any signs of parental influence and observed that the boy had attained sufficient age and degree of maturity for his views to be considered. Although the magistrate judge accepted that the father's generosity might have to some extent influenced the child's preference to remain in the United States, he concluded that the boy had a clear insight into the positions of his parents and had not been particularly tempted by wealth in forming his views. In reaching his conclusion, the magistrate judge placed reliance on the fact that the child's decision to remain in the United States was a result of ongoing discussions with his father and therefore represented a considered and honest decision. Accordingly, the return application was refused. On appeal, no error was found in the District Court's conclusion that the child should remain in the United States, and the appeal was dismissed. The court found the circumstances of this case to be sufficiently exceptional so as to justify a refusal to return based solely on the Article 13(2) exception.

The legal reasoning applied in the case of *De Silva v Pitts* was followed in a number of District Court decisions. These included 2007–2009 decisions in the cases of *Kofler v Kofler*,[250] *Leites v Mendiburu*,[251] *Man v Cummings*,[252] *Di Giuseppe v Di Giuseppe*,[253] *Matovski v Matovski*,[254] *Ago v Odu*,[255] *Andreopoulos v Nickolaos*

[248] *De Silva v Pitts* 481 F 3d 1279 (10th Cir 2007).

[249] The court held: '[U]nder the unusual circumstances of this case, it is appropriate to refuse repatriation to Canada solely on the basis of Jonathan's desire to stay in Oklahoma.'

[250] *Kofler v Kofler*, Slip Copy, 2007 WL 2081712 (WD Ark, 2007).

[251] *Leites v Mendiburu*, Slip copy, 2008 WL 114954 (MD Fla, 2008).

[252] *Man v Cummings*, Slip copy, 2008 WL 803005 (D Or, 2008).

[253] *Di Giuseppe v Di Giuseppe*, Slip copy, 2008 WL 1743079 (ED Mich, 2008).

[254] *Matovski v Matovski*, Slip Copy, 2007 WL 2600862.

[255] *Ago v Odu*, Slip Copy, 2009 WL 2169857, (MDFla, 2009).

Koutroulos[256] and *Castillo v Castillo*.[257] In *Kofler v Kofler*,[258] the court noted that the child's objections exception only needed to be established by a preponderance of evidence, as opposed to the grave risk of harm exception that was the subject of a stricter burden of proof.[259] This analysis led the court to the conclusion that the Article 13(2) exception to return was intended to be applied. Having considered the facts of the case, namely that the children felt unloved by their father but had a close relationship with their mother, and that they had better living conditions and opportunities in the United States, the court concluded that the children's objections should be taken into account. The court concluded that the Article 13(2) objection (and the Article 13(1)(b) objection) had been established and declined to order the return of the children to Germany. In *Leites v Mendiburu*, the court was satisfied that the exception of Article 13(2) was made on the basis of the child's preference for the United States because she enjoyed her school and friends there and because her father's home in the United States provided her with a calmer environment than she had in Argentina.[260] Similar reasoning was used in *Ago v*

[256] *Andreopoulos v Nickolaos Koutroulos*, Slip Copy, 2009 WL 1850928, (D Colo, 2009).

[257] *Castillo v Castillo* 597 F Supp 2d 432 (D Del, 2009).

[258] *Kofler v Kofler*, Slip Copy, 2007 WL 2081712 (WD Ark, 2007). This case involved a return application of a father who sought the return of his three minor children, aged 15, 13 and 11, to Germany. The children had been wrongfully removed by their mother to the United States. The mother contended that the children preferred living in the United States than in Germany and that they were of such ages and maturity that their wishes should be considered by the court. The children were interviewed twice and additionally, they were given the opportunity to express their feelings in letters addressed to the court. All three children were heard by the court in chambers. The eldest child, aged 15, testified that he had a good relationship with his mother but a poor relationship with his father as the father had never shown much interest in the children. The father's apartment was occupied by his girlfriend and her two daughters. Consequently, when the children wanted to visit their father, there was no room for them. Moreover, the father's girlfriend did not wish to have all the children there and therefore, access visits with the father 'never worked out'. The statement of the younger child, aged 13, also indicated a lack of interest in the children on the side of the father. The girl stated that visitation with the father had caused her considerable anxiety. The youngest child, aged 11, was quite shy and did not express her opinion on the matter. In addition to the hearing, each of the children wrote a letter to the court, stressing that they desired to remain in the United States. Following the letters, the mother filed a motion for hearing. Despite the father's objection, the court found it 'proper to permit the parties' children to testify, should they wish to do so, before the court *in camera*' and granted the motion. Afterwards, a supplementary hearing was conducted. During this hearing the children were again interviewed separately in chambers. They repeated their wish to stay in the United States and pointed out that, since the initial hearing in the case, their father had not made any effort to contact them. The court found that the views of the children were not unduly influenced by the respondent mother and that all three children were sufficiently mature to form and express an opinion on the matter.

[259] The court pointed out that '[t]his difference in stringency of examination is expressly mandated by ICARA, 42 USC § 11603(e)(2)'.

[260] This case involved a 13-year-old girl who had been wrongfully retained by her father at the end of an access visit in the United States. Following the retention, the mother of the child filed a petition for the return of her daughter to Argentina. The father argued that the girl objected to being returned. The court conducted an *in camera* examination of the child. The interview led the court to the conclusion that the girl was extraordinarily bright and had attained a sufficient degree of maturity for her views to be considered. According to the court, her reasons for not wanting to return to Argentina were genuine and independent. The child showed fondness for both parents, but clearly indicated that she wished to live with her father in the United States. Upon conclusion of the interview, the court exercised its discretion and dismissed the mother's return application.

Odu, where a 14-year-old boy felt that life was better in the United States than in Italy and that he was more comfortable in his new surroundings.[261] In *Man v Cummings* and *Andreopoulos v Nickolaos Koutroulos*, the successful invocation of Article 13(2) was based on the availability of better educational opportunities in the United States than in Hong Kong and Greece respectively;[262] and in *Castillo v Castillo* an 11-year-old girl successfully objected to returning to Colombia on the basis that in Colombia, she 'received little help with homework, performed poorly in school, was often unable to play outside due to safety concerns, spent much of her time at home alone, and had few friends'.[263] In *Di Giuseppe v Di Giuseppe*, the children involved successfully opposed their return claiming that they had been victims of parental neglect and abuse in the hands of their mother.[264] Finally, in *Matovski v Matovski*, the exception was made out on the basis that the children had witnessed incidents of domestic violence and felt settled in the new environment.[265]

[261] *Ago v Odu*, Slip Copy, 2009 WL 2169857, (MD Fla, 2009) 14.

[262] The child involved in *Man v Cummings*, Slip copy, 2008 WL 803005 (D Or, 2008) was a 13-year-old girl who had not returned to her father in Hong Kong following an access visit to her mother in the United States. The father initiated return proceedings. During an *in camera* interview with the court the girl testified that she had an affectionate relationship with her father and wished to maintain contact with him; however, she desired to remain in the United States with her mother. The main reason for her decision was the availability of better educational opportunities in the United States than in Hong Kong. The court did not find any signs of undue parental influence and concluded that the child had attained sufficient maturity to decide whether to remain in the United States. Consequently, the father's return application was dismissed. *Andreopoulos v Nickolaos Koutroulos*, Slip Copy, 2009 WL 1850928 (D Colo, 2009) involved a 14-year-old boy who during an interview in chambers testified that he preferred school in the United States because it was 'easier' than his former school in Greece. He further stated that he had made friends in the United States and perceived greater educational opportunities if he stayed in the United States.

[263] *Castillo v Castillo* 597 F Supp 2d 432 (D Del, 2009) 441.

[264] In the instant case, three children, aged 12, 11 and 10, did not return from a visitation of their father in the United States. The mother of the children filed a petition for their return to Canada. The court conducted *in camera* interviews with each of the children and concluded that all three children demonstrated sufficient maturity for their views to be taken into account. The children were found to have testified truthfully, free from any form of parental influence. The children claimed that they had been victims of parental neglect and abuse in the hands of their mother. The children said that the mother's behaviour was unpredictable; she used to slap and beat them frequently and without apparent reason. The court concluded that the children's objection to return to Canada was based on a justified fear for their safety and decided to grant their request to be allowed to remain with their father in the United States.

[265] In this case, a father of three children petitioned for their return to Australia. The children, two girls and a boy aged 12, 11 and five respectively, were removed from Australia and brought to the United States by their mother in May 2005. In June 2006, the father initiated the return proceedings. The mother argued that the children were settled in their new environment and objected to being returned to Australia. The court interviewed the two eldest children in chambers. On the available evidence, the court concluded that the mother had been a victim of domestic abuse for many years prior to her departure from Australia. The children testified that they had witnessed the incidents of domestic violence and indicated that, although they loved their father, they did not feel safe with him. Both girls expressed a preference to remain in the United States. They enjoyed a more stable life there than they had in Australia and felt settled in their new environment. The court found that both girls had attained an age and degree of maturity at which it was appropriate to take account of their wishes and their opinions were not unduly influenced by either parent. According to the court, both girls responded truthfully to all questions and their wishes were a product of careful consideration

Contrary to the District Courts' understanding of the importance of the voice of the child, post-*De Silva v Pitts* appellate jurisprudence, unfortunately, indicates a return to the traditionally narrow approach.[266] In *Yang v Tsui*,[267] the court concluded that the child's attachment to her environment in the United States developed because of the passage of time that was a consequence of her wrongful retention. It further held that if the Article 13(2) exception was applied in this case, it would reward the abductor father for violating the respondent mother's custody rights and thus defeat the policy of the Convention. Referring to older, that is, pre-*De Silva v Pitts* authorities, the Court of Appeal pointed out that: 'As with any of the affirmative defences under the Convention, this decision is to be construed narrowly',[268] and that: 'The exceptions are construed narrowly so their application does not undermine the express purposes of the Convention'.[269] The conservative approach was adhered to also in a Court of Appeal decision in the case of *Kufner v Kufner*.[270]

and mature understanding of their situation. Consequently, the court concluded that, based on the preponderance of evidence, it was appropriate to take account of their views. Accordingly, the father's petition was denied.

[266] Additionally, the restrictive approach has been adopted by at least one post-*De Silva v Pitts* District Court decision. In particular, in *Wasniewski v Grzelak-Johannsen*, Slip Copy, 2007 WL 2344760 (ND Ohio, 2007), the District Court on several occasions pointed out 'the traditionally narrow application of the exception in the United States' and added that this approach was in accordance with the established case law, as well as the Convention itself. The child involved in the instant case was found to be of an insufficient maturity to have his wishes taken into account. Nevertheless, the court added that, given the Convention's intention that the age and maturity exception 'be interpreted in a restrictive fashion', under the facts of this case it would have been inappropriate to give weight to the opinion of the child, even if he had been found to be of sufficient maturity.

[267] *Yang v Tsui* 499 F 3d 259 (3d Cir 2007).

[268] Reference made to *England* 234 F 3d 268, 272 (5th Cir 2000).

[269] Reference made to *Feder v Feder* 63 F 3d 217, 226 (3rd Cir 1995).

[270] *Kufner v Kufner* 519 F 3d 33 (CA 1 (RI), 2008). In the instant case, a father sought return of his two sons to Germany. The boys, aged nine and eight, had been wrongfully removed by their mother from Germany to Rhode Island. The District Court of Rhode Island appointed a guardian who was to act also as an attorney for the children. The guardian was asked to prepare a report recommending, among other issues, what role the children should play in the proceedings. The guardian reported that the children expressed a preference to stay in the United States and to live with their mother and repeatedly highlighted the fact that they had been very much attached to her. The guardian, however, pointed out that when the children were interviewed in Germany for the purpose of custody proceedings, they consistently answered that they wanted to live in Germany. Having considered this evidence, the trial judge concluded that, given the children's young age, the views they presented were most likely a result of a strong parental influence as each parent had been attempting to 'poison' the boys against the other. Moreover, the judge concurred with the view of the guardian that the children 'had taken an unhealthy view of their power and responsibility in the custody determination [in Germany], and that any more involvement of the children in the [return] proceeding would be significantly harmful'. Consequently, the judge decided not to take account of the children's views. The trial court's decision was appealed by the mother. The Court of Appeal, however, rejected her appeal and affirmed the first instance decision in all points of her defence, including the Art 13(2) objection to return.

During 2010 and 2011, many District Courts aligned their jurisprudence with appellate case law and followed the return to the pre-*De Silva v Pitts* approach.[271]

D. Conclusions

The principle of the automatic inquiry into the views of the child introduced by Article 11(2) of the Regulation appears to be 'unheard of' in all three major non-EU jurisdictions. This finding points to the inescapable conclusion that the developments in Europe (England and Wales and Ireland in particular) exhibit a more child-focused approach than the current trends outside of the borders of the European Union. Undoubtedly, to a large extent, the credit for this goes to the Regulation.

As regards the problem of the exercise of discretion, save for the temporary period that followed the decision in the case of *De Silva v Pitts* in the United States, current trends in the above non-EU jurisdictions reflect a fairly restrictive approach towards the exception of Article 13(2). In particular, in Australia and Canada it appears to be a general pattern that, when discretion is exercised, considerations such as the Convention's policy or the objective of keeping siblings together are routinely given more weight than the child's views or feelings. Similarly, in the United States, a child's objections were traditionally given strictly limited space in return proceedings. Although following the 2007 Court of Appeal decision in the case of *De Silva v Pitts*[272] there was an indication of a more liberal approach towards the defence of child's objections, the more recent Court of Appeal decision in the case of *Kufner v Kufner*[273] pointed to a return to the traditionally narrow interpretation of the defence that marked the period prior to *De Silva*. Against this background, developments in Australia, Canada and the United States do not appear to be in accord with the increasingly child-centred approach advocated in Europe (in particular in England and Wales).

[271] See, eg, *Haro v Woltz*, Slip Copy, 2010 WL 3279381 (ED Wis, 2010); *Etienne v Zuniga*, Slip Copy, 2010 WL 2262341 (WD Wash, 2010); *Falck v Sinclair*, 692 F Supp 2d 147 (D Me, 2010); *Trudrung v Trudrung*, 686 F Supp 2d 570 (MDNC, 2010); *Carnelli v Paz*, Slip Copy, 2011 WL 1983360 (DNJ, 2011), and *Johnson v Johnson*, Slip Copy, 2011 WL 569876 (SDNY, 2011).

[272] *De Silva v Pitts* 481 F 3d 1279 (10th Cir 2007).

[273] *Kufner v Kufner* 519 F 3d 33 (CA 1 (RI), 2008).

8

Conclusions

Since the entry into force of the Treaty of Amsterdam in 1997, the European Union has steadily been legislating in the area of private international law.[1] One of the major undertakings in this respect has been the adoption of the Brussels II bis Regulation in 2003. The Regulation was the outcome of four years of preparation; however, despite the lengthy groundwork, in the area of child abduction the instrument was a huge disappointment. The preparation of the new intra-EU return mechanism provided an opportunity to assess the operation of the 1980 Hague Abduction Convention, to identify the limitations of the Convention return mechanism, and to address them at the regional level. Regrettably, however, this chance was missed. Instead of targeting real problems (the most pressing being the safety of the returning parent and the child in Article 13(1)(b) cases, especially those involving allegations of spousal/child abuse),[2] the Regulation focused primarily on tightening the Convention return mechanism. As a result, under the procedure established by Articles 11(6)–11(8) of the Regulation, a court of the habitual residence can now 'trump' an Article 13 non-return order through a custody decision entailing the return of the child. No less importantly, Article 11(4) of the Regulation requires the court of the requested State to order the return of the child even if it will put the child at risk, if it is established that measures have been taken in the requesting State to protect the child upon the return. It is submitted that Article 11(4) suffers from a number of legislative defects (see below). These defects give rise to concerns over the standard of protection of the child and the returning parent, especially in abductions motivated by spousal/child abuse.

A critical assessment of the development of the new intra-EU child abduction regime has revealed a number of serious shortcomings. Among these, the underlying problems were an obvious reluctance by the Commission to take on board objections raised by a number of Member States, and a complete lack of expert

[1] J Basedow, 'Worldwide Harmonisation of Private Law and Regional Economic Integration—General Report' (2003) 8 *Uniform Law Review* 31, 31.

[2] Importantly, this problem has recently been formally identified by the Hague Conference as one of the major current issues in relation to the operation of the 1980 Hague Convention. See Permanent Bureau of the Hague Conference, 'Conclusions and Recommendations of the Sixth Meeting of the Special Commission to Review the Operation of the Hague Convention of 25 October 1980 on the Civil Aspects of International Child Abduction, 1–10 June 2011' part I, paras 35–43, available at www.hcch.net/upload/concl28sc6_e.pdf.

involvement in the drafting procedure. This resulted in the legislative quality of the scheme having been seriously compromised as a number of useful provisions that had appeared in earlier drafts of the Regulation were left out of the final version of the instrument. These included the provision of Article 23 of the revised Commission proposal from May 2002 on Provisional Protective Measures Not to Return the Child, which guaranteed the right of the child to remain in the requested State pending the adjudication of custody by the courts of the habitual residence. Another useful provision that was omitted from the Regulation was the proposal to draw up guidelines for special cases such as those involving domestic violence, contained in the report of the European Parliament on the revised Commission proposal from November 2002. It is submitted that had the above provisions become a part of the intra-Union child abduction regime, the quality of the new scheme would have significantly improved, as the major drawback of the Convention return mechanism would have been adequately addressed.

The process of preparation of the regional return mechanism was characterised by a total lack of adherence to the Union's official law-making policy and standards of good legislative drafting. In particular, the following elements of Union law making were assessed: the principle of subsidiarity, the principle of proportionality, and the obligation to consult widely on the proposed legislation. It is submitted that in case of child abduction the principle of subsidiarity was supposed to be applied in 'upwards' fashion (so called 'reverse' subsidiarity). Accordingly, in order to justify the separate intra-EU return mechanism, the Commission had to prove that the existing international Regulation (the 1980 Hague Abduction Convention) was not achieving the aims of the proposed initiative (the necessity criterion), and that these aims could have been better achieved by action on the part of the European Union (the efficiency criterion). The generally ambiguous character of the term 'objectives of the proposed action' coupled with the 'multi-layer' character of the proposed objectives of the Brussels II bis Regulation cast doubts on the reliability of the necessity test. It is suggested that every 'layer' of the objectives should be regarded as individual aims, and checked against necessity. It appears, however, that the Commission carried out the necessity test only in relation to the primary objective of the Regulation (that is, the objective to guarantee a child's fundamental right to maintain contact with both parents) but failed to carry out the necessity test in relation to sub-objectives of the Regulation (such as the aims to tackle parental child abduction, and to ensure a prompt return of an abducted child to the country of his/her habitual residence). No less importantly, advantage was taken of the ambiguous character of the principle of subsidiarity. The elastic character of subsidiarity allowed the pro-reformists headed by France and supported by the Commission to flout the rules embodied in the principle's constituents, the necessity test and the efficiency test. Similarly, being more of a political than a legal concept, the principle of proportionality was found to have had very little practical effect on the drafting procedure. Had the principle of proportionality been taken seriously, the proposal for the new child abduction regime would have concentrated on how to increase the effectiveness of the existing global instrument rather than on how to create a separate intra-Community solution. Finally, the obligation to consult widely on the proposed legislation throughout negotiations was flagrantly disregarded by the Commission, resulting in a complete lack of involvement of child abduction specialists in the Commission's drafting procedure. No effort whatsoever was made to support the assertion of the non-efficiency of the Convention summary return mechanism by empirical research into the operation of the Convention.

Given the restricted scope of the researched area, the above findings do not justify sweeping generalisations. Nevertheless, several commentators have indicated that legislative techniques akin to those applied throughout the negotiations on the new child abduction regime are standard practice in Union law making in the area of family law.[3] It is therefore suggested that further research be undertaken into legislative methods of the European Union to explore and assess the general level of compliance with the EU's standards of good legislative drafting. Problematic areas should then be highlighted and those responsible should be requested to mend their ways.[4]

The initiative was sought to be justified by the argument of an overuse of the Article 13(1)(b) grave risk of harm defence. Apart from a conclusion drawn from a rather superficial examination of the 1999 statistical survey, however, no credible evidence of a misuse of Article 13(1)(b) was presented by the Commission. The book assessed the credibility of the claim of the indispensability of the separate intra-EU child abduction regime through a detailed examination of all accessible resources, including the 1999 statistical survey, the Hague Conference Special Commissions' documents, conclusions of conferences and judicial seminars, and

[3] See P McEleavy, 'The New Child Abduction Regime in the European Union: Symbiotic Relationship or Forced Partnership?' (2005) 1 *Journal of Private International Law* 5, 6: 'Research and consultation, essential elements one might think for the long-term viability of any legislative initiative, are engaged in on a very *ad hoc* basis in the field of Justice and Home Affairs (JHA)'. Also P Schlechtriem, 'EC Directives, Common Principles, and Law Reforms' (2001) 75 *Tulane Law Review* 1177, concluding that 'Law-making methods of the drafters are often very poor'. In a more general way, De Geest criticises the Commission for lacking consistent comparative law methodology. He writes: '[T]hey have no methodology: they select on the basis of intuition and sometimes, compromise (in trying to please the lawyers of all legal families)'. G De Geest, 'Comparative Law and Economics and the Design of Optimal Legal Doctrines' in B Deffains and T Kirat (eds), *Law and Economics in Civil Law Countries* (Amsterdam, Elsevier Science BV, 2001), per VV Palmer, 'From Lerotholi to Lando: Some Examples of Comparative Law Methodology' (2005) 53 *American Journal of Comparative Law* 261, 287. In a more specific way, criticism has been expressed about the preparation of the Rome III Regulation (choice of law in divorce) (proposal for a Council Regulation amending Regulation EC No 2201/2003 as regards jurisdiction and introducing rules concerning applicable law in matrimonial matters). See A Fiorini, 'Rome III—Choice of Law in Divorce: Is the Europeization of Family Law Going Too Far?' [2008] *International Journal of Law, Policy and the Family* 178.

[4] Nevertheless, it must be acknowledged that an improvement has been shown recently with a more careful preparation for dealing with issues surrounding the problem of matrimonial property. However, it remains to be seen whether this trend will continue or whether a reversion to old ways should be expected. See Commission Green Paper of 17 July 2006 on Conflict of Laws in Matters Concerning Matrimonial Property Regimes, Including the Question of Jurisdiction and Mutual Recognition, COM(2006) 400 (not published in the Official Journal), available at www.europa.eu/legislation_summaries/justice_freedom_security/judicial_cooperation_in_civil_matters/l16018_en.htm.

academic literature. The primary aim of the analysis was to reveal the truth about the asserted abuse of Article 13(1)(b).

The 1999 statistical survey as a first comprehensive piece of research concerned with the functioning of the 1980 Convention was of the utmost importance in assessing the practical application of this international instrument. Generally, evidence obtained through surveys of this kind is of high importance, as it may 'help to dispel myths, for example, that … a particular exception to the obligation to order a return is too frequently relied upon'.[5] Detailed analysis of the findings of the 1999 survey has revealed that the Convention was working well, whereas no overuse of Article 13(1)(b) was detected. The same conclusion was arrived at by the fourth Special Commission of the Hague Conference, which met in March 2001 to review the practical operation of the 1980 Convention. This forum formally assessed the results of the 1999 survey, concluding that the survey had demonstrated a very strict interpretation of the Article 13(1)(b) exception to return by the courts in the Contracting States. Contrary to the contention of the European Commission, the Special Commission did not find a particle of evidence of a misuse of Article 13(1)(b) in the survey. Against this background, one feels prompted to ask how one piece of research can lead to two contradictory conclusions. Additionally, none of the remaining Hague Conference Special Commissions that met in parallel with the preparation of the Brussels II bis Regulation (that is the first Special Commission held in October 1989; the second Special Commission held in January 1993; or the third Special Commission held in March 1997) identified the abuse of Article 13(1)(b) as a real problem.[6] This leads to an inescapable conclusion that the European Commission either missed out the Special Commissions' documents from its preparatory research, or, being aware of their content, deliberately ignored these important materials. The former would constitute gross negligence and ignorance of the obligation to consult widely on proposed legislation. The latter, however, would point to an alarming conclusion that the Commission acted with the intention of fabricating evidence.

No evidence of an abuse of the Article 13(1)(b) exception to return was found by participants of relevant conferences and judicial seminars either. Quite the contrary, the International Judicial Seminar on the 1980 Convention held in the

[5] N Lowe and K Horosova, 'The Operation of the 1980 Hague Abduction Convention—A Global View' (2007) 41 *Family Law Quarterly* 1, 59–104 and 60.

[6] Similarly, the fifth Special Commission meeting to review the operation of the Convention that took place two years after the adoption of the Regulation acknowledged that Article 13(1)(b) had been interpreted narrowly. The fifth Special Commission concluded: 'The Special Commission reaffirms Recommendation 4.3 of the 2001 meeting of the Special Commission: "The Article 13, paragraph 1 b), 'grave risk' defence has generally been narrowly construed by courts in the Contracting States, and this is confirmed by the relatively small number of return applications which were refused on this basis"'. See Permanent Bureau of the Hague Conference, 'Report of the Fifth Special Commission Meeting to Review the Operation of the Hague Convention on the Civil Aspects of International Child Abduction and the Practical Implementation of the Hague Convention of 19 October 1996 on Jurisdiction, Applicable Law, Recognition, Enforcement and Co-operation in Respect of Parental Responsibility and Measures for the Protection of Children, 30 October—9 November 2006', available at www.hcch.net/upload/wop/abd_2006_rpt-e.pdf.

Netherlands in October 2001, for example, expressly agreed that Article 13(1)(b) had been interpreted narrowly. Similarly, the participants of the fourth UK-German Family Law Conference at Trier in Germany in September 2002 concluded that the Convention had been working well, both within and outside the EU, and that any attempts to improve the operation of the Convention summary return mechanism should remain 'within the context of that global instrument'. Even more relevantly, the participants challenged the plan to establish a separate intra-EU child abduction regime, and called for the removal of the child abduction provisions from the draft Regulation.

Finally, the review of academic literature has revealed that, overall, only a small proportion of commentators believed that Article 13(1)(b) had been interpreted more widely than intended by the drafters of the Convention. The majority of specialists acknowledged a generally strict interpretation of the defence in most jurisdictions. Moreover, voices were raised in support of a more liberal approach towards Article 13(1)(b), especially in cases involving domestic violence or child abuse.

Despite the lack of credible evidence of an improper use of the Article 13(1)(b) grave risk of harm defence, the plan to tighten the Convention return mechanism through a separate intra-Union child abduction regime was pursued. Given the serious defects of the drafting procedure, it is now of immense importance to carefully monitor the functioning of the instrument. Bearing this in mind, an empirical study into the effectiveness of the child abduction provisions of the Brussels II bis Regulation was carried out. The research took the form of a statistical survey and involved a detailed analysis of return applications made within the European Union under the Brussels II bis Regulation between 1 July 2005 and 30 June 2006. The study was the first comprehensive statistical analysis of the functioning of the new intra-EU child abduction regime, and therefore represents a particularly valuable contribution to the understanding of the practical operation of the new Hague Convention-Brussels II bis arrangement. Admittedly, however, given the relatively limited research period caution must be exercised and broad generalisations should be avoided when assessing the outcomes of the survey.

So how did the Brussels II bis Regulation perform in the first year of its application? In terms of quantitative findings, the survey produced relatively clear results. It revealed an upward trend in the number of intra-EU abductions (363 return applications as opposed to 301 return applications in 2003); confirmed the widely held view that mothers as taking persons are in the majority (75% of all alleged abductors); and showed a rising trend in the proportion of mothers as alleged abductors 'going home' (62% as opposed to 60% in 2003). The survey recorded a slight decrease in the proportion of judicial refusals (3%) in relation to both overall outcomes and outcomes of the applications that went to court. No less importantly, the Regulation achieved a significant reduction in the percentage of judicial refusals based on Article 13(1)(b). The proportion of these refusals fell by 11% (from 30% in 2003 to 19% in 2005/06). When all the reasons are analysed, the reduction was even more significant, by 12% (from 35%

in 2003 to 23% in 2005/06). A decrease was also recorded in relation to two other Article 13 grounds for judicial refusal. In particular, the proportion of refusals based on Article 13(1)(a) not exercising rights of custody and Article 13(2) child's objections fell by 7% and 4% respectively, if the overall reason for judicial refusal is considered; and by 10% and 3% respectively, if the reason for judicial refusal combined is considered. In terms of the overall time to the final judicial decision, only 20% of all judicial decisions were made within the six-week deadline; no judicial refusals were made in less than six weeks; and 24% of judicial return orders took less than six weeks to make.

Classifying 'success' in terms of qualitative findings is, however, not so straightforward and rather controversial. First, in terms of overall outcomes, the Regulation achieved a 3% decrease in the refusal rate; nevertheless, this was accompanied by a 10% drop in the proportion of returns, pointing thereby to a conclusion that no improvement was achieved in terms of overall outcomes. A small improvement, however, was shown in relation to the outcomes of the applications that went to court. In particular, the refusal rate here fell also by 3%; however, unlike overall, the decrease was accompanied by a corresponding rise in the proportion of judicial returns (3%).

Second, as intended by the drafters of the Regulation, in the first year of its operation, the instrument achieved a marked reduction in Article 13(1)(b) refusals. There is, however, no reason to celebrate this 'accomplishment'. Quite the contrary, given the failure of the Regulation to effectively regulate the safety of the returning parent and the child in Article 13(1)(b) cases, the rise in the proportion of children returned despite allegations of a grave risk of harm may mean a corresponding increase in the percentage of children and parents whose safety is compromised upon their return to the requesting State. This development is of particular concern in relation to abductions motivated by domestic violence. It must, however, be noted that the 2008 survey did not confirm the trend towards a decline in Article 13(1)(b) refusals. On the contrary, the 2008 survey surprisingly recorded a marked increase in the proportion of judicial refusals based on the Article 13(1)(b) exception, and thus to some extent reduced, but not removed, the concern over the safety of the child and the returning parent in Article 13(1)(b) cases. Although Article 11(4) of the Regulation states that in cases of a proven grave risk of harm a child can only be returned if adequate protective measures have been taken by the requesting State, the provision does not address the question of who is to demonstrate that these arrangements are indeed in place. Article 11(4) does not indicate whether it is for the left-behind parent to demonstrate that protective measures are in place in the requesting State, or whether it is to be assumed that adequate arrangements to protect the child have been made unless the alleged abductor shows otherwise. The lack of clarity as to the allocation of the burden of proof is considered as one of the principal flaws of Article 11(4).

Another serious limitation of the Article is a complete lack of consideration for the safety of the returning parent. Indeed, the provision pays no attention to the fact that frequently it is not only the child but also the returning parent whose safety is at risk upon the return to the requesting State. This deficiency is a source of serious concern given the high proportion of mothers as taking persons in intra-EU abductions (75%), and the increasing occurrence of domestic violence within the scope of the grave risk of harm defence. In abductions committed against the background of spousal abuse, it is highly unrealistic to rely on the efficacy of undertakings as a form of protective measures. The fact that undertakings are unenforceable in the majority of EU jurisdictions means that in wrongful removals motivated by domestic violence these promises given to a court by the applicant form a very dangerous basis for ordering return.

Another defect of Article 11(4) is that it is based on an idealistic assumption that all Member States are capable of providing the same level of protection to the returning child. It ignores the reality that the level of protection of the child will depend especially on financial resources available in a particular jurisdiction and on the efficiency of co-operation between authorities involved; and that consequently, children returned to different jurisdictions will inevitably enjoy a different standard of protection.

Yet another weakness of Article 11(4) is its silence on the extent of investigations that should be conducted where the grave risk of harm is raised. It is unclear from the wording of Article 11(4) whether it is expected from the requested court to first establish whether 'grave risk' exists and then proceed to the examination of the availability of the protective measures, or whether the requested court should assess only the availability of the protective measures without investigating the presence of the 'grave risk'. Older Brussels II bis case law indicated that there was a tendency towards the first approach.[7] An extreme version of the first approach was also advocated by the European Court of Human Rights in its controversial decision in *Neulinger and Shuruk v Switzerland*.[8] The UK Supreme Court in *Re E (Children)*,[9] however, rejected the interpretation of the Convention given by the European Court of Human Rights in *Neulinger* and showed an inclination towards the second approach.[10] The major disadvantage of the first approach is that it may undesirably prolong the return proceedings and turn the 'grave risk' defence into a 'best interest' inquiry. Nevertheless, it is submitted that balance should be found between the two approaches in each individual case as it does not appear to be realistic to assess the adequacy of protective measures without having first obtained information about the actual nature and severity of the harm invoked. The final flaw of the Regulation in relation to the protection of the

[7] Not much reliance can, however, be placed on this finding for the reason that only two older relevant cases were made publicly available. Moreover, both judgments were given by English courts so only a geographically limited picture is available.

[8] *Neulinger and Shuruk v Switzerland* (App no 41615/07) ECHR 6 July 2010.

[9] *Re E (Children)* [2011] UKSC 27, [2012] 1 AC 144.

[10] In particular, the Supreme Court stated: 'Where there are disputed allegations which can neither be tried nor objectively verified, the focus of the inquiry is bound to be on the sufficiency of any protective measures which can be put in place to reduce the risk. The clearer the need for protection, the more effective the measures will have to be'. *Ibid*, para 52.

returning child is the failure to clearly define the responsibilities of the Central Authorities in facilitating a safe return.

Third, another finding that gives pause for thought is an indication of avoidance of the use of Article 13. Generally, there was a decrease in the number of judicial refusals based on the Article 13 defences (in particular, the lack of the exercise of the rights of custody; the grave risk of harm; and the child's objections). Interestingly, a concurrent increase was recorded in relation to judicial refusals grounded on the non-Article 13 defences (in particular, Article 12, Article 20, and the lack of habitual residence of the child in the requesting State). It is submitted that this highly undesirable development may be indicative of an adverse effect of Articles 11(6)–11(8) of the Regulation—game playing by judges to avoid refusals based on Article 13 through adopting a more liberal interpretation of non-Article 13 concepts. The above supposition was, however, neither confirmed nor rejected by the 2008 survey[11] or by further research. In particular, a comprehensive analysis of Brussels II bis refusals based on non-Article 13 grounds revealed that initially the Brussels II bis interpretation of Article 20 in Ireland markedly departed from established jurisprudence (in Ireland as well as in Australia, Canada and the US).[12] This indicated avoidance of Article 13(1)(b) in favour of Article 20; however, it was only in one case and the approach was not followed subsequently.[13] On the other hand, the understanding of habitual residence in the Brussels II bis case of *B v G*[14] strictly adhered to the traditional interpretation of the concept in Ireland. Despite the lack of conclusive evidence it is, nevertheless, recommended that further research be carried out into the topic. If the presumption of a more liberal interpretation of non-Article 13 concepts as an adverse effect of Articles 11(6)–11(8) of the Regulation was correct, then this disturbing development must clearly be identified, and steps must be taken at the relevant level to reverse this trend.

The fourth major point of concern highlighted by the survey is an apparent inability of the EU Member States to comply with the six-week time limit imposed by the Regulation. Moreover, the survey revealed that the 2003 statistics had showed better timing than the 2005/06 survey, pointing to a conclusion that applications governed by the Convention are resolved faster than those governed by the Regulation. This in turn suggested that the Regulation itself might present an obstacle to a more effective disposal of the intra-EU return applications. In particular, efforts to act expeditiously in Regulation cases may in some cases be

[11] The 2008 survey provided only some limited evidence in support of the above hypothesis. In particular, the survey recorded a decrease on the 2003 proportions of judicial refusals (reason for judicial refusal combined) in relation to all Article 13 exceptions, except from Article 13(1)(b) and Article 13(1)(a) acquiescence. In contrast, an increase of 9% was recorded in the use of Article 12. The proportion of Article 20 remained the same as in 2003 (0%) and although the proportion of Article 3 the lack of the habitual residence of the child in the requesting State decreased, it was only by 1% (from 16% in 2003 to 15% in 2008).

[12] *Foyle Health and Social Services Trust v EC & Anor* [2006] IEHC 448, [2007] 4 IR 528.

[13] *Nottingham County Council v KB and another* [2010] IEHC 9.

[14] *B v G* [2009] IEHC 104.

hindered by the procedural requirements of Articles 11(2) and 11(5) (the right of the child and the requesting party to have the opportunity to be heard). In other cases, delays may result from the application of Article 11(4) as courts await information on the availability of protective measures in the requesting State or negotiate undertakings or safe harbour/mirror orders. The survey further revealed that appeals took significantly longer to dispose of than unappealed cases. Last but not least, the survey demonstrated that the most efficient European jurisdiction in dealing with child abduction cases is England and Wales; nevertheless, overall, even courts in this jurisdiction struggle to meet the six-week target.

Finally, the survey has indicated a disturbing pattern of a major difference in the effectiveness of the application of the Regulation/Convention in different groups of EU Member States, in terms of both outcomes and timing. In particular, it has been revealed that the 'new' EU Member States operate the Regulation far less successfully than the 'old' EU Member States. This disparity is closely linked to the historical differences between the two groups of EU Members. The post-communist judiciary of the 'new' Member States suffers from numerous shortcomings, including the lack of experience with the application of international law, and a generally rigid mindset. These defects present formidable obstacles to an effective application of European law, including the child abduction provisions of the Brussels II bis Regulation. It is submitted that before the 'new' Member States can improve their performance, a total replacement of the old judiciary by a young generation of judges trained in the spirit of democratic values is indispensable.

Recital 29 of the Regulation imposes on the Commission a duty to monitor the proper functioning of the Regulation. The Commission is also bound to propose amendments to the Regulation, if it appears necessary. In order to alleviate at least some of the above points of concern, the following amendments to the Regulation are suggested. First, in order to afford better protection to the returning child, the burden of proof should expressly be placed on the applicant in all types of protective measures except undertakings. Second, it should be recognised that in cases involving spousal violence, a return to the requesting State exposes the abductor mother to a serious physical and psychological threat. Accordingly, Article 11(4) should be amended to take into consideration the need to secure not only the protection of the child but also the safety of the abductor mother. Third, if undertakings are to serve as effective tools in the operation of Article 11(4), the Regulation must impose on the Member State the obligation to guarantee the enforcement of undertakings. Also, an obligation should be imposed on the requesting Central Authority to oversee the compliance with undertakings. In case of a breach of the undertakings, the Central Authority will be required to initiate enforcement proceedings on behalf of the abductor parent. In the meantime, the Central Authority will be expected to take all necessary measures to eliminate any risk to the child and/or the returning parent that might be associated with the breach of the undertakings. Fourth, a provision listing specific duties of the Central Authorities in facilitating a safe return should be included in the Regulation. In particular, in abductions motivated by domestic violence, these obligations would range from a responsibility to secure safe temporary accommodation for the returning parent and the child pending the custody proceedings; a removal of criminal sanctions against the returning parent; and a duty to ensure that appropriate child welfare and child protection agencies are not only alerted but actively involved if the child and/or the abducting parent are in danger upon their return to the requesting State. No less importantly, the Central Authorities would be responsible for initiating substantive proceedings before an appropriate court, if no court had been seized with the matter prior to the abduction or pending the return proceedings. Throughout the proceedings, the Central Authorities would be under the duty to ensure the safety of the child and the abductor parent by monitoring the child's situation. A compulsory progress report would then be prepared by the requesting Central Authority and sent to the Central Authority in the requested State. If the requested court expressed an interest in the progress of the case, the requested Central Authority would then be able to keep the judge informed of developments and/or forward him the progress report. Finally, with a view to addressing the problem of timing, the feasibility of the six-week time limit should be reconsidered, and appropriate steps should be taken to amend this target to make it more realistic.

Alternatively, given the fact that the above points of concern relate to some extent also to Convention applications, at the global scale, an effective reform could be accomplished by the adoption of a protocol to the Hague Abduction Convention. With respect to the intra-EU applications, the protocol would achieve an improvement in those areas that are not covered by the Regulation. Consequently, all the above defects but timing could be alleviated in intra-EU cases through the protocol. The only shortcoming of the protocol is that signatory States to the Convention are not bound to participate in a protocol initiative. This would, unfortunately, lessen the value of the Protocol; nevertheless, it is submitted that even a protocol with a limited number of participating States would represent an improvement on the current situation.

Finally, the book sought to acknowledge those aspects of the Regulation that represent an added value in the area of child abduction. Accordingly, the final Chapter was devoted to the analysis of the obligation to hear a child in return proceedings, set out in Article 11(2) of the Regulation. The examination revealed a trend towards the acknowledgement of the importance of the voice of the child in family proceedings generally. The Regulation was found to be working towards the reinforcement of this general trend, with effects being produced beyond the scope of intra-EU return applications. In particular, in England and Wales, the obligation of Article 11(2) has become a principle of 'universal application'. Through *Re D (a child)*,[15] the principle was declared as being applicable to all Convention proceedings. In England and Wales, the Regulation also reinforced the trend of lowering the minimum age at which a child must be given the

[15] *Re D (a child)* [2006] UKHL 51, [2007] 1 AC 619.

opportunity to express his/her views in return proceedings. In accordance with legitimate expectations the Brussels II bis Regulation has, however, had no direct impact on the established principles of the exercise of discretion. The analysis also revealed that in the major non-EU jurisdictions (Australia, Canada and the United States) children are heard in Hague proceedings only in those cases where the defence of child's objections has been invoked (either as a sole exception or in conjunction with other defences). The principle of the automatic inquiry into the views of the child appears to be 'unheard of' in all three jurisdictions, pointing to the conclusion that the developments in Europe exhibit a more child-focused approach than the current trends outside of the borders of the European Union. Undoubtedly, to a large extent, the credit for this goes to the Regulation.

INDEX